THE VICE PRESIDE

THE VICE PRESIDENT'S
BLACK WIFE

THE UNTOLD LIFE OF
Julia Chinn

AMRITA CHAKRABARTI MYERS

A Ferris and Ferris Book
The University of North Carolina Press
CHAPEL HILL

This book was published under
the Marcie Cohen Ferris and William R. Ferris Imprint
of the University of North Carolina Press.

© 2023 Amrita Chakrabarti Myers

All rights reserved
Set in Calluna and Mrs Eaves
By Jamie McKee, MacKey Composition

Manufactured in the
United States of America

Cover photo of Daniel Franklin Pence quilt,
part of the Pence Family private collection, courtesy of the author.

Library of Congress Cataloging-in-Publication Data
Names: Myers, Amrita Chakrabarti, author.
Title: The vice president's Black wife : the untold life of Julia Chinn /
Amrita Chakrabarti Myers.
Other titles: Untold life of Julia Chinn
Description: Chapel Hill : The University of North Carolina Press, [2023] |
"A Ferris and Ferris book." | Includes bibliographical references and index.
Identifiers: LCCN 2023020738 | ISBN 9781469675237 (cloth ; alk. paper) |
ISBN 9781469675244 (ebook)
Subjects: LCSH: Chinn, Julia, -1833. | Johnson, Richard M. (Richard Mentor), 1780–
1850. | Enslaved women—Kentucky—Biography. | Enslaved persons—Kentucky—
Social conditions—19th century. | Interracial couples—Kentucky—History—19th
century. | Kentucky—Race relations—History—19th century. | BISAC: SOCIAL
SCIENCE / Ethnic Studies / American / African American & Black Studies |
HISTORY / United States / 19th Century
Classification: LCC F455.C45 M94 2023 | DDC 973.5/7092 [B]—dc23/eng/20230512
LC record available at https://lccn.loc.gov/2023020738

For my grandmothers,

Nilima Chakraborty

and

Usharani Chakraborty

Contents

LIST OF ILLUSTRATIONS | viii

A NOTE ON TERMINOLOGY | ix

PREFACE. Searching for Julia: *July 28, 2015* | xv

INTRODUCTION. Telling Stories | 1

CHAPTER ONE. Beginnings: *Bluegrass and Black Slaves* | 17

CHAPTER TWO. Mistress of the Parlor: *The Black Woman of Blue Spring* | 39

CHAPTER THREE. Campus Conflicts: *Racial Collisions at Choctaw Academy* | 61

CHAPTER FOUR. Disorderly Communion: *The Johnsons Go to Church* | 91

CHAPTER FIVE. Town Talk: *Locals Draw the Line* | 117

CHAPTER SIX. Affairs of State: *The Nation Speaks of Sex* | 135

CHAPTER SEVEN. End of Days: *Privilege, Property, and Passing(s)* | 165

EPILOGUE. Past Meets Present: *History and Memory* | 193

POSTSCRIPT. The Search for Julia, Redux | 213

ACKNOWLEDGMENTS | 215

NOTES | 221

BIBLIOGRAPHY | 251

INDEX | 261

Illustrations

FIGURES

Ward Hall—Main house | xvii
Ward Hall—Slave cemetery | xvii
Ward Hall—Remains of slave cabin | xvii
Great Crossing Baptist Church—Johnson Family Cemetery (2015) | xviii
Blue Spring Farm—Choctaw Academy dormitory building | xviii
Blue Spring Farm—Slave quarters building | xxi
Blue Spring Farm—Scenic view | xxi
Portrait—Rev. Thomas Henderson | 47
Great Crossing Baptist Church—Cemetery, historic marker | 94
Great Crossing Baptist Church—Cemetery (2022) | 94
Great Crossing Baptist Church—Original building | 97
Portrait—Daniel B. Pence | 109
Cartoon—"An Affecting Scene in Kentucky" | 154
Pendant—Richard Mentor Johnson | 171
Pence Family Farm—aerial view | 178
Headstone—Imogene J. Pence | 189
Headstone—Daniel B. Pence | 190
Pence Family Farm—1990s | 195
Eleutherian College, Madison, Indiana | 206
Daniel Franklin Pence quilt | 214

MAP

Map of Kentucky and Scott County | 19

A Note on Terminology

*L*anguage from the eighteenth and nineteenth centuries often doesn't match that of our own time. I thus use primary sources where necessary and place terms in quotation marks, so readers are aware that the words I use are from the era in question and not my own. This is particularly important when using race, gender, and/or color terminology, such as "negro," "wench," or "mulatto," terms that were common in Julia Chinn's time but are not in use today and are offensive to twenty-first-century readers (and with good reason).

Readers will notice that I move between using the words "enslaved" and "slave" as well as "enslaver," "owner," and "master" when referring to those persons forced to labor in the United States against their will and to those who owned the rights to their labor, respectively. Historians have discussed the use of the word "slave" versus "enslaved."[1] The latter is seen as the more appropriate term for people who were kidnapped, brought here against their will, generationally exploited, and made to work and reproduce for the benefit of Europeans and white Americans. That persons of African descent were violently enslaved is something I affirm, as opposed to placing upon them the identity of "a slave." I thus use "enslaved" wherever possible, but to avoid repetition and awkward phrasing I also use "slave," "laborer," and "bondsperson." For similar reasons, I use "enslaver" as well as "owner" and "master" to further the flow of prose.

The identifiers "African American" and "Black" are both used in this text, often interchangeably. And, like "African American," the word "Black" is capitalized. This is a conscious choice. It is the result of my own community work as well as my ethical and political beliefs. As much an ethnic group as Germans, Irish, or Dutch people, as W. E. B. Du Bois stated long ago, "I believe that [these] Americans are entitled to a capital letter."[2]

Throughout this text, I use the terms "Indigenous," "Native," and "Native American," as well as specific tribal names, to refer to those persons who are members of what we in Canada call First Nations Peoples. The term "Indian" is used only when referencing primary sources or titles from the era, such as "Indian Agent" or "Indian Territory." I consulted with my colleague Dr. Liza Black, a member of Cherokee Nation, about this matter, and I thank her for her insights on Indigenous terminology (and so much more). Any missteps here are my own.

A NOTE ON TERMINOLOGY

It is near impossible to know how Julia self-identified. Given how others referred to her, however, she was almost certainly a mixed-race person. I thus refer to her as either "Black" or a "woman of color" when I am not using primary sources that directly discuss her appearance. Because of the time and place in which she lived, as well as her social location as an enslaved woman, she wouldn't have been seen as white, which played a critical role in what she was and was not able to accomplish over the course of her life. This is, of course, foundational to the story I am telling.

This brings me to the word "wife." I have been asked at times why I refer to Julia as Richard's wife. Moving away from definitions of marriage based solely on the performance of ceremonies or the acquisition of state documents, I call Julia "wife" for several reasons. The first is that Richard Johnson referred to Julia as his wife. Additionally, several antebellum states, including South Carolina, acknowledged that marriage was a civil contract and that proof of such a union needed nothing but "an agreement between the parties in good faith." It was, then, about the behavior of two people, and how they acted toward each other, as opposed to the execution of any rites or the possession of a piece of paper.[3]

This is, in many ways, in line with the scholarship of the historian Tera Hunter, whose groundbreaking work on Black marriage in the nineteenth century reveals that, far from being monolithic or replicating the white ideals of Christian ritual, ideas of marriage and kinship in the Black community were complex, flexible, and creative. Enslaved and free Black relationships were also always precarious, particularly in the face of racial and economic inequities.[4] Utilizing Hunter's work as a frame, in addition to Richard's own words, I thus accord Julia the title of wife. Given the labor she performed for Richard and their household, the way that Richard treated Julia and their daughters, and how she was regarded by various members of their local community, she more than earned the label. Additionally, limiting oneself to legal/state definitions of marriage would have been problematic in Kentucky, which refused to recognize unions even between two free Black persons until 1825.[5]

Referring to Julia as Richard's wife is not, however, about conferring equity. Patriarchy meant that marriage in the nineteenth century was never about equity for women, regardless of race. And the Chinn-Johnson relationship in particular always involved two partners of uneven position and power due to differences in their race, gender, and free status. Still, it was an alliance in which the parties came together, and remained together, in order to achieve certain goals, both shared and singular. The initial "pact," however, was unlikely to have been voluntary on Julia's part, given her status as an enslaved laborer, legally the property of the man who became her husband.

The Families of Julia Chinn, Imogene Johnson Pence, and Adaline Johnson Scott

JULIA CHINN'S FAMILY

Henrietta (Color unknown, Enslaved) possible sexual relationship with [First name unknown] Chinn (W)

- Julia Ann Chinn (b. ca. 1790–97, d. 1833, MR, Enslaved) married Richard Mentor Johnson (1780–1850, W)

    -- Imogene M. Johnson (1812–1883, MR, Free)

    -- Adaline J. Johnson (c. 1814–1836, MR, Free)

    Richard possible sexual relationship with a woman known only as "The African" (Enslaved)

    -- [Number of generations unknown]

        --- *William Hatley McIntyre (1931–2022, B)*

- Daniel Chinn (MR, Enslaved) married Patience (Color unknown, Enslaved)

    -- Parthene (MR, Enslaved)

    -- Marcellus (MR, Enslaved)

    -- [First name unknown] (female) (MR, Enslaved)

IMOGENE PENCE'S FAMILY

Imogene Johnson married Daniel Brown Pence (1804–1891, W)

- Richard M. J. (1831–1834, W)

- Amanda Malvina Pence (1833–1907, W) married Robert M. Lee (W)

    -- Mary Elizabeth ("Lizzie") (1851–1917, W)

    -- Robert (1863–unknown, W)

    -- D. Franklin (male) (1875–1889, W)

- Mary Jane Pence (1835–1894, W) married second cousin Josiah "Joe" O. Pence (1827–1914, W)

    -- William Henry ("Willie") (1852–1941, W)

    -- Robert (1855–unknown, W)

    -- Anna Mary ("Annie") Pence (1857–1943, W) married James L. Jackson (ca. 1849–1911, W)

        --- William Claude Jackson (ca. 1881–1970, W)

    -- Thomas Pence (1860–unknown, W)

    -- Daniel B. ("Junior") (1862–1928, W)

    -- Alice (1864–unknown, W)

    -- Emma F. (b. 1867, d. between 1898 and 1961, W)

- Daniel Franklin ("Frank") Pence (1850–1919, W) married Ella Davis Smith (1861–1913, W)

    -- Grace Maria Pence (1884–1962, W) married second cousin William Claude Jackson

        --- Imogene Ella Jackson (1910–1979, W)

            ---- *Brenda Gene Brent Wilfert (b. 1939, W)*

        --- A. Claude Jackson (1913–1990, W)

            ---- *William "Bill" French Jackson (b. 1948, W)*

-- William Collis Pence (1885–1968, W)

--- Frank Durham Pence (1918–2002, W)

---- Mary Pence McMillan (b. 1951, W)

---- *Harriet Elizabeth Pence Gray (b. 1953, W)*

---- *Margaret Ellen Pence Brooks (b. 1955, W)*

- Albert (1852–1853, W)

- Edward Herndon Pence (1858–1922, W) married Ida Cooper (1865–1945, W)

Edward sexual relationship with Amanda Thomas (Enslaved [Manumitted], B)

-- Susan (B)

-- Mary Elizabeth ("Betty") (B)

-- Nellie Pence (1891–1985, B) married Harrison Taylor (B)

--- *Unknown*

---- *Unknown*

----- *Obie Taylor Sr. (b. 1969, B)*

ADALINE SCOTT'S FAMILY

Adaline Johnson married Thomas West Scott (1808–1885, W)

- Robert Johnson Scott (c. 1834–1905, W)

   1st wife, name unknown

     -- Edward Bion (ca. 1859–unknown, W)

     -- Thomas Frederic (ca. 1861–unknown, W)

     -- Frances (female) (ca. 1863–unknown, W)

   2nd wife, Emily "Emma" A. Johnson (1851–unknown, W)

     -- Ira (ca. 1871–unknown, W)

   3rd wife, Maud Crawford (W)

     -- A. J. Scott (female) (ca. 1884–unknown, W)

     -- Stone (male) (ca. 1887–unknown, W)

     -- Robert Bruce (ca. 1890–unknown, W)

     -- Ruth R. (ca. 1893–unknown, W)

LEGEND

B: Black

MR: Mixed race

W: White

Italics: Interviewed by the author

PREFACE

SEARCHING FOR JULIA

July 28, 2015

B*y the time we got to Blue Spring Farm* that afternoon, it had already been a long day. And as was typical in the Bluegrass region for that time of year, it was hot and humid. Ann Bolton Bevins and I had started by having lunch at her home in Georgetown. Ann is *the* historian of Scott County, Kentucky. There isn't much about the area that Ann doesn't know. A longtime journalist who has published more books and articles than I could list here, Ann's passion for history is matched only by her love for God and her family and by her joy in helping other people make historical connections. If not for her, getting my book project off the ground would have been far more difficult, and the end result would have been nowhere near as rich. The debt I owe her cannot be repaid.

We spent the first part of the afternoon at Ward Hall, the home of Junius Richard Ward—Richard Mentor Johnson's nephew—and his wife, Matilda Viney Ward. Junius was the son of Richard's sister Sally Johnson Ward and her husband, William Ward. Now restored and open to the public for tours a few days each month, Ward Hall is Kentucky's only Greek Revival antebellum plantation mansion. Ann is on the board of Ward Hall, and as her guest, I was able to get a walk-through of the entire facility that day. The grounds were of particular interest to me because preservationists had recently discovered a cemetery with several graves believed to hold the remains of some of the Ward family's enslaved laborers. There was also one small outbuilding, partially intact, that had been a slave cottage.[1]

After leaving Ward Hall, we made our way to the office of Dr. Chip Richardson, an ophthalmologist. Chip and his wife own a piece of Blue Spring Farm, the plantation that had once belonged to Richard M. Johnson, congressman, senator, and ninth vice president of the United States. The farm had also housed Choctaw Academy, a Native American boarding school run by the federal government on Blue Spring Farm from 1825 to 1848. The sole remaining Choctaw Academy building sits on the Richardsons' land, and Chip is committed to having the entire property declared a national historic site. He and others in the local area have been working diligently to save the building from collapse.[2] Chip would like to see the Choctaw and other Indigenous groups be able to use it for gatherings.

Our next stop was Great Crossing Baptist Church, just down the road from Blue Spring Farm. The church that the Johnson family helped found in 1785, it was where Julia Chinn, Richard Johnson's enslaved wife, was baptized and where she and Richard worshipped. Although the first sanctuary was destroyed by a tornado in 1923, the cemetery behind the building is the original and contains markers dating back to the 1790s. Many a Johnson is buried in this tiny, stone-walled graveyard, including both of Richard's parents.[3] Richard himself is buried in the state cemetery in Frankfort, amid many dignitaries, and an enormous monument marks his gravesite. As for Julia, Ann thinks she's buried across the way from Great Crossing, in a large field that used to belong to the church and where it's believed numerous bodies are buried in a second church graveyard of sorts. It's perhaps the only thing on which we disagree. I was saddened to see that the cemetery at Great Crossing was overgrown with grass and weeds. Even the tallest markers were barely visible, and it was impossible to read the stones. Both Ann and I sighed as we got back in the car.

Our final stop that day was Blue Spring Farm, the home of Julia, Richard, and their daughters, Imogene and Adaline. The property is no longer in the hands of the Johnson family and belongs to four different owners. The Richardsons gave us permission to visit the part they own, on which the Choctaw Academy building is located. That's on the left-hand side of the driveway as you enter the property. Two other sets of people own the land on the right-hand side of the driveway. The land behind the end of the driveway is owned by a fourth party. That person has his house at the end of the driveway. Apparently, his property goes upward, past his own home, to where the "Big House" used to stand. Supposedly all that remains there now are foundation stones. I can't say for sure because I haven't

Main house; slave cemetery; and remains of a slave cabin. Ward Hall, Georgetown, Kentucky (2015).

All images courtesy of the author.

Johnson Family Cemetery at Great Crossing Baptist Church, Georgetown, Kentucky (2015).
Image courtesy of the author.

The last remaining Choctaw Academy building at Blue Spring Farm, Georgetown, Kentucky (2015).
Image courtesy of the author.

been up that way. The owner wasn't home that day, so we couldn't get permission to go onto his property, and there also didn't appear to be a safe way to do so. The growth was tall and fierce, and the possibility of snakes was high. We took no chances and stuck to the driveway and small side paths.

Even so, what I did see that hot July day made me both glad and sad: Glad that after all these years, with Ann's help, I had stepped foot on the land where Julia, Imogene, and Adaline had lived, worked, laughed, loved, raged, cried, and died almost two centuries ago. Desperately sad to see how empty and neglected it all was. Choctaw Academy alone had originally boasted five school buildings at Blue Spring: One was a two- or three-story stone classroom building with two rooms on each floor, complete with fireplaces and windows, which held up to 120 students. A second stone building had functioned as a dining hall. Two other stone buildings, each two stories high, were used as dormitories, and there was a small frame house for the headmaster and his family.[4]

Four of these buildings were demolished decades ago. The only remaining Choctaw Academy structure is clearly visible off to the left from the long and winding driveway one uses today to enter the Blue Spring property from the main road. It's the first building I saw once I made it onto the old plantation site. The grass and brush had been cleared away from all around it, but the building itself, built of dry-laid stone around 1818, wasn't in great shape. Thought to have been one of the dormitories, the doors and windows were boarded over, the roof open at the front. It looked as if a good old-fashioned thunderstorm, the kind the region is famous for, might take it out. And indeed, just such a storm caused major damage to the structure the very next spring, caving in the building's roof and back wall. Sadly, while the building has been on the National Register of Historic Places since 1972, preservationists hadn't taken up serious restoration work on it until recent years. This was due not to any lack of local interest or efforts but to a shortage of funds.[5]

On the right-hand side of the driveway stood another, antebellum-era building. Also made of stone, it was so overgrown with weeds, grasses, and brush that it was barely visible, and I couldn't get close to it. There were holes in the roof and broken glass in the windows, but it looked sturdier, somehow, than the Choctaw Academy building. Ann said that it was believed to have been one of the slave cottages or a kitchen building at Blue Spring. It was too small to have been Julia Chinn's residence. That structure, also built of stone, was large enough to house a three-room library. Additionally, Julia's home would have been closer to the Great House, which was made of brick and sat up high on the hill.[6]

I sighed as I looked around. The main house at Blue Spring was gone, the cemeteries on the land had disappeared to the naked eye, and the two remaining antebellum-era buildings were falling into the ground. The very air of the ninth vice president's farm reeked of sadness and neglect. On the other hand, just a few miles away, thousands of visitors streamed through the impeccably maintained gardens and halls of Ashland each year. Ashland was the home of Henry Clay, Johnson's political peer and Kentucky's other great antebellum statesman, and the contrast between the two sites couldn't be any starker. For me, the difference lies in how the two men conducted themselves in matters of race and sex. Richard Johnson's decision to go public about his relationship with Julia Chinn and Clay's choice to hide his Black mistresses played an enormous role in the way the two men are remembered today. I'm convinced it's why Clay is a name known to so many lay historians and Johnson to hardly any. It's why Ashland is a major historic attraction, selling tickets at twenty dollars a head for tours and available to rent for weddings, and why Blue Spring Farm has all but disappeared—and why Choctaw Academy lies in ruins.[7]

Ann, in better shape in her eighties than me in my forties, was speedily walking as far as the overgrown brush and small pathways would allow; I followed slowly behind, taking pictures of the structures and the land. She chatted away from her reservoir of knowledge about the area, the buildings, and its people. I wondered what it all would have looked like here, back in the 1810s, '20s, and '30s, when it was a busy, productive plantation and school with almost 100 enslaved laborers on-site. We eventually reached a clearing and stopped. While Ann continued to speak, for me everything began to fade away. Things became still, and a heaviness descended on the afternoon. My skin broke out in goose bumps, despite the sweltering heat. I wondered if we were going to get another thunderstorm. We'd already been caught in a fierce one earlier that afternoon at Ward Hall. But the sky was clear. And then, in the quiet of the moment, I realized what it was. We were standing on hallowed ground.

I have always believed that Julia Chinn and her younger daughter, Adaline Johnson Scott, are buried at Blue Spring Farm. It's the most logical location. That's what most antebellum farming families did. They buried their kin on their land. They also had a graveyard for their enslaved laborers, like the one we had seen earlier that day at Ward Hall. Julia wouldn't have been buried at Great Crossing. Although the church was progressive in some ways, Julia was still Black. And she was enslaved. It's as simple as that. She would have been buried by her family on the land where she had lived, worked, and died, land which by that point rested in the hands of her younger daughter, Adaline, and Adaline's husband, Thomas Scott. Adaline was likely laid to rest next to her mother when she herself died just a few years later. It makes sense. It's just that the house and all three of the graveyards at Blue Spring (one for the family, another for the enslaved laborers,

Slave quarters or kitchen building at Blue Spring Farm, Georgetown, Kentucky (2015).

Image courtesy of the author.

Scenic view, Blue Spring Farm. This is where Julia Chinn is likely buried. Georgetown, Kentucky (2015).

Image courtesy of the author.

PREFACE

and a final one for the students of Choctaw Academy) have all disappeared from view. But Julia and Richard's older daughter, Imogene Johnson Pence, is buried on the land her parents gave her when she wed, land which sits across Elkhorn Creek, just a mile or so away. Her husband, Daniel, lies next to her.[8] The house and the cemetery at the old Pence farm are both still standing.

There are two, intertwined tragedies here. The first is that Julia Chinn's final resting place remains unknown and unacknowledged to this day. The other is that no one has ever tried to unearth the full story of her life. This is because, for so many years, neither the remains nor the stories of enslaved Black women were considered important enough to mark or mention.

The inability to find the exact location of Julia's grave made me even more determined to tell her story. And while no author ever has the last word, I hope this book helps bring Julia's life some small measure of justice. May this be the beginning of her and her daughters receiving their long-overdue flowers.

THE VICE PRESIDENT'S BLACK WIFE

INTRODUCTION

TELLING STORIES

---

*In Kentucky the general banter was always
"Oh well... we all have Black blood in our history."*

—WILLIAM "BILL" FRENCH JACKSON,
July 13, 2016

This is the story of an American family. Set in Great Crossing, Kentucky, in the early nineteenth century, it's a tale that seems typical at first glance: a plantation owner was sexually involved with an enslaved woman and had children with her. The union of Julia Ann Chinn and Richard Mentor Johnson, a congressman from Kentucky who became vice president of the United States in 1837 under Martin Van Buren is, however, anything but standard. Lying at the crossroads of race, sex, and politics, Julia's life illuminates how some Black women in the Old South utilized interracial partnerships to negotiate and acquire a modicum of power for themselves and their families while simultaneously highlighting the clear limits of that power: the farther away the Johnson women moved from home and their networks of privilege, the less authority they had.

The Vice President's Black Wife also reveals the ways in which even white men of wealth and influence had to follow an interracial playbook that dictated the proper forms of sexual conduct in antebellum America or lose the privileges that came with white manhood. Assaulting Black women was understandable. Claiming them as wives was not. Sex with Black women behind closed doors was acceptable. Public displays of interracial intimacy were not.

INTRODUCTION

Additionally, Julia's story clearly, and at times painfully, highlights how white supremacy wounds *everyone* in the United States. An unfree woman in a hostile time and place, Julia became complicit in helping to maintain slavery so that her kin could acquire upward social mobility. The Old South didn't leave enslaved women with a wide range of options. Julia thus allied herself with Richard, ran his businesses, managed his enslaved laborers, and appears to have maintained social distance from the field hands at Blue Spring Farm, all in order to give her daughters a fighting chance at a better life than she herself ever had. Her descendants, having seen firsthand the violence and victimization that was attached to Blackness in the United States, used enslaved labor on their own plantations, passed land and Black bondspersons down to their children, married into white families, and eventually crossed the color line.

Erased from the memory of her own descendants for close to a century, the story of Julia Chinn is, finally, one of reclamation. Laying bare the constructed nature of race, it is a poignant tale of passing, history, and memory that reveals how we all, individuals, families, and the nation at large, continue to feel the effects of slavery and interracial sex down to the present moment. And while there are those who would prefer to keep women like Julia dead and buried, others, including Brenda Brent Wilfert, are tired of all the secrets. A direct descendant of Julia and Richard through their older daughter, Imogene Johnson Pence, Brenda has devoted the last two decades of her life to putting the pieces of her family history together. "I'm for throwing it [the truth] all out there."[1]

WHO WAS JULIA CHINN?

Julia Ann Chinn was an enslaved Black woman. Born sometime between 1790 and 1797, Julia was originally owned by Richard's parents, Robert and Jemima Suggett Johnson. Trained to be a domestic servant, Julia moved to Richard's home, Blue Spring Farm, around age fourteen and became his housekeeper. The pair began having intercourse shortly thereafter, and Julia gave birth to the couple's first daughter, Imogene, in early 1812. Although Julia remained legally enslaved for the rest of her life, she and Richard apparently "stood up" in front of a preacher and lived together as man and wife until her death from cholera in 1833.[2]

Richard never married a white woman, and he referred to Julia as his wife. He also never denied his paternity of the couple's two daughters: he introduced Imogene and Adaline to his colleagues, had both girls educated, and gave them substantial property during his lifetime. And because his political work kept him in Washington, DC, for six months each year, it was Julia who handled the daily operations needed to run the plantation and Richard's other businesses in Kentucky. She dealt with local contractors, was responsible for the farm's finances, managed the estate's enslaved laborers, took care of visitors, planned all social functions, and helped operate Choctaw Academy, the boarding school for Native American boys located at Blue Spring.[3]

Kentucky whites appeared to tolerate Julia and Richard's relationship in certain ways. The couple attended a nearby Baptist church that Richard's parents had helped found; Scott County merchants did business with Julia when Richard was away; neighbors attended large parties at Blue Spring Farm; and two local white men eventually married the Johnsons' daughters. There were limits to the toleration, however. The couple's younger daughter, Adaline, was excluded from attending a Fourth of July celebration alongside the county's white women; area newspapers published angry editorials when Adaline married her white husband; and neighbors protested when Julia was seen riding around in the family carriage, a marker of white ladyhood.[4] Black women who behaved like white women blurred the line between slavery and freedom. This also set a precedent of racial and social equality that couldn't be allowed to stand, at least not without pushback.

The union of Julia Chinn and Richard Johnson reveals how most Americans of the day, not just Kentuckians, felt about interracial sex. While DC insiders had long known about Julia and Richard's connection, it was mainly "pillow talk." Even most news columnists referred to Richard as a bachelor—until he ran for the vice presidency. That was when editors, politicians, and laypersons all began engaging in public mudslinging about "amalgamation" (the antebellum term for miscegenation or interracial sex), publishing articles that attacked Julia, Richard, and their daughters. All this, even though Julia had been dead for almost three years. Their comments made it clear that white folks cared less that the couple had a sexual relationship and more about the open nature of it. People were particularly outraged that Richard had tried to place his now-deceased wife and their two daughters on an equal social footing with white women.[5]

The Vice President's Black Wife not only highlights the existence and the limits of enslaved Black women's power and privilege; it also illuminates a gap that existed between the ideals that Americans projected about themselves and life on the ground in their society. Antebellum whites engaged in rhetoric that was at odds with their behavior. They wrote pamphlets and preached sermons claiming that interracial unions didn't exist or that they only took place among white persons from the lowest orders of society, who lived with their Black lovers in secrecy and shame. There was a divide between these public outcries against amalgamation and the real, private toleration that often existed in the face of such relationships, particularly at the local level.[6]

Consider Julia and Richard, who entertained visiting dignitaries in their home and defied racial conventions of the day by appearing in public places together, such as church. This gap between what I call "rhetoric and reality" held its course, from the eastern seaboard to the new frontier, from urban ports to rural areas, from the Deep South to Washington, DC. Equally true was that toleration was not true *tolerance*, and even grudging accommodation could vanish in an instant.[7] Julia Chinn literally lived with the daily reminder of her vulnerability. An enslaved Black woman who was owned by her husband, she was subject to his every whim. Had Richard died or tired of her, she could have found herself on the auction block. Julia also had no real protection from the law. If she or her daughters became the victims of sexual violence by outsiders, for example, there would have been no recourse through the Kentucky courts, which held that only white women could be rape victims.[8] Richard's protection was all they had, and it was a thin shield from the many horrors that the antebellum South held for enslaved women.

As for Richard Johnson, his disdain for convention eventually cost him friends, financial stability, social credibility, and his presidential ambitions. From the Carolinas to Kentucky, from the backwoods to the nation's capital, even white men of wealth and standing had to obey the interracial rule book of antebellum society or risk losing the privileges that came with white manhood. A code of conduct existed for engaging in sex across the color line. The issue was not *if* a white man had interracial sex; it was whether he was *discreet* about it and didn't try to force his peers to accept his relationship beyond certain, understood boundaries. If a white man went from exploiting Black women, which was accepted, to placing them on an equal footing with white women, with all the rights, privileges, and protections thereof, he wasn't just breaking with decorum; his behavior threatened to disrupt the raced and gendered hierarchies of power that governed nineteenth-century society. To put it simply, what a man did with a Black woman in private could be ignored, but if he brought it into the light of day, into the *public* realm, his behavior wouldn't, and couldn't, be tolerated.

Stories of violent, coerced sex in the Old South are common. Given the pressure to keep relationships like Julia and Richard's under wraps (and out of the record books), however, studies of Black women who had sex with white men and managed to wield some level of authority are rarer.[9] Indeed, even the last biography of Richard Mentor Johnson (which does discuss his relationship with Julia) was published in 1932.[10] *The Vice President's Black Wife* is the first full-length study of Julia Chinn and her daughters, Imogene Johnson Pence and Adaline Johnson Scott. Bringing the Johnson women in from out of the shadows and placing them at the forefront of US history, it's a story that highlights the complicated nature of Black female privilege in the Old South while illuminating anew what life looked like for enslaved women in the nineteenth century.

What the tale reveals is that there were white folks in rural areas of the United States who were willing to extend certain privileges to Black women who were in partnerships with wealthy white men.[11] Great Crossing, Kentucky, wasn't a port city like New Orleans or Charleston, which had large, autonomous free Black communities, but Julia's daughters acquired a good education, and they and their mother dressed like elite women, attended the church that Richard's parents had helped found, and mingled with white visitors of note on their plantation, including foreign dignitaries and former US presidents. And nobody seemed to mind that Julia Chinn, an enslaved woman, ran that farm and oversaw Richard's business interests while he was in Washington for six months each year.

The limitations to their privileges became apparent, however, when Julia and her daughters attempted to behave in certain ways, enter particular spaces, or acquire social capital that Americans believed was reserved for white women alone. While it was fine for the Johnson women to do what they wanted on their own property, exercising their privileges off of Blue Spring Farm or away from Great Crossing Church, which made exceptions for them, wouldn't be tolerated. Their circles of power were small. Sitting among white women at town functions, marrying white men, owning property, and riding in carriages were markers of white ladyhood. Such conduct was forbidden to women like Julia and her daughters, no matter whom they were related to or how educated, wealthy, and refined they might be. They were Black, and legally, they were enslaved. Their attempts to "live as ladies" thus disrupted every hierarchy and upended every raced and gendered system of power. Such behavior couldn't be allowed to stand. Ultimately, having sex across the color line wasn't the problem. But trying to move up the social ladder was, as the Johnson women came to discover.

FINDING JULIA

In 2009, as I was preparing to teach the first half of the US history survey at Indiana University, I came across a brief mention of a vice president from Kentucky named Richard Mentor Johnson in a textbook. Johnson, vice president under Martin Van Buren in the late 1830s, never married a white woman but supposedly lived in open "scandalous concubinage" with several different enslaved women.[12] Held up by northern politicians and abolitionists as an example of how immoral southern plantation owners sexually abused enslaved Black women at a time when the nation's political parties were disintegrating over the issue of slavery. I wondered who this man was and how I had never heard of him. I bookmarked the page and resolved to return to it at some point.

The following year I had a conversation with a colleague, Christina Snyder, who had just begun her research on Choctaw Academy.[13] She told me that this Native American boarding school, located in Scott County, Kentucky, was on the farm of a prominent politician who later became vice president of the United States: Richard Mentor Johnson. I remembered the passage from my survey text and asked Christina if this was the same man who had engaged in sexual relationships with several of his enslaved laborers. She confirmed it was, although it was more complicated than my survey text had suggested: Johnson had lived with one of the women, Julia Chinn, for over two decades and they had two daughters together, Imogene and Adaline. Nobody had ever written a sustained study of Julia or her daughters, however. "Well, somebody should write a book about her," I said. "We need to know more about Black women in the Old South, particularly those whose lives can help us to better understand interracial relationships, as well as Black female freedom, power, and privilege." Christina replied, half-jokingly, "Isn't that kind of what you do?"[14]

I went home that day and began looking up Julia Chinn online. What immediately struck me was how little scholarly material I found. There was a biography of Richard that had been written in 1932 and a handful of articles about Choctaw Academy dating back to the early twentieth century. I also stumbled across some websites and newspaper articles that focused on the "boozing and bounding" ninth vice president, a man who supposedly enjoyed having affairs with the wives of his colleagues "on the hill" in addition to having a fondness for enslaved Black women. There was also Wikipedia, which had some decent factual material. So much of what was available had no citations. It was gossip, used for shock value. And very little of it was about Julia.[15]

Having already written one book that pieced together antebellum Black women's lives from fragmentary public records including wills, census documents, tax records, city directories, legal cases, government petitions, church registers, and more, I had some idea of what I was getting myself into if I took on this project.[16] I assumed this would be easier, though. Richard Mentor Johnson was a career politician who had lived in the public eye for well over forty years. Congressman, senator, and vice president, he would have left behind a huge collection of archival materials. And while I wasn't interested in writing a book about Richard, I knew I would have to use his records to write about Julia. That I would have to go through him to get to her.

This is one of the more frustrating realities of the work I do: that in order to reconstruct the lives of enslaved women, to write Black women back into the historical narrative, I must use materials created by white folks, white men, who never intended for their documents to highlight Black women's voices. To recover the stories of eighteenth- and nineteenth-century Black women, who left behind few firsthand accounts of themselves, we must, then, be willing to ask new questions of the archives, to use different kinds of source materials, and to use innovative methods of analysis with existing records.[17]

The challenges in doing this kind of work are many. How do we use data created by the very people who exploited Black women, data that was never supposed to tell Black women's stories, to reconstruct their lives? How do we read between the lines and give flesh to skeletal remains, responsibly analyzing the silences? How can we ensure that Black women remain at the center of our work and are not overshadowed by the men in their lives, men who created the paper trail we rely on and about whom more information exists? How do we maintain a responsible ethic of care so that we don't (re)inscribe violence onto the women we study, women who were subjected to terrors most of us cannot begin to imagine and who carried the physical and psychic scars of those horrors to their graves?

I expected these challenges as I prepared to write Julia's story, but I wasn't ready for the fact that there was no large collection of Richard Mentor Johnson archival materials. Richard spent forty-four years in state and national politics, but there was no major repository of his papers anywhere in the country. Not in Washington, DC, where the Library of Congress had only a small collection of about 160 letters, almost entirely related to financial matters and business correspondence.[18] And not in his home state of Kentucky, where I spent six years scouring private and public libraries and archives in Louisville, Frankfort, Georgetown, and Lexington in my efforts to discover any information that I could about Julia Chinn and her daughters.[19] I was initially confused and surprised by the lack of family papers.

I'm now fairly certain that when Richard died in 1850 his surviving brothers, John T. Johnson and Henry Johnson, destroyed his records in an attempt to erase all evidence of the existence of Julia (by then deceased) and the couple's two children. This was partly so they could inherit what little property their brother died still owning and partly because they were ashamed that he had been involved with a Black woman for almost a quarter century and had descendants by her. Claiming that Richard died without a will, and with the help of a racist local probate judge, a man who would have known that Richard had a daughter and grandchildren still living in the area, John and Henry got away with robbing Imogene Johnson Pence of what remained of her father's estate.[20]

INTRODUCTION

SOURCES AND STORIES

I was horrified when I realized what John and Henry had likely done and the lengths to which they had gone to try to erase the Johnson women from existence. Julia and her daughters, unlike most southern Black women of their time, were literate. Among the papers the men destroyed, then, would have been the letters the three women wrote to husband and father during the months he lived in Washington each year while they remained in Kentucky, caring for the family's business interests—letters Richard referenced in his own correspondence, but which have never been recovered. What the Johnson brothers couldn't do, however, was destroy the letters that Richard wrote to other people. They couldn't erase the church registers and newspapers, government correspondence and census materials, or the deed books and estate papers. Nor could they eradicate the churches and gravestones, homesites and school buildings, or the memorabilia and photographs passed down by Julia and Richard's kin. These materials, when added to oral histories and descendant interviews, and laid against corroborating evidence from the lives of other enslaved women, comprise the foundation of *The Vice President's Black Wife*.

This book is significantly different from other work that exists on Julia Chinn. While there are brief commentaries about Julia online, and she shows up in larger discussions on Richard Johnson's life, at times as a "concubine" or mistress, she has not been the subject of any stand-alone published historical research.[21] The first major study of her and her daughters, this book required the kind of reconstructive research that those of us who do Black women's history in the early period struggle with. The challenges of being a historical private detective and wrestling with archival silences, of (re)building Black women's experiences from fragmentary, white (male) sources, are numerous, painful, and time consuming. The only other choice, though, is to leave the narratives of women like Julia, Imogene, and Adaline untold. To allow the silences in the archives, and the resulting gaps in the literature, to remain unchecked. This is not an option for me. To do so would be to perpetrate yet more violence on the lives of enslaved women.[22] And so, armed with an understanding of the word "source" that goes beyond written documents, and carefully wielding tools such as informed speculation, I have woven together the fabric of Julia's life from the threads that have been left to us to try and capture the essence of her existence.[23]

The first chapter of *The Vice President's Black Wife* introduces readers to Julia; her mother, Henrietta; and frontier Kentucky. It focuses on Julia's childhood, analyzes how her sexual association with Richard began, and compares their union to other interracial relationships of the time. This was always an alliance composed of partners of uneven status and authority due to gender, race, and free status. Like many military or trade coalitions, however, which are often made up of stronger and weaker allies, Julia and Richard each used their relationship to further their own interests, goals more easily accomplished together than alone.

Chapter 2 examines the day-to-day lives of Julia and her daughters on their plantation, Blue Spring Farm. Enslaved women in interracial families had surprising authority within the first "circle of power," that of their households, which came with a wide range of accompanying rights and privileges. They also enjoyed more acceptance from white persons in their local communities than we might imagine, even in rural spaces.

The next chapter focuses on Choctaw Academy. Blue Spring Farm was a private home, a working farm, and the site of a federally funded boarding school for Native American boys. The story of Choctaw Academy, open for almost two decades, illustrates how the violence of settler colonialism led white Americans and certain Indigenous nations to hold similar ideas about Blackness, racial hierarchies, and chattel slavery. While the academy was the second circle of power for Julia and her daughters, and a space where the Johnson women exercised considerable authority, it was also a place where battle lines were drawn because of the long arms of federal power, anti-Black racism, and white supremacy.

Moving out from the home, chapter 4 provides a close look at the life of one southern Baptist church. Founded by a group of Virginians that included Richard's parents, Great Crossing Baptist Church came to function as the third circle of power for Julia, her daughters, and other Black community members. Though a place where the Johnson women were accorded privilege and respect beyond what was normally reserved for Black people in white spaces in the nineteenth-century South, Great Crossing's continuing tensions over race reflected similar divisions over slavery and abolition within churches across the Old South and the nation.

The advantages that Julia and her daughters enjoyed because of their ties to Richard didn't extend far. Chapter 5 reveals how small the Johnson women's circles of power really were, and the limits of their rights and privileges. Homing in on Georgetown and Lexington, Kentucky, this chapter highlights how whites closed ranks when Black women tried to enter into spaces reserved for white women. No matter how educated, wealthy, or refined they may have been, Julia and her daughters were still Black, and they were still enslaved. Their attempts to ride in carriages, marry white men, and attend local events, to "live as ladies," disrupted the larger raced and gendered hierarchies of the South. Such behavior wouldn't go unchallenged.

Chapter 6 continues to interrogate the limits of privilege, turning to the national political scene. Here, it becomes clear that even powerful and wealthy white men stood to lose everything if they chose to disregard public opinion about Blackness and spit in the face of society's codes of appropriate sexual conduct. It wasn't interracial sex that destroyed Richard's political career; it was *publicizing* it. In America, white men's influence depended on their adherence to the rule book of interracial conduct and upholding the virtue and social position of white women. Richard chose to ignore an age-old motto: discretion is the better part of valor. It would cost him in the end. In a chapter examining Richard's fall from power, we never turn the spotlight away from Julia. Although deceased, she is always present precisely because her race, her gender, and her very public role as Richard Johnson's wife dominated national perceptions of Richard, even years after her death.

The final chapter follows Julia and Richard's daughters and their offspring to explore how race is socially constructed. Sources reveal that as early as 1850, the descendants of Julia Ann Chinn and Richard Mentor Johnson crossed the color line and began living as white people. One branch of the family did this undercover while living in Illinois and Missouri. The other did it openly, at home in Scott County, Kentucky. Both sets of family members had the privileges of freedom, education, and wealth to aid in their transition. This chapter interrogates what led these folks to take such measures; what they gained by passing for white; and what, if anything, they lost in the process.

Using interviews conducted with Chinn-Johnson descendants, woven together with archival materials, the conclusion gives the living and the dead a chance to speak to issues ranging from slavery and sex to politics, marriage, and family. It is an opportunity to explore history and memory as well as acts of individual and national forgetting and remembering.

WHY JULIA, WHY NOW?

I believe it's critical to broadcast Julia Chinn's tale far and wide for several reasons. First, Black, white, and Native people have been sexually involved since they initially encountered one another. Interracial sex was, and is, so common in the Americas, between people of all classes and races, that Julia's story can't have been unique. But there are more records on Julia than on most other enslaved women who were in such relationships except, perhaps, for Sally Hemings.[24] Because Julia was married to a politician of national importance, it meant more people were talking about her than would have normally happened. So there are more public sources on her, particularly newspapers. It's partly what helped me write this book, even though we don't have Richard's personal papers. This means we can not only re-create parts of Julia's story; to a certain extent, we can use that information to make reasonable assumptions about what life might have been like for other Black women in similar situations.[25] Julia's narrative can thus help us better understand what life was like for enslaved women about whom we may have less direct source materials.

A quintessentially American family saga, when examined in its entirety, the story of Julia and her daughters also reveals how the United States is still struggling with the effects of slavery and interracial sex almost 160 years after the end of the Civil War. While conducting research, I was saddened, but not surprised, by how Julia, like most enslaved women, had been all but erased from US history. Few people today know her name. The truth is that Julia and Richard are both victims of a continued, national refusal to acknowledge our history of slavery and interracial sex. This has played out in various ways, including but not limited to a long-standing, and violent, commitment to segregation; the corresponding construction of the "one-drop rule" of Blackness; an unwillingness to accept the existence of biracial persons, even after *Loving v. Virginia* legalized interracial marriage in 1967; and a comparable inability, until recently, for people to self-identify as multiracial on government forms and records.[26]

The reality of historical erasure, of people's dilemmas with a Black-white binary created by structural racism, and of the struggle with history and memory was driven home to me when I met and interviewed some of Julia and Richard's descendants. It wasn't something I ever thought would happen. I'm a slavery scholar. I research dead people. The thought of meeting any of Julia's family members hadn't occurred to me, and when I did, their stories surprised me. Because none of them knew until much later in life that they were descended from a vice president and his enslaved Black wife. This was not an accident. Julia Chinn hadn't just been removed from the history books of the nation; she had been erased from the memories of her own kin. At some point in the early twentieth century, members of the Pence family stopped telling their children about their family's lineage. Although "in Kentucky the general banter was always 'Oh well . . . we all have Black blood in our history,'" white families never admitted that they, in fact, actually *had* Black ancestry. When I asked Bill Jackson, a direct descendant of Julia and Richard through their older daughter, Imogene Johnson Pence, why he thought his family lineage had been hidden from him for much of his life, he remarked, "You know . . . it's a closeted secret. It is not something that people were necessarily proud of. . . . I know that it's certainly been hush-hush in our family, and whenever it comes up in other families . . . it's just as hush-hush."[27]

The Pences are your typical American family. As one descendant concluded, if you've been here long enough, and you go back far enough, people are "all mixed up together."[28] Native, African, European. This is the southern story. The American story. It's sex. It's race. It's slavery. It's also a story many folks still deny. It's why Julia and her daughters were written out of the history books and hidden from the memories of their own descendants. It's uncomfortable. *Because Richard owned Julia.* Because Blackness was and still is treated as a stigma by countless people. Because some folks still believe in the myth of white superiority. Because our history of slavery and settler colonialism has yet to be fully acknowledged. It's why some people are trying to eliminate teaching chattel slavery and other historical realities, including Indigenous genocide, in our schools. They claim that educating children in "critical race theory" (CRT) is divisive. Not only do these folks not know what CRT is; the problem is not CRT.[29] The issue is that these folks are terrified of the truth. It's about retaining power. It's about the maintenance of white supremacy. Long dead, Julia Chinn still poses a threat to the Ron DeSantises, Rand Pauls, and Mitch McConnells of our time. Keeping Black women like Julia buried is crucial for men like them. To acknowledge her intellect, her achievements, and her very existence in the midst of what she endured, amid generational slavery, overturns everything they stand for and against. It is no wonder that Florida is fighting so hard to keep AP African American Studies out of its high schools. Ignorance is the key to maintaining control.[30]

If we want to begin the national process of healing and move forward in any meaningful way, stories like Julia's are what we must embrace. We must face the history of this nation. People of color will be the majority of the US population by 2043. It's time we step into that future by accepting the country's interracial past and all that comes with it. By bringing Julia and her daughters front and center into the American narrative, that is what we begin to do. By acknowledging who we were and are, we begin to see a more realistic vision of who we can and will be. Reconciliation can only begin with truth, and that means an honest accounting of our intertwined, collective, and painful histories. The only way out is through.

This is why *The Vice President's Black Wife* is such a crucial history of reclamation, particularly now. The protests that erupted in the summer of 2020 began a new chapter in the ongoing Movement for Black Lives in the United States, one that has fueled interest for more histories of Black people, especially Black women. This intersects with persistent calls by Black women themselves, who have long waged a multifront offensive for race *and* gender justice. Fighting an intersectional battle that is different from that of both Black men and white feminists, Black women strive for rights and protections in every aspect of their lives. From equity in health and medical care, financial and educational opportunities, equal pay and career advancement, fair treatment by the police and legal system, religious and sexual protections, and more, Black women across this land demand to not just survive but *thrive*.

There have certainly been moments of Black Girl Magic and Joy, including the swearing in of Kamala Harris to the second highest office in the land in January 2021 and the confirmation of Justice Ketanji Brown Jackson to the top court in the nation in the spring of 2022. Their stories are in many ways a testament to Julia's success. From the enslaved partner of a vice president to women of African descent becoming vice president and serving on the Supreme Court, we can see how far we've come and the sacrifices it has taken to get us here. The sacrifices of Black women who were committed to ensuring their families' freedom. To doing the best they could with what they had. To making a way out of no way.

Stories of sacrifice are not always pleasant. They often contain truths we don't want to hear. Julia's story reveals how white supremacy warps everyone. This isn't a romance novel. Richard M. Johnson was always an enslaver. He held close to 100 Black souls in bondage, including Julia Chinn. He flogged many of those folks, sold some of them "downriver" as punishment, mortgaged others to escape from debt, and engaged in coercive sex with several of the women he owned. Julia and her daughters may have been the exception to the rule in some ways, but that didn't make Richard an exceptional slaveholder. In fact, his treatment of Julia and their daughters reveals that the exception *upheld* the rule: he differentiated between "his family" and "his people." For Richard, Imogene and Adaline Johnson especially, and Julia Chinn to a lesser degree, were "his family." They thus merited better treatment. But that doesn't mean that he saw Black people *as a whole* as worthy of better treatment. It's much the same way with people today who claim they aren't racists because they have a Black friend or family member, all while supporting policies that harm Black people as a group. To those individuals, their Black friends or relatives are different, not like "other Black people." These people thus engage in a kind of magical thinking that allows them to enact harm upon entire ethnic groups while telling themselves they aren't racists because of their personal relationships.

Julia Chinn and her daughters were also damaged by white supremacy. Living in a time and place that left Black women with few options for freedom or upward social mobility, Julia was neither total victim nor absolute heroine. The story of her life is, instead, a tale of *survival*. It illuminates what people are willing to do to stay alive in the midst of the most oppressive and dangerous of circumstances. For Julia, Imogene, and Adaline, this meant becoming overseers and slave owners to get ahead in a society where success was measured by owning land and laborers. When the choice was to be owned or to own, they chose the latter.

Becoming complicit in the institution of slavery, the Johnson women engaged in what one of my friends called "shady behavior." They focused on the freedom and prosperity of their family, and their family alone. Theirs is not a story of mass advocacy or activism. Time and place didn't allow for that. Instead, their lives illuminate that racism and slavery didn't and don't just warp white people; to varying degrees, they infect every piece of fruit from the American tree. White supremacy taught enslaved people that Blackness was impoverishing and dangerous and that whiteness held opportunity, privilege, and safety. It's not surprising, then, that some Black women sought to escape the shackles of slavery by allying themselves with white people, owning slaves, segregating themselves from other Black people, or passing. We can still see the remnants of this mentality today among those who purchase skin lighteners; in the money some people spend on plastic surgery, desiring features that conform more closely to Eurocentric ideals of beauty; and in the actions of folks such as Daniel Cameron, Clarence Thomas, and Herschel Walker, all of whom have allied with those who claim that white supremacy and systemic racism are lies.

These are some of the more blatant examples of the diseased fruit that has grown from the poisoned tree of American white supremacy. The roots of this tree run deep under the soil of the United States, however, undergirding every system and structure in the nation. It is impossible to have been raised here, or to have lived here for any length of time, and *not* have been impacted by white supremacy in ways both large and small. What we need to ask ourselves is, How *deeply* have we been affected? What are we willing to do to detoxify ourselves? And finally, how do we pull up the roots of this tree, once and for all?

I never thought I would live to see our first Black president, our first Black and South Asian woman vice president, or our first Black female Supreme Court justice sworn into office. These are certainly milestones to celebrate. However, I find myself saddened that in 2023, we are still celebrating "firsts." It has been my privilege and my honor to spend this last decade getting to know Julia (and her family) and writing her story. I sincerely hope this book does her life some small measure of justice. I also hope that her legacy of sacrificial love, of taking the long view, and of working tirelessly to make a way out for future generations spurs us on as we continue the urgent and necessary work of building Dr. Martin Luther King Jr.'s "beloved community" so that, one day, the nomination of Black judges or the election of Brown presidents will no longer be historic events but rather celebrations both great and commonplace.[31]

I write these words at what is hopefully the tail end of a terrifying pandemic that has taken so many Black lives, amid an ongoing national racial crisis that has taken so many more. I do so in an attempt to bring Julia's story, a story filled with both sunshine and shadows, back into the center of the American narrative while simultaneously shining a lens on Black people's, *Black women's*, continuing struggle for justice in the here and now. To highlight their ongoing fight to *not be erased*, as Julia was for so long. To stand and demand their rights, to say with their foremothers, as they have for centuries, "Aren't I a woman?"[32]

We have a long way to go. Until we can embrace the totality of our history, the good, the bad, and the ugly, men such as Payton S. Gendron and Dylann Roof will continue to fall prey to white supremacists who spout dangerous philosophies, including fears of white genocide and "replacement theory."[33] Indeed, the Federal Bureau of Investigation has reported that the most serious terror threat in the United States today are ethnonationalists, white supremacists intent on carrying out acts of "violent domestic extremism."[34]

So I turn now to Julia's story. For it is in looking back that we may yet see a path forward. *A luta continua.*

CHAPTER ONE

BEGINNINGS

Bluegrass and Black Slaves

*J**ulia Ann Chinn was born*** sometime between 1790 and 1797 in the Bluegrass region of Kentucky, into an economy becoming increasingly dependent on slavery. Home to the state's largest free Black population, the Bluegrass was also the site of Kentucky's biggest plantations, dedicated to growing hemp and staple crops such as wheat and corn. Julia and her mother, Henrietta, belonged to Robert and Jemima Johnson. One of the wealthiest couples in the state, the Johnsons owned over 65,000 acres of the region's finest agricultural land.[1]

Kentucky was the frontier. Viewed as the "wild west" of the nation, having been settled by whites after 1776, it was a vast swath of rich, fertile land. While nearly half the area was covered with cane, between the brakes there were large spaces of open ground, as if "God Himself had intended for fields to be planted there one day." A profusion of weeds grew across the countryside, as did wild grasses, rye, and clover. The dew lay heavy in the mornings, and while the summer days were hot and muggy, the nights were cool. Early explorers marveled at the number of trees that could provide both sugar and salt but complained that the dense undergrowth made the land appear more even than it was and prevented exploration. Honey locust, black walnut, sugar trees, hickory,

Map of KENTUCKY & TENNESSEE

Exhibiting the
Post Offices, Post Roads, Canals, Rail Roads, &c.

BY

David H. Burr.

(Late Topographer to the Post Office.)
Geographer to the House of Representatives of the U.S.

Statute Miles.

References

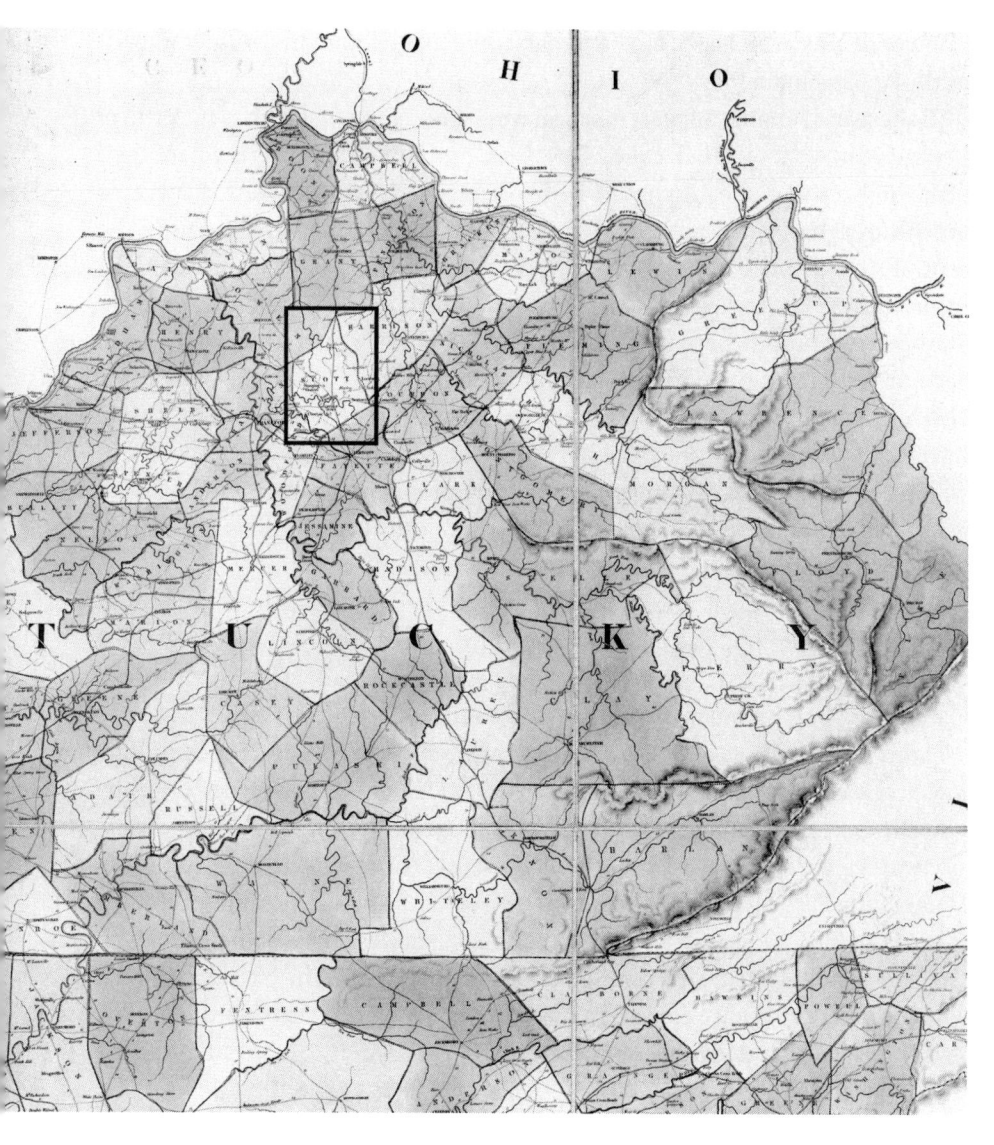

Top: Kentucky, 1839, with Scott County outlined in bold.

Map of Kentucky and Tennessee Exhibiting the Post Offices, Post Roads, Canals, Rail Roads, &c., by David H. Burr, 1839. Image courtesy of the David Rumsey Historical Map Collection, www.davidrumsey.com.

Inset: Scott County, with Georgetown, Great Crossings, and Blue Spring Farm marked.

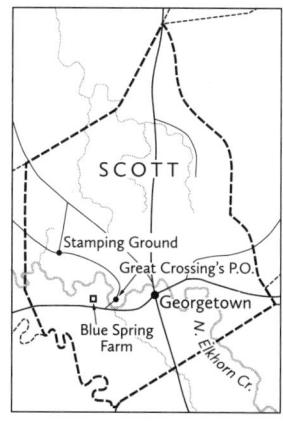

CHAPTER ONE

ironwood, hoopwood, ash, elm, and oak could all be found in this region west of the Appalachians.[2]

Robert and Jemima Suggett Johnson were among the first whites to settle in Kentucky, in what was then called Beargrass, now Louisville. This is where their fifth child, a son named Richard Mentor, was born in 1780. Robert, a surveyor for the area, had his eye on the rich farmlands in the Bluegrass region in the central part of the territory, however. In 1783, he relocated his growing family from Beargrass onto several thousand acres of prime land by Elkhorn Creek at Stamping Ground, where the buffalo were known to cross, near what would become Georgetown, Kentucky. He and Jemima bought the land from Patrick Henry and built what came to be known as Johnson's Fort or Johnson's Station. Enclosed by a wall to protect the families within from attacks by Native tribes who were understandably angered by white settlement, it was a good place to get buffalo wool, which could be used to make cloth. The Johnsons built a mill inside their stockade, along with log cabins, barns, and corncribs.[3]

Robert used his position as a surveyor to locate the best land in the state, and by 1812 he and Jemima had acquired one-third of the land in what is now Scott County. Highly respected, Robert was a delegate to the Kentucky Constitutional Convention in 1792 and represented what was then Woodford County as a state senator. He was also a county judge, and when Woodford was divided in June 1792 to create Scott County, Georgetown became the new county seat. Over the years, Robert was named a town trustee, a judge of the Court of Quarter Sessions, and a state director of public buildings. An active member of the Kentucky Democratic Party, he signed the new state constitution in 1800 and served in a number of elected positions until 1814. Robert and Jemima also helped found Great Crossing Baptist Church, even donating the land for the church building. The Johnson family attended Great Crossing, as did their enslaved laborers, and both Robert and Jemima served the church in a variety of capacities during their lifetimes.[4]

During the decade in which Julia Chinn was born, Kentucky's Black population boomed. Slavery was a part of Kentucky's landscape from the start. The region's earliest settlers brought their human property with them from their home states to help "tame the frontier." The legal status of enslaved people wasn't settled until 1792, however. That year, Kentucky became the fifteenth state to join the Union and formally legalized slavery by including the institution in Article IX of its new constitution. And in 1798, the state adopted an elaborate slave code that relegated both free and enslaved Black people to an inferior position in all aspects of life. As a result, the enslaved population grew from just under 12,000 in 1794 to over 40,000 by 1800.[5]

The central Bluegrass counties experienced the largest Black population growth. Scott County, where Julia was born and raised, was over 30 percent African American by 1810. And while the Bluegrass counties were primarily rural, most had a town center, where Black people made up a sizeable proportion of the population. Lexington, in nearby Fayette County, was 25 percent Black in 1800 and never less than 30 percent Black during the antebellum era. Up the road, in the state capital of Frankfort, persons of color made up 42 percent of the population in 1800. By the 1820s, the capital was almost 50 percent Black. Georgetown, the county seat where Julia grew up, had 912 enslaved persons and was 63 percent African American in 1840. Slavery was thus vitally important to the economy of the smaller towns in the Bluegrass region that would dominate Julia's life.[6]

Established in 1784, Georgetown was barely a blip on the map when Henrietta gave birth to Julia in the 1790s, however, and life at Johnson's Fort in those early years was hard. Like most enslaved women in frontier Kentucky, Henrietta was up before dawn each day. She would have put on a simple homespun dress, sewn from cloth woven right on the Station, dyed with colors from wild berries. She likely had only two dresses, and they had to last her all year. One was probably blue, the other brown, and chances are that they were made from the coarse, linen-and-wool-blended "linsey" that was typical of most "slave clothing" in those days, although dresses made out of wool, cotton, and durable osnaburg weren't unusual. In the winter, she would have received socks and one pair of shoes, russet-colored brogans, but if the untanned leather footwear wore out before spring, she would have gone barefoot. The clothing was meager, but what Henrietta had for her children was worse. Julia and her brother, Daniel, like other enslaved children, probably ran around with only rough, tow-cloth shirts to cover them, made from poorer-quality flax. As the children got older, and taller, these shirts were barely long enough to cover their nakedness.[7]

Like most enslaved mothers, Henrietta had to leave her children in the care of other Black laborers in order to go to work each day. That childcare was performed by those too young, too old, or too lame to be otherwise productive. After feeding and dressing her children, Henrietta took them to the childcare area and then went to work alongside her owners. While the men cleared and plowed the land, looked after the horses, mules, and oxen, and drove the cattle and sheep to pasture, she and the other women at the Fort saw to the chickens and slopped the hogs. And though she was a woman, Henrietta also worked in the fields, especially during harvest season, helping to maintain cash crops such as hemp, wheat, and corn while tending to sweet potatoes, shelling corn, and weeding and harvesting garden vegetables for everyone's daily consumption. Anything that the residents of Johnson's Fort didn't eat, Henrietta and the other laborers took to sell at the local market. Elderly, young, and lame bondspersons were also put to work carding wool, spinning thread, weaving and dyeing cloth, and tailoring clothes. There were no idle hands at Johnson's Station.[8]

Exhausted after a full day of work, Henrietta returned to her quarters each night where she still had to feed and care for Julia and Daniel. The home she came back to, like those of most enslaved people of the era, would have been a one-room cabin built of logs, with a roof made of wooden shingles, located away from the main house. An individual cubicle, 100–200 square feet in size, the cabin likely also had a loft of equal length, accessed by a ladder. The family's small home would have had a single door, a brick or stone fireplace, and maybe one window. Many slave cabins in Kentucky had no windows, however, and almost all had dirt floors. And while some were well constructed, others had walls where the cracks were so large, you could "shoot a gun through them." If they were lucky, Henrietta and her children had the cabin to themselves, but on many farms, slave cabins were shared by up to three families. As late as 1849, it was estimated that housing a bondsperson in Kentucky cost enslavers only five dollars per year, which translates to about $194 today. This shockingly small amount reveals just how poor accommodations were for enslaved folk in the state.[9]

Henrietta's cabin was sparsely furnished with items that had all been made at Johnson's Station, right down to the cooking spoons. There would have been a tall bedstead for her and a smaller trundle bed for the children that she pushed underneath her own during the day to open up space in the small, one-room cabin. The mattresses were straw-ticks, and the bedcovers were rough patchwork linsey quilts made from worn-out clothing, put to good use in their second life. A simple wooden table, a couple of chairs and stools, and a storage chest would have completed the furnishings of the humble home. The fireplace, which dominated one wall, provided the family's warmth and was also their cookstove. Pots hung over the fire on racks and tripods, and every member of the family had their own eating utensils.[10]

What Henrietta was able to feed her children on a daily basis was repetitive and nutritionally inadequate. Given the labor she performed, it wasn't enough food for her, either. On larger farms, rations were distributed on a weekly basis, like they were in the Deep South. It's possible the Johnsons did this as well, doling out four pounds of pork, a peck of cornmeal, and a half gallon of molasses to each of their laborers every Sunday. The gardens that Henrietta and other enslaved workers maintained were used to round out this diet, providing beans, potatoes, cabbage, black-eyed peas, greens, and other produce. Henrietta may have also had access to milk, cheese, and other dairy products in addition to fruit such as apples, peaches, and cherries. Many enslaved persons in Kentucky complained of having "mush and milk" diets, however, few vegetables, and the "poorest kind of fat meat." Some ate only two meals a day. Most, in addition to growing their own personal gardens to supplement the food their owners gave them, raised chickens and sold their surplus produce at local markets for cash if they could. Male laborers also added to their families' diets with wild fish and game, hunting opossums, squirrels, birds, and rabbits. There's no indication that Henrietta had an enslaved husband on-site to hunt for her, but that doesn't mean that others in the slave community didn't provide her family with wild game in exchange for eggs, chickens, or garden vegetables she might have grown.[11]

Both of Henrietta's children used the last name Chinn as adults, perhaps to connect themselves to the man they believed was their father. Given the references to Julia as a light-skinned woman, he was likely a white man and member of a local Chinn family, of which there were several. It's unclear how Chinn met and fathered two children with Henrietta. He may have been a regular visitor to the Johnson farm, and the sex with Henrietta may or may not have been physically violent or emotionally coercive. Home was never a safe space for Black women in the Old South. Though only white women were seen as rape victims by the courts, it wasn't uncommon for guests on southern plantations to "help themselves" to enslaved women for a night or for enslavers to send Black women to their male company as a display of "hospitality."[12]

We don't know exactly why Julia and Daniel took the name Chinn. They may have hoped it would earn them some benefits, perhaps even their freedom. Mr. Chinn, of course, wasn't obligated to acknowledge his enslaved children or provide them with anything. US law stated that children followed the legal condition of the mother. If a woman was free, so were her children. If a woman was enslaved, so, too, were her children. Paternity didn't matter. Julia and Daniel were thus born into bondage because Henrietta was enslaved. There were some white men (and their families), however, who, when pressed by the mothers of such children, bought the enslaved offspring, educated them, gave them property, and/or set them free. This was what the father of Harriet Jacobs's two children eventually did.[13]

Henrietta may have hoped for a similar outcome for her children and encouraged them to go by the name Chinn. Of course, the decision to take the Chinn name could have been one that Julia and Daniel made as adults. They weren't the only enslaved people to use a white man's last name, however. Sally Hemings, the longtime partner of President Thomas Jefferson, and her mother, Elizabeth, were both known by the last name of Elizabeth's father, known only as "Captain Hemings." The name of Elizabeth's mother isn't known. The violence of the colonial archives and the erasures of slavery mean that we know her only as "an

African woman." Perhaps Julia, Daniel, Elizabeth, and Sally all held on to these white men's last names as a way of claiming this part of their identity, of defiantly being *remembered*. This may have been their way of refusing to be ignored and erased from existence by white America, no matter what the law said about the irrelevance of enslaved people's paternity and their supposed kinlessness.[14]

It didn't matter to the Johnsons that Henrietta had been impregnated by a white man, willingly or otherwise. Any child she had was theirs by law and only made them richer.[15] This point was driven home to Henrietta one fateful day, when Julia was still very young, when Jemima Johnson appeared down at the quarters. She was looking for a child to train up as a house servant. As she looked over all the children, her eyes eventually settled on Julia. Noting that the child was light-skinned and "almost pretty," Jemima decided she was perfect. It's unlikely that Henrietta was happy with the decision. Julia would be living in the main house now, and mother and daughter would only see each other on Sundays, when enslaved persons had their one day off a week from work. Henrietta didn't have a say in the matter, however. What Mistress Johnson wanted Mistress Johnson took. The fear of familial separation that enslaved persons lived with every moment of their lives would have bloomed large in Henrietta's heart that day.[16]

Of course, Henrietta knew that there were certain advantages to being a domestic. Julia could have access to more food, and a larger variety of food, because leftovers from the white family's table often went to those who served up at the main house. She might receive better clothing, since domestics were often given hand-me-downs from white family members. She could gather important information while waiting on tables, and she might learn how to read and write. Most important, being a house servant would keep Julia out of the fields. Field hands were arguably the most exploited laborers with the worst working conditions, and they had the least opportunity for advancement. And working in the hemp fields was the hardest, dirtiest, most labor-intensive task in Kentucky agriculture. Hemp was used to make rope and rough cloth, and growing hemp was the most profitable use of slave labor in the Bluegrass. Since tobacco cultivation had shifted to the western part of the state, this is what farmers like the Johnsons would have grown for a cash crop, in addition to staple crops such as wheat and corn.[17]

Having worked in the fields, Henrietta surely wanted Julia to avoid the horrors of growing hemp, which included "hemp pneumonia," a nasty lung condition that resulted from inhaling hemp particles. Still, Henrietta knew that being Jemima's servant didn't mean Julia's life would be easy. Training for house girls and boys was intense. Former Kentucky bondsperson and houseboy Lewis George Clarke remembered that from the tender age of six, he was building fires in the morning, rocking white children to sleep at nap time, and making sure that there was always water in the house. By the time he was seventeen, Lewis knew how to spin, weave, and sew and had all the skills needed to run a large household. Additionally, while close relations with their owners offered some domestics an opportunity for freedom, their daily proximity to those same people meant they were also subject to their masters' and mistresses' fits of rage and constant whims, as well as the potential for sexual violence.[18]

Henrietta knew all the pitfalls that might befall her little girl up in the main house, but she had no choice but to let Julia go. Like any mother, if she had the chance, she would have told her daughter the last night they were together in their cabin, "Be careful, pay attention to the older folks you're working with, mind Mistress Johnson, and stay out of trouble." Even enslaved children were beaten with a fire-hardened hickory switch on their legs if they failed at their tasks. One wonders if Henrietta sent Julia off that final morning with a brisk hug and a "See you on Sunday," as if everything were fine, or if she turned her head away so that her daughter wouldn't see her shaking lips and tear-filled eyes. Their little cabin would never again be the same. Parting would have been difficult for Julia as well. Likely no more than six years of age, she was leaving behind the only home she had ever known, her mother, her brother, and all her playmates, to go and live with strangers. Even though the main house was in the same compound, it was the start of a whole new life for her, and she wouldn't be coming back to sleep in the quarters ever again. She must have been terrified.[19]

Julia was now an apprentice, and her days would have started early as, laboring alongside Jemima and the senior house slaves, she learned to perform the typical and tedious tasks required to run a home. Her first job upon waking would have been to build the fires in the L-shaped, timber-frame house that had, by this time, replaced the Johnson's original log cabin. After that, she milked the cows and then helped prepare breakfast for the Johnsons. A large part of the domestic staff's morning was spent cleaning the farmhouse, with its wraparound porch and ash-wood floors, and then washing all the family's clothes with lye soap in a pot of boiling water in the yard. When that was done, it was time to begin prepping the noon and evening meals, after which she and the others would make and mend clothing, help tend to the sick at the Station, and do the ironing. Julia would have also been expected to care for any of the Johnsons' small children and those of their visitors. There was no "downtime" for those who were training to be house servants. It's certain that the little girl fell into her bed exhausted every night, although she was always "on call" and had to wake up, ready to work, if a member of the family called for her, no matter the time. That bed was likely tucked away in the loft of the Johnsons' house. Even today, just after you enter the house through the back door, there is a closeted staircase off to the right that provides access to the attic. There, pegs joining the original hewn wooden timbers were visible until recent years, when they were covered over by wallboard.[20]

One wonders how hard these first days and weeks were for Julia, and how homesick she must have been. The child may have cried herself to sleep at night. It's possible that one of the older enslaved women of the house took her under her wing and helped her get adjusted. What we do know is that learning the ins and outs of household management was a difficult job, but it's one at which Julia excelled. By the time she was fourteen years old, she had learned to cook, clean, sew and weave cloth, read, and write, had gained a fair amount of medical knowledge, and was known for being a good hostess, all in addition to the washing, ironing, and childcare tasks mentioned above. Jemima and the laborers at Johnson's Fort had trained the young girl well.[21]

Julia's playmates down in the quarters, while not chosen for training as domestics, were also put to work. Childhood ended early for enslaved persons. By age five or six they were taking care of babies, and by age ten they were responsible for all kinds of chores, including bringing water to thirsty field hands, collecting the mail, and caring for livestock. Many enslaved children spent their days pulling weeds in the gardens, gathering tomatoes, sweeping the yard, collecting firewood, gathering eggs, feeding the pigs, and shelling corn. Some were also sent to the fields. Using a smaller hoe designed for young workers, they walked up and down the rows, following the adults, chopping weeds and turning the soil, although they weren't expected to do the work of a full adult hand until they were fourteen years old. Children were also apprenticed to elder laborers to learn a skilled trade. Just as Julia learned household management from Black women at the main house, Johnson's Station had enslaved carpenters, tanners, spinners, weavers, distillers, blacksmiths, and others who made the products that all the residents, Black and white, used. It was crucial to pass these skills on to enslaved children, who would carry them forward into the next generation.[22]

Despite the hard work and long hours, there was still some time to relax. After work wrapped up on Saturday afternoons, the laborers at the Fort were free until Monday morning. While the Johnsons and their bondspeople attended monthly services at Great Crossing Church, depending on what Jemima needed from her, Julia would have spent Saturday evenings and Sundays with her family and friends down in the quarters. How she must have looked forward to the weekend! While the adults played horseshoes, sang, told stories, visited, held quilting bees, went fishing, and played musical instruments, she and the other children played. And until they reached ten or twelve years of age, when enslaved children began to work more regular hours, all the children on the farm, Black and white, male and female, played together. The boys played games such as marbles, whereas Julia and her girlfriends played with dolls, jumped rope, or participated in ring-and-line games including "sheep meat," where one person who was "it" had a ball of yarn and tried to hit someone with the ball in order to make an "out." She and the other girls also pretended to dress up, keep house, cook food, serve meals, wash dishes, and care for their doll "babies." Without money to buy toys, Julia and the other enslaved children used whatever was at hand, including clay, rags, string, acorns, branches, pine needles, and their imaginations to make marbles, dolls, horses, cups, saucers, and more.[23]

Saturday nights were also a popular time for Black adults to dress up and get together for a variety of amusements in the woods. Sports and games of all kinds took place: foot races were popular, as were wrestling and boxing matches. Illicit dance parties were what the enslaved enjoyed most, however, and it's not hard to imagine Henrietta dancing with other enslaved women and men under the stars while the banjos and fiddles sang merrily in the night air and the liquor flowed. These gatherings were risky; white folks could show up at any time to break up the frolics, demanding to see people's passes and doling out beatings. It was worth it to be out, however, to feel alive and free, dancing the double shuffle, flirting, drinking, and courting after a week of backbreaking labor. It was an act of reclaiming one's body for hardworking women like Henrietta. Styling their hair, decorating their simple dresses with flowers, and stealing their owners' gowns at times, she and the other enslaved women from the Fort stole off to make merry in the woods.[24]

On Sundays, if she had the money, Henrietta may have taken Julia and Daniel to Lexington. Going to town was a popular pastime for many enslaved laborers. A town of almost 1,800 people with a population that was 25 percent Black by 1800, Lexington would have offered Julia a whole new world. So many pretty things in the stores, and beautiful houses to look at! Once there, the family could buy pastries and sodas from a variety of merchants and visit with friends from other farms as well as those who lived in town. Like other enslaved persons, they would have gone to town on Christmas Day, too, dressed in their best clothes to celebrate the holiday. Laborers generally received the whole week off between Christmas and New Year's Day, in addition to getting an extra allotment of food. Adults were also given a ration of whiskey. Henrietta may have had her whole family under one roof that week, although visitors would have kept Julia up at the main house. More food meant Henrietta could cook better meals for her children to celebrate the holidays. Julia and Daniel, like all enslaved children, probably received a stick of hard candy as a gift from Master and Mistress Johnson, plus whatever gifts Henrietta made for them. As part of the house staff, Julia likely also received extra gifts from the Johnsons, perhaps clothing or other items for herself and maybe even for other members of her family.[25]

Not every enslaved person looked forward to the holidays. This was because in Kentucky, as in other parts of the slaveholding South, January 1 was Slave Hiring Day. The hiring of enslaved persons was financially advantageous to slave owners and nonowners alike. It gave enslavers the chance to rent out their excess laborers for extra income with minimum risk, while small farmers without the capital (or perhaps the desire) to purchase enslaved persons could acquire workers on an as-needed basis. From the earliest years of Kentucky's founding, and then throughout the nineteenth century in small towns and rural areas of the state such as Scott County, small farmers rented bondspersons from their neighbors on an informal handshake basis. They were usually looking for people with particular skills to perform specific tasks and thus hired laborers for a day, a week, or a month, returning Black workers to their enslavers when the job was done.[26]

In larger towns and cities, slaveholders leased their laborers out on a more formal basis. They drew up written contracts with their neighbors that contained details about payment, food, clothing, medical care, housing, and work conditions for their bondspersons, or they auctioned their slaves off to the highest bidder. Contracts ran from January 1 to December 25 and were renegotiated during the week between Christmas and New Year's Day. In December, newspapers in urban locales were filled with ads from buyers and sellers, either requesting enslaved persons with specific skill sets or hawking persons with particular qualities. On January 1, slave hiring auctions were held in the public squares of almost every sizeable town in the slaveholding states, and at day's end, newly hired people departed with their masters for the year, often leaving behind family and friends on their home plantations as they headed into the unknown. The holidays thus cut like a double-edged sword for many enslaved persons.[27]

It doesn't appear that Julia or her immediate family were ever subjected to the hiring market. Still, they would have known people affected by it, so it would have never been fully absent from their minds during the Christmas season. In this and other ways, although Julia Chinn and Richard Johnson both grew up at Johnson's Fort, they had very different childhoods. It's also doubtful that they spent much time together while growing up given their age difference. Jemima wouldn't have started training Julia before the age of six. If the girl was born in 1790, that wouldn't have put her in the main house before 1796. Richard, sixteen years old that year, was unlikely to have had much interaction with a six-year-old girl. Given that he supposedly studied law at Transylvania University in 1800 before being admitted to the bar in 1802 and then elected to the Kentucky House of Representatives in 1804, it's possible the two had little or no contact when they were younger. Richard then moved to Washington, DC, in 1806, after he became the first native-born Kentuckian elected to Congress. If Julia was born in 1796 or 1797, however, and didn't arrive at the main house until 1802-3, then she and Richard likely didn't cross paths at all until 1810.[28]

Eighteen hundred ten. That's the year everything changed. While Julia's life had taken a serious turn at the age of six, the day Jemima Johnson came to the quarters and pointed at her, her world was completely transformed the day she was forced to move to Blue Spring Farm, a couple of miles up the road from Johnson's Station, leaving her mother, Henrietta, behind. That was the day any remaining fragments of her childhood vanished. Richard Mentor Johnson owned Blue Spring. A gift from Robert Johnson to his son, Julia came to Blue Spring, along with 100 other laborers from Johnson's Fort, to help Richard set up his new home. Richard was by then a congressman in Washington, DC. Julia was literate, knew a fair bit of frontier medicine, and had a reputation for being a great cook. Richard was a lawyer by training, rode horses, was a good dancer, and was popular with the young society women in Kentucky and Washington. He was then thirty years old and had reddish hair. Julia, according to oral tradition, was about thirteen or fourteen years old that year and weighed only ninety pounds. She was Black. He was white. She was enslaved. He was her new owner.[29]

Sending 100 laborers to Blue Spring rocked the lives of every Black person at Johnson's Station. There is no enslaved family that wouldn't have been affected by such a massive movement of people. Robert would have sent the laborers Richard needed most to get his plantation up and running, including field hands, skilled craftsmen, and household staff. Black families would have been divided to serve Richard's interests. Henrietta's household was absolutely devastated by Robert's "gift" to his son. She not only lost Julia; her son Daniel was also sent to Blue Spring. It didn't matter that they were only two miles away. She couldn't keep an eye on them anymore; she couldn't cook for Daniel, watch him sleep at night, or take care of him when he was sick. There was even less chance of her being able to protect her beautiful young daughter from sexual assault. Two miles might as well have been 200.

Every enslaved parent feared being separated from their children. They all knew that their owners' debts or deaths could lead to Black families being torn apart to raise money or to fulfill inheritances. In one way, Blue Spring was a best-case scenario for Henrietta. Her children were still in the neighborhood, and they belonged to her owner's son. She would be able to see them at church on Sundays, if not spend the day with them, and could likely run up the road in case of an emergency. But that would have been of cold comfort to her the day her children were marched off the Fort and up the road to Blue Spring, leaving her alone in her small cabin. There is no telling what Henrietta thought or did when she heard her children were going to be moved from the Station. An enslaved man named

Robert recalled that his mother threw fits when he was sold away from her as a child until they were reunited. Other mothers killed themselves at such news. Margaret Garner chose to commit infanticide rather than see her children taken from her and returned to slavery. Henrietta may have been more like Rose, who put together an emergency pack for her daughter Ashley when she discovered that they would be parted by sale. Placing a tattered dress, three handfuls of pecans, and a braid of her own hair in a cotton sack, Rose told her daughter that, most important, "it be filled with my love always." In the face of the lie perpetuated by enslavers that African-descended women had no maternal instincts or feelings, Black women showed, in a multitude of ways, on a daily basis, that *everything* they did was out of love, for the survival and betterment of their descendants.[30]

Julia went up the road to Blue Spring Farm with no idea about what her new life would be like. She had just left her mother behind, along with the only home she'd ever known. The young girl was surely terrified and grief stricken. Daniel was with her, but there was no telling if they would be living together or what her role at Blue Spring would be. She had never had any significant interactions with Richard Johnson in the past, so she had no clue if he would be a cruel or kind master. He also lived in Washington for half the year, and it wasn't clear who would be in charge when he was away. Julia was also probably anxious to see the main house and the quarters in order to determine what her new work and living conditions would be like.

It must have been quite a sight, marching up the long, winding driveway at Blue Spring that first day. Although the main house was not quite finished, it was an impressive two-story brick mansion set into the hillside, and two rows of brick cabins had been constructed below it for Richard's enslaved laborers. Julia, who grew up in a log cabin for the first six years of her life and then lived in a timber-frame home, all surrounded by the thick walls of a stockade to stave off attacks from Native tribes, may have been awed by the plush surroundings. She settled into the quarters with the other laborers, awaiting her new assignment.

When the house was finished, Richard's mother came to help him furnish his new home. It was Jemima who once again changed the course of Julia's life. She told Richard that he needed a housekeeper capable of keeping things in order for him. The housekeeper wouldn't do the work herself but would oversee everything at Blue Spring. Jemima then told Richard that she had already gone down to the quarters and selected "Henrietta's girl," fourteen years old, "well trained and almost pretty," for the position. Mrs. Johnson was enthusiastic about young Julia's qualities as a potential housekeeper, stating that the girl was "neat and trim, quick in movement and will not grow up bulky and awkward. She weighs only ninety pounds and will look well around the house." The matter was settled.[31]

Although Julia had trained as a domestic servant for the last eight years of her life, this was a big step. Being a housekeeper, especially for a bachelor politician, was no small task. With no wife on the premises, it meant managing Richard's large home and overseeing the household staff, as well as organizing the fabulous parties for which Richard was known. Enslaved housekeepers were powerful persons on large plantations. Julia would carry the keys to the estate clipped to her belt, choose the daily menu, do all the shopping, handle deliveries of and payments for all goods and supplies, organize and oversee work assignments for the household staff, handle minor punishments, take care of the needs of all houseguests, and more. There were also real risks to being a housekeeper, however. It was common for white men who engaged in sexual relationships with enslaved women throughout the Atlantic world to refer to their Black mistresses as their "housekeepers" or for their housekeepers to be their mistresses. Indeed, there appeared to be a fine line between the two. One wonders if this long history of sexual relations between masters and housekeepers was on Julia's mind as she prepared to take on the role of Richard's *ménagère*, as they were called in French-speaking areas such as New Orleans. Certainly, it didn't take long for this to happen. By 1811, when Julia was fourteen or fifteen and Richard was thirty-one, the pair had begun having sex. It was an arrangement that continued for the next twenty-two years and produced two daughters.[32]

It's unclear how this relationship began, whether with physical force, psychological coercion, or "gentle persuasion." We will likely never know. What we do know is that this became a long-standing alliance, but one of always unequal partners. Each person had goals that the other could help them acquire, and by collaborating, both were able to achieve things they may not have been able to attain on their own. For Julia, allying with Richard meant upward mobility for her descendants: a proper education, legal manumission, and generational wealth. For Richard, Julia was a sexual companion, a hostess for his political soirees, and an unpaid manager for his home and business enterprises while he lived in Washington. But race, gender, and freedom meant that Richard Johnson always had the upper hand. Of course, had he married a white woman, his positionality as lord and master would have remained unchanged: households and families were seen as "little commonwealths" where husbands and fathers reigned supreme, the rulers of their wives, children, servants, and slaves.[33] Unlike a white woman, however, Julia was in a relationship with a man who could actually sell or kill her and their children without fear of legal reprisal. It's highly unlikely that she ever forgot that.

Jemima Suggett Johnson came to regret making Julia her son's housekeeper. She dropped in at Blue Spring regularly to make sure that things were running smoothly at her son's home, and it was during one of these trips that she discovered Julia Chinn had become a mother. The young girl was moving throughout the house, going from room to room and overseeing her duties while holding baby Imogene in her arms. Jemima, who appeared not to know who the father of Julia's baby was, told Richard to get another housekeeper. Nobody, she said, wanted to see a maid dragging a baby around with her. She told Richard to send Julia back to the quarters and get someone else. At the very least, if he wanted to keep Julia in the house, he had to send the child back to the quarters to be cared for by some of the "old darkies."[34]

Six months later, Richard's mother returned and discovered that Julia and her baby were still in the main house. When she confronted Richard about the matter, her son refused to send Imogene to the quarters, admitting then that she was his child. Jemima was horrified and said that he sounded "almost proud" of having a Black child. Richard claimed that he *was* proud of being a father, but Jemima told him that he had nothing to boast about and that if anything happened to him, the baby and its mother would both be sold, along with all the other laborers he owned. When Richard said that perhaps he could do something to prevent this, she told him he couldn't; if he freed Julia and the baby, they could still be forced back into slavery. Jemima told him, "Just sell them both and get it off your mind. . . . Be sensible."[35]

An oral history, these materials refer to the girl who had Richard's child as "Imogene." This was likely just a mistake due to the passage of time. Julia's first daughter with Richard was named Imogene, so the couple's ex-slaves, who recounted this story in the 1870s after having relocated to an all-Black settlement in Kansas, probably confused Julia's name with that of her daughter. It's not the only time that facts about Julia have been mixed up or exaggerated. For instance, some people claimed that Julia and her daughters lived with Richard in Washington when Congress was in session. Others stated that Julia was "a prominent figure of . . . Washington life" and that when Vice President Johnson was not "delightedly breaking ties in Senate votes . . . he and Julia would run off to Kentucky to manage the hotel he built . . . at White Sulphur Springs."[36] Julia supposedly served as the vice president's official hostess in Washington, while the couple's daughters were educated in their "magnificent house on E Street, given the Johnson name, and were welcomed at Ward Hall," one of the extended Johnson family homes in Kentucky. Still others claim that when DC socialites refused to accept Julia at their parties, Richard stopped going out almost entirely.[37]

While this certainly makes for exciting, even sexy, reading, there's no evidence that Julia, Imogene, or Adaline ever lived in Washington. Richard lived and worked in Washington for part of each year, and the Johnson women lived in Kentucky, taking care of the family's plantation and business interests while he was away. Richard stayed in a boardinghouse while Congress was in session, and he was publicly referred to in DC circles as a "bachelor."[38] Additionally, Imogene and Adaline were educated at home by a private tutor named Thomas Henderson, and Julia passed away before Richard became vice president in 1837. She couldn't have acted as the vice president's official hostess in Washington or "run off with him" to the hotel in Kentucky whenever the mood struck.[39] In addition to these conflicting reports about her life, it's also unclear what Julia Ann Chinn looked like, because no confirmed portraits of her are known to exist. Everyone agrees that she was a person of African descent. She has, however, been variously referred to at different times and in numerous places as a "negro," an "African," mulatto, brown, yellow, and an octoroon who was "fair enough to pass for white."[40]

The nature of Julia and Richard's relationship is also up for debate. Was she Richard's legal wife, his "willing" partner, or his coerced mistress? Some people considered the pair to have been married, concluding that since Richard treated Julia like his wife, she probably was.[41] According to the couple's former laborers, Richard asked Julia to marry him after the argument he had with his mother, when Jemima discovered he was baby Imogene's father. Concerned about his family's safety, Richard, after obtaining some legal counsel from a friend, apparently decided that marrying and freeing Julia was the best way to protect both her and their child.

Richard galloped home after talking to this friend and found the young woman sitting on the settee in front of a blazing fire, knitting, while their daughter slept in her crib. He sat down beside Julia and asked her if she wanted to get married. She looked at him in confusion and asked, "Why?" He said, "Well, I want you to marry *me*, wouldn't you like that?" She then responded with a joyful "Yes, and I will be so glad then my baby won't be sold." It's worth noting that Julia's first response, her focus, was not affection for the man she had just agreed to marry but relief about her daughter's safety. Whereas slavery and racial capitalism were built on the lie that Black women lacked maternal love—and the even greater lie that Black people were kinless—enslaved mothers made clear choices, each and every day, that revealed that what mattered most to them *was* their kin.[42] Richard assured Julia that neither she nor their daughter would ever be sold, and he went to town the next day and brought home yards of pink silk for her wedding dress. The enslaved seamstresses at Blue Spring then made her a beautiful dress, the cook baked a cake, and invitations were sent out to a short list of guests.

The night of the wedding, violins played somewhere out of sight, and the sound of the popular wedding ballad "I Will Be True" could be heard as Julia and Richard walked across the parlor and stood in front of Reverend Hayes, who married the pair. After cake and other refreshments were served, a number of voices, accompanied by those same violins, sang several popular songs. The Johnsons' former laborers concluded their oral history by stating that the couple's married life was a happy one and that they eventually had another daughter together.[43]

Although an emotionally satisfying account of Julia and Richard's story, it's unclear whether things happened this way. Nobody named Hayes, who supposedly married the couple, appears in the Scott County census records. Since the Johnson family had a history with Great Crossing Baptist Church, which they had helped found, it would have made sense for Richard to ask Thomas Henderson, one of the preachers at Great Crossing (and in later years headmaster of Choctaw Academy and tutor to the Johnsons' daughters), to marry him and Julia, given his long connection to the man. Capt. John Wilson, a contemporary of Richard's, claimed that the couple had, in fact, been secretly married by Henderson, although there is nothing in Henderson's personal papers to suggest he married the pair.[44] Additionally, no "free papers" have ever been discovered for Julia or her daughters, nor has a marriage license been recovered for Julia and Richard. Perhaps Julia was never enslaved, and the license could have been lost or destroyed by fire, a common enough occurrence at the time. Still, documents as late as 1828 refer to Julia as "belonging to Col. Johnson," suggesting she was never freed.[45]

Despite the lack of paperwork, and Kentucky's refusal to legally recognize interracial unions, some people clearly believed that Julia and Richard were a married couple. Judge James Y. Kelly, who knew Richard when Kelly was a young man, stated that "Old Col. Johnson had a mulatto wife."[46] And Richard himself referred to Julia as his wife. In a letter to a friend, Richard mentioned "my bride," and he supposedly released a statement to the press during the election of 1836 that concluded that "unlike Jefferson, Clay, Poindexter and others, I married my wife under the eyes of God, and apparently He has found no objections." Since all three of the politicians referenced were sexually involved with Black women, we can assume that Richard was talking about Julia in this letter. Although the state didn't recognize their partnership, Richard clearly believed that the laws of God trumped the laws of Kentucky.[47]

Despite these recollections, it's impossible to know how *Julia* felt about Richard. Though she was literate, we don't have any sources written by her. The accounts that have been passed down were mostly written by Richard or his contemporaries, and they're often written as love stories. Given the pair's significant age difference, however, and Julia's lifelong status as an enslaved person, it's doubtful this was a consensual relationship, at least in the beginning. Indeed, if this had been a love story, he likely would have freed her. And make no mistake:

Richard could have freed Julia. There were no laws in Kentucky that prevented owner manumission. Unlike other states, where the slave codes stated that freed Blacks had to leave the state, Kentucky had no such clause during Julia's lifetime. As long as Richard could prove that she would not become a financial charge to the county, there was nothing in the Kentucky Constitutions of 1792 or 1799 that would have prevented him from freeing her had he wanted to. After 1800, Kentucky didn't even require that manumissions be witnessed. It doesn't appear that Richard wanted to emancipate Julia, however. Perhaps he feared that if he freed her, he would lose his hold over her. She might leave him. She might choose to leave the state. She might even choose another man.[48]

Although sexual unions in the Old South between white slave owners and Black enslaved women were common, these "relationships" were always complicated affairs, where enslaved women had limited options, none of which were good, and little choice in the matter because of the intersection of slavery, racism, and patriarchy. Julia couldn't say no without incurring possible retaliation from her owner. Of all her "choices," then, the best one—if not for her, then for her descendants—was to ally with Richard. Such an alliance had the potential to give her children all the things she herself never had: a formal education, church marriages, ownership of property, and legal manumission. In short, significant upward mobility. It was a sacrifice on her part, but perhaps it was worth it when taking the long view from the perspective of an enslaved woman born in the 1790s when there were no other visible roads to emancipation.[49] According to the couple's former bondspersons, when Richard asked Julia to marry him, her first response was one of relief, because now her baby would never be sold. This suggests that Julia Ann Chinn was thinking along these very lines.

Certainly, interracial sexual relationships in the slave South were not all the same. They ranged from horrifyingly violent and abusive to more partner-like in nature and could have been onetime assaults or lasted for decades. The overarching shadow of slavery, however, which made words such as "choice" and "consent" complicated at best and entirely absent at worst, was never entirely eliminated, even in the best of situations.

The life of an enslaved woman named Celia stands at one end of the spectrum. Sold at auction in 1850 at fourteen years of age to the widower Robert Newsom, then sixty years old, Celia was raped by her new master that very first night on their way back to Newsom's farm in Missouri. This set the stage for the hell that became Celia's existence for the next five years. During this time Robert continued to rape her, on his farm, surrounded by his grown daughters and grandchildren, and Celia gave birth to two of Robert's children. After five years of assaults, Celia snapped. It's possible she had met someone, an enslaved man, and saw the chance for a different life with a person she cared about. During her third pregnancy, Celia begged Robert to leave her alone. She told him she was sick, and she warned him that she would hurt him if he didn't stay away from her. He refused to listen and came to her cabin that very night to claim her body as he believed to be his right, a cabin he had built for her so that he could be alone with her whenever he wished. That was the night she killed him.[50]

Although it had taken her five years to get to this point, and she had acquired some material privileges, such as the cabin, as a result of their sexual interactions, this wasn't a relationship. There had never been any choice on Celia's part. She had done nothing for five years, however, because where could she go? Robert's daughters were of no help. There was no way out for Celia, no prospect of freedom or upward mobility for her or her children. She had been purchased to be a sex slave, and there was no such crime in the Old South as the rape of an enslaved woman. People could do as they wished to their laborers. In some states, they could even murder them without penalty.[51]

If Celia and Robert are at one end of the spectrum when it comes to the kinds of sexual interactions that occurred between slave owners and enslaved women, then the relationship of Zephaniah Kingsley Jr. and Anta Madgigine Jai Kingsley is at the other end of the continuum. Kingsley stated that Anta was a woman of "truth, honor, integrity, moral conduct [and] good sense... who has always been respected as my wife."[52] Anta, or Anna as she came to be known, was only thirteen years old when she was captured by raiders in Senegal in 1806, eventually ending up in Havana, where she was purchased by Kingsley, a forty-one-year-old slave trader. Afterward, he took her back to his home in Spanish Florida. By the time the pair arrived at Zephaniah's plantation, Anna was already pregnant with his child.[53]

The couple lived together openly with their children for the next thirty-seven years until Zephaniah's death, and he always referred to Anna as his wife. "A fine, tall figure, black as jet, but very handsome," Anna was affectionate, faithful, trustworthy, and capable, and she could run the plantation as well as Zephaniah in his absence.[54] Formally freed by Zephaniah in 1811, along with their three young children, Anna not only remained with her husband after she was emancipated; she continued to actively manage his home and lands. She also became a plantation owner and slave owner in her own name and was apparently an excellent businesswoman, helping to oversee her family's financial affairs.[55]

Between these two ends of the spectrum lie a range of Black-white relationships. There was Judge Nathan Sayre and Susan Hunt, who lived in antebellum rural Georgia. Nathan built a hidden set of apartments within his Greek Revival mansion, Pomegranate Hall, while it was being constructed, in order to secretly house his family of color so he could live with them but no one would ever see them. While Nathan never married anyone else, white or Black, all three of the couple's children carried Susan's last name, were never legally or socially recognized by Nathan, and don't appear to have been formally educated. Still, the family lived together for over twenty years at Pomegranate Hall, and Susan and her children acquired most of Nathan's personal household goods before he died. Nathan also left shares of railroad stock for Susan upon his death, although they were in the hands of a trusted white male friend.[56]

While Nathan Sayre completely hid his Black family from sight, Sally Hemings and Thomas Jefferson's relationship was hidden in plain sight. Sally was only fifteen years old when the relationship began, and the future president was forty-four; the pair came together in Paris, where the law said Sally was free. Jefferson, apparently, wasn't the type to physically force himself on a woman; he instead chose verbal methods of persuasion to convince women to sleep with him. In fact, when Jefferson began packing up to return to Virginia, Hemings told him she was going to stay in France with her brother, also one of Jefferson's laborers, where they could live as free people. Hoping to convince her to come back with him, Jefferson promised the young woman that he would free any child the couple had together when that child turned twenty-one years of age.[57]

We know Sally Hemings chose America and Jefferson over France and the unknown and that Jefferson freed all five of her children who survived to adulthood. And while Jefferson never publicly acknowledged Hemings or their children, it was a poorly kept secret. Hemings led a relatively comfortable life at the president's estate at Monticello, and she was able to negotiate certain privileges for her children and for members of her larger, extended family. It also appears that both parties came to care for each other over the course of the thirty-eight years they spent together. Not only did Jefferson free the couple's children and find good apprenticeships for them, but Hemings had no children during Jefferson's long absences from Monticello, suggesting she was faithful to him. She may have had other options, as she was, by all accounts, an attractive young woman.[58]

Unlike Sally Hemings, Julia Frances Dickson was only thirteen years old on a cold February day in 1849 when she was yanked from the field where she was playing and raped by David Dickson, her owner's son. Julia was a tiny girl who hadn't even had her first period when she was assaulted by the large, heavyset man in his early forties. Her childhood ended the same day her daughter, Amanda America Dickson, was so violently conceived. And while her descendants remembered that Julia held the keys to the Dickson plantation and controlled everything on the property, and that she and her mother, Rose, lived in a nicer house than most of the other Dickson servants, Amanda was also taken from Julia as soon as she was weaned and lived in the main house with David's mother, Elizabeth.[59]

Julia and David Dickson were known to be intimate in many ways, kissing in front of visitors to the plantation and discussing business matters in the parlor or in David's bedroom, behaving, some said, like sweethearts. Deep down, however, Julia never fully forgave David for what he had done to her. In addition to Amanda, she had two other children by two other men, one white and one Black, and she eventually stopped sleeping with David altogether. It was a complicated partnership that never really survived that first, brutal assault, and Amanda Dickson was the one who benefited most from this union. She acquired an education as well as most of her father's fortune at his death, making her the largest landowner in Hancock County, Georgia, and the wealthiest Black woman in the post–Civil War South.[60]

Interracial sex between white male slave owners and enslaved Black women was widespread in the Old South, but it was also complicated. Patriarchy, slavery, and racism made it impossible for these interactions to be anything *but* complicated. Constantly having to walk a fine line to keep their partners happy, enslaved wives lived lives that were never secure. While their relationships gave them certain privileges, everything could change if their husband's favor was removed. Power, freedom, wealth, even access to their children—everything could vanish in an instant. What this book illuminates is where on the spectrum of master-slave unions Julia Chinn and Richard Johnson's relationship fell. It examines what the Johnson women's lives were like on a daily basis and in the long run; how people responded to this relationship, at home and across the country; where the lines of privilege were drawn for Julia, for Adaline and Imogene, and for Richard; and whether the choices and sacrifices Julia made ended up benefiting her descendants in the ways in which she had hoped.

CHAPTER TWO

MISTRESS OF THE PARLOR

The Black Woman of Blue Spring

The people of Georgetown were in a tizzy. Lafayette was coming! *The* Lafayette—the man who had been imprisoned for five years for his democratic political convictions. Friend of George Washington. Hero of the Battle of Brandywine. Champion of *liberté, egalité,* and *fraternité* in revolutionary France. Hoping to catch a glimpse of the Revolutionary War hero, Kentuckians of all races and ages eagerly lined the roadways for fifteen miles between Lexington and Georgetown to cheer on the marquis as he made his way toward Blue Spring Farm, home of Julia Chinn and Richard M. Johnson, on May 18, 1825. They roared their enthusiasm alongside the din of cannon and musket fire as Lafayette rode past in a parade that included generals, prominent citizens of the state, and Governor Joseph Desha. The "Spirit of 1776" was very much alive that day as the marquis went through Fayette and Scott Counties on his way to an "elegant dinner" that had been prepared for him at the Johnson residence.[1]

While the afternoon's parade was a sight to behold, it was nothing compared to the gala that took place at Blue Spring Farm that night. Well-dressed bondspeople poured vast quantities of wine and punch, and the sound of music carried into the air as hundreds of people of all classes streamed toward Julia and Richard's home, which was lit up for the celebration. Every girl in town was dressed for the occasion, and for just a few hours everyone, rich and poor, came together to make merry as a community. Each household in the neighborhood had helped prepare various parts of the feast, since the festivities were beyond the capabilities of any one family. Trenches had been dug by enslaved laborers along an actual branch of the Blue Spring for cooking roasts, and ladies from the area reportedly made a cheese weighing 500 pounds in honor of the occasion. Other accounts mention that there were 500 cheese balls. The entertainment included a stirring speech from young Richard M. Johnson Jr., the twelve-year-old nephew and ward of Richard Mentor Johnson, piano performances by "certain female guests," and exhibitions by various students from Choctaw Academy, the Native American boarding school on the Johnsons' property. When Lafayette finally left Blue Spring that day, "he entered his carriage amidst the hearty greetings of a large assemblage of citizens who had gathered to take their last leave of him."[2]

Most of the work for this feast was done by the enslaved laborers of Blue Spring Farm, and it was Julia Chinn who oversaw the entire event and made sure that everything was prepared perfectly, given her role as "the chief manager of the domestic concerns of the house." And Julia and her daughters almost certainly met the marquis during his visit to their home. Not only did Richard recognize Julia "as his wife, the mistress of his parlor, and the mother of his household, which was confirmed by everyone who knew him; he unblushingly treated the girls as his daughters, placing them at the same table with the most honorable of his white guests."[3]

Visitors who went to Blue Spring to see Lafayette that day verified that Imogene and Adaline Johnson attended the party; they were the "certain female guests" who played the piano for the general that evening. The girls were thirteen and eleven years old, respectively, when the marquis came to visit, wearing gowns as fine as money could buy. These were dresses that Julia either carefully purchased or had specially made for the occasion. Local papermaker Ebenezer Stedman remarked that to anyone who didn't know them, Imogene and Adaline would have been mistaken for white, since they were as light-skinned as any of the other ladies at the party that evening. And there were a good many white folks from all walks of life at Blue Spring the day the Marquis de Lafayette came to visit. Rich and poor, Black, white, and Native, male and female, the residents of Georgetown all ate, drank, and danced well into the night, making many a toast to the Revolutionary generation along the way.[4]

A stirring scene, this wasn't the first time, nor would it be the last, that Julia Chinn stood in the parlor at Blue Spring and directed matters as mistress of the manor. And since Richard's political career kept him in Washington, DC, for six months each year, it was Julia, like many white women of her day, who ran the family business while her husband was away. In this case, that business was Blue Spring Farm, a 2,000-acre plantation where hemp and corn grew and that had a tavern on the premises, along with grist-, hemp-, and sawmills and a workforce of roughly eighty enslaved laborers. At Blue Spring, their private home space, Julia Chinn and her daughters wielded significant authority over enslaved people, over the students of Choctaw Academy, and even over certain white persons.[5]

White women were frustrated after the end of the American Revolution. They had sacrificed much to see the United States win the war against Britain, and they considered themselves to be patriots, just like their fathers, husbands, sons, and brothers. Some had followed the Continental army, working as cooks, laundresses, and nurses. Others disguised themselves as men and fought on the front lines. Still more managed their family's farms and businesses while the men were away, which gave them confidence in their abilities to think and act on matters normally reserved for men. When the war ended, and the men came home, many women were unwilling to return to the status quo. While the new US Constitution excluded them from voting or holding political office, large numbers of women, knowing their capabilities, refused to be denied civic roles entirely. They also demanded that marriage and motherhood be adjusted to new standards. "I object to the word 'obey' in the marriage-service," wrote one woman, "because it is a general word, without limitations or definition. Obedience between man and wife . . . ought to be, mutual."[6]

As female subordination in the home became a subject of debate, a growing number of people began arguing that women ought to have more rights with regard to the state. They insisted that a successful American republic needed "virtuous citizens" and the only way to develop such citizens was by creating "virtuous mothers" to serve the republic. This led to calls for higher education for women. The belief was that educated women would make better mothers, who in turn would raise up better (male) citizens. This concept, known as "Republican Motherhood," was advocated by men and women alike, although some of the women who called for it did so for different reasons than the men. Judith Sargent Murray wrote in 1790 that she favored education that would make women "self-confident, rational beings," stating that both men and women had "equal intellectual abilities" and thus deserved equal education. She hoped that sensible, informed women would improve their minds and not rush to marry but would eventually instill republican ideals in their children.[7]

An early feminist, Murray emphasized educating women in the values of liberty and independence to strengthen the virtue of the new nation and ensure they passed those values on to their children. While women might gain literacy and knowledge, the main objective was to create better male citizens; women still had to put their husbands and families first. Republican Motherhood did, however, push the urban upper classes to begin founding schools for girls in large numbers after 1780, providing US women with their first real opportunities for advanced education. These prospects didn't extend to Black women, however; that they also might have the capacity for virtue (and intellect) was inconceivable to those writing about female virtue at this time.[8]

Despite the educational advances that came with Republican Motherhood, women still faced significant legal obstacles in the United States during the early national period. Once they married, women went from being able to transact business in their own names to ceasing to exist as persons in the eyes of the law. No longer considered autonomous legal beings, married women couldn't buy or sell goods or services, enter into legal contracts, own property, sue or be sued, or conduct any business apart from their husbands. They weren't even entitled to their own wages if they worked outside the home. By law, upon marriage women became femes covert, literally "covered women," unable to transact any business on their separate and exclusive account or benefit, unlike single women, who were legally seen as femes sole.[9]

Julia Chinn, shackled by these limitations due to her gender, was further bound by her race and by her status as an enslaved person. Yet she, like many other married women, still exercised significant authority, both at home and in her local community. A savvy, literate businesswoman who also possessed the skill of numeracy, Julia handled Blue Spring's finances and oversaw its slave labor force. She used the cash Richard left her each year to pay the plantation's employees, contracted with area merchants to have furniture made for the farm, and, using Richard's lines of credit, purchased a wide range of goods and services for her family, from wine and clothes to home repairs. Julia also interacted with the headmaster and students of Choctaw Academy, the boarding school for Native American boys located on the Johnsons' property. Founded at Blue Spring Farm in 1825 thanks to Richard's political connections, the school ran smoothly because of the oversight of Julia Chinn, who helped perform and oversee a number of tasks for the students. This included making their clothes, taking care of them when they fell ill, organizing their housing arrangements, and distributing spending money to them. The school remained in operation until the late 1840s. That a Black woman helped manage the plantation and the school would become an issue for some of the young men who attended the academy.[10]

Although they had just become parents in the spring of 1812, Julia and Richard spent little time together with their new baby; Johnson left Blue Spring shortly after Imogene was born. The United States had officially declared war against Britain in what would later be called the War of 1812. Commissioned as a colonel, Richard resigned his seat in Congress and raised two regiments of mounted regulars from Kentucky to follow him to the front.[11] Involved in decades of conflict with each other, Britain and France each worked to block the United States from trading with the other nation in an attempt to prevent supplies from reaching their longtime enemy. In 1807, Britain took the blockade to new heights, requiring that all neutral countries obtain a license from England before trading with France or French colonies. Frustrated by England's policies, which were crippling the American economy, the United States was further enraged by the British Royal Navy's continual searches of US merchant ships at sea and the subsequent seizures of its seamen. England claimed these men were British deserters, and they forced the sailors to serve in the Royal Navy. These issues led many young "war hawk" politicians, including Richard, fellow Kentuckian Henry Clay, and John C. Calhoun from South Carolina, to press for and eventually vote in favor of the War of 1812.

With a newborn at her breast, Julia watched Richard ride off to war, not knowing if he would ever return or what would happen to her and Imogene if he died. Over 2,000 acres of prime real estate and eighty enslaved laborers were now under her authority. One wonders what went through Julia's mind as she surveyed the land and its laborers. Her mother, Henrietta, wasn't there to give her advice, having been left behind at Johnson's Station. Her brother, Daniel, however, was at Blue Spring and worked in the main house with her. If there was anyone she could talk to and trust, it would have been him. Daniel's wife, Patience, was also a member of the house staff. Still, with Richard gone, and letters from the front being few and far between, the brunt of running the large planation fell on the shoulders of the new, fifteen-year-old mother. Farming, overseeing the work and disciplinary issues of the estate's slave labor force, hosting guests for weeks or months, sewing clothes, cooking, cleaning, paying the bills, making purchases for the farm at local stores, taking care of Blue Spring's livestock, gardens, and mills, and raising her daughter, along with a hundred other things, were now her responsibility. She had to have been lonely, even scared. But it's doubtful she let anyone see it. She couldn't. With Richard away at war, Julia was truly the mistress of Blue Spring Farm. She was in charge, and if she wanted the respect of the farm's workforce, and of her white neighbors, she had to act like it.[12]

Richard wouldn't return to Blue Spring until the fall of 1813, after the Battle of the Thames. On October 5, in a bloody encounter in Upper Canada, near

Chatham, Ontario, Richard led his men in a brave, "forlorn hope" maneuver that helped win the day for the American forces who were under the overall command of Maj. Gen. William Henry Harrison. Taking twenty of his trusted Kentucky horsemen and charging straight at the Native Americans allied with the British, hoping to draw them away from the main US contingent (led by his brother James Johnson), Richard was hit by at least five bullets, his beautiful white horse shot out from under him, his left arm and hand badly shattered.

This clash at the Thames made Richard a national hero. Horribly wounded, not only did he and his troops help the Americans win a great victory that day, retaking Detroit from the British, but the Shawnee chief Tecumseh died in the conflict. This eroded Indigenous resistance in the area, and Richard took credit for Tecumseh's death. Reports from later years, however, strongly suggest that it was William Whitley, a Revolutionary War veteran, and not Richard Johnson, who killed the famous Native warrior.[13]

Imogene, a newborn when Richard rode off to war, was over twenty months old when her father, badly broken and close to death, was carried home on a stretcher after the Battle of the Thames. The toddler likely didn't remember him. And although his injuries were severe, Richard wasn't interested in staying in bed. Julia, an excellent physician, had her hands full. By late November, Richard was already up and walking on crutches, and he attended a public dinner in his honor in Lexington in January. In late February, shortly after Imogene's second birthday, although not fully recovered, Richard hauled himself up on a horse and began the long trip back to Washington, determined to rejoin Congress. He had stayed home just long enough to leave Julia pregnant with their second daughter. Arriving back in DC to a hero's welcome, he took his seat in the US House of Representatives on March 1, 1814, although he still hadn't regained the full use of his left arm and hand and was unable to participate in floor debates until the next session of Congress. This came to be the pattern of the couple's life together for the next two decades: Richard came and went, spending months at a time away from Blue Spring. When Richard was at home, sex with her husband was added to Julia's other labors. This work included planning and hosting the many social functions that came with being a politician's wife, including the 1825 gala for Lafayette.[14]

In many respects, Julia's day-to-day existence looked like that of the white plantation wives in her local area. It also looked very much like Anna Kingsley's life in Florida. Zephaniah Kingsley, like Richard Johnson, was away from home much of the time. A slave trader who was often on the road, Zephaniah trusted his Black wife with his affairs, a woman he said could run his plantation as well as he could. Organized and efficient, Anna managed Zephaniah's home and lands whenever he was away, took care of the couple's children, and oversaw the family's financial affairs. She stayed with Zephaniah and continued to perform these functions even after he manumitted her and their three children in 1811. This, of course, was one significant difference between Anna and Julia Chinn; the latter woman was *never* legally freed.[15]

A slave on paper, Julia lived the daily existence of a busy plantation wife. Like other farms in the area, Blue Spring was a business, working to turn a profit from hemp and corn. And like the nearby plantations of Henry Clay and others, it had an absentee landlord for a large part of each year. It also had a young mistress overseeing things while trying to raise her children and care for both house and farm. There was also an enslaved labor force that, unsurprisingly, didn't want to work. What made Blue Spring Farm different from its neighbors was the existence of Choctaw Academy on its premises, which brought white teachers and Native students together with the farm's mistress, her daughters, and their enslaved laborers. There was also the fact that the aforesaid mistress and her children were enslaved Black women themselves. Even if some local whites didn't treat them that way. Even though the Johnson women didn't *behave* as if they were enslaved.

For example, while Julia and her daughters lived at Blue Spring, they didn't stay in the slave quarters. It's not clear if Julia and Richard lived together, however. It appears that Julia and the girls stayed at the main house when Richard was in Washington, and Julia certainly helped host galas there. There were several buildings on the property, however, including the brick dwelling that Richard called his "Great House." Newspaper articles claim the couple lived together when Richard was in Kentucky, but Julia also had her own place at Blue Spring, a "stone house." In this way, her life also mirrored Anna Kingsley's. Anna lived in a pretty, two-story brick-and-wood-frame house with her children, just steps from the main house, occupied by her husband, Zephaniah. Like Anna, Julia appears to have earned the privilege of having her own home: a place where she could retreat from the labors of the day and prying white eyes, as well as potentially hostile Black and Indigenous ones. It was likely a place to escape from Richard on occasion, too. Julia may have negotiated this home, a structure large enough to house a three-room library, as part of the couple's "relational arrangement."[16]

That is what young Julia Dickson did after David Dickson pulled her out of the fields and raped her, leading to the birth of their daughter, Amanda. While laborers, visitors, and relatives all mention that Julia and David Dickson behaved as lovers, kissing and sitting in the parlor or by the fire in David's bedroom, Julia and her mother lived in a house of their own, separate from the other Dickson bondspersons, on the edge of the Dickson property. As an enslaved person, however, Julia Dickson, like Julia Chinn, wasn't legally permitted to own anything;

this was never really her house. Slave owners like David Dickson and Richard Johnson made it clear that their plantations, and everything on them, were their property. Richard told Thomas Henderson, headmaster of Choctaw Academy, that if more space was required for the students, he would just take over Chinn's house: "At any time I could appropriate that whole house if necessary." One wonders how Julia felt, knowing she could be turned out of her home by the father of her children whenever he chose. These kinds of situations would have reinforced to her that she was, fundamentally, unable to own property because, to Richard, she *was* property.[17]

Having a separate house would have been convenient for both Julia and Richard. Family and friends regularly visited Blue Spring Farm, staying for weeks or even months. Richard's sister Sally Johnson Ward and her husband, William, lived with Julia and Richard for several years before moving to Choctaw Nation, where William became the Choctaw people's Indian Agent for the federal government. And while guests could be a source of excitement, bringing news to the quiet rural area, as well as gifts, companionship, and playmates for her children, they also greatly increased Julia's workload. She had to entertain the visitors, arrange for any special needs they might have, and be sure their rooms were cleaned. It meant extra food shopping, cooking, expenses, and possibly childcare. This was in addition to her regular duties in terms of running the farm, tavern, and mills, overseeing the gardens and enslaved laborers, and raising her two daughters. Depending on who the guests were, Julia may have wanted to escape to her own place during these visits. And if Richard was in Kentucky, it would have been a convenient place for him to come and spend time with Julia or their daughters.[18]

An enslaved woman, Julia Chinn walked a fine line between having privilege and being property. Still, like white wives in the area, she exercised considerable oversight as manager of Blue Spring. And, like Zephaniah Kingsley, Richard Johnson relied on his Black wife to make sure that things ran smoothly in his absence. Holding the keys to the estate firmly in her grasp like other plantation mistresses, Julia attended to a variety of matters at Blue Spring. Probably her most important task, however, other than raising her daughters, was directing the farm's enslaved laborers. It was her job to make everyone "do their duty," behave, and be industrious. Thomas Henderson was there to aid her in case she fell sick and to make sure that the slaves didn't "get out of hand."[19] Julia, however, was responsible for telling Thomas which of Blue Spring's laborers acted "well" and which ones acted "ill." He, in turn, was supposed to "support her authority." This meant that Thomas was supposed to flog the bondspersons who didn't obey Julia's orders.[20]

Thomas Henderson came to his post at Blue Spring because of his long association with Great Crossing and its most famous family. Born June 15, 1781, in

John J. Audubon portrait of Rev. Thomas Henderson.

Image courtesy of the Filson Historical Society, Louisville, Kentucky.

Henry County, Virginia, Thomas married Nancy M. Terrill in Charlottesville, Virginia, on April 28, 1803, and was ordained as a Baptist minister in that state in 1808. By September 1810, Thomas and his family were living in Kentucky, and he was one of the ministers of the Baptist Church of Christ at Bullittsburg. In 1812, Thomas moved his family from Boone County to Great Crossing in Scott County, where he became the fifth pastor of Great Crossing Baptist Church. Founded by a group of Baptists from Virginia that included Richard's parents, this was the church Richard grew up in and which he and Julia attended. Thomas preached at Great Crossing and developed a close relationship with Richard. A gentle, well-read man who was opposed to corporal punishment, Thomas believed in educating people of all races and backgrounds. He took over as headmaster of Choctaw Academy in 1825, a position he acquired because of his connection to the Johnson family. He continued to preach at Great Crossing on a rotating basis, balancing that with his duties at Choctaw Academy, where he remained headmaster until 1841.[21]

Thomas wore many hats at Blue Spring because Richard didn't hire an official overseer for the farm until 1828. Until then, Thomas and Julia essentially functioned in that role as a team. Coleaders and virtual equals, she took care of most of the day-to-day tasks of running Blue Spring when Richard was away, as a plantation wife would, and Thomas stepped in and "disciplined" the male field hands when they needed to be reminded that Julia was in charge. Julia oversaw all matters for the house party, including punishments. Richard likely didn't hire an overseer on purpose, preferring to leave certain things in the hands of his longtime friend. It was less expensive, plus who else could be trusted in the position? Not many white men would have taken orders from the enslaved woman running things on the Johnson place.

The Black mistress of Blue Spring Farm definitely had issues maintaining control when her husband was away. In December 1825, Julia Chinn was having real trouble. Choctaw Academy had just opened, so she was busier than usual. In the midst of dealing with her increased workload, one of the students had fallen ill, and she couldn't get two enslaved laborers, named Daniel and Jerry, to help her take care of him. This was a problem on a number of fronts. Julia and Richard couldn't afford to have a student die; that kind of negative publicity could harm funding for the school. To make things worse, all the male field hands had snuck off and left the plantation, except for two men named Sandy and Jacob Chace. The bondspeople likely hadn't gone far; it was Christmastime. It was customary for the enslaved to have the week off between Christmas and New Year's Day. They were probably visiting friends and family on nearby farms. What isn't clear is why twenty-eight-year-old Julia hadn't given her laborers the standard time off, causing them to have to sneak away. She surely remembered holidays as a child, spending time with her mother Henrietta and her brother, Daniel. Since the school had just opened, perhaps Julia needed "all hands on deck," so she canceled Christmas break. Whatever the reason, it appears the Johnson slaves were unwilling to forgo their annual holiday. This aggravated Julia, partly because these kinds of "disciplinary issues" arose every winter when Richard was in Washington. Unhappy, she wrote to her husband about what was happening.[22]

Richard was furious. Over the next three months, he wrote several letters to Thomas Henderson about this situation. He told him to talk to Julia, figure out who had been causing her problems, and then whip the offenders. If he didn't want to flog the men himself, Thomas was ordered to call a constable to come and beat the laborers in question. As a last resort, the troublemakers were to be sold to Edward C. Johnson's cotton farm. It's clear from even this one incident that the enslaved laborers at Blue Spring didn't respect Julia's leadership and that Richard was perfectly willing to use violence to uphold her authority, and his own. While many slave-mistresses had similar issues when their husbands and fathers were away, the problems at Blue Spring Farm were surely aggravated by Julia's race. In what appears to be a case of "while the cat's away the mice will play," the field hands at the Johnson place pushed to see how far they could go when Richard was in Washington. Julia, like many white plantation mistresses, had to call on white men, including Thomas Henderson, local constables, and her neighbors, to help carry out the disciplinary actions needed to enforce her authority, because she was unable to punish the offenders herself. And while it's possible that she was unwilling to discipline the bondspersons at Blue Spring, the fact that she wrote to Richard about her troubles suggests otherwise, since she likely knew how he would react.[23]

Julia Chinn was clearly the manager of Blue Spring Farm. She appears to have had authority over every part of the plantation, including the lives of other enslaved people, and she seems to have taken that role seriously, informing Richard about everything that happened in his absence, including when their laborers broke the rules. This would have strengthened Richard's faith in her. In turn, her willingness to report on other bondspersons probably gave Julia the ability to ask favors of Richard, and his growing trust in her likely meant that he was more willing to say yes to her suggestions. For example, Julia's brother, Daniel, eventually became Richard's body servant. Daniel's wife, Patience, along with the couple's daughters, wove, sewed clothes, did laundry, and performed other tasks that kept them out of the fields. As members of the house party, Daniel and Patience's daughters also acquired an education, since Thomas Henderson tutored the house staff at night, alongside Imogene and Adaline Johnson.[24] Years of strategic choices eventually made Julia Chinn Richard Johnson's right hand at Blue Spring Farm. She then used her position to protect and promote the interests of her extended family.

Julia's relationship with those who worked in the fields was more complicated, and contentious, than her connections to the members of the house party, many of whom were her kin. It was the field laborers at Blue Spring who challenged her authority. They were also the ones whom Julia turned in to Richard when they "misbehaved." It's doubtful, then, that Julia had family among the "outhands." These laborers led very different lives from Julia and her daughters, from the small cabins they lived in to the homespun clothing they wore and the fatback and mutton they ate. Even the domestic staff at Blue Spring wore clothes that set them apart from the farm's field hands, and the Johnson women wore head-turning dresses, garments made from expensive, high-end fabrics. Their outfits were a regular topic of conversation among their white neighbors and in the local press. And though the Black folk at Blue Spring all attended Great Crossing Baptist

Church, Julia sat on the main floor of that church with Richard. All other enslaved persons, as well as free Blacks, sat upstairs in the gallery.[25]

It's not surprising, then, that men such as Daniel and Jerry refused to take orders from Julia when Richard was away, while the male outhands all "walked off the job." The field hands likely resented the mistress of Blue Spring Farm, an enslaved woman who, from their perspective, was no different than they were but who had it better than them: she lived in a nice home, ate good food, wore expensive clothing, did cleaner work, and socially segregated herself from the other Black laborers on the farm. Their frustration would have come to the forefront when that same enslaved Black woman tried to tell them what to do. Richard, ever the enslaver, thus turned disciplinary matters over to white men such as Thomas Henderson, and later to a man from a local family, Edward H. Pence, in order to reinforce his wife's authority.[26]

Although the situation at Blue Spring meant that Julia occasionally needed Thomas's help, he wasn't in charge of her. We already know that Julia was a literate woman and that she wrote to Richard to tell him what was happening in Kentucky while he was in Washington. It was in one of those letters that Julia complained to Richard about the situation with Daniel and Jerry. She also told Richard whether Thomas Henderson was doing his job.[27] In January and February of 1826, Julia was in better spirits, in part because the headmaster was being very helpful. The man had recently given Daniel, "the problem slave," a stern lecture. He was also regularly visiting the couple's house to hear Adaline's and Imogene's lessons (which had a good influence on the girls), and he had been of great help in making the field hands behave. Richard wrote to thank Thomas for his good work.[28] While he may have been grateful to the man for keeping up his end of their deal (tutoring the couple's daughters and helping Julia maintain discipline at Blue Spring in return for his job and free housing on the farm), it's also likely that Richard wanted Thomas to know that if he *didn't* do his part, Richard would find out. Clearly, Julia Chinn wasn't only relaying information about Blue Spring's enslaved laborers to Richard M. Johnson.

In addition to overseeing matters at Blue Spring Farm, Julia's other significant responsibility was helping Thomas manage Choctaw Academy. While Thomas was headmaster, Julia oversaw the practical tasks that kept the institution functioning. This was a boarding school: the students needed food, clothing, medical attention, and more. It was Julia who directed a team of skilled Black seamstresses at Blue Spring who made the students' clothes. An excellent cook, she likely also oversaw some of the school's food preparation along with Jerry, the academy's enslaved cook.[29] Because Julia had been trained as a house servant by Richard's mother, Jemima Johnson, it's possible that it was Jemima who taught Julia how to read and write. She likely learned how to sew and cook under the apprenticeship of the talented enslaved seamstresses and cooks at Johnson's Station. Some of her knowledge of cooking and sewing, along with her medical skills, could have also been passed down to her by her mother, Henrietta.

Julia regularly drew on all these skills after she moved to Blue Spring Farm and became Richard's wife, the mother of his children, and the "mistress of his parlor." Responsible for every soiree at the Johnson residence, big and small, Julia would have handled the arrangements for President James Monroe's visit to Kentucky in 1819. While in the Bluegrass State, Monroe spent one night at Johnson's farm as he traveled from Frankfort to Lexington. Although there was a public dinner for the president in Frankfort one evening, which Richard Johnson and Andrew Jackson both attended, the men all relaxed and ate at Blue Spring on a Thursday afternoon in July and then stayed there overnight before traveling to Lexington the next day.[30]

Richard was known for his hospitality. Indeed, when he was home from Washington, he loved to entertain, and entertain lavishly. Contemporaries said they were treated so well when they visited Blue Spring, they just "loved to go."[31] Adam Tunno was like Richard in this respect. Although Tunno wasn't a politician, he was wealthy and well respected. A prominent merchant in Charleston, South Carolina, Adam imported Madeira wine and was involved in the city's most distinguished mutual-aid organization, the St. Andrew's Society; his social circle thus included men of power and influence. He also enjoyed the finer things in life, regularly hosting wine and dinner parties at his home on Charleston's illustrious East Bay. It was Adam's wife of forty years, Margaret Bettingall, who organized these parties. A Black woman who may have been enslaved, Margaret, like Julia, was a God-fearing woman. A communicant at St. Philip's Episcopal Church, Bettingall ran Tunno's home, raised the couple's children, oversaw the work of the enslaved laborers who lived in small dwellings scattered about the couple's yard, and carried the keys to the estate on her belt. Known as the "head and front" of the Tunno home, Margaret was acknowledged as the "mistress of Adam's household" by white Charlestonians, just as Kentuckians knew that Julia Chinn was the mistress of the parlor at Blue Spring Farm.[32]

James Monroe wasn't the only visitor to Blue Spring. Julia got used to hosting events, big and small, often on the spur of the moment. For example, when Richard came home from Congress in 1824, he and some of the neighbors decided to invite the entire township out to Blue Spring on July 3 to celebrate the nation's birthday. Given the numbers expected, Julia was one of many women in the area cooking and preparing for the gathering. Since the party was going to be held at Blue Spring, however, most of the work for planning the spectacle fell to Julia and the Johnsons' enslaved laborers. And what a spectacle it was! A special table, 300 feet long, was built just to hold all the food, and the Georgetown Light Infantry made an appearance and fired off a special salute on the hillside in honor of the occasion. They were answered in return by artillery that had been planted at the (blue) spring. Cannons were shot off at 11:00 a.m. to start the festivities, and the crowd listened to musical selections such as "Yankee Doodle." Speeches were given, and a special reading of the Declaration of Independence was made by none other than Richard himself. When all the speeches and toasts were finished, the guests, old and young, rich and poor, sat down together to enjoy a magnificent dinner that lasted over two hours. It was a perfect day, the kind that made Richard beloved in his community. It was also the kind of day that was only made possible by an enormous amount of enslaved labor. Carpenters. Cooks. Waitstaff. Cleanup crew. And Julia Chinn, who organized and oversaw everything, like any good political wife and hostess. The only difference was, she was an enslaved Black woman.[33]

Given her experience directing such affairs and receiving dignitaries such as President Monroe, Julia was more than ready to host the Marquis de Lafayette in May 1825. She was probably excited to meet the man, known as he was for his abolitionist views. It's doubtful that the French hero, on a tour to visit the friends he had made during the American Revolution, would have visited tiny Georgetown had it not been for Richard Johnson, then at "the noon tide of his prosperity."[34] Richard was popular in the 1820s. He was a war hero, the supposed slayer of Tecumseh, and a sitting US senator. He also belonged to one of the "First Families of Kentucky." His parents had helped found the state, moving to Kentucky from Virginia, and then established one of the most important Baptist churches in the area. His father, Robert, was, among other things, one of the signers of the Kentucky State Constitution. The Johnson men, thanks to Robert's position as a territorial surveyor, owned tens of thousands of acres of the best land in the state and among them counted congressmen, federal judges, and, one day, a vice president of the United States. The women married into other powerful families across the state and the nation, connecting the Johnsons to planter wealth in Mississippi and beyond.[35] It's no exaggeration to say that Richard M. Johnson belonged to his century's version of the 1 percenters. Richard's family's connections and wealth, along with his military service, catapulted him to a position of political and social power.

Given his background, Richard should have married a white woman from a family as powerful as his own, further expanding the Johnson family's wealth and their civic reach. But he never did, even when it would have been in his own best interest to do so. The fact is that Richard, who was good-looking, popular with the ladies, and a smooth dancer, was also almost always in debt, scrambling to hold on to the appearance of wealth. This is partly because he tended to loan money to people who never paid him back. He was also a terrible businessman. Hoping to get in on the ground floor of westward expansion, he and his brothers made several unwise deals over the years, leaving Richard skating on the edge of bankruptcy for most of his adult life. Unwilling to give up the good food, fine wines, and extravagant parties he enjoyed, he was regularly in and out of court, trying to collect money from those who owed him and holding off his own creditors. This may have been one of the reasons why Richard didn't hire an overseer to help Julia with things at Blue Spring until the late 1820s. He couldn't afford it. In fact, things got so bad in 1824 that he mortgaged most of his property, including several of his enslaved laborers, in order to raise the cash he needed to pay his bills. A steady stream of letters from his desk in Washington to creditors, bankers, and lawyers in Kentucky and elsewhere reveal the dark underbelly of Richard's lavish lifestyle. These financial woes surely kept Julia on edge. Although Richard supposedly never treated Julia as a slave, he also never freed her. Had he gone bankrupt, she and their daughters, unlike a white wife and children, could have ended up on the auction block to satisfy the bill collectors. Such thoughts likely kept the woman up at night.[36]

We'll never know why Richard never married a white woman. Although Julia Chinn performed all the duties of a wife, Richard could have taken a white wife and still maintained his relationship with Julia, like so many of his contemporaries did, benefiting from the intimate *and* economic labors of both their white wives and their Black "housekeepers." Given his financial situation, it would have been the most logical choice. While not all southern planters had overseers, most had wives who could help to run their plantation enterprises along with the couple's enslaved laborers. Richard Johnson, however, chose not to marry a white woman. His housekeeper and his wife thus remained one and the same. Why?

Johnson family legend has it that Richard and his mother argued over his relationship with a poor white seamstress (or maybe it was a northern schoolteacher) at some point prior to the War of 1812. Richard wanted to marry the girl, but Jemima objected to having a daughter-in-law who didn't come from money. She knew her son could do better. Richard supposedly ended the romance but told his mother she'd regret her actions one day. That day came when he took Julia as his lover, after his father gave her to Richard as part of the younger man's inheritance. Because Jemima had trained Julia by hand and saw her as her "special pet," this horrified her on a whole host of levels. This, then, was the perfect revenge on Richard's part, although it fails to explain why he remained with Julia after Jemima's death and why he never married a white woman.[37] Maybe Richard actually cared for Julia. Perhaps no respectable family would marry one of their daughters to Richard, given his open relationship with Julia. Given his numerous sexual entanglements with Black women over the course of his life, there's also the possibility that Richard M. Johnson simply wasn't attracted to white women.[38]

In no way was Blue Spring your everyday plantation and Julia and Richard your commonplace farm couple. Indeed, after hosting Lafayette and the large number of guests his visit brought to their home, Julia welcomed a crowd of 700 to her home in 1827, all of whom came to Blue Spring to see performances given by the students of Choctaw Academy. Under her supervision, dozens of enslaved laborers bustled between the kitchens and the exhibition area that day, carrying bowls and trays heaped with all kinds of tasty dishes. Julia may have seen this party as being particularly important for her family. Having Choctaw Academy at Blue Spring allowed her and Richard to quietly educate their daughters at home with Thomas Henderson. It was important they impress these visitors, then, many of whom were public officials and tribal elders. If the federal government and the Choctaw chiefs were happy with the school's performance, they would continue to fund the academy and send students to the school, which would keep Thomas at Blue Spring.[39]

While Julia organized many a party at Blue Spring and was known for being a wonderful hostess, she and her daughters also attended these gatherings. In July of 1832, there was an electioneering barbecue at Choctaw Academy. The event overflowed with good food and wine, and everyone who attended the barbecue "had much fun and sport." This included "Miss J****** (you know whom I mean)," who was "dressed in the most brilliant manner, and really looked very pretty; the color of her dress was adapted with much taste to her complexion; and she was the greatest belle present." Although the lady's first name isn't mentioned, the comment about the woman's "complexion" suggests the anonymous letter writer was referring to Julia; her younger daughter, Adaline, was light enough to be mistaken for white by anyone who didn't know her family. It's doubtful the piece, which was published in a local paper, was about Julia's older daughter, Imogene; already married by 1832, she would have been known as Mrs. Pence.[40]

Richard Johnson was a fortunate man. He could afford to be away for six months every year because he knew his home and business interests were in good hands. He felt confident in turning every aspect of Blue Spring Farm over to Julia whenever he left, just like other absentee plantation owners did with their wives. From larger decisions concerning their laborers and state dinners, to smaller details regarding household purchases, there was nothing she couldn't handle. And it's no surprise that she raised her daughters not only to succeed in every aspect of life but to exceed her. This was Julia Chinn's main mission. Like

Black mothers well before her and those who would come long after, every step she took was carefully planned so her descendants would rise up higher, and go much further, than she herself *ever* would.

Imogene Johnson was born February 17, 1812, and Adaline Johnson sometime in 1814. The family's former enslaved laborers, who moved to Kansas after the Civil War, recalled that both were beautiful young women. One was a brunette with wavy hair that flowed to below her waist, the other a blonde who supposedly showed no signs of her African heritage. The Kansans described both girls as "well-trained," having been educated in private schools.[41]

Neither Johnson girl attended formal schools, however, private or otherwise. Instead they were tutored at home by Thomas Henderson. Their father frequently corresponded with Thomas about his daughters' education. Julia and Richard were fanatical about Imogene and Adaline's schooling. They knew how critical a good education would be to their daughters' ability to rise in America, socially and economically. Such behavior was hardly unusual among the planter class: it was common practice for mothers and then tutors to serve as the early educators of elite white children before they attended formal schools. The Johnsons' treatment of Imogene and Adaline, then, and the focus on their education thus mirrored what other elite white parents did for their children. The added layer here was Julia and Richard's understanding that their daughters faced additional obstacles in the United States due to the hierarchy of race.[42]

Julia wrote to Richard on a regular basis to keep him up to date on their daughters' lessons and Thomas's commitment to tutoring their girls. Richard, in turn, constantly asked the headmaster to pay attention to his family. He repeatedly reminded the man to continue his "evening visits to my house, if you stay only 30 minutes," and asked him to "oblige me to continue to hear lessons from my girls whenever you can at nights so as not to make it a burden to you." Richard apparently thought that tutoring his daughters and the house staff at night would make things easier on Thomas, who already had a job that kept him busy seven days a week.[43] He also alternated between praising the man for his efforts (promising to reward him financially for his work) and criticizing him for not keeping Richard up to date on his daughters' academic progress. There were also the not-so-subtle hints that Thomas's job as headmaster depended on his success with Imogene and Adaline: "Whenever you are well & able, visit my house as I requested to hear their lessons. You will understand that it is a matter personal to me & has had & will have influence in my arrangements for you with the Govt."[44]

If Thomas Henderson took the job at Choctaw Academy thinking that Richard's absence for six months each year would make things easier on him, he was sorely mistaken. Julia was a literate, savvy businesswoman who was deeply invested in her daughters' education. She had never been formally educated, and she knew how critical it was for Black women to have every tool at their disposal to help them in their quest for freedom and upward social mobility. That's why she wrote to Richard on a regular basis and kept him informed as to what was happening at home in general and with their daughters' lessons in particular. When Richard thus thanked Thomas for his "kind attention to the learning of my house party in my absence," Thomas probably understood that this was as much an acknowledgment of his hard work as it was a way of letting him know he was under surveillance.[45]

Because Imogene and Adaline were tutored by Choctaw Academy's headmaster, it's no surprise they received an education that put them on par with the white elite of their day. By the time Imogene was fourteen years old, she was studying grammar and punctuation, which led to advanced levels of English literacy. Her superior reading, writing, and patterns of speech allowed her to mingle with the most elegant of company. It makes sense that Julia and Richard wanted their daughters to be able to converse with the most educated people of their day: visitors to Blue Spring included local gentry, former presidents, and foreign dignitaries. Their education and social skills would make the girls more eligible marriage partners when they grew up and also allow them to avoid the low-wage jobs and grinding poverty that was the lot of most free Black women in the United States. Thomas also taught the girls the Italian method of bookkeeping and accounting, a skill that helped them manage the property each received from her parents when she married.[46]

Adaline and Imogene's training was supposed to be a private matter, although Kentucky had no laws against educating enslaved persons.[47] While Thomas was expected to visit the main house every night to tutor the Johnsons' daughters, and on those Sundays when there were no church meetings, Richard regularly referred to the headmaster's visits to the house to hear lessons as a personal matter: "It is best to keep our arrangements to ourselves & do our own duty."[48] Legal or not, Julia and Richard were probably worried about how their white neighbors would react to news that the girls were being educated and concerned that it might generate backlash.

The Johnsons' demands placed an enormous burden on Thomas, but it paid off for the girls. In 1835, when Richard was running for the vice presidency, Thomas, at Richard's urging, wrote a letter to the *Daily Globe* about Julia and the couple's daughters. In it, he claimed that if anyone unaware of Adaline and Imogene's parentage met them, they would never suspect that they were "the children of a colored woman." He also wrote that, at Richard's request, he spent his evenings, after his workday at the academy was over, tutoring several of Richard's house servants, in addition to these two young women. "I soon discovered such uncommon aptness in those two girls to take learning, and so much decent, modest, and unassuming conduct on their part, that my mind became much enlisted in their favor. I continued to give them lessons until their education was equal or superior to most of the females in the country."[49]

Thomas's letter, meant to help win voters to Richard's campaign, was a detailed, almost avuncular introduction of Richard's daughters to the country. They were very intelligent, although it's not clear whether Thomas thought the "uncommon aptness in those two girls to take learning" was because Imogene and Adaline were girls, persons of color, or both. They were also virtuous and humble, dressing and behaving like respectable young ladies. And their training went well beyond the basics; it was "equal or superior to [that of] most of the females in the country." Given the terrible, often illegal conditions under which antebellum Black people were educated, even those who were free, Thomas certainly meant *white* women. This was high praise, coming from an ordained minister.[50]

Imogene and Adaline were publicly known to be Julia Chinn's daughters by Richard Johnson. Although their father worked to keep their schooling a secret, he made no attempt to hide their parentage. He never contradicted statements that he was married to Julia or that her daughters were his own. Newspaper editorials claimed that Richard, using the influence of his name and his money, sought to have the girls, who went by the last name Johnson, recognized in society and forced them into the highest, most fashionable circles of the community. Some even claimed that he brought them into the ballrooms of the nation. It's true that white visitors of all classes interacted with the Johnson girls at Blue Spring and that Julia and her daughters attended Great Crossing Baptist Church. It doesn't appear that Richard tried to take his daughters to high-society engagements off his own farm, however, and there's no indication that Julia or her daughters ever visited Richard in Washington. This is consistent with the behavior of men such as Adam Tunno. While Tunno and his wife, Margaret Bettingall, entertained white visitors at their home on Charleston's East Bay, and Bettingall attended St. Philip's Episcopal Church, there is no indication that Margaret or the couple's daughters accompanied Adam to functions hosted by the prestigious mutual-aid society he belonged to. Adam educated and manumitted the couple's daughter, Barbara, raised Margaret's older daughter, Hagar, as his own, and left all three women a large estate at his death. Barbara even went by the last name Tunno before she married. But there were certain lines that Adam Tunno still wouldn't cross.[51]

The Johnson girls clearly received certain advantages because of who their father was. They went to lavish parties and wore fancy dresses, while their enslaved counterparts wore cotton or linsey outfits and served and cleaned up at those same parties. At Christmas, the Great House at Blue Spring was filled with pretty stockings, numerous kinds of candy, oranges, holiday packages, and pies for the Johnson family. The sheer material abundance of Julia and her daughters, when contrasted with the lack experienced by their enslaved laborers, can be summed up in the recollections of Addie Murphy, a young girl who waited on tables at the "Big House." Addie's mother was the Johnsons' cook, and her daughter blacked boots every morning, but she ate more blacking than she used, because it "tasted kinda sweet." This was apparently the only "treat" Addie ever got while working for the Johnsons.[52]

Although Adaline Johnson had a privileged childhood compared to Addie Murphy, she still grew up laboring on the plantation. She helped her mother with many of the chores associated with running Choctaw Academy, as it was too much work for any one person to oversee both the school and the farm. From the age of fourteen onward, Adaline worked with a team of enslaved women who sewed, distributed, washed, and mended the students' clothes throughout the school year. When she was older, Adaline, like Julia, wrote to Richard in Washington and kept him informed on plantation matters, including problems with their enslaved laborers, financial concerns, and disciplinary issues with students at the academy.[53] In later years, after her mother had passed away, Adaline took on even more of the responsibilities that Julia had carried while she was living. She became indispensable to her father. In a letter he wrote to his daughter in December 1833, Richard, after discussing the academy at length, as well as the farm's slaves, and a wedding he had attended, stated how happy he was with Adaline and her work ethic.[54]

Julia and Richard's older daughter, Imogene, was also raised at Blue Spring, educated by Thomas Henderson, and trained up under the care of her mother. Imogene appears to have had a different childhood than Adaline, however. There's no indication that she did much of the physical labor needed to maintain either the farm or the school while she was growing up. It seems odd that Imogene didn't have more responsibilities as a child, given that Adaline shouldered heavy burdens from a fairly early age. Perhaps this was a sign of favoritism toward their older daughter on the part of her parents. It's also possible that since Imogene married and left Blue Spring to start her own household in 1830, it was left to Adaline to help her parents manage the various family businesses.[55]

Julia Chinn and her daughters were busy southern farm women. And at least on the surface, it appears that local whites accepted the Johnson women and Julia's relationship with Richard. Educated, well dressed, trained to play the piano, and serving as planters, slave owners, hostesses, and managers, the Johnson women led lives that looked in many respects like those of the white plantation women in their community, people they socialized with at their home and at church. There were limits to the "toleration" of their neighbors, however. Indeed, some of these lines of tension and conflict appeared even before the Black women of Blue Spring stepped outside the boundaries of their own farm.

Even in these early years, and despite her position as "mistress of the manor," Julia always knew that the privileges she enjoyed were dependent on the goodwill of the man to whom she was married and that, for the sake of her daughters, she needed to keep herself in his good graces. She had no real authority over Richard. While he might listen to her on some matters, her powers of persuasion had their limits. This was brought home to her in the most devastating way in the fall of 1821 when Richard mortgaged her brother, Daniel Chinn, and Daniel's wife, Patience, in order to pay off his ever-mounting debts. While Richard never sold the couple, he was still willing to put them at risk, despite the fact that they were Julia's kin.[56] When it came to his own financial stability, Richard treated Daniel and Patience like any other property he owned, not family.

Enslaved people knew that an owner's debts or death always put them at risk of being sold away from their loved ones, because they could be "liquidated" in order to pay bills or fulfill an inheritance.[57] Whatever authority Julia held at Blue Spring Farm, it was never enough to fully protect those she loved from the man who would always have the final word on how things ran at Blue Spring. Like other enslaved women across the South, Julia Chinn thus worked to do the best she could with the tools she had: she focused on using both body and mind to "make a way out of no way" in order to ensure that Imogene, Adaline, and their families obtained a secure, legal, lasting freedom so that they would never, *ever* find themselves placed in such a position of risk.[58] Would she—could she—succeed?

There were many forces arrayed against the Johnson women. Some of these would come from the outside, in the form of the state and strangers. Others bore the faces of neighbors and fellow parishioners. There was also up-close hostility from some of the students at Choctaw Academy. There was no safe place for Julia and her daughters to lay their heads. Even Richard couldn't be fully trusted. The home, while supposedly a private space, was no refuge for Black women in the Old South, not even those women involved with powerful and wealthy white men. In fact, their public relationships with white men would make the Johnson women a target of both white and Native anger.

CHAPTER THREE

CAMPUS CONFLICTS

Racial Collisions at Choctaw Academy

*T*he men were drunk. They may have broken into and stolen whiskey from the storerooms on the plantation, a regular problem at Blue Spring Farm, or slipped off the farm to purchase alcohol from local free Blacks who sold liquor to folks throughout the county.[1] Regardless, David Wall and Peter King, both students at Choctaw Academy, were inebriated. And as the pair staggered up to the main house at Blue Spring on that cold December night in 1827, they had one thing on their minds: getting into the Big House.

It was late when they arrived at the house. Julia and her daughters, thirteen-year-old Adaline and fifteen-year-old Imogene, were in for the evening. Julia's brother, Daniel Chinn, was with them, as was his wife, Patience, and other members of the house staff, including the enslaved woman Parthene, who worked alongside Adaline, sewing and mending clothes for the students of Choctaw Academy. What happened next was a nightmare: David and Peter began beating on the door, trying to break it down and get into the house. Those inside were terrified. Julia feared that the men intended to sexually assault her and the other women of the house party, including her daughters and nieces.

CHAPTER THREE

The house party barricaded the entrances, doing everything they could to ward off the attackers. Richard was in Washington and the nearest neighbors were miles away, too far to hear the screams of the group that night. Thankfully someone else on the farm, whether a slave from down in the quarters or headmaster Thomas Henderson, who lived with his family in a separate house on the property, heard the commotion and managed to run off and return with the magistrates before David and Peter succeeded in breaking down the door to the house. Despite the shocking nature of the attack, however, the two men got off with just a warning. It wouldn't be the last time the Johnsons had problems with the students of Choctaw Academy. For Julia and Richard both, 1827 became a defining moment that shaped their actions moving forward.[2]

Blue Spring Farm was a private home, a working farm, and the site of a federally funded residential school for Native American boys known as Choctaw Academy.[3] Richard used his political connections to have the school placed at Blue Spring in 1825; it remained there until it closed in 1848. Julia, her daughters, and the farm's enslaved laborers all worked to ensure that every student was fed, clothed, and housed, their clothing and bed linens maintained, and their rooms cleaned. Julia also negotiated with local stores to purchase supplies for the academy and contracted to have larger items, such as bed frames, made for the students. The key to the school's success was Julia's hard work and good management, as well as the unpaid labor of Blue Spring's enslaved Black women who, along with Julia and her younger daughter, Adaline, sewed, distributed, washed, and repaired the students' clothes. The plantation's enslaved laborers also tidied the students' rooms, laundered their bedding, cooked their meals, and cleaned up after them in the dining hall three times a day.

The academy's presence at Blue Spring Farm led to ongoing problems, as the plantation became a space where the lines between public and private crossed and recrossed on a daily basis, often with disastrous results for Black women. Many of the students came from Indigenous nations where Black slavery was legal. In the first Choctaw census of 1831, for example, there were 521 enslaved Africans among the roughly 20,000 Choctaw residents of Choctaw Nation. The Pitchlynns, one of the leading families of the Choctaw Nation, sent several family members to Choctaw Academy, including future headmaster Peter Pitchlynn, also known as Snapping Turtle. The Pitchlynns owned sixty Black slaves, making them the largest enslavers in Choctaw Nation. Enslaved laborers at the Pitchlynn estate performed a variety of tasks. They planted corn and cotton, took care of herds of cattle and hogs, cleared the land, and dug wells.[4]

Seeing women such as Julia Chinn and her daughters, whose legal status as free people was never certain but who were literate, well dressed, and in positions of authority, confused many of the students. They likely found Richard's behavior hypocritical. The boys had come to Blue Spring with preconceived ideas (learned from white settler colonials) about Black women, slavery, and racial hierarchies. Yet here was a white man who held some Black people as enslaved laborers while treating other Black bondspersons as kin, leaving them in charge whenever he was away. Some of the young men thus saw the Black women of Blue Spring as property to do with as they wished, and on more than one occasion they attempted to break into the Big House to steal alcohol or assault the women of the house party. There were also consensual sexual relationships and friendships between the academy's pupils and the plantation's enslaved laborers. This caused serious anxiety for the Johnsons, who wanted to abolish all contact between "their people" and the Choctaw scholars. This proved impossible, given the limited space in which everyone at Blue Spring lived and worked.

The story of Choctaw Academy illustrates what happens when rhetoric meets reality, when public outcries against "amalgamation" come face-to-face with the private "toleration" of mixed-race relationships.[5] And it all took place at the crossroads of Blue Spring Farm, where the most private of spaces became the most public of places. Although the academy rested on the Johnson women's homesite and was thus a place where they exercised influence, the farm also became an openly contested hot zone, a "rival geography" where Julia and her daughters found their power tested by the students.[6] The history of the school thus reveals the tense relations that existed between Indigenous, Black, and white persons at Blue Spring Farm. The story of the academy is, at its core, the story of Julia Chinn and the other Black women of Blue Spring whose labor made the school's existence a reality but whose authority, even on their own property, unnerved so many folks. The fracture lines around these pressure points, between slavery and freedom, gender and power, and the overarching issue of interracial sex, were never fully erased.

The Choctaw had been on their ancestral lands in Mississippi, Louisiana, and Alabama since time immemorial. The greed of white southern slave owners had also kept the Choctaw embroiled in wars and treaties with various European nations and the US government for many years. Indeed, they were in a constant state of land encroachment by whites, followed by treaty negotiations, from after the American Revolution through to the days of Jacksonian Indian Removal (1786–1830), losing roughly 21 million acres of land during those years. In 1831 alone, the Choctaw Nation ceded 11 million acres of land to the US government.[7]

It is critical to note that the events at Blue Spring Farm and Choctaw Academy unfolded in the years just before and during Choctaw removal, at which point the Choctaw had been battling the settler colonials for centuries. The academy itself grew up out of the Treaty of 1825, also known as the Treaty of Washington City. Frustrated with the encroachment of white people on their lands, Choctaw leaders traveled to Washington to remind US politicians of their long-standing alliances, seek the expulsion of the settlers, or receive compensation for the loss of their land. While the Choctaw ended up ceding land to the United States as a result of these discussions, the Treaty of Washington City also contained funds *in perpetuity* for Choctaw education to the tune of $6,000 per year. This led to the eventual founding of Choctaw Academy, a collaboration between the Choctaw Nation and the federal government. Placed under the control of the War Department, which oversaw Indian affairs at the time, the academy was the only school directed in this manner except for West Point. Both schools were founded as elite institutions, and the plan was to offer a secular education to rising leaders in the respective communities that each school served.[8]

Up until this point, educational opportunities for Indigenous children had been in missionary schools located on Native lands. Choctaw elders wanted more than the evangelizing and vocational education offered by those schools, however; they wanted their children to learn law, politics, and the sciences so they could economically compete with white people. While they had little love for white culture, they wanted their sons to receive a "white" education so that they could compete with Americans on a more level playing field, particularly in things such as treaty negotiations. Because the Choctaw wanted to establish an academy outside of their homelands in Mississippi (in order to minimize cultural contact with outsiders), they reached out to William Ward to see about setting up a boarding school that would provide such an opportunity for their children. William, the Choctaw's federal agent, was also Richard Mentor Johnson's brother-in-law, having married Richard's sister Sally.[9]

Deep in debt due to some bad business ventures and desperate for cash, Richard told William and the War Department to look no further. He had "a house with three rooms, 20x20 feet, which I shall appropriate exclusively to their accommodation. Another house with four rooms, twenty feet square, which will do for a teacher to live in, and one room for a school room. The whole establishment will be within my fences, so no time shall be lost."[10] Richard was also the one who suggested Thomas Henderson, whom he knew from Great Crossing Baptist Church, for the position of headmaster. Richard wrote that Thomas was a preacher and a man of science, "eminent for his literary talents and his amiable disposition, a man of business, industrious, dignified and conciliatory in his manners." The government agreed to the plan, placing the academy under the local supervision of the Baptist Church Board of Missions.[11]

Given the money that would come in to fund the school from Choctaw Nation and the US government, plus what Richard hoped to save by using his own laborers, as well as food and materials from Blue Spring, it's easy to see why the man was so excited about having the school on his property. As he said in private, "The more scholars I have the more profit." For Richard, this wasn't about helping the Choctaw. He made it clear that if he didn't get "reasonable compensation" from having the school on his farm, he would "quit the business."[12] The fact is, Richard Johnson did everything he could to capitalize on the school to enrich himself. The federal government, in turn, used Choctaw donations to help run the school, all while maintaining the appearance of paternalistic benevolence as they helped to "civilize the savage."

Choctaw Academy eventually brought together students from a number of different tribes, although the majority of the boys were from Choctaw Nation, and the pupils did receive the classical education their elders wanted. Subjects included reading, writing, arithmetic, English grammar, geography, practical surveying, astronomy, natural philosophy, history, moral philosophy, and vocal music. And while each day opened with prayer and the boys had to attend church, unlike at the older missionary schools, instruction at the academy was excellent. It was so good, in fact, that "respectable" white families from the region wanted their sons to attend the school. They eventually obtained permission to send their children to the academy, making it one of the first interracial schools in the United States. Science subjects were eventually added to the curriculum, and in the 1830s, the school opened shops on the premises and introduced manual training. Skilled craftsmen were brought in to instruct the students, and land was set aside so the boys could also learn how to farm.[13] Still, despite the excellence of the academy, one can't overlook how difficult it must have been for the students to go to school in this strange new place, leaving their homes and families so far behind. While their families sent them there, and they would one day return to lead their nations, the homesickness and culture shock they experienced must have been wrenching.

In addition to the money the school brought in, Julia and Richard were happy to have the academy at Blue Spring because it meant they could educate their daughters without their neighbors knowing about it. It makes sense that Richard recommended Thomas Henderson for headmaster. He and Julia needed someone they could trust in the position. One wonders if Thomas understood what he was getting into when he took the job, however. He had to oversee the school and its teachers, "promote order and industry and good conduct among the Indian boys while absent from school," and help Julia discipline Blue Spring's enslaved laborers. He was also expected to teach Imogene and Adaline Johnson, along with other members of the house staff, on evenings and weekends. This was a tall order, and Thomas may not have been overly happy when Richard told him that the government had agreed to pay him a salary of $500 a year, which Richard claimed he had already "determined in my own mind to give you . . . on account of your kindness in teaching Imogene, Adaline & the girls." Thomas and his family also lived at Blue Spring, in the four-room house mentioned earlier.[14]

The Johnsons surely knew they were asking a lot of Thomas Henderson. But Julia may have found this to be a fair trade. For her, having the academy at Blue Spring was a double-edged sword. While it was beneficial for her daughters and nieces, allowing them to acquire an education, it also increased her own workload. Since Richard was in Washington for six months each year, it was Julia who oversaw all the daily operations needed to maintain the farm. She had taken this on at the age of fifteen when Richard rode off to war, and now, at twenty-eight, she shouldered the burdens of running the school as well. Julia and the enslaved laborers she oversaw had to ensure the pupils were clothed, fed, and housed, their clothing and bed linens cleaned, and their rooms maintained. This was no small task, even though the incoming class in the fall of 1825 had just twenty-five students. And as early as December 1825, Richard was angling to get more funds from Choctaw Nation so he could renovate existing buildings at Blue Spring and expand to host sixty scholars. "If I could get $12,000 a year for boarding etc. you see what affect would follow," he wrote to his brother Maj. John T. Johnson.[15]

There was a reason Julia Chinn had a reputation for being "the chief manager of the domestic concerns of the house." Already juggling a multitude of tasks, she stepped into her new roles at Choctaw Academy with grace. In addition to the duties mentioned above, Julia was also responsible for the students' medical issues, being "as good as one half the Physicians where the complaint is not dangerous." Her work in this area was significant; she lost only one student over the course of many years, and Richard didn't hire a full-time doctor for the academy until after her death.[16] Julia likely acquired her healing skills from the enslaved women of Johnson's Station and from Richard's mother, Jemima Suggett Johnson. Like most plantation mistresses, especially those on the frontier, Jemima would have had basic medical knowledge, necessary to survive in rustic conditions. Given that enslaved women passed down herbal remedies, midwifery skills, and other medicinal knowledge within their families, Julia probably learned most of what she knew from other Black women, however, including her own mother, Henrietta.[17]

Her new duties meant that Julia worked closely with Thomas Henderson. Every summer, after asking the headmaster how many students were expected in the fall and their ages, Julia went about setting up the boys' beds and making their bedding. After assigning each new student their living quarters, she first bought "coarse linen" from William Johnson's store in town to make the bedticks (mattresses). She then negotiated with a local craftsman named Campbell to construct the actual bedsteads (frames). It's unclear how much of the physical labor of sewing and stuffing mattresses Julia did herself and how much she delegated to the team of enslaved laborers she oversaw, although it was a large enough job to have required a number of workers. There is also no indication as to whether Johnson or Campbell had any serious issues doing business with the Black woman overseeing matters at Blue Spring.[18]

Julia also consulted with Thomas about the clothes the incoming students would need. Although she purchased some things ready-made, she also bought vast quantities of cloth. She and Blue Spring's team of skilled Black seamstresses then spent weeks sewing the items requested by the headmaster before the students arrived. In this way, Julia saved the household money by "furnishing some things at home with her own labour." Richard, however, claimed that if Julia had to "purchase everything" for the school, he wouldn't object. In fact, while discussing plans for the school's expansion, he stated that "as to everything else, Julia has the means and can accomplish it; perhaps she may want some aid in having a contract made for the bedsteads for the upper part of the library."[19]

Julia Chinn clearly provided a substantial amount of labor, both manual and managerial, to ensure the smooth running of Choctaw Academy. From medicines to mattresses, there was nothing, great or small, she didn't oversee. Indeed, it's not possible to estimate how *much* work Julia did for Richard, all without compensation. Had he not had Julia Chinn in his life and on his farm, most of what Richard accomplished at Blue Spring would have been impossible. He would have had to marry a white woman, hired an overseer, or both in order to obtain the breadth of talent and supervisory oversight that Julia furnished him without pay.

In addition to providing him with free labor, Julia also handled Richard Johnson's money for him when he was away. Not only was she literate; she also had the skill of numeracy. When Richard stated that if Julia had to "purchase everything, I do not object," or that "as to everything else, Julia has the means and can accomplish it," he may not have meant that she had access to substantial amounts of cash, however. It likely meant that Julia could shop for the household, place orders, sign for materials, and enter into contracts with local vendors for whatever was needed at Blue Spring, since most businesses in antebellum America functioned on credit. This is significant, however; if Julia could draw on Richard's local lines of credit, it meant that area merchants recognized her right to do so. It means that in the Bluegrass region, Julia Chinn was legally able to transact business as Richard Johnson's wife.[20]

Like white antebellum wives, Julia also had access to some physical currency in addition to signing authority on the family's lines of credit. She paid employees at the school and seasonal laborers at the farm and handed out allowance money to students at Choctaw Academy. In February 1826, Richard told Thomas that if the students were short on cash, Julia would hand him "$10 for distribution for spending money."[21] Like other plantations where white men functioned as overseers, Thomas Henderson had to ask the mistress of Blue Spring for funds. This wouldn't have been unusual, except for the fact that the mistress here was an enslaved Black woman. Nothing suggests that Thomas was dismayed by the need to work so closely with Julia Chinn, however, or by her position as manager, wife, and mother.

Julia's skills, work ethic, and business savvy meant that Richard relied on her to run things in Kentucky during his absences. He could afford to be gone for months at a time because she could "accomplish everything." Even the fact that "she may want some aid in having a contract made for the bedsteads for the upper part of the library" suggests she could handle the matter. Julia was literate and capable of negotiating contracts. It wasn't that she couldn't do this; it was that she "may" have wanted "some aid." Thomas could provide it—if Julia requested it. It's possible she asked him to intervene if the carpenter, Campbell, was being difficult. It would have been useful for Julia to have a white man on hand if Campbell was hostile or tried to cheat her. It's doubtful that every merchant in the area was comfortable dealing with the Black woman running things at Blue Spring Farm.

A hard worker, Julia couldn't take care of everything needed to make both Blue Spring Farm and Choctaw Academy a success. She was just one person. The key to making the plantation and the school run smoothly was that she was also an excellent supervisor; she knew how to delegate. While she thus shouldered new responsibilities with the opening of the school, so did everyone else at Blue Spring, including her daughters. Imogene Johnson, for example, regularly acted as a go-between for Richard and the headmaster, providing Thomas Henderson with a variety of school supplies, materials she would have kept at home and doled out as required. In 1826, Imogene, then fourteen years old, received a number of religious tracts in the mail from her father, some of which she handed over to Thomas for the students to read. She also gave Thomas pencils for the pupils, and when Richard sent her "a small paint Box & some brushes," she turned a portion of those items over to Thomas "for any of the Boys who may have a taste for drawing." Even the instruments she received from her father to help with "plotting & making maps" were to be given to the headmaster if he needed them for the students. And when Thomas ran out of paper and sealing wax, Richard sent him those items, but it was Imogene who provided the "seal or stamp.... Imogene also has sealing wax which she will furnish if I should not forward enough."[22] It appears that Richard trusted not just Julia but also his Black daughters to help maintain his business enterprises.

Imogene's work as a go-between is revealing. While she may have enjoyed reading religious literature, it's more likely that Richard was trying to parent his teenaged daughter from afar, hoping to infuse Christian morals and values into her. And while Choctaw Academy was a secular school, it still opened each day with prayer, and students attended Sunday services at Great Crossing Baptist Church. For Richard to send tracts to the boys was thus in keeping with the larger goals of the academy, which was under the local authority of the Baptist Church Board of Missions. Drumming Christian principles into the students was part of the overall educational project of this and other Indigenous residential schools, which strove to "educate the man" while simultaneously engaging in policies of cultural eradication, or "killing the Indian."[23]

In addition to reading religious literature and learning grammar and punctuation, Imogene, like elite white girls of her era, pursued ladylike pastimes such as painting and drawing, which her father encouraged with gifts of paints and brushes.[24] She also spent time honing her scientific knowledge, creating maps using the instruments her father sent her. By age fourteen, then, Imogene Johnson was receiving a well-rounded, classical education in religion, English, art, and the sciences, and her father was deeply involved in her training, both moral and scholarly, even from a distance. He was also constantly cutting corners, given how he divided materials between his daughter and the students of the academy, expecting Imogene to regularly share her school supplies with the Choctaw scholars. Given his financial situation, he may have even used school funds to purchase items for his children.[25]

As Imogene got older, she took on more serious responsibilities, giving Thomas Henderson not only seals and stamps for the academy but money as well. When she was just a few months shy of her sixteenth birthday, Richard asked Imogene to distribute $100 cash to Thomas and a teacher at Choctaw Academy named Rood. Although this was a significant amount of money (the equivalent of just over $3,000 in 2023), it doesn't appear that Imogene's contributions to the academy were ever physically difficult. While she supplied the headmaster with materials that benefited the school's students and teachers, Imogene Johnson didn't engage in any manual labor for either the plantation or the academy.[26]

This is strikingly different from the relationship that her mother and sister had with the school. Younger than Imogene by roughly two years, Adaline Johnson, from about age fourteen onward, helped sew, wash, and mend the students' clothes. As the academy grew from twenty-five scholars in 1825 to over 200 pupils in the 1830s, and Julia's workload increased accordingly, Adaline began working with Thomas Henderson to compile the boys' required clothing list each term. While her parents continued to purchase certain items ready-made, including the students' summer overalls, Adaline labored with Julia and the farm's enslaved seamstresses to sew most of the items that were needed. She then took charge of distributing the clothes directly to the scholars, which was a large task. She was assisted in this by one of the "house girls," Parthene, who also helped Adaline wash and mend the boys' shirts and other items throughout the school year. This was a more difficult job than it sounds. Not only was all the laundry done by hand, but the Johnsons claimed that the students were hard on their clothes, so things required constant cleaning, sewing, and patching. It was also the rationale given for why the sturdiest, and cheapest, overalls were purchased for the boys' summer wear.[27]

Adaline's responsibilities at Blue Spring evolved over time. For example, she began writing to her father in Washington. While much of the correspondence would have revolved around news from church and town, she also wrote Richard about troubles at the school. One letter concerned a student named William Frayham. William had left the academy and returned to Choctaw Nation, where he was "running down the school" to anyone who would listen. His comments made their way back to Kentucky via letters to current students. When Adaline heard the rumors, she reported the news to her father.[28] Richard also noted in an 1834 letter to Thomas Henderson that Adaline had written him several times about the behavior of one "insolent and spoilt" Washington Frahern.[29] Adaline Johnson thus continued her mother's tradition of keeping Richard updated in writing on all matters concerning the farm and the school, including issues with so-called "problem students." Indeed, Julia had probably trained her daughter to do exactly this, understanding that it would build trust between Richard and his daughter and thus benefit Adaline in the long run.

Although Adaline married in 1832 and had a son around 1834, her commitment to Blue Spring Farm and Choctaw Academy never wavered.[30] Richard, in turn, regularly commended his daughter. He told his "dear child" in late 1833 that he was delighted to hear from her, both because her health had improved and because she had, despite her recent illness, exceeded all his calculations in terms of the number of garments (fifty-six) the house staff could complete in one week. That, he said, was deserving of high praise, and "I think you and Miss Margaret entitled to a due proportion of credit for encouraging others by your own example." He then stressed to Adaline the importance of ensuring the "goodness of the work" and urged her to make sure that Parthene examined everything and "report[ed]" back to her. He ended by telling the nineteen-year-old that he trusted her, "my dear child to think & reason & exercise your best judgement & discretion and manage to the best advantage to help me all you can for everything looks well & I give you very great credit."[31] Here again was evidence that Richard relied on Black women to see to it that his business enterprises ran smoothly while he was away and that he believed they were able to think and reason, set good examples, ensure a high quality of work, and use good judgment and discretion. It didn't hurt that they came cheap, since all of these women, those who were related to him and those who weren't, worked without compensation.

Adaline and her father appear to have been close, and it's obvious that Richard trusted her to help run things in his absence. Like Julia, Adaline performed her own labor at Blue Spring in addition to overseeing the work and the workers of the farm; women such as Parthene "reported" to her. It's also clear that Richard was just as, if not more, concerned about the amount and "goodness of the work" Adaline helped produce as he was about her health. Indeed, his praise of her was based on her excelling in her duties for him and helping him "all you can."

What is confusing is why one daughter did so much work for the farm and the school and the other so little. In most households, it's the older children who do more physical labor to support their families, simply as a matter of birth order. One wonders, then, why Imogene didn't do more for the academy and the plantation, especially since her younger sister appears to have had health issues. As early as 1828, when Adaline was fourteen years old, Richard wrote that he had been distracted for almost a week by sickness in his family, "but God is gracious." Then, in the spring of 1832, he thanked Thomas for his "kindness towards Adaline." It's possible that the eighteen-year-old, who got married later that year, was unwell. She was definitely recovering from some ailment when her father wrote to her in December 1833, praising her for her industry in spite of having been ill.[32]

Whether because of favoritism or something else, Imogene didn't have much to do with the upkeep of Choctaw Academy or Blue Spring Farm, either before or after her marriage in 1830.[33] Equally clear is that while Julia and Adaline both did an enormous amount of work to keep home and school running smoothly, things would have fallen apart without the coerced labor of the enslaved women and men of Blue Spring Farm. The duties they performed were critical to the success of the plantation, and their already heavy workloads increased once the academy opened. It was the farm's enslaved laborers who set up and then tidied the students' rooms, sewed their garments, laundered and mended their clothing, cooked their meals, and cleaned up after them in the dining hall. It was their unpaid labor that would yield Richard the profits he hoped to squeeze from the money that the Choctaw Nation and the federal government sent for each student's tuition, room, and board.

The Johnsons had twelve enslaved laborers as early as 1810. They owned seventy-two people in 1820 and maintained roughly forty-five bondspersons for the next twenty years. By the time Richard died in 1850, he had divested himself of most of his workers (many of whom he gave to his daughters); that year he owned seven elderly slaves. During the years that the academy was open and at its peak, however, from the mid-1820s to the mid-1840s, the Johnsons controlled the labor of well over forty individuals. One-third of these people were women, many of childbearing years. This was a young, healthy, productive, and reproductive labor force, meant to enrich their owners.[34] The question is, how did they feel about their increased workloads when Choctaw Academy came to Blue Spring Farm in 1825?

Some of Blue Spring's enslaved laborers were likely pleased that the school was on the premises. For the "girls" of the house, including women such as Parthene, it meant an indoor job, such as sewing or mending, the opportunity to avoid field work and accompanying conditions such as hemp pneumonia, and the chance to be tutored at night by Thomas Henderson. There was also the hope of manumission at some point and a job in an urban area with a larger free Black community, such as Louisville or Lexington, where knowing how to read and write could help you get ahead.[35] For those who labored in the kitchens and the dining hall, however, who cleaned the students' rooms and washed their clothes, or who continued to do field labor, the opening of the school just meant more work.

There were problems other than increased workloads that accompanied the arrival of the Choctaw scholars. Many of the students were teenagers. There were bound to be some disciplinary issues, especially because a number of the boys were away from home for the first time. Additionally, coming as they did from elite families, often from slaveholding nations that viewed Black persons as their social inferiors (a cultural construct they had learned from settler colonials), their arrival at Blue Spring Farm, a plantation run for six months each year by Black women, was confusing for some of the students.[36] They quite literally found themselves living among well-dressed and educated young Black women, some of whom held positions of authority on the farm. And yet their associations with Europeans and Americans had taught them that Black folks were "less than" and that Black women were property to be used as laborers, sexual commodities, or both. Trouble was not long in the making.[37]

Some of the issues were what you might expect from teenaged boys. For example, Julia and Richard discovered that someone was breaking into their storerooms and stealing whiskey. Letters flowed back and forth between Kentucky and Washington about how best to set a trap to catch the thief by "evidence of their drunkenness." Then, there were those students who sold their clothing to buy alcohol from local free Blacks whom they met up with at night. While free Blacks under Kentucky's slave code could be fined anywhere from $50 to $300 if they were caught manufacturing or selling liquor, that didn't stop some of them from continuing to do so.[38]

While these sorts of things could be passed off as pranks, young men blowing off steam, more serious was what happened that night in December 1827 when David Wall and Peter King tried to break into the main house. Although no one was injured, the Johnsons were shocked when both students were let off with nothing more than a tongue-lashing. This was their home. Their sanctuary. The most private of spaces. Didn't such behavior warrant "severe chastisement"? Richard fumed, "Whether I leave black or white to Keep my house in my absence it is as sacred by the Laws & the Constitution as if I was in it myself—I am deeply mortified to think that such a scandalous and forceable entry of my house in my absence should be passed over with words & a reprimand."[39]

The magistrates respected Julia and Richard enough to come out to Blue Spring that night and prevent a possible assault, but they weren't willing to punish David Wall and Peter King the way they would have had the women in the house been white. And here, the issues were laid bare: Julia was mistress of Blue Spring Farm and Richard Johnson's wife, but she was still an enslaved Black woman, and her daughters may have been enslaved as well. Even though they lived as if they were free people, they were still people of color. While Julia and her daughters asked that their ladyhood be validated and protected through a public demonstration of legal power, and Richard demanded that his masculinity and whiteness be upheld by affirming his sacred roles as husband, father, and master, the magistrates' actions revealed that mixed-race families and Black women didn't have quite the same levels of protection that white families and white women did. Their behavior suggested that it did, indeed, matter whether it was "black or white" who kept Richard's house in his absence and that the "Laws & the Constitution" did not apply equally in all cases.

The magistrates would have seen this as a case of Native-on-slave crime or Native-on-Black crime, which likely removed any desire on their part to get involved. It's also possible that they feared retaliation from the Choctaw if more severe penalties were laid against David and Peter, especially since the men didn't manage to actually get into the house and harm anyone. Tensions at crossroads spaces such as Blue Spring Farm thus highlight the limits to which local officials were willing to go to protect and tolerate amalgamation in general and Julia Chinn and the Johnson family in particular. It also reveals that the students, who came from elite families in matrilineal, slaveholding nations, regarded Julia and her daughters not as Richard's kin, as wives and daughters, but as slaves. Outsiders. And they had learned by watching white men that it was acceptable to terrorize or brutalize women, especially enslaved women who held no status and who, as kinless folk, stood outside of a community's social structure.[40]

Julia and Richard were angry that David and Peter walked away from this situation, but they also feared it might happen again. Julia would have been especially worried for the safety of her daughters and nieces, while Richard was frustrated with Thomas Henderson. Not only did Wall and King's conduct "disgrace the most abandoned characters," but it showed a total disregard for the headmaster's authority. Richard wanted Thomas to make an example of the pair in order to bring the rest of the students back in line. He was also intent on trying to hide the incident from the War Department: "It will be impossible much longer to keep such scandalous conduct from the government, which would have a very bad effect and induce a belief that the Boys feared neither god, nor devil, nor man." According to Richard, the only way to prevent this from ever happening again was "severe chastisement" and to "lay it on with power and vigour." This meant floggings, which Thomas had always avoided but which Richard had long wanted.[41] His desire for corporal punishment suggests that he saw the Choctaw students on the same level as his Black enslaved laborers, whom he regularly whipped. One wonders if Richard would have been so eager, or willing, to flog the boarding school's students had they been white.

None of the Johnsons ever forgot that night in December 1827. Richard certainly didn't. He had been humiliated, emasculated by the students and the magistrates. Concerned that the government would close the school or move it to another location if the War Department lost faith in his ability to control things on his own plantation, Richard hid what was happening at Blue Spring from Washington politicos. His rage was evident, however, when he told Thomas in 1830 that "when Dave Wall & Peter King attempted to force into my house after the girls they ought to have been dismissed in disgrace or their backs tanned with a hickory or cowhide."[42] Although Wall and King never made it into the house, Richard believed they intended to go "after the girls." That information would have been given to him by Julia, her brother, Daniel, and others who were in the house the night the two men tried to break in. That Richard embraced this belief years after the events in question suggests that Julia Chinn and others at Blue

Spring continued to discuss what had happened that night, emphasizing what they clearly felt was a sexualized attack.

Richard's anger stemmed from the fact that the students tried to break into *his* house and came after *his* family and *his* slaves. It was all about protecting *his* property:

> If the boys find women or any body outside of my yard I would say nothing to them but to permit them to go into my Great House & get into my beds with my Negro wenches or to permit any of them to be doging [sic] into my house or sellars [sic] after the girls are things which I can not & will not bear. In all such cases my people no matter which or who shall have the cowhide on her back but in every case a disgraceful dismissal or the hickory shall be the portion of such students.[43]

Like other colonizers who had taught Indigenous men that women, especially Black women, were sexual property, Richard made it clear that he didn't care what the boys did as long as it was to *someone else's* wife, daughter, or "Negro wench."

His fury was also fueled by the fact that he saw himself as a father figure to the students, so for them to treat him this way was doubly horrifying: "Is it not infamous in the extreme in Boys that we are educating & acting as kind Parents that I should have my dwelling House invaded, my family degraded & my peace destroyed by a few scoundrels." Like a true patriarch, Richard concluded that if this ever happened again, he would call the magistrates and have the criminals lashed. He would also punish any of "the girls" who were sexually involved with the scholars via a "cowhide on her back," whether or not she was a willing participant.[44]

It was inconceivable to Richard that his family should be "degraded." Richard was raised in a time and place where white men understood that white women in general, and their female relatives in particular, were to be protected from assault because of their proximity to patriarchal whiteness. Because they were *not* kinless. The Indigenous students at Choctaw Academy, however, almost certainly had friends and family members who had been raped by white men. They thus learned about the interconnected nature of gender, race, rape, and kinship status because of the power dynamics of settler colonialism. It isn't surprising, then, that some of them grew up to use against others the tactics they saw wielded against their own people.

Although Richard had a long-term alliance with a Black woman and had two daughters with her whom he cared for, he clearly didn't treat all Black persons, or all Black women, with respect. He was still a white male slaveholder. That he drew a line in the sand between his family and his slaves is evidenced by his willingness to flog potential rape victims and by his use of terms such as "Wenches," "my people," and "the girls" to refer to the Black women who worked in the house with his family. Some of these "girls" were Julia's nieces and sisters-in-law. Additionally, when an enslaved woman named Dicy had a consensual sexual relationship with a student named Pierre Juzan, Richard forgave Pierre (after he confessed), but he thought Dicy should have been flogged. And when Julia's sister-in-law, Patience, got into a fight with a student named Daniel Folsom, Richard's response was telling. Even though Patience was Daniel Chinn's wife and a part of the house staff, Richard believed Thomas should have beaten her for "having anything to say or to do with any of the Boys no matter how rude on their part."[45] The fact that Thomas didn't whip Patience is irrelevant; he didn't believe in corporal punishment. The point is that being married to Julia's brother wouldn't have saved Patience had Richard been home. Despite Julia's power at Blue Spring, there were limits to her authority. Richard was still master of the plantation; he would have lashed Patience and poured salt in her wounds, just like he did to any of his other Black laborers who "misbehaved." She was a slave, and he was her owner. Her being a Chinn didn't change that or grant her extra protection.[46]

Even though the enslaved women at Blue Spring knew what would happen if they got involved with the school's students, it didn't keep some of them from sleeping with the young men of Choctaw Academy. In addition to Dicy and Pierre, a member of the house staff named Lucinda and one of the Folsom men were also in a consensual relationship. Lucinda apparently let her lover into the main house, believing nobody would catch the couple, but the pair were discovered having sex in one of Richard's beds. While Lucinda's "back paid for it," Folsom walked away, "permitted to pass and go on with his villainy with impunity." Fearful of losing the money the school brought in, as well as the education it provided their daughters, the Johnsons hid what was happening at Blue Spring from both the War Department and the Choctaw elders. So, while he fumed at the various misdeeds taking place in his house, Richard beat his slaves and watched the academy's students escape punishment. It's clear that Blue Spring was contested space and that the Johnsons were in a battle for control of this "rival geography" with both the students of the academy and their enslaved laborers.[47]

One thing did change after that night in December 1827; the Johnsons finally hired an overseer. Julia and Thomas had been functioning in that role as a team. While this had worked for years, things changed after David Wall and Peter King attacked the house. Worried for her daughters and nieces, Julia probably asked Richard to hire someone for the family's protection. It's unlikely he would have done so otherwise. It was expensive, and frankly, who could be trusted to hold this post? Who would take orders from Julia and not turn on her or the couple's daughters when Richard was away? Here, again, the public and the private came to a head at Blue Spring. It had been easier to allow Thomas to quietly function as a pseudo-overseer because his role as headmaster of Choctaw Academy meant he was already living on the farm. But it was the very presence of the school at Blue Spring that caused the tensions that required a full-time overseer and one who wouldn't have issues reporting to a Black woman.

The Johnsons eventually hired a man from a local white family: the Pences. It was a family they knew well. In fact, their older daughter, Imogene, would marry Daniel B. Pence in 1830, but in 1828 the couple hired Daniel's brother Edward H. Pence to enforce order among "black and white and red" alike at Blue Spring Farm.[48] Even so, the issues didn't stop. In January 1828, Julia wrote letters to Richard that filled him with "great uneasiness." It seemed impossible to keep the peace between the scholars and the couple's enslaved laborers. Refusing to acknowledge the powder keg he had created, Richard begged Thomas to do everything he could to address the "little things," such as student complaints about food, so they didn't become big things. If Thomas and Julia couldn't handle something, they were to call the school's trustees, or even the town magistrates, to help address matters. Richard was also willing to blame "his people," as he called Blue Spring's bondspeople, for the trouble. "I am sorry that any of the young men or large boys should have difficulties at my house with any of my people. If any of my slaves follow them to the school house to insult them I should be very severe. . . . I should be glad if every person would let my negroes alone till I get home & if any improper conduct on their part let it be conveyed to you."[49]

Keeping the students and the farm's enslaved laborers away from one another was easier said than done. Everyone at Blue Spring ate, slept, worked, and studied just a few feet from one another. One of the main school buildings was only 100 feet from the Great House, and the scholars, the slaves, and the women of the house party walked past each other throughout the day while going to work and class. On weekends, they worshipped together at Great Crossing Baptist Church while the students fished at nearby Elkhorn Creek and attended cockfights alongside the farm's laborers.[50] Additionally, Julia, Adaline, Parthene, Miss Margaret, and other women responsible for sewing, washing, and mending the students' clothes interacted with the boys on a regular basis, while the kitchen staff saw them in the dining hall. They prepared their food, served their meals, and cleaned up after them, three times a day. It was foolish to think relationships, good and bad, platonic and sexual, wouldn't develop in such close quarters. Julia did her best to keep the two groups separated, however, so when Thomas asked if a few of the school's older students could board in the main house instead of in the dorms, the answer was an unequivocal no. She was likely shocked that he even asked, given that her daughters and nieces lived in the house and that David Wall and Peter King had tried to break in just three months before the request. The fear of assault was clearly still at the front of her mind, and Richard agreed, stating, "It is important to make that distinction [between the students and my family] & you know that my family is no fit place for them to mingle."[51]

Despite Julia's and Richard's best efforts to keep matters at Blue Spring under control, tensions erupted again shortly after they hired Edward Pence. The trouble began in February 1828. Edward had rounded up several of the farm's enslaved women to be flogged. Their offenses appear to have been sexual in nature, since they were referred to as a "parcel of outrageous strumpets whose disgraceful conduct deserves almost hanging" and "abandon [sic] wenches, who are a disgrace to city Brothels." As the women stood there, stripped to the waist and shivering in the winter air, likely trying to cover their breasts as they awaited the lash, a Choctaw student named John Riddle stepped in and stopped the overseer from laying the cowhide on the women's naked backs. Why he did this is unclear, although his brother, William, was supposedly in a relationship with one of the house staff, and she may have been one of the women lined up to be whipped that morning. If so, Julia Chinn, in charge of the house party, would have been responsible for turning her in for punishment. After stopping the flogging, Riddle, a member of a slave-owning family in Choctaw Nation, then disobeyed a direct order from Thomas Henderson. Told by Henderson to step aside, he refused. Riddle also threatened to fight the headmaster and told the school's younger students not to obey the man. Revolution had come to Blue Spring Farm.[52]

A Choctaw student had stopped a white man from whipping a group of enslaved Black women. He then threatened to beat the white headmaster of the school and commanded his fellow students to disobey that same man. Upending the racial hierarchy on the plantation, this was a rejection of white patriarchy *and* white supremacy. This couldn't be allowed to stand. Horrified, Richard wrote, "If he can do all this with impunity, then of course he is your Master & my master, and superior to the laws of our state which authorizes a man to keep order among his slaves." John Riddle couldn't get away with this. Not only would he become the ruler of white men; it would cause unrest among the enslaved. Thomas was told to "persist in your exclusion of that mighty gentleman, be sure not to permit his reentry without the most abject submission to your laws, & if he goes home, be sure to put as large a black patch on his back as you can by fairly representing his infamous conduct to Col. Wm. Ward and each of the Chiefs."[53]

John Riddle became the first and only student to ever be expelled from Choctaw Academy. There were scholars who had engaged in far more serious acts of violence, including trying to break into the Johnsons' home. These occurrences had made Julia Chinn fear for her safety, and that of her daughters and nieces, which had led her husband to hire an overseer at Blue Spring—but the perpetrators remained at the school. One wonders if Julia ever asked Richard to expel David Wall and Peter King and how she felt when Riddle was expelled. It would have been blatantly obvious to her that Richard was so concerned with the school's image, the threat to his own honor and masculinity, and maintaining his cash flow that it wasn't until a student threatened white supremacy and the authority of white men that they were removed from the academy. Perhaps she realized yet again that all of these things superseded any concerns he may have had for his Black family. It likely reinforced to her that she had to work even harder to protect her daughters and her kin. Who else would?[54]

Richard Johnson was supported in his decision to expel John Riddle by a wide range of white men, from federal officials to local school board trustees. This was one situation Richard wasn't afraid to publicize, because he was so sure of being backed up by other white patriarchs. In fact, since there were folks who likely questioned his allegiance to the racial hierarchy due to his relationship with Julia Chinn, the Riddle affair gave Richard the perfect opportunity to proclaim his commitment to the ideals of Black chattel slavery and white supremacy.

The trouble didn't end with John Riddle's expulsion, however. Arriving in Choctaw Nation, John began telling anyone who would listen about the unconventional power structures at Blue Spring Farm, complete with references to "Black Masters and Negro Mistresses."[55] Using a white man named George Harkins as his go-between, John wrote to Richard, claiming it was Julia who had expelled him. Richard stated, "I suppose he has gone home with that lie in his mouth. It was too ridiculous for me to answer it on paper."[56] And this *was* a stretch. There is no indication that Julia's reach at Blue Spring extended that far. One can imagine that if it did, Peter King and David Wall would have been sent home before John Riddle. But the accusation was a sign of how much power she did have. It was no secret to locals that Julia oversaw Blue Spring Farm and its enslaved laborers for six months each year. That she worked with Thomas Henderson to run Choctaw Academy. Or that she had access to Richard's cash and lines of credit. And everyone knew that Julia was Richard Johnson's wife and the mother of his children. Riddle wasn't afraid to take this commonly known information and use it to "out" the inverted power hierarchy on the Johnson plantation, in writing, using a white man as his ally.

Despite his smear campaign, conducted to try and overturn his expulsion, destroy the school, or both, John Riddle never returned to the academy, and the school remained open. According to Richard's brother-in-law, Indian Agent William Ward, even the Choctaw Nation's chiefs and elders were sorry that John had behaved in such a manner and that Thomas Henderson had been forced to take such extreme measures against the young man.[57] In this, Choctaw and US government officials apparently found themselves in agreement. While both sides may have murmured against Richard's personal life behind closed doors, neither disputed his right to own enslaved laborers and treat them as he wanted.

After the trials and tribulations of 1827–28 and the Riddle affair, things settled down at Choctaw Academy. For a while. It wasn't until 1830 that tensions flared again. Julia likely wasn't surprised that it happened in the dining hall. She and Adaline had let Richard know that the students had serious complaints about the food at Choctaw Academy. The boys also sent letters home to their families, writing about the dreaded mutton that was so often served (a meat they had never before eaten); asking for more dessert items (and sugar in general); and saying that they needed better-quality coffee. Good coffee was something they were used to drinking back home. The stuff at Blue Spring was watered down, "mixed with rye," and "badly prepared."

Many of the students were also upset that they were being served the same "fatback and cornbread" as Blue Spring's enslaved laborers, which they found insulting. They were the sons of Choctaw elders. The future leaders of their nation. Far from home, missing their families and familiar foods, they didn't appreciate being under the authority of white and Black persons at Blue Spring, let alone being treated like enslaved people. Back home, many of their families owned Black people, and settler colonialism had taught them about social and racial hierarchies and the place of Black bondspeople within those hierarchies. The Johnsons, of course, were trying to save money by providing the pupils with the cheapest food and drink they could. This meant feeding the students like they fed their outhands, two groups they clearly saw as similar in some ways. It's doubtful the couple would have done such a thing had the students been white. While it may not have occurred to them that the students would realize what was happening and take offense, the coffee issue was more important than either Julia or Richard realized. The students' complaints were not "little things."[58]

The food wars came to a head in 1830. The dining hall had long been one of the most contested spaces on the farm, a place where the struggle for control over rival geographies came into sharp relief. The large, two-story building was staffed by five or six enslaved laborers, all of whom were women or children. Patience Chinn, Julia's sister-in-law, managed the lower room with the help of a woman named Fanny, while a woman named Lucy and her two children worked in the upper room. The staff served 300 meals each day to the students, prepared by the head cook, Jerry, and then washed dishes and cleaned the hall between each meal. Older student monitors were supposed to keep the younger boys in line, but things were strained. Insults were regularly hurled at Patience, Fanny, and Lucy by the pupils. Many of the boys referred to the waitstaff, who dressed in clean, country dresses, just like other respectable women in the local area, as "insolent" and "dirty" in appearance. The women, frustrated by the students' demands and verbal cruelty, sometimes challenged the scholars in return, following them to the schoolhouse on occasion to hurl their own abuse. It's very possible, given her work assignment, that an altercation in the dining room is what had led to Patience Chinn and Daniel Folsom's argument in 1827.[59] That day in the spring of 1830, however, matters got out of control. The issue with the coffee escalated beyond verbal complaints. The students began rioting and threw their coffee at the serving staff; they had had enough of the foul-tasting stuff. Some of the young men and boys then hurled rocks at the Black female laborers.

After hearing about the "Coffee Riot" from Julia, Richard told Thomas that he had to crack down on such behavior. If any of their people were "guilty of crime or neglect you know they are subject to the lash if proper complaint is made to you or to Mr. Pence." The Johnsons' main concern was preventing disorder inside their yard and home; this led them to try to lessen and then abolish all contact between their slaves and the students instead of addressing the root cause of problems at the farm. For example, ignoring the students' long-standing frustrations with their food, Richard said he was pleased that the boys and Blue Spring's laborers appeared to be getting along "better than at any other session of congress when I am absent, and I hope there will be a calm and good order and good conduct.... When they have any complaint let it be made to you and not by dashing coffee etc. and throwing stones at my people." Mentally placing both groups on a level with each other and using language that minimized the riot, Richard refused to acknowledge the real anger underlying this incident and was unwilling to admit that the students and his bondspersons were not getting along any "better" than they had in the past.[60]

It wasn't long before things heated up again at Blue Spring Farm. Just weeks after the coffee clash, two scholars, William Riddle and an unnamed Creek student, broke into the main house and raped two of the plantation's enslaved Black women: "one of the girls" and "one of the Negro women, Lewis' wife," named Rose. Lewis must have been outraged by the violation of his wife. Julia would have been angry as well, and terrified. She and Rose attended church together, and the attacks happened inside the home where she and her daughters worked, ate, and slept.

All of the memories from that night in December 1827 likely came rushing back. Richard was furious when he got the news. Viewing the rapes as further assaults on his and Julia's authority, Richard instituted a series of severe punishments for the farm's enslaved laborers and the school's students. "In all such cases my people no matter which or who shall have the cowhide on her back but in every case a disgraceful dismissal or the hickory shall be the portion of such students."[61]

Julia Chinn was responsible for the women of the house party in all matters because they were under her supervision. Their behavior was a reflection on her, and she was now told to investigate their role in any case of possible assault and take her findings to Thomas Henderson. He would then judge "what course to pursue." Richard concluded, however, "I know my people in all such cases are as much or more to blame and in all such cases the cowhide has been put on their backs freely & shall be . . . if such things are repeated. . . . I will call up the magistrate and have the lash put upon the Criminal. . . . I am willing that my determination should be known to the whole school." It appears Richard believed the centuries-old tales of Black women being "immoral wenches," seductresses who led men astray with their insatiable sexual appetites.[62] In spite of his relationship with Julia Chinn, or perhaps because of it, Richard seemingly did all he could to make sure people knew he was committed to upholding the racial hierarchies of the day.

Richard's determination finally rubbed off on Thomas Henderson. While Thomas still refused to flog the students, overseer Edward Pence whipped the enslaved laborers as ordered, even women who may have been rape victims. And Thomas became more rigid in his oversight of the farm and the academy, keeping "a strict and watchful eye over all things at the Brick House that every part of the system may reflect honor and not shame and disgrace as heretofore."[63] One wonders if the previous "shame and disgrace" belonged to the students or to Thomas and Richard for allowing things to get out of hand. Perhaps it was Julia who had brought shame to Blue Spring, since she answered for the women of the house, women who Richard implied were harlots and temptresses. Women who didn't even merit the right to a name of their own unless they were someone's wife. Just another "one of the girls."

The Johnsons took additional steps to protect their family in light of this new attack on their home. In 1831, they relocated Choctaw Academy about two miles away from their house at Blue Spring Farm to land they owned at White Sulphur Spring, seven miles from Georgetown. The public explanation for the move was that there was more firewood at the new location and that the school had outgrown its old quarters since more students had enrolled at the academy. This was also when Thomas Henderson asked for a raise; since the school had expanded, so had his workload. His salary thus went from $500 to $800 per year. He was also given $400 to hire assistant teachers. These terms continued until Thomas left the school in 1841.[64]

The timing of the move suggests this wasn't about firewood or space. The "old" academy buildings at Blue Spring were built of stone, for example, and were much nicer than the new ones, which were constructed of logs. The move seems to have been an attempt to get the students away from the Johnsons' home, remove them from the rival geography, and eliminate the sexual intercourse, both consensual and forced, that was taking place between the scholars and the "girls" of the main house. In fact, Richard was so desperate to keep the two groups separated that he even suggested bringing Indigenous girls to the school as students, hoping that would keep the male students away from the Black women of Blue Spring; the secretary of war refused to even consider the idea. Thomas was then told that the boys were to be marched to the dining hall and back three times a day under a teacher's supervision in order to maintain discipline; that they were to be kept away from the Johnson family; and that he should "cut off the evil of former familiarity with my negroes." There was no contact too small that could be permitted between the Johnson family and the Choctaw students. In Richard's absence, Thomas was to "protect me and mine from the rudeness and improper conduct of the boys."[65]

Keeping the scholars and Blue Spring's bondspersons apart proved to be a difficult task. Two miles wouldn't stop a healthy young man from taking a walk to see his girlfriend. It also didn't stop some scholars from attacking the main house. A student named Calvin and a group of other young men got drunk one night and broke down the kitchen door, supposedly trying to get to the women inside. Another night, a student snuck in and hid behind the basement door inside the house, apparently waiting for "the girls." That same student, Samuel Long, somehow had himself appointed, or appointed himself, some kind of "monitor." He was charged with patrolling the Johnsons' yard at night to "keep order" and ensure that no trouble erupted, an odd position for someone who was himself a source of trouble. For the Johnsons, having Samuel watch the main house was like "appointing profligate young men to go into the Houses of black people to keep order, which is done by driving away their husbands if they have no pass & then get into their places." Richard didn't differentiate between assault and consensual relationships among his laborers and the students, however. He assumed "his people" were also and always at fault, and thus many of the Johnsons' young female slaves were flogged and then sent "downriver," sold to sugar planters in New Orleans for having had sex with the students, whether they were rape victims or not. For Richard Johnson, "Black woman" seems to have equaled "wench."[66]

CHAPTER THREE

Although the Johnsons' older daughter, Imogene, got married in 1830 and moved across Elkhorn Creek to the land she received from her parents as a wedding gift, Adaline and Julia continued to live at Blue Spring after the academy relocated to White Sulphur Spring in 1831, as did the other "house girls."[67] Richard remained in Washington for half of each year, and Thomas kept working with Julia. The Johnsons expected him to continue assisting her in maintaining "the order and decorum of black and white and red upon the premises."[68] Adaline, who got married in 1832, helped Julia with the increasing amounts of labor needed to keep things afloat at Choctaw Academy. With over 200 boys to cook and wash for, it was a running battle to keep dorm rooms tidy and students outfitted with clean clothes. The latter became a significant issue.

By April 1833, the problem of clean shirts was widespread at Choctaw Academy. Whenever the headmaster found a student with a dirty shirt, he was supposed to ask the boy why he was wearing a dirty shirt or send him to Adaline. If the washerwomen couldn't immediately provide a clean shirt, Thomas was to take the student to Parthene, who would "always furnish a shirt." Adaline was to relay all of this information to Parthene, the only one that Richard "trust[ed] to attend to this matter." Parthene apparently knew when each of the boys had last received new shirts, so she could estimate if a boy's shirts had all worn out or not. It appears that the students, instead of taking whatever shirts were ready at the laundry, tried to get new shirts made when they ran out of clean ones. That wouldn't do; the cost would ruin the Johnsons. This led to the dirty shirts: the boys apparently preferred to walk around in their own, dirty shirts before wearing whichever clean ones were ready at the laundry, shirts that may or may not have belonged to them. Richard trusted Adaline and Parthene to fix the problem. Still, there was apparently "more confusion in the washing department than in any other."[69]

The "confusion" with the washerwomen at Blue Spring may have been deliberate acts of resistance. Washerwomen had grueling jobs, but doing laundry was a skill, and one that was in high demand, like sewing and cooking. Laundresses thus often banded together to ensure they weren't mistreated, knowing the power they literally held in their hands in the form of cherished, often expensive, items of clothing. If the Johnsons, or the students, insulted the laundresses the way the dining hall staff seem to have been abused, they may have retaliated with damaged shirts, missing garments, or more. That's certainly what their sisters in the postbellum era did.[70]

While Adaline, Parthene, and Thomas collectively handled the clothing crisis in the spring of 1833, Julia Chinn wasn't involved. This seems odd, given her position as mistress of Blue Spring for over two decades, attending to all issues, great and small. Instead, Richard's letters in April 1833 focused on Adaline's work partner, Parthene, the only person he could "trust" to attend to the matter of dirty shirts. It's striking that Julia, who had borne so much responsibility for the farm and the school, including handling Richard's money, didn't oversee the shirt shortage. Instead, the headmaster, long her partner in dealing with school and farm concerns, was to "consult with Mr. Pence & advise with Adaline" on this and other problems.[71]

This letter was written no more than two months before Julia passed away in the cholera epidemic of 1833. It's possible that Julia's responsibilities in caring for the many persons who fell sick from that dreaded disease at Blue Spring had already begun to take her away from her other duties. This means that Adaline and Parthene would have had to take on more work. It's also possible that Julia had been replaced in Richard's affections by the spring of 1833. In December 1833, just six months after her mother's death, Richard wrote to Adaline, "I want you to tell Parthene that I am very much pleased to find that she is so high on your list of industry & I hope her conduct will be equally good."[72] The remark about her "conduct" seems out of place here and suggests that Parthene may have been more than just another worker to Richard.

The Johnsons' relationship was, of course, never a love story. Richard was always a slaveholder. Julia was always his property. She had a limited range of options, none of them good; staying with him gave her daughters the best chance at a better life than she alone could provide. Keeping him happy was a constant negotiation, however, and angering him could result in being replaced in his affections. At worst, it could mean being sold away from her daughters. After over two decades together, having him turn to another woman might have been the least of her concerns, especially since Imogene and Adaline were, by then, married and had estates of their own. In fact, it's unclear whether Julia and Richard even shared a bed in the years before her death. Julia had always had her own house at Blue Spring. While she continued to live in the Brick House when Richard was in Washington, with their girls now grown, there is no way of knowing if the pair lived under one roof when Johnson was in Kentucky.[73]

While Julia disappeared from Richard's letters before her death, her passing deeply affected the life of everyone at Blue Spring Farm, and her husband came to miss her organizational capabilities. Within months of her death, students at the school flooded Choctaw Nation with a deluge of letters complaining about poor-quality food and clothing, suspect education, and dirty accommodations. Richard tried to address the concerns and persuade the Choctaw leaders not to take their sons back home. He stated, for example, that "I can pledge myself from the most correct information that there is not a day in the year that coffee is not furnished for every Boy in the school & that of the best quality except during the cholera when there was some derangement in the cooking owing to the death of the formidable cook & the sickness of others." Richard was, of course, referring to the death of Jerry, the enslaved man who cooked for the students, and to the sickness of Julia Chinn, who spent months nursing the ill before passing away from cholera herself. He blatantly ignored the fact that the students had rioted because of poor-quality coffee as far back as 1830.[74]

Worried by the letters from Choctaw Nation, Richard asked Thomas to ensure that the boys kept their rooms and clothes clean. "Therefore, you must keep your eyes upon their Cloths, & if necessary you can get Adaline or Parthene to furnish any deficient so as to keep them to look well & this without exciting other Boys & without letting any person know the object for I have said nothing of these complaints even to Adaline. . . . Perhaps the Chiefs may be referring to letters soon after the cholera when matters were deranged."[75] This was the second time Richard used the word "deranged" or "derangement." It's clear that matters were "deranged" because Julia Chinn, who had always ensured that things ran smoothly at Blue Spring Farm and Choctaw Academy, had died, yet neither Richard nor the students were willing to speak this truth. Richard also tried to hide the attacks against the school from his daughter. He may have been worried about her emotional state, given that she had just lost her mother.

Julia Chinn's life had been one of unceasing and uncompensated labor. Without her, both Blue Spring Farm and Choctaw Academy would have fallen into disrepair early on due to Richard's regular and lengthy absences. Like white plantation mistresses across the South, Julia was responsible for raising her children, overseeing the farm's agricultural productivity and the work of the estate's slave labor force, entertaining guests, sewing, cooking, cleaning, paying the bills, making purchases for the home, and taking care of Blue Spring's livestock, gardens, and mills. This was in addition to the labor she performed to keep the academy profitable, from ensuring the students stayed healthy, were clothed, fed, and housed, their clothing and bed linens maintained, and their rooms kept up. She also purchased supplies for the school and contracted to have furniture items made for the students. Her daughters, particularly Adaline, assisted in this work, and since they were expected to take over her duties in case of her illness or death, Julia educated them in all aspects of running the farm and the school. In this she was like elite white women of her time who educated their children, particularly their daughters, in all the ways of running a household.

Richard couldn't easily replace Julia and everything she had overseen in his life. He told Thomas to confer with overseer Edward Pence, who would make sure that matters in the washing, mending, and cooking departments were taken care of by the enslaved laborers. The headmaster was then instructed to give directions to Parthene, so far as the work of the house party was concerned. Everything but the students' coats would be made by Parthene, who would have the neighbors make what she couldn't get done at home. Thomas, along with Edward, "was to take the whole Burthen of giving out the summer clothing."[76] What one person had managed was now divided up between numerous people, including the Johnsons' neighbors.

There was also the matter of the medical work that Julia had performed on the plantation, work that eventually killed her. In June 1834, Richard hired one Dr. Cotton to care for the students at Choctaw Academy, an expense he had long avoided because of Julia's expertise. Richard claimed there had never been a "faithful discharge of that duty which has always been that of the Superintendent and teachers to attend to the sick. That troublesome duty has principally devolved upon my black people. . . . But when Julia was alive I had no objection but that matter must be taken entirely from my shoulders." Richard seemed to feel that medical care was the responsibility of Thomas and his teachers but "his black people" had taken care of it, until now. With Julia gone, however, Richard could no longer be burdened with "that matter." Still, he eventually hired Cotton, because medical care wasn't something that Thomas appeared able, or willing, to add to his already long list of duties.[77]

It's obvious, given how much things changed after her death, that Julia Chinn contributed an enormous amount of unpaid labor to the smooth running of Blue Spring Farm and Choctaw Academy. Equally clear is how much responsibility Adaline had shouldered while her mother was alive and that her workload increased once Julia was gone. Already writing regularly to her father to keep him informed about daily issues, overseeing the sewing, washing, and mending of clothes, and furnishing the boys with their summer clothing, Adaline's duties evolved once her mother was gone, as she strove to balance everything at the farm and the school with the tasks that came with being a wife and mother.

In 1834, Thomas Henderson was ordered to "keep your eyes upon their [the students'] Cloths, & if necessary you can get Adaline or Parthene to furnish any deficient so as to keep them to look well." Adaline also outfitted students who were leaving the school with any clothes they might need for the journey home.[78] Further, whenever Thomas received new students at the academy, he was to tell Adaline what was needed "and it will be furnished." This included preparing the students' "bedticks and bed cloths," just as Julia had done when she was alive. It's clear that Adaline had stepped into her mother's shoes and that Richard came to depend on her for all things related to both home and school. She was incredibly industrious and helped keep everything organized for him. What's hard to believe is that Adaline was no more than nineteen years old when her mother died in 1833.[79] All of these burdens, however, along with the duties that came with being a wife and a mother herself, proved to be too much. Adaline died less than three years later, in February 1836, no more than twenty-two years of age. The timing of her passing (her marriage in 1832, and the birth of her son, Robert, circa 1834), suggests she may have died in childbirth with her second baby. Having been her father's right hand for several years, she left Richard "unhappy in mourning her loss."[80]

Choctaw Academy remained open for several more years, although its most successful period, when Julia and Adaline were there to ensure the school's smooth operation, was over. Thomas Henderson and his family moved off of the property in 1839, although Thomas remained headmaster of the academy for another two years before being replaced by the federal government with Peter Pitchlynn of Choctaw Nation.[81] Pitchlynn, however, wasn't invested in keeping the school open. Having been removed from their homelands in Mississippi and relocated to Indian Territory as part of President Andrew Jackson's removal policies, Choctaw Nation was moving toward opening its own schools in what is now Oklahoma, where they could educate their children themselves. Choctaw Academy officially closed its doors in 1848.[82]

When considering the events that unfolded at Choctaw Academy, many of which highlight intersecting nodes of gendered and racialized violence, we can never forget that white enslavers and tribal nations are not interchangeable groups. What this story reveals, yet again, is how settler colonialism and white supremacy warps *everyone*. There was ugliness to spare at Blue Spring Farm. Perhaps the only innocent people there were the enslaved laborers—not the members of the house party, the extended Chinn family, but the "outhands." At its core, however, this is a story that is less about innocence and more about gradations of violence and victimization. Far from the students being one-dimensional characters, tropes of the "Violent Indian Man," they were both the perpetrators and the recipients of violence, as were many of the Black folks they interacted with at Blue Spring.

Julia Chinn, though enslaved, behaved as an overseer and enslaver in these spaces. She used her authority to maneuver her relatives into positions of privilege and handed out medicine and other supplies to the students, all while helping police those same students alongside the enslaved laborers on the plantation. Her mission was always to better the lives of her daughters and kin. If she felt any distaste for what she had to do to the students, and to the other bondspersons at Blue Spring, it wasn't evident from her actions. As for Richard Johnson, he was first, last, and always a slaveholder who was committed to turning a profit. For him, Choctaw Academy was not about Native education; it was about making money. He also viewed Indigenous people as "others." Ranking them lower than himself and his family, in his mind the students deserved the kinds of punishment, food, and clothing that were doled out to Blue Spring's enslaved laborers, particularly the "outhands."

The Indigenous students disliked Richard intensely. Although they had been sent to Choctaw Academy by their families, Richard was still a representative of the government that had robbed them of their homelands and was systematically destroying their culture. As an individual, Richard was a penny-pincher who rationed supplies and gave them "slave" clothing and food. He was also in an open relationship with an enslaved Black woman and had two daughters with her. Because he was so often gone, it was these women who ran the farm and the school for much of the time. This was a problem, because decades of interactions with white settler colonials had taught these young men that Black folks were kinless "others." In fact, many of the students came from nations that had transitioned away from enslaving other Native peoples as prisoners of war to practicing generational Black slavery, behavior they had learned from Europeans and Americans.

All of this set up conditions at Blue Spring Farm that made it a tinderbox ripe for explosion. If any one person could be said to have lit the match, it was Richard Johnson. It was his greed that led him to bring Indigenous students, his Black family, and the enslaved laborers of Blue Spring into close proximity. That same greed made him continue on with the experiment, despite every piece of evidence suggesting it was an unhealthy situation for everyone involved.

In the midst of this, it's obvious that if not for the work of Julia Chinn, her daughter Adaline, and the enslaved laborers of Blue Spring Farm, Choctaw Academy would have never been as successful as it was for as long as it was. It was the uncompensated labor of Black people, and Black women in particular, including Julia's sister-in-law, Patience Chinn, Parthene, Miss Margaret, Lucinda, Rose, Fanny, Lucy, Dicy, and a host of others, that made this venture possible. It was the work of Black women, some of whom received an education but most of whom did not. Black women who were flogged, insulted, and assaulted. Black women who washed, mended, served, and sewed. Black women who cooked and cleaned. Black women who found themselves sold "downriver" for having sex, consensual or not. Without Black women, the school would have never even existed, let alone made a profit.

Yes, Native, Black, and white folks had strained, often contentious interactions on Blue Spring Farm. In a place both private and public, Choctaw Academy forced teachers, local magistrates and school board officials, the US government, Choctaw elders and students, enslaved laborers, Julia Chinn, Richard Johnson, their daughters, and extended Johnson relations to all converge in this one space. With conflicting ideas about race, class, kinship, and gendered power, these groups clashed at a site where enslaved Black women held a certain amount of authority in opposition to the rhetoric maintained by the larger, white, settler-colonial society. A contested hot zone of "rival geographies," Blue Spring Farm also became a "geography of containment" where various groups of men attempted to police enslaved Black women by reinscribing the racial and social hierarchies to which they themselves adhered.[83]

These same groups of people, white plantation owners, Indigenous students, enslaved laborers, and Johnson family members, would come into contact with one another in a different venue, just two miles away from Blue Spring Farm. In a small building set in a curve in the road, men such as Thomas Henderson would preach the Good News one Sunday a month at Great Crossing Baptist Church. There, white Kentuckians would come face-to-face with Julia Chinn, Imogene and Adaline Johnson, the scholars from Choctaw Academy, and their own enslaved laborers. Here, in this public space, yet one supposedly dictated by the laws of God and not of man, they would wrestle with what it meant to be "Brethren in Christ." While it sounded good in theory, it would prove to be more complicated in practice, as making room for Black church members in general, and the Johnson women in particular, exposed more fully exactly when, and to what degree, the white folks of Scott County were willing to accommodate, if not exactly accept, the amalgamationists in their midst.

CHAPTER FOUR

DISORDERLY COMMUNION

The Johnsons Go to Church

Imagine the sight as you come around a bend in the road: people of all races and ages, enslaved and free, sitting on the grass as far as the eye can see, spreading out from a small brick church. It's 1828, springtime. Horses and wagons are lined up on the grass, the smell of food rises up from campfires, the sound of music fills the air, and a man stands on a table that has been placed "in the sink just south of the meeting house." He preaches by lantern light that spills out from the church and pops up over the hills as daytime turns to evening.[1]

Week after week, month after month, the Revival of 1828 brought hundreds of folks to Jesus, and enslaved laborers from the area's farms were among those who gathered on the grass to sit with friends and loved ones to talk, sing, pray, and ponder on the state of their souls. Then, on a still-chilly day in April 1828, the spirit of the Lord touched the heart of a Black woman from Blue Spring Farm out on the grass, and she walked into Great Crossing Baptist Church to have her "conversion experience" heard by Rev. Silas M. Noel. And on Sunday, April 20, 1828, Julia Chinn was baptized by Noel in the cold waters of Elkhorn Creek and became an official member of the church she had attended for years.[2]

Great Crossing Baptist Church lies nestled in the curve of a quiet country lane just outside Georgetown, Kentucky, not quite two miles from Blue Spring Farm. Founded in 1785 by sixteen white Baptists originally from Virginia, a group that included the parents of Richard Mentor Johnson, Great Crossing in Julia Chinn's day had a congregation consisting of a handful of free Blacks, numerous enslaved laborers and white plantation owners, and students from Choctaw Academy. Julia and several of the Native students were baptized at Great Crossing during the Revival of 1828. Although Julia wasn't the only Black person who worshipped at Great Crossing, her position at the church differed from that of other Black attendees. Understood to be Richard Johnson's wife, she didn't sit upstairs in the "slave gallery" with the other Black congregants. And although Kentucky didn't recognize interracial marriage, she was never charged by the church board with fornication. Richard's position as the prominent son of a wealthy founding family led church officials to treat Julia with a certain measure of respect.

Great Crossing wasn't a radically progressive church. But within its walls, as white Kentuckians came face-to-face with the Johnson family, the students of Choctaw Academy, and their own enslaved laborers, they were forced to confront what it meant to say that they were brothers and sisters in Christ. It was complicated. Tensions over slavery started schisms in many churches during the antebellum era, leading to the creation of northern and southern branches of several Protestant denominations, which continue to the present day.[3] Great Crossing, part of the Elkhorn Association of Baptist Churches, refused to "meddle with emancipation from slavery or any other political subject," although prominent Kentucky Baptists including David Barrow and Carter Tarrant preached antislavery from their pulpits, while other associations in the region banned slave owners from their communion tables.[4] Great Crossing never went that far, but it did make certain accommodations for Julia and her daughters, including performing the wedding of the Johnsons' older daughter, Imogene, to Daniel B. Pence, despite state laws against interracial marriage.[5]

The privileges at Great Crossing did, at times, extend to other Black parishioners, including permitting the church's Black members to hold their own separate worship services for many years.[6] The church was able to do this because, while it was a public-facing organization, Great Crossing was also a place that in many ways policed itself. Standing outside of state governance due to the separation of church and state, houses of worship were liminal arenas. Positioned on the line between private spaces and public places, Great Crossing could choose to extend certain liberties to its Black congregants and to women inside its own walls. Still, these benefits only existed to a point, both for the Johnson women and for the church's Black congregants as a whole. Although she was recognized as Richard's wife, Julia wasn't buried in Great Crossing's cemetery alongside his white kin. And as the nation drew closer to war in the 1850s, the church's Black attendees found their separate service privileges revoked. Toleration, then, was never tolerance. Accommodation was not acceptance.

The small cemetery behind the sanctuary at Great Crossing Baptist Church, cordoned off by a stone wall, contains gravestones and markers dating back to the 1790s. The building itself is more modern, however; the small brick meetinghouse that Julia worshipped in was destroyed by a tornado in 1923. Despite this, the current congregation takes great pride in its history. The quiet little cemetery is now a historic landmark, reminding visitors that Great Crossing traces its founding back to Kentucky's frontier period, when parishioners carried their rifles to church to defend against attacks by Native Americans who were frustrated by settler colonials encroaching on their lands.[7]

In the late eighteenth century, while settlement was still underway, Baptist churches were already beginning to appear in Kentucky. Great Crossing was among the first. Richard's father, Robert, who spent these early years working as a surveyor, was able to scout out the best land in the region. By the early 1800s, he owned roughly one-third of the land in what is now Scott County. After building their home, the first thing Robert and Jemima Johnson did was move to establish a church. Devout Christians, the Johnsons were already members of Blue Run Baptist Church in Virginia. Great Crossing Baptist Church was organized at a meeting held in their home "at the Big Crossing, on Saturday the 28 and . . . 29 of May 1785."[8]

At that meeting were sixteen people whose names became synonymous with the elite of Georgetown in the years to come, including William and Susanna Cave, brothers John and James Suggett, and Robert and Jemima Suggett Johnson. The Johnsons also donated the land on which Great Crossing erected its building, just a few hundred feet from their home at Johnson's Station. Both Robert and Jemima held different leadership positions in the church over the years, and Robert represented Great Crossing at the region's Elkhorn Baptist Association meetings thirty times between 1785 and 1814. It's fair to say that over the course of his life, Robert Johnson became one of the Bluegrass region's most respected Baptist elders.[9]

Like other churches, Great Crossing met once a month to conduct business, on a Saturday; they gathered the next day to worship.[10] Eventually, the congregation began to meet for worship twice a month, on the first and third Sunday of the month, but still conducted business once a month. This information is preserved

Historic marker and Johnson Family Cemetery at Great Crossing Baptist Church, Georgetown, Kentucky (2022).

Images courtesy of Kyle Holland.

in the church's ledger books, which date back to 1793.[11] Those records reveal that Great Crossing, like other white churches, struggled with how to integrate its Black congregants into the fold. The church wasn't unusually tolerant of its Black members, nor did it make exceptions for most of its white parishioners when it came to those behaviors it labeled "sins." It did, however, walk a fine line when it came to Julia Chinn and her daughters, assigning the women positions that were neither slave nor free, Black nor white. Instead, the women occupied a uniquely in-between space, in large part because they were members of Richard Johnson's family.

Deeply religious, the senior Johnsons raised their children and their enslaved laborers at Great Crossing, and both Jemima and Robert are buried in the tiny, stone-walled cemetery behind the church building on Stamping Ground Road. Richard, however, didn't become a member of the church until after the War of 1812. On the first Saturday of June in 1815, just a few months before his thirty-fifth birthday, Richard was baptized and then admitted into the fellowship of the church. It makes sense that Richard was thinking more deeply about spiritual matters at this point in his life. He had been badly injured in the Battle of the Thames during the War of 1812 and sent home to recover from his wounds in the fall of 1813. Additionally, his mother and his brother William both passed away in 1814. These things likely took a toll on his emotional health, prodded him to think more deeply about his own mortality, and ultimately led him to place his faith in God in the midst of so much loss. That same faith would have helped him deal with the death of his father just a short time later, in October 1815.[12]

Julia Ann Chinn, a pious woman of faith, also attended Great Crossing Church. Because she grew up at Johnson's Station, she would have gone to Great Crossing from the time she was a child, along with her mother, Henrietta, and her brother, Daniel. The Chinns attended services in the very first meetinghouse that Great Crossing built in 1796, a structure "40 Feet Long by 30 Feet Wide, with Gallery's compleat [sic]." Julia and her family weren't the tiny church's only Black parishioners, however; Great Crossing had a sizeable number of Black members, mostly the enslaved laborers of the church's white congregants, including the bondspeople who worked alongside Julia and her family at Johnson's Station.[13]

It's unknown whether Black people were forced to attend services at Great Crossing by their owners, but they *were* made to sit upstairs, in a separate section of the church known as the "slave gallery." Formerly enslaved persons remembered years later that "Negro members of the church were expected to occupy the back seats" of the sanctuary and that Richard sat at the back of the room with his wife because "he would not embarrass her."[14] Church records from 1802 reveal that the "gallary [sic] at the south end of the meeting house" was set aside "for the accommodation of the slaves or black brethren." Additionally, "two seats at the south east corner of the house" were reserved for Black members of the church. The seats at the back of the room where the Johnsons supposedly sat are likely these same two seats in the southeast corner of the sanctuary.[15]

These seats would have been convenient for the Johnsons. They also highlight the in-between status the couple held at Great Crossing and the tightropes communities walked when it came to handling interracial relationships in public spaces. The seats kept the Johnsons (who blurred lines of race and freedom) away from the Black parishioners up in the gallery. They also kept them near (but not entirely with) the white attendees on the floor, who didn't have to actually look at the couple seated at the back of the tiny church. They could, in some ways, pretend the Johnsons weren't there. It was an elaborate game of "see no evil," since everyone inside the small, 1,200-square-foot meetinghouse could easily see everyone else. To visitors, it suggested that Julia Chinn was not like the other Black members of the church. It also signaled that she and her husband were more, but not exactly, like the white congregants of Great Crossing. Indeed, when Richard chose to sit in those seats, next to Julia, he took on a symbolic cloak of Blackness. His actions, in effect, made him *socially Black* because he chose not to "embarrass" his wife. These kinds of choices would eventually cost him.

It's unlikely that such an accommodation would have been made for the couple at any other area church, which may explain why Julia and Richard attended Great Crossing. Not only was it the church closest to their home, but the Johnson family's history with Great Crossing meant it was the church most likely to bend the rules for Richard, a son of one of its founding families. And since Richard lived in Washington, DC, for half of each year, Julia attended church on her own, or with the couple's daughters, much of the time. That would have intensified her need to find a church where she felt at ease and where she was treated with dignity. Knowing those seats existed might have made all the difference in the world to Julia Chinn.

Julia likely also felt comfortable at Great Crossing because it was the church that Thomas Henderson attended and where he preached the third Sunday of every month. Given the pair's work relationship, that would have made life easier for Julia. Thomas knew Julia from their interactions at Blue Spring and he appeared to respect her, noting years after her passing that she "sustained a good character as a pious, humble Christian to the day of her death."[16] Additionally, Great Crossing may have appealed to Julia because, in addition to having them attend regular services, the church allowed its Black congregants to hold their own worship meetings. The Black brethren of the church asked if they could "assemble themselves for the purpose of religious worship" as early as October 1802, and

Original meetinghouse of Great Crossing Baptist Church, Georgetown, Kentucky. This building was destroyed by a tornado in 1923.

The author would like to thank Ann Bolton Bevins and Ellie Caroland for tracking down this image for her.

such services took place for many years.[17] Black members apparently became too bold in their use of the meetinghouse, however, which led to a reprimand in 1824: "It is to be understood that in future when any privilege is wished by the black brethren of the use of the meeting house, they will first obtain the liberty of the church."[18] After twenty-two years of holding services in the sanctuary, Black congregants, for reasons that went unrecorded, were reminded that their use of the church building was not a universal right but a privilege to be decided on a case-by-case basis.

Whether Julia Chinn attended these separate Black worship services is unknown. She may not have been welcomed by the other congregants, most of whom would have been enslaved people, some of them bondspersons from Blue Spring Farm. They may well have seen her as a collaborator. A snitch. It's also possible that she chose not to go. As a woman who desired upward social mobility for herself and her daughters, she knew the dangers of associating too closely with enslaved folk. On the other hand, she may have looked forward to these gatherings, where friends and family from Johnson's Station would have been in attendance, including her mother, Henrietta. It may have been the only place outside of her own home where she could be herself. Perhaps there, away from the constant gaze of white people, she was able to let down her guard, to laugh, shout, pray, dance, testify, and sing. It's possible she brought her daughters to these meetings so they could spend time with their kin.

The ledger books contain no information about these Black meetings, not who attended them or what they were like, so we can only speculate about what happened at the gatherings. Given how important independent religious spaces were to Black people throughout the Old South, and the roles that enslaved women played in them as Bible study leaders, Sunday school teachers, ministers, prayer warriors, and community revolutionaries, the Black services at Great Crossing likely mirrored those that arose in other, white-affiliated Baptist churches in nearby Lexington and Louisville. There, Black gatherings were enthusiastic. Unlike white services, the singing and preaching in Black meetings were loud, and testifying was common. There was also exuberant dancing, rhythmic clapping, and the patting of feet.[19] Given the chance, Julia Chinn may well have walked down that road from Blue Spring Farm to attend Great Crossing's Black services, mingling in one of the few social spaces available to her in this quiet rural locale.

Communities of Black worshippers, at Great Crossing and in churches across the state, saw themselves as just that: a community. These were people who lived on farms and in urban neighborhoods, who labored together in factories and in the fields and kitchens of white families. While some were forced to attend church by their enslavers, others chose to worship together. This didn't mean that things always went smoothly. One Sunday in May of 1825, Julia, Imogene, and Adaline went to church as they always did. Richard may not have been with them. Although Congress wasn't in session, his attendance at church was inconsistent.[20] It was Communion Sunday. As the music played, there was a commotion of some kind up in the slave gallery. Some of the people on the floor probably craned up their heads, wondering at the noise. There were likely shocked gasps or murmurs. Julia, seated at the back of the church, underneath the gallery, wouldn't have seen a thing, although she surely heard the disturbance. It's doubtful she got involved, however. She couldn't afford to be associated with troublemakers. She had to think about the futures of thirteen-year-old Imogene and eleven-year-old Adaline. Unlike at Blue Spring, where she gave orders with authority, Julia's position at Great Crossing was more tenuous. She probably kept her head down and hustled her daughters out of the meetinghouse as soon as it was safe to do so.

At the next board meeting, the elders noted that "it is discovered that some disorder existed at our last communion among our brethren of colour. In order to remedy the evil, [four white brothers] are appointed by the church to attend to our black brethren on communion days and rectify any disorder which they may discover among them, and should they find any difficulty in rectifying or suppressing any disorder they will report the case to our Brother deacons."[21] Unfortunately, there are no details as to what the "disorder" was, and no further mention of any "evil" on Communion days. Perhaps someone had been denied Communion and caused a scene. It's possible that one or more of the Black congregants "caught the holy ghost" and fell over or began shouting, dancing, or testifying. Here, again, the silence of the ledgers, and the fact that there is no documentation on (or from) the separate Black services, where the matter would have been discussed by Black folks themselves, leaves frustrating gaps.

These tug-of-war moments over separate meetings and "disorderly communions" are just two examples of the ongoing struggles Great Crossing had with its Black congregants over the years, struggles that had to do in part with the church's efforts to ensure that all its members obeyed its vision of "morality." Great Crossing expected no deviation from the rules when it came to "sin." And its catalog of "sins" was lengthy. From speaking "inadvisedly" and talking disrespectfully to or about one's neighbor to attending a picnic or barbecue; from playing ball to drinking too much; from calling the law out on another member to lying; from fornicating to dancing, fighting, horse racing, not attending service, engaging in rowdy behavior, or committing adultery, the list of sins a member could commit was long.[22]

Baptist churches at the time were set up so that any member could "cite" another member for a violation. A person could even cite themselves, and women had "a right when they are distressed with a brother or sister to bring him or her before the church, also to vote in all cases of deception, and moreover to vote to fill up the various offices of the church."[23] This is noteworthy because women couldn't vote in the larger society at the time. The person cited was then called to appear before the church to answer to the charge. If found guilty, they could be temporarily suspended from fellowship if the offense was minor. Even if a person admitted their guilt, they could still be suspended until they had mended their ways, or they could be censured. For more serious offenses, a person would be excluded from the church. If, after a time, a person showed repentance, appeared to have changed their behavior, and sought readmission, they might be brought back into membership.[24] Great Crossing Church, then, was a public instrument, used by the community to enforce law, order, and morality on the frontier. In particular, the church policed race, gender, and sex, working to keep whiteness, masculinity, and the slavocracy in control by judging "morality." And while members could be charged for "calling the law out" against one another, they were encouraged to use the church morals board to keep one another in line.

CHAPTER FOUR

Great Crossing found itself flooded with morals charges made against its congregants, on top of trying the civil cases of its members. It also accepted calls from other churches to act as a mediator, to deal with matters those churches couldn't resolve.[25] This kept the board busier than anticipated, to the point where it couldn't handle all its business on that one Saturday a month. So in April 1802, the church decided it would "meet at Ten O'Clock in the morning, on every Lord's day at our Monthly meeting when Business requires to hear and determine all Difficulties that arise amongst our Black members." Not only did the church decide to hear the cases of white and Black parishioners separately, the original word following "Black" was "Brethren." It was then scratched out and "members" written in its place.[26] One wonders about the change; it implies that while Black congregants of Great Crossing were members of the church, people like Julia Chinn and her daughters may not have been seen as part of the church family.

Great Crossing clearly struggled with this question. Black members enjoyed equity with the church's white congregants in certain ways. In addition to attending Sunday worship, they could hold their own separate meetings, and they were brought up on the same morals charges as white parishioners. On the other hand, Black attendees had segregated seating at the main Sunday service, their separate meeting privileges could be revoked at any time, and white members were warned not to let Black people cross certain social lines. For example, in 1808, white congregants of the church were advised "never to have Black people collected at corn shuckings without written leave from their masters."[27] Apparently, there was concern that Black folks might cause trouble if allowed to gather without white permission or oversight. Additionally, and significantly, though white members could charge each other or Black members with morals violations, and Black folks could charge one another, Black members couldn't bring charges against white members of the church.[28]

In these and other ways, Great Crossing mimicked the larger slave society in which it stood. As for Julia Chinn and her daughters, they occupied a literal "third space" within the church, neither fully white nor fully Black. Indeed, while it's possible the Johnson women went to the aforementioned corn shuckings, it's just as likely that they signed permission slips for enslaved laborers from Blue Spring to attend those same events. What is clear is that the church continually reminded Black parishioners that people of color were under surveillance, that they needed to be controlled, and that whatever privileges they enjoyed could be revoked at any time. While Black attendees at Great Crossing may have been part of the family of Christ, their status in that family wasn't quite the same as that of the white congregants of the church.

Consider that while few white people were ever cited to appear before the church board, charges were continually brought against the enslaved members of Great Crossing, to the point where extra meetings had to be scheduled to hear them all. And while white persons who appear in the ledgers were often "complaining against themselves" for improper behavior, and were usually forgiven, Black persons were often cited by their owners. It appears, then, that the white enslavers of Great Crossing used the church as another way to discipline their slaves and maintain the racial hierarchies of the larger society in which they lived. Take the case of John T. Johnson, Richard Johnson's brother, who confessed to fighting with a white man. He admitted his conduct was improper and that he had "sinned against God and his brethren." The church first voted that the case be held over or continued so people had a chance for "reflection and consideration." They then decided to "bear with John T. Johnson on his acknowledgement of wrongdoing."[29]

Contrast this case with that of Billy, an enslaved man who belonged to Martin Hawkins. Charged by Martin with fighting and using bad language, Billy was "excluded for fighting and riotous behavior." It's unclear whether Billy testified on his own behalf.[30] Whereas the church could "bear with" John T. Johnson, a war veteran, a white man, the son of a founding family, and a man whose sin was fighting another white man, Great Crossing drew the line with Billy, a Black man who exhibited violent behavior, possibly against a white man who was also his owner. That couldn't, and wouldn't, be tolerated "in a community dedicated to upholding whiteness, patriarchy, slavery, and Christ."

Matilda's situation sheds light on the church's commitment to policing race, gender, and sex. The bondsperson of Johnathan J. Johnson, Matilda was first cited to appear before the church board in November 1811. Her case was held over, however, month after month, because Matilda never showed up for her hearings, claiming she was "too unwell" to attend meeting. Finally, in March 1812, the church brothers were sent out to cite Matilda yet again. She was to appear at the next meeting and answer to a new charge. When they showed up at her door, they discovered that Matilda had recently given birth. This explains why she hadn't shown up at meeting for so long; she was probably trying to hide her condition, although her pregnancy also may have made her too sick to attend church.[31]

In April, the brothers reported back on their meeting with Matilda. They were of the opinion that not only had Matilda had a child but the father of her baby was a white man, not her husband. She still refused to attend meeting. After considering the case, the church concluded that Matilda was guilty and should be excluded from fellowship. It's unclear what the charge was, although it was probably adultery. Regardless, no charges appear to have been filed against the unnamed white father, who may have been her owner, Johnathan J. Johnson. There is also no information as to whether or not this child was the result of assault. It's possible that Johnathan had forbidden Matilda from going to church in order to cover up his own crimes. Here again, the ledgers are silent. All we know is that a Black woman was excluded for having a baby with a white man who wasn't her husband. This verdict upheld the rhetoric against adultery and amalgamation, expectations about appropriate feminine behavior, and raced and gendered hierarchies of power. It was Matilda, the enslaved Black woman, not the father of her child, who was punished for giving birth to their light-skinned child.[32]

The way this case was handled may have worried Julia Chinn. Matilda gave birth to a child supposedly fathered by a white man in February or March of 1812. This was exactly when Julia had her first daughter, Imogene. The two women's circumstances were similar in certain ways, including the fact that both Julia and Matilda may have been in coercive sexual situations. It's unclear how Julia and Richard Johnson's relationship began. At one end of the spectrum, Julia may have been an enslaved woman of twenty who entered into a relationship with Richard with her eyes wide open, knowing that her options were limited and that this was her best "choice" out of a handful of bad options. At the other, she may have been a fourteen-year-old girl, forced into sex by a man in his thirties, who then bore his child, not knowing if she or her baby would be sold to hide the evidence of her master's "indiscretions." While one scenario is more physically violent than the other, neither is free of slavery's constraints and coercions.

When Julia heard about Matilda's exclusion, she may have wondered if the next knock at the door of Blue Spring Farm would reveal the brothers of Great Crossing, come to cite her. Known for her piety, this would have been of great concern to Julia. It never happened, however. Despite the church's stance against interracial sex and fornication, the way Richard treated Julia and the authority he invested in her, when added to the Johnson name and money, allowed the pair to live together more openly than one might have thought possible in this small, religious community. Additionally, the fact that Richard wasn't married to a white woman, the couple's apparent monogamy, and the rumors of their wedding ceremony all seem to have helped people at Great Crossing look the other way when it came to Julia and Richard's relationship. Richard had no other wife, Julia no other husband. Unlike Matilda's situation, then, this wasn't a case of adultery. And unlike Richard Johnson, the father of Matilda's new baby didn't appear to treat Matilda as a wife or partner.

Whether this scenario was good or bad for Julia is uncertain: the rules were bent at Great Crossing not for Julia's sake but to protect Richard, his white family members, and the church. The many Johnson relations who attended the tiny church were already embarrassed by Richard's unconventional life. They, and the church elders, likely hoped to avoid the public scandal that would develop, for the family and the church, if Great Crossing suspended or excluded the politically prominent Johnson nephew and brother or his Black wife. It wasn't about making life better for Julia, Imogene, and Adaline; it was about shielding the extended Johnson clan from possible economic, social, and political fallout.[33]

Matilda's refusal to come and be judged may not have surprised Julia; it was a common theme among the enslaved folks at Great Crossing. Another, similar case hit even closer to home. The enslaved woman Fanny was cited in October 1815 and told to appear at the church's next meeting to answer the charge against her. Fanny, however, chose not to attend meeting in November. She probably reached out to Julia Chinn for help: Richard was Fanny's owner. In the future, Fanny and Patience Chinn, Julia's sister-in-law, would work together in the dining hall at Choctaw Academy.[34] The three women likely knew each other well, then. As a member of the house party, it stands to reason that Fanny confided in one or both of the Chinn women, hoping that Julia or Patience would speak to Richard about her situation and that his influence with the church board would help her case.

Unfortunately, neither her connection to the Chinns nor the fact that Richard Mentor Johnson was her owner helped Fanny in the end. The church had a different set of rules for the Johnson women than it did for other Black people, even those who worked at Blue Spring Farm. There's also no guarantee that Richard actually interceded on Fanny's behalf. While he had a long-standing relationship with one Black woman and held great affection for their two daughters, Richard was still an enslaver who viewed Black women on the whole as loose and immoral "wenches," who flogged enslaved women for having sex, and who sold bondwomen "downriver" when they displeased him.

Charged with adultery, Fanny was found guilty by the church board, which voted to exclude her. As in Matilda's case, the name of the man Fanny was having sex with wasn't recorded in the ledgers. And like Matilda, Fanny knew that by not showing up for her hearing, the only possible verdict was exclusion. Still, she decided she would rather be excluded from the church than ask for forgiveness or defend her actions to the all-white panel that would sit in judgment over her in the small brick building at the Big Crossing. At some point in the future, however, Fanny apparently atoned for her sins and was readmitted to the fellowship of the church. She then continued to worship at Great Crossing until her death from cholera in the summer of 1833.[35]

The refusal of enslaved persons to show up for hearings could have been a show of defiance, a sign of fear, or a suggestion of shame. It also indicates that at least some of the Black congregants at Great Crossing didn't come to church of their own free will but were forced to attend by their owners, who were also members of the church. In fact, some enslaved persons may have deliberately "sinned" in order to be removed from the church. Clearly, the enslavers at Great Crossing didn't have total control over their bondspeople, who rebelled against the church's morals code and chose exclusion over repentance. While they may have pressured them to attend services, the complaints that churchgoing slave owners filed against their own bondspeople, and the charges that other whites in Scott County filed against enslaved Black persons, make it clear that all was not quiet in the church pews or in the neighborhood.

Great Crossing was, then, a microcosm of the larger society in which it stood. While the church made some exceptions for the Johnsons, it was not a haven for most Black people. One wonders, then, if Julia Chinn and Richard Johnson made church attendance mandatory for Blue Spring's enslaved laborers or if their bondspeople willingly sat in the slave gallery at Great Crossing. Certainly for Julia and her daughters, church attendance was a prerequisite for upward social mobility. It was something they needed to do in order to attain respectability in a nation that viewed Black women as inherently lewd, promiscuous, and immoral. Still, while Julia was known for her piety, the Johnsons discovered that, despite their standing in the community, even *they* were not above being cited by the mighty morals board at Great Crossing Baptist Church.

In April 1820, two brothers knocked at the door of Blue Spring Farm. Julia may have opened the door with her heart in her throat. They weren't there for her, however. They wanted to speak to her husband, but Richard wasn't home. Congress was still in session, and he wouldn't be back in Kentucky for another two months.[36] Julia's mind was surely racing. What did the men want? With two children to raise, dignitaries to entertain, and a 2,000-acre farm to run, Julia was a busy, privileged woman. Her relationship with Richard was the gateway to her social mobility, however. If something were to happen to him, if he fell from grace, so would she. Great Crossing wasn't just a place of worship for Julia. Given its position in the community, and the public power it held as both mediator and enforcer of morals for women and men, Black and white, enslaved and free, if the church suspended or excluded Richard, regardless of his wealth, it could be catastrophic for his quasi-free Black family. It would be particularly damaging for Imogene and Adaline, who needed to shake off any remaining stains of enslavement.

When Richard returned home later that spring, the brothers from Great Crossing explained that they had come to charge him, to demand he come to church and explain "why he has absented himself from meeting so long." The matter is puzzling. The church surely couldn't expect him to come to meeting while Congress was in session. This implies that when he was in Kentucky, Richard wasn't as faithful about attending church as his pious parents had been or as devout as his enslaved wife. The charge was directed at Richard alone, suggesting Julia, Imogene, and Adaline attended services without Richard, even when he was at Blue Spring.[37]

The forty-year-old war hero and sitting US senator was likely frustrated by the charge. Richard's views on God were different from many others' of his day; a decade after this, in what came to be known as the Sunday Mails Battle, Richard Johnson stood up in Congress and supported continued delivery of the Sunday mail against strong religious opposition to postal delivery on the Sabbath.[38] Still, he responded to the matter at hand. While the issue was held over in May, probably because he was still in Washington, Richard appeared before the board in June to plead his case, and the church agreed "to Bear with Br. Richard Johnson hoping he will bee [sic] more attentive in coming to meeting." There are no other notes in the ledger. Once again, the Johnson family name, along with Richard's race and gender, appears to have helped him avoid censure, suspension, or exclusion. Evidently, the board felt his explanation for his absences, whatever it was, was valid, and no other charges were brought against him. Richard likely made more of an effort to attend meeting after this brush with the board, if for no other reason than to protect his daughters from possible harm.[39]

Great Crossing was supposedly serious about their members attending service. While they let Richard off with a mild warning, they were far more rigid when it came to their Black members missing church, as they were with other offenses. In 1826, Benjamin Davis suggested "this church advise those of their black brethren who reside at so great a distance from the place that they cannot attend our meetings to join some other Baptist church more convenient to them."[40] The church passed his motion. This was before the 1827–28 revival, when hundreds of new converts were added to the church's membership.[41] In 1826, then, the church couldn't necessarily afford to turn away new members. Still, it seems they felt they could turn away Black ones, especially those whose behavior the white brethren couldn't monitor. Great Crossing clearly took its role as community watchdog seriously, at least when it came to its Black congregants. Keep in mind that Richard Johnson, who lived just up the road, wouldn't have been able to use distance to explain his absences in 1820, yet the church agreed to "bear with Br. Richard." The rhetoric of the church thus differed from the reality, as it often did, when it came to handling the powerful and wealthy interracial family at the center of its congregation. Like the larger society to which Great Crossing belonged, church justice wasn't (color-)blind.

CHAPTER FOUR

The revival in the late 1820s changed the lives of hundreds of Black people across the state, including that of Julia Chinn. While Julia had attended Great Crossing for many years, she wasn't an official member of the church. She was what is known today as an adherent. You could only become a member of a Baptist church after being baptized by full water immersion. That could only happen if you first had a conversion experience, received Christ as your Lord and Savior, and then publicly testified to that experience. It works the same way today.

At Great Crossing, 359 people were converted in 1828 alone. Many of those persons were African Americans, enslaved and free, as well as several of the Native American students who attended Choctaw Academy.[42] Much of this was in keeping with the times. By 1828, the country was deep in the throes of what came to be known as the Second Great Awakening. As religion spread across the land through emotional preaching and mass meetings or revivals that lasted for days or weeks, hundreds and then thousands of people, especially white women, Black folks, and Native Americans, were converted to new Protestant denominations. Beginning in the 1790s with an outpouring of religious fervor on what was then the new western frontier of Kentucky and Tennessee, and stretching down into the 1830s and 1840s with mass meetings in places as far flung as Rochester, New York, and Charleston, South Carolina, the Second Great Awakening gave rise to the Methodist, Presbyterian, and Baptist denominations and helped birth numerous social reform movements across the United States.[43]

Great Crossing had already experienced a major revival early on during the Second Great Awakening, in 1800–1801, when 376 new members were baptized into the church. Julia was just a child, perhaps no more than four years old, during that "Great Kentucky Revival," when "the beautiful waters of the Elkhorn were parted by burial in baptism by hundreds who now trod the shores of immortality."[44] She likely had friends and family who had been impacted by the experience, however. Her mother, Henrietta, may have been one of the 376 persons baptized during that revival. It's thus no surprise that Julia Chinn became a lifelong churchgoer, faithfully attending Great Crossing even before the fires of revival swept back into Scott County when she was a grown woman of about thirty-two. Rev. R. T. Dillard did much of the preaching during that second revival in 1828, along with John Bryan, J. D. Black, and Julia's colleague from Choctaw Academy, Thomas Henderson. When asked about the 1828 revival years later, Dillard remembered,

> A table was placed in the sink just south of the meeting-house for him to stand on while preaching, the crowds being so great that the house would not near hold them—that while he was preaching the people would sit on the grass on the hillsides around in

great numbers, giving earnest and close attention, while the pastor, Rev. S.M. Noel, would be in the house, with crowded aisles and benches, hearing experiences related—that the people would come, not only from this county, but also from counties adjoining, and stay with the members near at hand, for days together, leaving their homes and worldly matters to attend to the preaching of the gospel.[45]

During the revival, at a meeting at Great Crossing on Sunday, April 20, 1828, a number of persons were received for baptism. Number eight that day was "Julia a woman of colour belonging to Col Johnson."[46] It's significant to note that despite all the accommodations that Great Crossing made for Julia and her daughters, and all the authority and privilege she held at Blue Spring Farm and Choctaw Academy, Julia Ann Chinn was still viewed by the church elders as an enslaved woman, the property of "Col Johnson."

The church left no records as to what its baptism services were like. We don't know if there was special scripture read or celebratory music. It's likely that the baptisms were performed at Elkhorn Creek, however, as they were during the Great Kentucky Revival of 1800. Although Richard was still in Washington when Julia was baptized, the couple's daughters surely witnessed the moment, along with Julia's brother, Daniel, his wife, Patience, and other family members.[47] Perhaps Julia's mother, Henrietta, was there to see her baby girl "born again." There may have been a special meal back at Blue Spring to mark the occasion. Baptisms are cause for celebration even today, and they are often seen as a person's "spiritual birthday." There were many such reasons to celebrate in the months to come, because Julia was not the last person from Blue Spring Farm whom Silas Noel baptized during this revival. A number of enslaved persons and seventeen students from Choctaw Academy, from Stephen Grayson on May 3 to Jackson McAfee on November 15, found Jesus at Great Crossing that year, although for the Johnson family, Julia's baptism would have been the most significant.[48]

Its proximity to Blue Spring Farm and Choctaw Academy meant that Great Crossing had a unique congregation. It also had men such as Silas Noel and Thomas Henderson in the pulpit. Thomas believed that all persons, regardless of race, should know how to read the word of God, and he spent his evenings, after he had wrapped up work at the academy, teaching enslaved persons at Blue Spring how to read. His students included members of Julia Chinn's extended family as well as the Johnsons' daughters. Silas Noel was known to be concerned with faith, repentance, and living a godly life over worldly hierarchies or status, and he regularly reached out to "invite the poor, the halt, the blind and lame, with every other soul to seek the salvation of God" and come to the Communion table. His attitudes were reflective, in many ways, of preachers who rose to prominence on the frontier during the Second Great Awakening.[49]

This might explain why Noel was willing to baptize Julia Chinn, a woman whom other, more traditional white preachers would have dismissed as a harlot. Since Julia lived with Richard Johnson in a monogamous relationship like a wife, bore his children like a wife, and ran his farm, businesses, and household like a wife, Silas Noel accorded her the courtesies of a wife and baptized her upon her profession of faith. He didn't see her as a fornicator. This is likely also why he performed the wedding ceremony of Julia and Richard's older daughter, Imogene, to Daniel B. Pence in 1830, despite state laws prohibiting interracial marriage.[50]

The Pences trace their family line back to one Johann Georg Bentz in Germany, and locals attested that Daniel B. Pence was a "Dutchman."[51] Bentz and his wife, Anna Barbara Bullinger, had a son named Adam in 1735 who immigrated to the United States. It was Adam who changed the family's last name to Pence, likely to Anglicize it for ease of use and perhaps to avoid the hostility directed at foreigners in his new homeland. Adam and his wife (whose name is unknown) had two sons: George, born in Shenandoah, Virginia, in 1774, and Adam Jr., born in 1780. George, who moved to Kentucky at some point before 1804, married a woman whose last name was Brown, and he died in Scott County, Kentucky, in 1847. It is this couple who became the parents of Daniel B. Pence. Born in Kentucky in 1804, Daniel Brown Pence married Imogene Johnson in 1830. Like the Johnsons, then, Daniel's family had been in Kentucky for several decades by the time of his marriage, after having arrived from Virginia.[52]

It makes sense that Silas Noel married Imogene and Daniel, given the Johnsons' long-standing ties to Great Crossing and both families' roots in the community. Still, it's doubtful the pair were married at the meetinghouse. That might have been going too far, even for Silas, considering that, technically, Imogene may have been enslaved, even though Richard always treated his daughters as free people and they behaved as such. Great Crossing's role as public enforcer of law, order, and morality might have made it difficult to explain to people in the larger community why the pair were married at the church. It's more likely that Silas performed the ceremony at Blue Spring, balancing that public-private line the church so carefully walked. Still, these were the kinds of rites and relationships that kept the Johnsons at Great Crossing.

After the excitement of the revival, Great Crossing thrived. It continued to have issues with its Black congregants, however, perhaps because it had integrated so many new members into its flock. Not all of these cases were filed by white people: some Black members worked the system at Great Crossing to

Portrait of Daniel B. Pence, husband of Imogene Johnson Pence. While the portrait has Daniel's middle name as "Boone," family records indicate that his middle name was "Brown," which was his mother's maiden name.

Image courtesy of the Pence Family private collection.

CHAPTER FOUR

their own advantage, citing other Black folks to rid themselves of their enemies. While there's no indication that Julia Chinn or any of the enslaved laborers at Blue Spring ever used the church to lay charges against other Black people, men such as "Brother Moses of colour" complained against Edward, another brother of color, for stealing. While Edward was charged to appear at the next meeting, there is no record of what happened to him. The ledgers do note what happened when Jackson, a Black man, complained against Jackson, Thomas, and Henry, all men of color. Brother Jackson charged the three men, who belonged to Brother Quarles, with drunkenness and bad language and then charged Winney, a woman of color, who belonged to Mr. Thomas Outon, for "profane and sinful conduct." In the end, Winney and the three men were all excluded. Jackson had gotten rid of everyone he had charged. What we don't know is the backstory. It's possible that the men had fought over something, or someone. Maybe over a woman. Perhaps it was Winney. Maybe she rejected Jackson, and this was his revenge. We have no idea what her "profane and sinful conduct" was. It's possible that she was involved with Jackson, and he caught her with one of the men he then charged. Here, again, the ledgers are frustratingly silent.[53]

Despite the church's role as community enforcer and mediator in issues of law, order, and morality, not all the Black parishioners of Great Crossing accepted the system. In addition to those who refused to appear at meeting when charged, one of the most enlightening cases was that of Moses, a brother of color charged by Brother William C. for drunkenness and other disorderly conduct. Moses was then cited to appear at the next meeting. Unlike most Black congregants, however, Moses actually appeared to speak to the charge. He also confessed to his behavior. He didn't ask for forgiveness, though. Instead, Moses said that he no longer wished to be a member of the church! Moses was likely tired of having his every move monitored by Great Crossing, on top of the surveillance he already had to put up with on his plantation. Moses wanted out. Moses thus chose expulsion. Moses chose spiritual, if not physical, freedom.[54]

In the midst of such hostile interactions, moments of kindness nevertheless did occur between the Black and white congregants of Great Crossing. Certainly Imogene, Adaline, and Richard Johnson must have appreciated that the church officially recorded the passing of their mother and wife, Julia Chinn, in July 1833: "Departed this life since our last meeting . . . July Chinn, Jerry, Jacob, Lucy, Rose and Fanny, all of the family of Col. R. M. Johnson."[55] Despite misspelling her name, by mentioning her death, placing her at the head of a list of persons who died at Blue Spring during the cholera outbreak that raged throughout Kentucky that summer, and noting that she was a part of Richard's family, Great Crossing acknowledged the position that Julia Chinn held in their congregation, on Blue

Spring Farm, and in Richard Johnson's life. Julia was not buried in the tiny graveyard behind the church she had faithfully attended for so many years, however. Not only was that space reserved for the white members of the church's founding families, but her death from cholera at the height of the epidemic ensured that Great Crossing wouldn't lay her to rest in their cemetery. Richard almost certainly buried her on the family farm, as was the practice of the day.[56]

Richard himself noted Julia's piety and the high regard in which she was held, telling a longtime friend of his a few years after her death that she had been for the "last 15 years of her life a member of the Baptist church at the Great Crossings as irreproachable as any member in it and as much respected in her place as a woman could be." A woman of "irreproachable" character and "much respected," Julia's example of Christian womanhood was evidently passed down to her daughters. When her older daughter, Imogene Johnson Pence, died fifty years later, she would be eulogized as "an exemplary member of the Christian church, a devoted mother, faithful wife, and a woman of rare intellectual achievements."[57]

Despite her many years of faithful membership, it's unclear how the other congregants of Great Crossing reacted to Julia's passing. One wonders if she had much to do with the white women of Great Crossing. We know little about the white sisters of the church, who seldom show up in the ledgers. Ann and Nancy Johnson made an appearance when they left the church for another society (likely another religious group), "for which they are condemned."[58] Sister Zerelda Burton was excluded for the sin of dancing. Most intriguing is the case of Brother Newton Craig, who complained against Sister Haney for her "unlawful dealing with negroes." As this case threatened to disrupt all expectations of appropriate white female behavior, given the dynamics of race, gender, (im)propriety, and (im)morality, the church immediately appointed a committee to inquire into the matter and report back to the board at their next meeting.[59]

Great Crossing couldn't afford to have a white woman caught up in a scandal involving Black people. And here, the double standard when it came to race and gender was laid bare; men, especially white men, didn't face any condemnation when they had relations with Black women—whether it was Richard Johnson, the man who fathered Matilda's child, or the man who had sex with Fanny. As the self-appointed judge and jury of morality in the community, however, the church always positioned itself as the public watchdog of sexual and racial impropriety. Sister Haney's case had the potential to cross both those lines. On the basis of the report, however, no details of which are given, the church agreed to "bear with Sister Haney." Haney thus escaped suspension or exclusion, but we have no clue what the supposedly "unlawful dealings" were that she had with Black people, nor do we know anything about the "negroes" with whom she was supposedly involved. They might have been enslaved or free, male or female. The dealings she was accused of could have been economic, sexual, or political. Perhaps she was involved with the Underground Railroad. We don't even know the connection between Craig and Haney. On these and other questions, the ledgers are, once again, entirely silent. One wonders if the board deliberately chose to leave these details out of the record, fearing that writing down such facts might lead to upheavals in their flock.[60]

What the ledgers do reveal is that Great Crossing's relationship with its members of color was complicated. There were moments when it seemed as if the church was learning to give its Black brethren more autonomy and respect. In spring 1842, "the church agreed to meet the members of colour the third Sunday evening in April and appoint a committee of their own body to adjust and hear all matters of complaint relating to themselves and report to the church such cases as may occur amongst them from time to time."[61] This was the first time that Great Crossing had ever granted Black parishioners the right to appoint a Black committee, which would hear Black-centered complaints and then report back to the larger church when needed. This was a significant step in the direction of racial sensitivity, and certainly one that Imogene Johnson Pence and others would have appreciated.

Just a little over a year later, however, the church began investigating "black religious worship" in a manner that was neither sensitive nor loving. On Sunday, May 7, 1843, the board appointed a committee "to ascertain what is the law in relation to the collection of blacks for the purpose of religious worship and report the same to the next meeting."[62] While the ledgers mention nothing about this in June, in July the "committee appointed at the last meeting to look into the law in relation to the collection of coloured persons for the purpose of religious worship report that the law is silent on the subject." Given the law's "silence," what happened next was shocking: "The church in future decline granting the people of colour the use of the meeting house for the purposes of religious worship."[63] With one stroke of the pen, the church overturned over forty years of practice and snuffed out separate Black meetings at Great Crossing.

Except for one note back in the 1820s that reminded Black parishioners to seek permission prior to using the building, there had been no mention of any problems with Black congregants using the meetinghouse. In 1843, however, Great Crossing radically altered its position, likely in response to matters *outside* of the church. By the early 1840s, the Baptist denomination was in crisis due to the abolition movement. At their annual convention, conservative northern Baptists came under pressure from abolitionists and proslavery southerners within the denomination regarding the slavery question. Hoping to allay southern fears, the convention's domestic and foreign missionary societies, which helped keep the nation's Baptist churches linked in a loose coalition, dismissed abolitionists from all positions of leadership and affirmed their neutrality on slavery. It wasn't enough. In 1845, proslavery Baptist churches broke away from the larger convention and established the Southern Baptist Convention, in addition to founding their own seminary in Greenville, South Carolina, where they could train proslavery ministers. That same year, a group of African American Baptist churches also broke away and formed their own convention, the American Baptist Missionary Convention, in opposition to the perceived proslavery stance of the larger organization's missionary societies.[64]

As Great Crossing eyed the growing national crisis, it was equally impacted by local matters. Kentucky had its own antislavery preachers and a number of influential Black Baptist churches. The Reverend William H. Pratt openly preached against slavery and the slave trade in nearby Lexington Baptist Church, while the Reverend Henry Adams, a free Black man from Georgia, founded First African Baptist Church (ABC) in Louisville in 1842, only one year before Great Crossing revoked separate services for its Black members. First ABC was the city's first independent Black church, and Adams nurtured Black Baptist congregations throughout the region. First ABC would go on to become the "mother church" of Kentucky's Black Baptist movement, hosting the formation of the State Convention of Colored Baptists in 1865.[65]

Men such as Henry Adams knew it was critical to expand the number of Black southern churches that were independent of white oversight and that Louisville, on the physical border between slavery and freedom, was the place to plant them. Such churches, and the independent schools they helped maintain, brought a powerful message of liberation to the state's enslaved and free Black populations. At the same time, however, local white evangelicals, in Louisville and across the state, came to see it as their duty to fight against the "aggressive spirit of abolitionism." In their opinion, one of the best ways to do this was by bringing enslaved people under the direct watch of the evangelical church. This meant reining in independent Black churches and establishing "slave missions" inside white churches, with white oversight.[66]

The decision at Great Crossing makes sense given the national and local contexts. In fact, the founding of First ABC in 1842 may have been a factor in the situation. The board at Great Crossing may have feared allowing its Black congregants to meet without white leadership, knowing what Adams was doing just up the road. The Black members at Great Crossing did not take this news quietly, however. Within a month, a new report was filed by A. Smith and G. B. Long, the authors of the original report that had led members of color to lose their meeting privileges. Undoubtedly prodded by the church's Black parishioners, Smith and Long moved to amend that first report, which they now said had an error in it: "The undersigned committee to ascertain what the law is in relation to assemblies of Blacks for religious worship find that we were led into error (by advice we received) in our former report and we ask leave now to correct the error. We find in a proviso in the law affixing a penalty for slaves meeting on the premises of persons other than their master that the 'going to Church and attending to divine service on the Lord's day, or any other day of public worship,' is excepted."[67]

First the law was supposedly "silent" on the issue, and now Smith and Long claimed to have been "led into error." The pair never stated who gave them the "bad advice" however, which may have been their way of covering up their own mistake or hiding the church's efforts at trying to squash Black worship services. They also didn't mention how they came to uncover the "error," perhaps because it was brought to their attention by the church's Black congregants. In fact, it's possible that the Black parishioners at Great Crossing were getting counsel from other Black Baptist churches in the area, including First ABC. It's equally telling that the records never mention whether the church reinstated its Black members' meeting privileges. It might have been easier for the board to just quietly return to doing so instead of formalizing it in the ledgers. The admission of error may have been too much. This would fall in line with the church's habit of not recording the details of cases involving its Black congregants. One can assume that the offensive new policy was revoked. This is upheld by the fact that in August 1859, as the nation edged closer to war, Great Crossing "decided that the colored people shall hold no more meetings in this church," implying, of course, that they already had been.[68]

A public-facing entity committed to serving God and policing the lines of race, gender, and sexuality in order to uphold patriarchy and maintain white supremacy and racial slavery, Great Crossing Baptist Church struggled with how to balance Blackness and brotherhood within the confines of its congregation. A white, slaveholding church, it made some exceptions when it came to Julia Chinn, Richard Mentor Johnson, and their daughters. Rhetoric and reality were blurred, up to a point. The church was willing to bend certain rules for Julia because of her connection to Richard. Never cited for fornication, Julia was baptized, the family had special seats in the meetinghouse, the couple's children had access to formal marriage rites, and more. In some ways, this isn't surprising. Across time and denomination, power and wealth have always paved the way for privilege. That's what the paying of indulgences was all about.[69]

Still, the church only extended the Johnson women benefits to a certain point. While it acknowledged that Julia was Richard's de facto Black wife, the emphasis was on the words "de facto" and "Black." There were lines that Chinn and her daughters could not cross, even at Great Crossing. Their seats were at the back of the sanctuary, Imogene's wedding probably didn't take place at the church, and Julia wasn't buried in the Johnson family cemetery behind the meetinghouse. The church elders, like the local magistrates who were unwilling to arrest or flog David Wall and Peter King after the attempted break-in at Blue Spring Farm in December 1827, made it clear by their actions that mixed-race families in general, and Julia Chinn and her daughters in particular, while more privileged than the other enslaved persons in their congregation, were not exactly like the white families and women in their midst either.[70]

The benefits that the Johnson women received at Great Crossing, already limited in scope, didn't translate into the broader community. While Great Crossing was a public space, it was also unique, both because of its leadership and because it was a religious body. It thus functioned as an entity separate from state intervention in certain respects because of the First Amendment. It was why women could vote in the church long before they could vote outside of it. The boundaries that Julia Chinn and her daughters crossed at home and at church were not so easily sidestepped in Georgetown, Frankfort, Louisville, or Lexington, however. The same people who were willing to dance and drink in their home, and who sat beside them in the pews, would draw a harder line when the Black women of Blue Spring attempted to enter into community spaces that were seen as being for white people, and particularly for white women.

CHAPTER FIVE

TOWN TALK

Locals Draw the Line

O n a hot summer day in *1831*, Adaline Johnson went to a barbecue with her father. It was the Fourth of July. Richard had been asked to speak at the local celebration in Georgetown, and he took his younger daughter with him in the family carriage to attend the outdoor festivities. Adaline was excited to accompany her father into town. Sixteen or seventeen years old, the teenager spent most of her time at Blue Spring Farm, studying with Thomas Henderson and helping her mother with the work needed to maintain Choctaw Academy. When she left the plantation, it was generally to go to services at Great Crossing Baptist Church. She probably felt quite grown up that day, accompanying her father to a public event. There would be music, food, dancing, and other people her own age to socialize with. Julia would have ensured that Adaline's outfit was of the highest quality, befitting her status as the daughter of an elected official and event speaker. One can imagine the thrill the girl felt, taking her father's arm as she exited the carriage.

Because Richard had to sit on the platform with the other speakers, Adaline went to join the other young women, many of whom were already dancing when the Johnsons arrived. When she took her seat under an awning that had been

CHAPTER FIVE

set up to shade folks while they rested, however, it caused a commotion. Several people who were sitting in the area got up and left, and the situation caught the attention of some of the event planners. Complaints were lodged. Some of the men were then sent to tell Richard that his daughter needed to leave the party. He protested, stating that she was "as well-educated as any lady there," but the managers said it was "not a debatable matter." Furious, Richard eventually escorted Adaline back to their carriage. There she sat, no doubt hurt and embarrassed, until Richard gave his speech. He left the gathering immediately afterward and went home with Adaline, refusing to join in the festivities.[1]

A day that had begun with such excitement and promise ended in humiliation for Adaline, Julia, and Richard. One can only imagine the thoughts that went through the young girl's mind as she sat alone in the carriage, waiting for her father to finish his speech. The ride home that day may have been filled with the sound of her sobs, Richard's angry rants, or a tense silence. One wonders what the conversation was like when the pair arrived back at Blue Spring earlier than expected and told Julia what had happened. Like any mother, she would have been heartsick that her daughter had been publicly humiliated, and for nothing more than the color of her skin. And because her mother was an enslaved woman. It wouldn't be the last time that the Johnson women became the center of public controversy due to their "boundary-breaking" behavior.

What white people thought of Julia Chinn and her daughters, and the battles that were played out in rural Kentucky over race, gender, sex, and power, have been preserved in the local press. Richard's political career meant that the Johnson family was regularly written about in area newspapers.[2] Had he been an ordinary citizen, it would have been more difficult to capture the details of the Johnson women's lives, let alone understand the anger they stirred up when they rode around town in carriages or attended social events. This is partly because although all three women were literate, none of their letters have survived. And while we have the letters Richard wrote to other peoples, the ones written to him have disappeared. All of these documents were likely destroyed by Richard's surviving white family members after his death.[3]

The story of the Johnson women's lives thus far seems to have been one that was fairly privileged for antebellum women of color. They appear to have had some degree of acceptance from their neighbors. White locals attended parties at their home. Adaline and Imogene were well educated, learned to play the piano, and interacted with visiting dignitaries at Blue Spring Farm. Julia had access to Richard's money, oversaw the plantation's labor force, managed her husband's various business enterprises, and entered into contracts on his behalf with local vendors. The family attended the church that Richard's parents had helped found, alongside the county's enslaved laborers, plantation owners, and students from Choctaw Academy. Additionally, Richard's reelection to public office year after year implies that his private life didn't damage his career. Still, the tensions that flared between some of the students at Choctaw Academy and the Black women of Blue Spring suggest that not everyone was pleased with the authority the Johnson women had.

In addition to the Choctaw students, there were local whites who were frustrated, if not disgusted, by the interracial family living at Blue Spring. Indeed, the benefits that Julia, Imogene, and Adaline enjoyed didn't extend far, not even to Georgetown or Lexington, respectively only five and seventeen miles from Blue Spring Farm. The brouhaha at the barbecue was not a solitary event. Although Great Crossing Baptist Church made certain accommodations for the Johnson family, there were limits to the women's privileges in the greater community. Local whites closed ranks when Julia and her daughters tried to enter spaces Americans believed were reserved for ladies (i.e., white women) alone. No matter how educated, wealthy, or refined their manners might be, the Johnson women were still Black, and they were still legally enslaved, although they lived as free people. Their attempts to thus "live like ladies" disrupted the larger raced and gendered hierarchies of the South, and the nation. Such behavior would not, could not, go unchallenged.

White folks in Scott County had, of course, always known about Julia and Richard. It was an open secret, and one they had long tolerated, if not accepted. The issue at heart, however, was "notoriety." It was about the fact that the Johnsons, at some point, began asking their neighbors to openly acknowledge their relationship; that they crossed over from living in private spaces to operating in public places. In doing so, they asked the people of Scott County to move from toleration to tolerance, from accommodation to acceptance. Had they stayed within the boundaries of farm and church, white locals would have likely continued to turn a blind eye to the family. But once the Johnson women left the confines of Blue Spring and Great Crossing and tried to integrate themselves into larger community spaces, protesters, who had before this limited themselves to gossiping behind closed doors, voiced their displeasure in action and in print.

The Fourth of July barbecue was one event that generated heated debate. On July 9, 1831, a few days after Adaline had been ejected from the picnic, the *Lexington Observer* published a brief paragraph on the matter. "DISGRACEFUL.

... On Monday last, a gentleman in a neighboring county, took his daughters to a Barbecue and Ball in his neighborhood, but they were not suffered to remain and partake of the festivities ... because they (the young ladies) were not so fair as some others that were there!"[4] The word "disgraceful" could be interpreted in multiple ways. It's unclear whether the writer meant that the removal of the young ladies was disgraceful or that their attempt to attend the event was disgraceful. Such subtle sarcasm, minus the use of any names, would have made this editorial easy to overlook or dismiss, unless you knew that Nicholas L. Finnell, editor of the *Observer*, was rabidly anti-Johnson.[5]

There was no misinterpreting the article that appeared eleven days later in the *Kentucky Reporter*. While they had heard about the incident in Scott County when it happened, the editors claimed they had chosen not to discuss it until now. But they felt duty bound, as "defenders of the purity of society," to tell their readers the facts as they heard and believed them to be. "Col. R. M. Johnson has a number of children by an African woman living in his family, either a slave or a manumitted servant. ... Perhaps he might be indulged and allowed in private to sing, 'I love you black Rose, Rose, I love you black Rose.' But it seems on the 4th of July he conducted in his carriage one of his daughters to a barbecue in Scott, where many of the ladies and daughters of respectable families ... were assembled." After outlining the events that led to Adaline's removal from the barbecue that afternoon, the editors concluded that "this attempt upon society in Kentucky was most unfortunate and highly censurable."[6]

By publishing this piece, the "defenders of purity" made their position clear: people could behave as they wanted in the privacy of their own homes, but crossing lines of race and gender in public would not be accepted. In other words, interracial sex would be tolerated by white Kentuckians, as long as the persons in these relationships didn't break the rules of appropriate social conduct and try to force the white community to openly accept or legitimize their unions.[7] Whatever went on at Blue Spring Farm, or even at Great Crossing Baptist Church, was one thing, but the good white people of Scott County couldn't permit a woman of color to ride around in a carriage or occupy the same tent as "respectable" (i.e., white) women without taking a stand.

Carriages were for women of the "master class." By coming to a local event in this way, the Johnsons declared Adaline was like any other woman in attendance. In fact, those were Richard's exact words when he was told his daughter had to leave; he protested, stating Adaline was "as well-educated as *any lady* there" (italics mine). This was irrelevant to the gatekeepers of social purity. Her education didn't matter. Her color, parentage, and free status did. Adaline had an enslaved Black mother; to white locals she would *never* be a lady. By arriving in a carriage and taking a seat under that tent, however, Adaline announced that she stood (or sat) on the same level as Georgetown's respectable ladies. Such behavior couldn't go unchecked. The boundary lines had to be policed. White womanhood had to be protected.

Already wounded from what had happened on the Fourth of July, articles like this would have further hurt and embarrassed Julia and her daughters. The wording surely stung. Power and privilege only went so far, it seems, even for Black women related to wealthy white men. And people had long memories. Years later, what happened at that barbecue was used to discredit Richard when he ran for the vice presidency. In 1835, Richard reached out to friend and supporter Francis P. Blair, claiming that his political enemies were engaging in "exaggeration" and making "false statements" about his character. He wrote Francis a lengthy letter that overturned each of the accusations against him. The main one was that he had tried to force his daughters onto white society. Richard wrote:

> The only circumstance upon which they pretend that I have pushed them [the two girls] upon the world is this—without my knowledge or consent, some white females carried Adaline, some 4 or 5 or 6 years ago to a 4th of July Barbecue *in the woods*, where every body went bond & free & without any act on her part to mingle with the company, she being only a child as it were of 13 or 14 & small at that. A few political enemies of mine pretended that her presence was disagreeable to some Ladies at the Barbecue. It was a most disgraceful scene on their part, & unoffending and innocent on our part. As to myself I was ignorant of the matter of her intention to go.[8]

This "Barbecue in the woods" has to be the infamous barbecue of 1831. Adaline, younger than her sister by about two years, was still unmarried in July 1831 and living at Blue Spring. Imogene, born in February 1812, was nineteen years old in July 1831. That year, she was already married and living with her husband Daniel Pence on their own farm. That means Adaline would have been about seventeen when she attended the barbecue in 1831, not thirteen or fourteen. Richard, however, who wrote to Francis Blair in 1835, thought the barbecue might have happened as far back as 1829. That year, Adaline would have been roughly fifteen years old, closer to the age Richard gave for her.

It's unlikely the incident happened as Richard recounted in his letter, as opposed to as in the numerous newspaper articles on the event in 1831. There are too many missing pieces, including how it was that Richard didn't know Adaline planned to go to the barbecue. It's doubtful Julia would have given her daughter permission to attend the party without her husband's knowledge, although Adaline, like many teenagers, may have snuck out to meet her friends because she feared she'd be forbidden from going. Still, who were these "white females" who supposedly whisked Adaline off to a gathering in the woods? There is nothing to suggest that Adaline or Imogene had friends among the local white girls. And, if this *was* a mixed-race affair, attended by everyone, "bond & free," it's not clear why the "Ladies" would have found Adaline's presence so "disagreeable." It's more likely that Richard, in 1835, was trying to put his best spin on the incident. Instead of an elected official taking his mixed-race, teenaged daughter to a formal event in the family carriage, a party with dancing and eligible young men, a young child went to a get-together in the woods with her friends. Most important, her father wasn't there and didn't know about it until afterward.

Whether a formal, white-only affair or a party in the woods attended by everyone, it's clear that Adaline's presence at the barbecue in July 1831 made people uncomfortable. She was a young woman of color who was, for all intents and purposes, free. She was also educated, beautiful, and of courting age, and she had crossed the private-public boundary line when she stepped out of the family carriage and sat down under that tent. This would not be the last time the Johnson women unnerved white folks at a social event.[9]

In July 1832, the Johnsons held an electioneering barbecue at Choctaw Academy. Julia was used to hosting all manner of events, large and small, and she pulled this one off with her usual flair. There was a wonderous feast of things to eat, the wine was flowing, and ladies from the district, including Julia and Adaline, were in attendance, wearing their summer best: "Miss J****** . . . was dressed in the most brilliant manner, and really looked very pretty. . . . She was the greatest belle present." An anonymous letter writer who reported on the event noted that Choctaw Academy yielded Richard "a clear profit of fifteen or sixteen thousand dollars a year, and enables him to dress his family so fine that many of his poorer neighbors are beginning to give up the little *colorable* objections they have heretofore had to associating with them." The writer concluded that while the barbecue was fun, "the company was rather too much mixed for my taste. You know, however, that I am . . . a little squeamish on such matters."[10]

There were likely many Scott County whites who, like this "old bachelor," were perfectly willing to help themselves to the "wine and cake and all sorts of good things" available at the parties out at Blue Spring but who were still uncomfortable attending such events because of the "mixed company," likely meaning the interracial makeup of the partygoers. And elite whites weren't the only ones with reservations about the family at Blue Spring. According to our "squeamish bachelor," poorer whites in the area had been unwilling to associate with the Johnson women until recently. These folks didn't have land or money, but they understood how race and slavery worked. They were free, and they were white. That meant they were supposed to have more social power than people like Julia Chinn and her daughters. They were only now beginning to give up their "little *colorable* objections" to the Black family next door, but only because their wealth allowed Julia, Adaline, and Imogene to dress in a manner "fine" enough to force a grudging toleration from even the poorest of the Johnsons' white neighbors.

Evidently money bought people of color at least superficial acceptance from some white persons. Adaline wasn't welcome at the county barbecue in 1831, but there were white locals willing to come out to Choctaw Academy in 1832, socialize with Julia and her daughters, and consume the family's food and wine. Still, the Johnson women's access to money and fine clothes bothered some people because they dressed like ladies, that is, white women. Their positions of privilege not only aroused confusion and violence among some of the students at Choctaw Academy, who were not used to seeing Black women dress and behave like free women, but it led to envy and anger among their white neighbors, many of whom feared that women of color who carried themselves like ladies might expect to be treated as such. These kinds of worries led to the passage of "anti-sumptuary" laws targeting Black women's hairstyles and clothing in US cities such as New Orleans and Charleston and across the Black Atlantic.[11] Adaline had already attempted to integrate one community event. What else might the Black women of Blue Spring do to try to blur or break the boundary lines between public and private, Black and white, slave and free?

That the Johnson women were uninterested in remaining quietly in their place, and that they were far from accepted by their white neighbors, became crystal clear in the winter of 1832, just a few months after the campaign party at Choctaw Academy. On November 8 of that year, Adaline J. Johnson married a local white man named Thomas W. Scott. She was about eighteen years old. It's unclear where the ceremony was performed, or by whom, but it's possible that Silas Noel, the minister at Great Crossing Baptist Church who had married Imogene Johnson and Daniel Pence in 1830, performed Adaline's wedding as well.[12]

Born in Montgomery County, Maryland, on December 2, 1808, Thomas West Scott was the son of Amos Scott and Nancy West Scott, both from that same county and state. "Trained in agricultural pursuits," Amos, who was of Scotch-Irish ancestry, moved his family to Kentucky in 1814 when Thomas was only six years old. The Scotts settled near Georgetown, and Amos engaged in planting until 1832. That year, the same year his son married Adaline Johnson, Amos and Nancy relocated to Buena Vista Township in Schuyler County, Illinois, where they spent the remainder of their days. The land they settled on was supposedly purchased for them by Thomas, who had lived in Rushville, Illinois, beginning in 1829. Opening a store in the little village, Thomas remained in the mercantile business in Illinois until he returned to Kentucky at some point before he married Adaline in 1832. It's unclear if the senior Scotts left Kentucky that year because they were dismayed by their son's marriage to a woman of color or if the move had already been planned. It's also possible that Thomas was able to purchase the land in Illinois for his parents as a result of the estate he received after marrying Adaline.[13]

Three weeks after the wedding, under the headline MARRIAGE EXTRAORDINARY! the *Lexington Observer and Kentucky Reporter* (*LOKR*) reported that Adaline, "a mulatto girl," was the "reputed, or acknowledged daughter of the *Honorable* **Richard M. Johnson,** *one of the representatives of the State of Kentucky in the Congress of the United States!*" Incensed, the editors wrote that a few days after Thomas became the "happy husband of the FAIR and lovely Adeline [sic]," Richard gave Blue Spring Farm to them, jointly, and to their heirs, forever. The writers noted that this was the second time the people of Scott County had been "shocked and outraged, by the marriage of a mulatto daughter of Col. Johnson to a white man, if a man, who will so far degrade himself; who will make himself an object of scorn and detestation to every person that has the least regard for decency, for a little property; *can be considered a white man*" (italics mine).[14]

The editors were, of course, referring to Julia and Richard's older daughter, Imogene, and her husband, Daniel Pence, who had married in June 1830. The *LOKR* informed its readers that shortly after their wedding, Daniel, like Thomas, was "rewarded for his degradation by being put in possession of a large farm and a number of slaves to cultivate it." The editors challenged the people of Scott County to do something about the matter:

> How long will the people of Scott County—of Kentucky—permit such ... violations of the laws of their state to be committed with impunity? How long will the moral and religious part of the community suffer such ... shocking examples to be set for their sons and the rising generation.... The laws of Kentucky forbid, under heavy penalties, a white man's marrying a negro or mulatto, or living with one in the character of man and wife. Why should Pence and Scott not be held amenable to the laws? What are the Grand Jury of Scott about.... Will they suffer Pence and Scott to go unpunished because they have become sons-in-law of Col. Johnson? We hope not.

There was also a rumor going around that Thomas Henderson, headmaster of Choctaw Academy, had performed Adaline and Thomas's wedding. The staff at the *LOKR* doubted this was true. They had "a higher opinion of Mr. Henderson than to believe he would be guilty of such an outrage against public opinion and the laws of his country."[15]

The basic facts *are* as the paper reported them: Adaline and Thomas *did* get married on November 8, 1832, and they *were* jointly given Blue Spring Farm the next day through a notarized deed.[16] Imogene and Daniel also jointly received numerous laborers and a large tract of land not far from the bride's childhood home shortly after their marriage in June 1830. The fact that Julia and Richard arranged marriages for their daughters, and that both couples received land and enslaved laborers after they wed, wasn't unusual. It was common for elite southerners to arrange marriages for their children. Marriages among the antebellum gentry were rarely for love. They were contractual family matters, and a large part of the premarital negotiations revolved around the transfer of real property: land and enslaved persons. In particular, it was about what property a young woman would bring with her into her marriage: her dowry. Many fathers, anxious to protect their daughters and future grandchildren from potentially crooked sons-in-law, gave their daughters their bridal dowries in a trust. A guardian, charged with protecting the woman's interests, oversaw the trust account. The other option was to give the dowry to the bride and groom jointly, so the woman had some control over her financial affairs.[17]

Given the standards of the day, there was no reason for community members, or the editors of the *LOKR*, to be disgusted by the transfer of property from Julia and Richard to their daughters and new sons-in-law. This was normal. The issue was that Imogene and Adaline, by openly marrying white men, used their family's wealth and power to cross the public-private boundary line that existed for interracial relationships and families. The newspaper editors were enraged, and terrified, because two women of color married white men in ceremonies with licensed ministers and because the transfer of property to each couple was recorded in the county clerk's office. Instead of keeping their relationships a secret, the Johnson family chose to make their domestic lives public. Legal. In doing so, they set an example that might be followed by other young people, members of the "rising generation." That couldn't be allowed to stand without a strong response. Once again, the Johnson women were behaving as if they were ladies. And it wasn't just that they were marrying white men; by acquiring land and laborers, Imogene and Adaline made the transition from being quasi-enslaved persons (although they had never been treated as such) to being members of the landed southern gentry, the most powerful group in the region. This drove the white men around them to the brink of fury and fear.

That the Johnsons were being persecuted because of the public nature of their actions was highlighted in a letter written and published by Nicholas L. Finnell, editor of the *LOKR*, on December 6, one week after the "Marriage Extraordinary" article was printed. An anonymous letter writer asked Finnell why he kept harping on the "*old and long since worn out* story" of Julia and Richard's relationship, and the editor responded that he had avoided the topic for years and would have continued to do so if Richard hadn't tried to bring his daughters into white society. Like everyone else, Finnell had always known about the family at Blue Spring Farm, but as long as they had played by the rules that US society had about interracial sex, he kept his opinions to himself. It wasn't until Daniel married Imogene that Finnell even hinted at the subject, because he didn't want to offend "the feelings of the numerous respectable relations of Col. Johnson." After Adaline and Thomas's wedding, however, Finnell felt it was time to "speak plainly on the subject . . . that . . . open and barefaced attempts to introduce intermarriage . . . did not meet the approbation of every one in Kentucky." His voice, he stated, would "ever be raised in opposition to an attempt . . . to break down the line of distinction that ever has existed, and ever should exist, between the whites and the blacks in this country."[18]

Finnell wasn't inclined to stand by and watch while "shocking examples" were set before the "rising generation" as commonplace. He wasn't alone. The *Baltimore Chronicle* argued that Richard was "the most powerful agent of amalgamation" and that he had used his wealth to lure white men, "greedy of money, but insensible to shame," to marry his interracial daughters. What would happen if others followed his lead?[19] Two weeks later, Finnell's newspaper reprinted an article from the *Dayton Journal* in neighboring Ohio. Titled "A Dark Deed," the piece reflected that "the difference in the colour of the human race in that state [Kentucky] is not regarded with so much *prejudice* as it formally was." The *Journal*'s rationale for this belief was "the marriage of a white man, to a lady *not* 'more than half white'—in other words a mulatto." The paper then named the bride as "the daughter of Col. R. M. Johnson, Member of Congress," and noted that after the wedding Richard gave the "happy pair a deed for a farm." The *Journal* concluded by stating that "another white man, some time ago, purchased a farm of Col. Johnson, with a similar encumbrance." According to the *Journal*, then, Imogene and Adaline (really all Black women) were "encumbrances," burdens to their husbands, men who had to be "encouraged" to take on these handicaps with offers of land, laborers, and money.[20]

While these pieces all speak to the concerns white southerners had with amalgamation, their greatest fears were laid bare in an essay published in the *Richmond Whig*. The editors were clear that if southerners accepted the Johnson women's marriages, then one day southern men might have to quietly stand by and watch while their daughters were "assailed by the sable hand of a crude depredator, or claimed to deck the chamber of some 'lusty Moor' as the new normal."[21] And there, of course, was the fear that lay at the heart of the matter. The oldest fear in the whole proverbial American book. A fear that so often caused, and continues to cause, fatal violence against Black men in the United States who continue to be positioned as the hypersexual "Black Beast Rapist," always seeking to assault white women.[22] If white folks gave in to the one scenario, they were opening the door to the other. That couldn't be allowed to happen. Particularly when one considered that slavery followed the condition of the mother—and white women were free. Private relationships between enslaved Black women and white men, understood to happen and tolerated to a certain point, couldn't cross the line to become codified, legal unions. To do so would be to allow for the possibility of the reverse scenario, consensual or otherwise. For the possibility that slavery might end. That the United States might one day become a free, and interracial, nation.

That white southerners viewed interracial marriage as unnatural was suggested again almost three years later. In 1835, the *LOKR* printed an article about a wedding that had taken place in Montgomery, Alabama. Under the headline MARRIAGE EXTRAORDINARY, the same title as the piece on Adaline and Thomas, the brief essay focused on the wedding of one Mr. Walter B. Wright to a Miss Pauline Snyder. Although both individuals were white, the bride had been born without arms and was "exhibited to the United States as a curiosity in consequence of that deformity." While "dame Nature" had thus been cruel to the lady, "Madam Fortune" treated her with more kindness and provided Miss Snyder with a husband. This, reflected the paper's editors, "whilst many an ivory arm and lilly [sic] hand is extended in vain by others whose youth and bloom the fickle goddess suffers to pine and fade away in hated withering celibacy." The writers couldn't fathom why Walter would marry someone "deformed" when so many women with arms were available for the taking. The title of the article had been used by the paper only once before, when Thomas Scott and Adaline Johnson were wed. It strongly suggests that Blackness was also seen by antebellum whites as a "deformity," and that Thomas's decision to marry Adaline was as "extraordinary" and confusing to his peers as Walter's decision to marry an armless woman who had been displayed as a "curiosity." Why would any "rational" white man marry a woman of color when there were so many beautiful (white) women available to wed?[23]

CHAPTER FIVE

The outcry over Adaline and Thomas's wedding had barely died down when Georgetown, Frankfort, and Lexington were all struck by cholera in the first days of June 1833.[24] Cholera regularly terrorized the United States in the nineteenth century, and 1833 was no exception.[25] Hundreds of people, Black and white, died in the Bluegrass region that summer. Over 500 persons died from the disease in Lexington alone, and people tried everything they could think of to contain the disease. For example, hearing that cholera was spread by poisonous vapors, city leaders burned pitch on every street corner and shot off cannons to purify the air. Additionally, a number of doctors published their "receipts" for curing cholera. Dr. Daniel Drake, who once taught at Transylvania Medical College in Kentucky, told people to go to bed at the first symptoms, "promote a perspiration," and send for the family doctor. He also suggested covering all the windows with netting to keep out "animalcules," tiny invisible creatures that supposedly filled the air at night, which Drake believed caused cholera. His actual cure included bloodletting for those who had a fever and "ten grains of Calomel and one of Opium mixed."[26]

While Drake's "cure" was fairly straightforward, other recipes were far more detailed, including this one, dated July 28, 1833:

— 20 drops ladnum

— 20 drops of Spirits of camphire

— 20 drops of tinker of assafoeditid

— 8 drops of Spirrits of harts horn

— 12 drops of acence of peper mint

— This is to be mixed together and Repeit the dose every 15 minutes untill the Vomiting Seases then give 30 or 40 grams of callamel and one half grane of opium this all congine together

— apply a blister plaster to the stomache of mustard Seed and to the Rist & ancles

— if cramp attend the limbs Rub industrious with french brandy & campor harts horn turpintine or Read pper tea, warm bathes Steam &c and if the calomel Should not opporate in six hours give oyl Ruberbe &c

— if it do not in three hours move give 20 granes of calomel and continue to give oyl injection &c until it do opporate then give oyl after the calomel has opporated Which will pirform a cure most asshuredly.[27]

Given the ingredients found in the "cures," as well as a lack of understanding that antebellum Americans had about the dangers of drinking polluted water, it makes sense that so many people died, and died quickly, during cholera outbreaks.

On June 19, 1833, the *Argus*, a pro-Johnson paper out of Frankfort, reprinted an article from the Lexington papers stating that the cholera, which had been raging in that city for about two weeks, appeared to be finally dying down. Far from celebrating, however, the editors commented on the "gloom and sorrow" on the faces of their residents, along with the "lonely and desolate appearance" of the normally lively city. Things were so bad, it wasn't even possible to give an accurate estimate of how many people had died, although the "list would be appalling" and include many of "our most worthy citizens," and "350 would not be too high an estimate." Of the names they did provide, all were white persons. They also noted that the "ravages of the Cholera have been severe in Georgetown." About twenty persons had died in that community. The paper listed the names of the nine white persons who had passed away in that small town. There were no names given for the Black folks who had perished, just a statement that "the balance [of the twenty dead] are all blacks."[28]

This was common for Kentucky newspapers. While editors from across the state updated people on the epidemic throughout the summer, they never named the Black persons (enslaved or free) who died during the deadly plague, whether in their own communities or elsewhere. The June 27 edition of the Lexington paper noted that the number of deaths in tiny Georgetown had risen to thirty-six and that cholera had broken out at Choctaw Academy. Twelve persons had died at the school up to that date, "one white person, six Indians, and five blacks." By July 11, the number of dead at Choctaw Academy had risen to twenty-one and included "one white person, nine Indians, and eleven blacks."[29]

The events at Choctaw Academy were laid out in greater detail in the published report of Samuel Hatch, a local doctor who visited the school a few times each year. According to Hatch, until cholera broke out, the health of the boys at the school had been marvelous: there had only been six deaths in the eight years the school had been open. As soon as cholera hit Georgetown, which was seven miles from the school, Hatch stated that he immediately sent medicine and instructions to the school's superintendent, Thomas Henderson, and its teachers, in case the epidemic reached the academy. Additionally, a rotating crew of area doctors was charged with visiting the academy on a daily basis, and strict attention was paid to diet and cleanliness. Despite these measures, cholera struck the school in early June and raged for the next month. A total of twenty-four people died over the course of that time: "nine Indian youths . . . fourteen black people, including five at the Blue Spring, and one white man."[30]

The situation at Choctaw Academy was terrible. Thomas Henderson and his family all came down with cholera and couldn't help take care of anyone. All the other teachers apparently fled, and classes were suspended. Hatch claimed that the lion's share of the burden of helping the sick thus fell to "Col. Johnson, aided by his black people and some of the Indian youths." He went on to state that

> his [Richard's] exertions through the day and night, to relieve and comfort the sick, demand the warmest gratitude from all persons. . . . We believe, that had he left the place during the existence of the malady, a large majority of the students . . . must have fallen victims to the disease. . . . Col. Johnson never left his residence more than a few hours during the three weeks that the malady existed; and by his . . . exertions and the timely and judicious arrangements made for the . . . attendance of physicians and the assistance of good nurses . . . many lives were saved.

Hatch also claimed that Richard came down with cholera twice himself, once very seriously, "brought on by excessive fatigue and watching [over the students]."[31]

A touching account, the story published in the *Argus* by Samuel Hatch made "the Hero of the Thames" a brave warrior once more, this time fighting the enemy known as cholera. What's missing, however, is any mention of Choctaw Academy's regular medical practitioner, Julia Chinn. The silence on this count is deafening. It was well known that, in addition to all her other duties at Blue Spring, she attended to everyone's medical issues, "being as good as one half the Physicians where the complaint is not dangerous." Indeed, Julia's work in this area was significant since Richard was able to avoid hiring a full-time doctor to help care for the school's students until after her death.[32]

It's hard to believe that Julia didn't oversee the cholera ward at Blue Spring and Choctaw Academy in the summer of 1833. And the truth is, she did. Samuel Hatch sent one report to the local newspaper that made Richard out to be the hero of the hour, but his report to the federal government's Office of Indian Affairs revealed that the care of the sick and dying fell to the academy's usual doctor, Julia Chinn, in whom he had great confidence. Having lost only one patient in several years, Julia took charge during the epidemic, drafting Richard and two Indian students, John Jones and Joseph Bourassa, to act as her nurses. Hatch credited Choctaw

Academy's medical team, led by Chinn, with saving many lives.[33] The white male doctor understood, however, that for readers of the *Argus*, Richard made for a better hero than his boundary-breaking Black wife. Politically pro-Johnson, the *Argus* remained tight-lipped when it came to publishing *anything* about Richard's personal life.[34]

Despite Julia's tireless efforts, Blue Spring lost twenty-four people to cholera that year, including nine of 129 Native students and fourteen bondspersons out of a total population of about sixty. It's not surprising that the death rate among the enslaved was so high (close to 25 percent), given their diets and working conditions.[35] What is tragic, but in hindsight foreseeable given her prolonged exposure to the sick, is that Julia Chinn, worn out from helping to care for the ill, contracted cholera herself that summer and passed away. One would never know that from reading Hatch's article in the *Argus*, however. It isn't surprising that Julia was left out of Hatch's report. It's likely that neither he nor the paper wanted to draw more attention to a woman who had already unsettled so many folks in life by highlighting her death.

This could explain why not one single area newspaper mentioned Julia's passing. Apparently, it wasn't appropriate to mention the "colored consort" of a local resident, not even when the couple had been together for over two decades and the husband was as prominent a man as Richard M. Johnson. It's worth noting, however, that the *LOKR* didn't run a scathing piece about Julia's death, or Richard's corresponding sorrow, since this was typically the kind of material they loved to exploit. Perhaps the epidemic kept Finnell and his staff too busy to worry about such matters. Or they may have thought that maligning the newly deceased was going just a bit too far. This might be why the only institution that acknowledged Julia's death was Great Crossing Baptist Church, the place where she was baptized and her religious home for many years. It's in the church's meeting minutes from July 6, 1833, that we learn that Julia, "of the family of Col. R. M. Johnson," had "departed this life since our last meeting." There was a meeting on June 1, so Julia Chinn died between June 2 and July 5, 1833. She would have been between thirty-seven and forty-three years of age at the time of her death. Like many enslaved women of her era, she died young, after having lived a life filled with compromise, coercive sex, and never-ending work, work that eventually killed her.[36]

While Richard didn't publicly mention Julia's passing, his letters reveal that her death greatly affected the life of every person at Blue Spring Farm and Choctaw Academy, including his own. Indeed, when the citizens of Indianapolis invited Richard to a public dinner in their city in late June 1833, he made it plain that he wouldn't be going to parties anytime soon: "The cholera has deprived me of ten of my family and six students of Choctaw Academy, who lived with me, and although it has greatly abated, some are yet on the sick list, and the derangement in my domestic economy is so great that I fear it will require my constant attention at home to repair it during the current year."[37] In letters written to Thomas Henderson months later, Richard claimed that matters at the academy after the cholera outbreak were "deranged." Given the enormous amount of labor that Julia provided to help run the school, and the fact that she was "the chief manager of the domestic concerns of the house," it makes sense that her death led to a serious "derangement" in Richard's personal and professional life.[38]

Once Julia had passed, her family likely assumed that white folks would stop talking about her relationship with Richard. What more was there to say, now that she was gone? It doesn't appear that Julia's death changed the behavior of the press, however, for a mere two months later, the local papers resumed their preoccupation with the couple's union. The *LOKR* noted, "He [Richard] has degraded himself ... so low in the scale of morality, that he could not well go lower.... By holding his conduct up to public view as a fit subject of castigation and reprehension, we have endeavored to deter others from following his example."[39] To the editors of the *LOKR*, Richard's flagrant behavior revealed that he was a man who did not respect community morals or standards, so they had no choice but to hold his behavior up to "public view" in order to "deter others from following his example." In other words, had Richard obeyed the antebellum rule book on interracial sex and kept his relationship with Julia in the shadows, the paper would have never printed a word about his private life.

Even Richard's supporters couldn't stop discussing his relationship with Julia Chinn. Writing from West Point, Jacob H. Holt noted in a letter to Thomas Henderson that given "what members of Col. Johnson's family died of Cholera etc. last season—I think he will be a prominent candidate for President at the next election. There are many in this state [New York] who would vote for him in preference to [Martin] Van Buren."[40] For Holt and others, the death of Richard's wife was enormously important: the fact that he was now a "widower" made the career politician a possible candidate for the highest office in the land.

This is, in some ways, unsurprising. Having sex with a Black woman and fathering children of color hasn't prevented other white men from running for political office in the United States. It certainly didn't have a negative effect on Thomas Jefferson's political career. The problem for Richard, however, was that he, unlike Jefferson, was *open* about his relationship with Julia. He never married a white woman for cover. Julia helped run his plantation and other businesses, she organized and helped host all major functions at Blue Spring, the couple lived together, and they went to church together. Richard also never contradicted statements that Imogene and Adaline were his daughters. He introduced them to visiting dignitaries, took them to local events, arranged marriages for them with white men, gave them large estates, and wrote letters about Julia and the girls to other people. Jefferson, on the other hand, was careful to keep his relationship with Sally Hemings confined to his plantation. He didn't take Sally or their children to public functions and they weren't present when he entertained at Monticello. Thomas Jefferson also never openly acknowledged the Hemingses as his family. His supporters were thus able to deny allegations that he and Sally were intimate or that they had children together.[41]

While it's tempting to compare Julia and Richard to Sally and Thomas, you don't have to go to Virginia to find a white politician involved with a Black woman or voters who understood the similarities in such situations. A comparable scenario unfolded just down the road from Blue Spring Farm. In a letter written to a friend in Connecticut, one L. Smith gave a detailed account of Henry Clay's relationship with a "yellow girl that attended to his poultry and fowls." When Clay's wife caught him "attending to the Yellow Girl more lovingly than suited her feelings," Clay sent the young woman and her children to Louisiana and had them sold. Noting that "there is not the least doubt but the children were Mr. Clay's," Smith concluded, "Much as has been said about Col. Johnson's *Negro* wife, he did not sell his Children as Mr. Clay has done. If the abolitionists can vote for Clay, they had better hang up the fiddle."[42]

Like many antebellum enslavers, Henry Clay engaged in interracial sex, but his reputation never suffered the way Richard Johnson's did, because he followed the rule book for interracial sex. Clay married a white woman, kept his enslaved mistress out back in the slave quarters, never publicly acknowledged her, and promptly "got rid of the evidence" after his wife caught him with the mother of his Black children. And so Clay is well known, both in Kentucky and across the nation, and remembered as the man who helped save the country from secession not once but twice. Johnson, however, has been largely forgotten, even in his home state. What people do remember of him is his relationship with Julia Chinn, because Richard, unlike Henry Clay and Thomas Jefferson, tried to take his Black family across the boundary line that separated private spaces from public places.

The Johnsons' neighbors were neither completely comfortable with nor fully accepting of the Black women of Blue Spring. While no southerner dared challenge a white man's right to have sex with his female slaves, the kinds of privileges the Johnson women exercised were reserved for white women. It wasn't appropriate for Black women to dress like ladies, to be educated like women of the white elite, to attend events with respectable folks on a level of social equality with white women, to ride in carriages like white women, to blur the color line by marrying white men, or to inherit real property, which would put them on par with the southern white gentry.

Many white Kentuckians were also repulsed by Richard—not because he was sleeping with a Black woman and had mixed-race daughters but because he didn't have the decency to keep quiet about it. His sin wasn't engaging in interracial sex; it was the public nature of his conduct. He wanted people to openly, legally, and socially accept his Black family as *his family* and, as such, as members of the community. He wasn't embarrassed by his behavior or by them. And that, for his peers, was embarrassing.

Although Julia Chinn was now deceased, the dilemma of what to do with the Johnson women, and with Richard, was far from over. Indeed, it would become the raging topic of the day as the nation headed into one of the most contentious presidential election campaigns in US history.

CHAPTER SIX

AFFAIRS OF STATE

The Nation Speaks of Sex

June 1835. They'd been planning this for months. The four of them had thought of everything, from what they would take with them to which route they'd follow through Ohio before heading for the Canadian border. Still, it was a risk. Parthene knew what Richard did to slaves who tried to escape. The beatings if they were captured. Salt poured into open wounds. Being sold "downriver" to Louisiana. But she couldn't bear sleeping with him anymore. She used the keys she carried around her waist as mistress of the plantation to take a check for $1,000, plus another $300 in cash, out of Richard's drawer. It was Sunday. Everyone had the day off, so it was the best day of the week to leave. Nobody would suspect that she and her cousin had run away until the next day. Their story of going to visit a friend would give them the head start they needed. The women would meet up with their two male companions (who had already left by carriage with four trunks filled with goods) in Lexington, and the four of them would head for Maysville. The women had their horses saddled up and headed out, their eyes set on freedom.[1]

CHAPTER SIX

When the story of "The Runaway Lovers" broke, it became a national sensation and threw fuel on the flames of Richard's nomination as Martin Van Buren's running mate in the presidential election of 1836. His opponents in the Whig Party were already dragging his relationship with Julia Chinn, dead since 1833, through the mud. There were also members of Richard's own party who hated him; that faction smeared him and Julia ahead of the Democratic National Convention and tried to persuade outgoing President Andrew Jackson not to support him. While Richard ultimately captured the nomination, it split both the party and the country. Richard hadn't just had sex with Julia; he had taken his relationship public and tried to place Julia and their daughters on an equal footing with white women. That was something white folks across the political spectrum agreed was unacceptable.

As white men attacked Richard for his relationship with Julia, the scandal involving Richard's new mistress broke. Parthene had grown up at Blue Spring Farm and, as we saw in chapter 3, she worked closely with Adaline Johnson for years, sewing and mending shirts and distributing clothes to the students at Choctaw Academy. A member of the house party, Parthene was one of the girls that Thomas Henderson tutored in the evenings, alongside Imogene and Adaline. She was most likely in the house that night in December 1827 when David Wall and Peter King tried to break in. And after Julia died, it was Parthene who took over many of her duties. His letters suggest that Richard may have begun sleeping with Parthene before his wife passed away, or he at least had his eye on her as a potential new sexual partner.[2]

Richard's sex life ultimately destroyed his political career. Neither his money nor his power could erase the fact that he had spit in the face of society's racial hierarchies and codes of appropriate sexual behavior. Although Julia Chinn had passed away, Richard's actions with Parthene kept his and Julia's relationship alive in the nation's memory and revealed his continued defiance of society's rules of interracial sexual conduct. The collective force of these things, when added to the existence of Julia and Richard's living Black daughters, imploded Richard's political dreams.

In 1835, Imogene and Adaline were grown women with children, married to white men, and they controlled substantial estates of their own. Richard was a sitting US congressman. Neither the father's political career nor the daughters' lives appear, then, to have suffered lasting damage from the fact that wife and mother had been an enslaved Black woman.[3] Everything was about to change, however, because 1835 was the year that people across the country openly took sides on the

Chinn-Johnson relationship. While Washington insiders had long known about Julia and Richard's union, it was cocktail party gossip until Richard was considered for, and then selected as, Martin Van Buren's running mate in the election of 1836. As early as spring 1835, editorials, letters, cartoons, and songs attacking Julia, Richard, and their daughters appeared in newspapers throughout the nation. Although Julia was dead, the ghost of her memory, and the living examples of her interracial daughters, led to raging debates over the issue of amalgamation.

Opposition newspapers didn't attack Richard for just his sex life, although that would become the focus for many papers, and not every paper engaged in the amalgamation battle.[4] Reporting the local and national news on a weekly basis, the *Argus*, published in Frankfort, Kentucky, was a pro-Democrat, pro-Johnson paper. It covered the national political conventions and election returns in detail but never once mentioned Julia Chinn, Adaline Johnson Scott, Imogene Johnson Pence, or interracial sex.[5] The *Kentucky Gazette*, out of Lexington, also a Democratic paper, expressed the opinion that the stakes in this election were too high to abuse *any* candidate. The editors said it would produce no good and only create enemies.[6]

One of the only Whig papers that didn't engage in the Julia debate was New York's *Albany Evening Journal*. The editor, Thurlow Weed, believed that one of the only sins greater than amalgamation was publishing personal attacks against a candidate. Weed reminded his party that in the past, when the opposition press had attacked candidates for their personal lives, it had backfired. This included Federalist charges against Thomas Jefferson about his relationship with Sally Hemings, as well as National Republican accusations about Andrew and Rachel Jackson's supposedly adulterous premarital affair. According to Weed, voters ended up sympathizing with Jefferson and Jackson and turned on the parties that had skewered them in the press. He thus called on his colleagues to stop using Julia and her daughters to attack Johnson. "The people will grow weary of seeing the newspapers filled with details about Col. Johnson's black wife and yellow daughters." Weed himself abandoned the issue after June 26, 1835.[7] This certainly wasn't out of respect for Julia or her daughters but because Weed worried that smearing Richard would cost the Whigs the election.

For papers that did dive into the murky pool of sex, it wasn't one they stayed in all the time. The Democratic *Kentucky Sentinel*, out of Georgetown, went back and forth between reporting on the upcoming election with no mentions of race or sex and wading into discussions of amalgamation. Prior to the Democratic Convention, which took place in Baltimore on May 20, 1835, the *Sentinel* stuck to fairly standard, pro-Johnson reports. This included editorials reprinted from the *Columbus Hemisphere* out of Ohio, which stated that Richard was "the most prominent man in the Democratic Party for the office of Vice President" and that it made no sense to support "Candidates for this office who are known to be unpopular, and who, no matter what their talents may be, cannot carry sufficient strength with them even to take the vote of a single State."[8]

The Democrats weren't united around a candidate before the convention, however. While Richard appeared to be the strongest contender, not everyone was happy about it, mainly because of the issue of interracial sex. Andrew Jackson's Tennessee friend and neighbor Alfred Balch wrote to the outgoing president on April 4, 1835, "I do not think from what I hear daily that the nomination of Johnson for the Vice Presidency will be popular in any of the slave holding states except Kentucky on account of his former domestic relations."[9] Judge John Catron, a justice on the Tennessee Supreme Court, also wrote to Jackson, urging him not to back Richard. Catron's objections were based largely on the fact that Richard had a Black wife and interracial children. He was positive the national media would have a field day with the story, attacked Richard for how he had "endeavoured often to force his daughters into society," and made note of how Julia and her girls were regularly seen riding around in carriages, which suggested the women "claimed equality" with white people. For men such as Balch and Catron, it didn't matter that Julia Chinn was dead. The memory of her boundary-breaking behavior, and the existence of her daughters, who were living proof of Julia's very public relationship with Richard, were intolerable, especially since this behavior had been encouraged by Richard himself. Catron concluded that "the idea of voting for him is loathed beyond anything that has occurred with us" in national politics. Jackson, however, ignored the advice of his friends and threw his support behind Richard, who ultimately won the Democratic nomination that year.[10]

While the convention ended with one ticket, neither the party nor the country was by any means united. The battle lines had been drawn, and they had been drawn on the grounds of race and sex. Ideas about interracial sex and families would come to the forefront over the next eighteen months as people from across the nation were confronted by, and confronted, their deepest fears about Blackness, interracial sex, social integration, and mixed-race people.

The most radical Americans—those who favored abolition and women's suffrage—said that Richard Johnson was a rapist, "the violator of the virtue of his female slaves."[11] Most white Americans, however, didn't care about the rights of enslaved women. They were concerned that, if elected, Richard would try to empower his Black family (and other people of African descent) and were disgusted by his relationship with Julia. The Democratic ticket was dubbed the "Black Ticket" by many people, and *US Telegraph* editor Duff Green wasted no time in making his feelings on the matter known:

> It may be a matter of no importance to mere political automatons whether Richard M. Johnson is a *white* or a *black* man—whether he is *free* or a *slave*—or whether he is married to, or has been in connection with a jet-black, thick-lipped, odoriferous negro wench, by whom he has reared a family of children whom he has endeavored to force upon society as ... equals. ... But thank God, to the great majority of the people of the United States we may with safety address ourselves on this subject, with a full conviction that in their breast we shall find a response to ... patriotic feelings.[12]

For Green and others, the fact that Johnson's daughters had been "forced upon society as equals" was as, if not more, problematic than the fact that Richard had had sex with a Black woman. While the latter was a private act, the former was a slap in the face that could not be forgiven. It's also telling that Green believed Richard had potentially lost his position as a "free white man" by marrying Julia. Indeed, his behavior was "unpatriotic." Green's feelings hadn't changed in September 1836 when he hailed Martin Van Buren as an advocate of "free negro suffrage," while Johnson was noted for "having been married to a negress of unredeemed blackness." For Green and other Americans of his time, Blackness was a stain on the soul, a sin beyond redemption, and it was a sin that Richard was now tainted with, because he had chosen to publicly partner with a Black woman.[13]

"Odoriferous negro wench." It must have been terrible for Imogene and Adaline to read such things about their deceased mother. It's no wonder that in the aftermath of the convention, Democratic newspapers found themselves forced to address personal, "domestic" matters they had never before had to acknowledge. The week after the convention, the editors of the *Kentucky Sentinel* responded to a statement made by George D. Prentice, editor of the *Louisville Journal* and a man long hostile to Julia and Richard. Prentice wrote, "The plain truth is, Col. Richard M. Johnson is the husband of a mulatto. The hands of the two have been joined by the priest; the ritual has been said, and the twain are one. Such truths half sicken us in the recital, but they must be told." The *Sentinel* claimed these were "villainous and downright lies," and "whether produced by the immediate influence of liquor or the effect of long habit, the result must be the same—it will add but one more shade to the black character of the perpetrator of the slander."[14] The *Sentinel* was bold to call Prentice a habitual liar (and a drunk), given the southern culture of dueling and because everyone in Kentucky knew about Julia. Indeed, Prentice had recently said that Richard's "chief sin against society" wasn't having sex with a Black woman, which was a common enough occurrence, but that he so openly crossed the color line, or "the publicity and barefacedness of his conduct."[15]

It's clear that the *Sentinel*, a local, pro-Johnson paper, felt it could no longer stay silent in the face of such remarks against Richard's private life. Still, this was never about standing up for Julia or her daughters; it was *always* about protecting Richard and his political career. While there used to be the occasional story in the opposition press about the Johnsons, usually after incidents like Adaline's marriage to a white man, over the next eighteen months, Julia and her daughters would become almost daily fodder for Whig newspapers. But while the *Sentinel* began making forays into the interracial sex wars that emerged in the local and national press, the paper never once mentioned Julia by name. Instead, it focused on the "greater sins" of Richard's competitors, cautioning the Whigs to step back from their attacks, because the things they charged Richard with were minor compared to the sins of their own idols, men such as John W. Taylor, Henry Clay, and Daniel Webster.[16]

The *Sentinel*'s August 26 story on Governor George Poindexter was one such example. It seems the Mississippi orator had been to Olympian Springs, a resort and spa in Kentucky where the elite went to bathe in the mineral springs. Poindexter had apparently rented a house there for himself and a Black female friend without telling the landlady who the occupants would be. Upon discovery, the landlady ejected him, the woman, and the bed, informing the governor that the house was open only to "respectable white persons." The pair sought shelter elsewhere. The bed was left to rot in the weeds.[17] What Poindexter chose to do in his own home was one thing, but by bringing his enslaved sexual companion with him on vacation, he opened himself up to criticism, both by the landlady, who made it clear that the governor was no longer respectable, and by the newspapers. He had attempted to take his Black lover, and his relationship, across the private-public boundary line, and that wouldn't be tolerated.

Although it's hard to decide which paper was the most offensive in its coverage, the *Lexington Observer*'s July 8, 1835, edition arguably had the most articles on "Sex, Race, and the Johnson Family" in one place. There were no fewer than *nine* pieces that had to do with Richard's "domestic relations" in some way, including one by editor Nicholas Finnell, who directly took on Gervas E. Russell, the editor of the pro-Johnson Frankfort *Argus*. Finnell was offended that Russell had had the nerve to ask in a previous issue, "Why is it that the opposition presses are groaning under the weight of low abuse and personal slander of the Hon. Richard M. Johnson?" The *Observer*'s editor believed that Russell, a member of a respectable church in Frankfort, had long given Richard a pass on his behavior because of his wealth and that Russell would never associate with a poor man who lived like Johnson. "Or would he . . . invite him and *his lady* to his house to spend a social hour or two with Mrs. R. . . . We cannot believe that he would encourage such shameless immorality, by inviting men who would be guilty of it, and their black wives, to his house . . . and their children to intermarry with his."[18]

This, of course, was the real problem. In confronting Russell, Finnell made it clear once more that the issue was not that Julia and Richard were having sex. Many white men in the United States were sleeping with Black women, particularly enslaved women whom they owned. It was about placing Black and white women on a level of equality and opening the door to intermarriage between the younger generations. This is what Finnell found to be "shamelessly immoral." These were the behaviors that had to be checked before they infected the larger population.

Blunt as it was, the piece directed at Russell didn't compare to the longest essay about Julia and Richard in this edition of the *Observer*. The column had originally appeared in the *Louisville Journal* and was titled "The *Georgetown Sentinel*—Col. R. M. Johnson." Responding to comments made by the *Sentinel* against the *Journal*, the editors of the Louisville paper claimed that perhaps the "maniac fury" of the editor of the *Sentinel* was because he was one of Richard's "mulatto sons" or he wanted to become one, having an eye on one of Richard's daughters, "aspiring to obtain a wife, who, like the offence of the King in Hamlet, 'is rank and smells to heaven.'" The *Sentinel* had accused the *Journal* of slander, arguing that Julia and Richard were never married.[19] The *Journal*, in response, stated it had simply reported what it had heard said a thousand times. Everyone had heard repeated stories of the wedding ceremony that had taken place at Blue Spring, and even northern papers referred to Johnson and Julia as husband and wife. The *Journal* pointed out that no one had ever seen or heard the statement contradicted, not even by Richard's own papers. "We were not the inventors, nor have we been the chief propagators of the tale. . . . Col. J's personal friends have suffered it to pass uncontradicted . . . because they knew, that report . . . had softened down the disgraceful deeds of their idol."[20]

The *Journal* then stated that while no one could perhaps say for sure whether Richard had ever married Julia, everyone knew how he was living. They knew he "recognized her as his wife, the mistress of his parlor, and the mother of his household." He didn't care what anyone thought, he did it all openly, raising a family of mixed-race children "at his fireside," and treating them as his own. He put them at the same table with his most honored guests, and he used his influence to try and force them into "the highest and most fashionable circles of the community." The *Journal* then recounted the story of the now notorious Fourth of July barbecue.[21] The editors wondered, if the woman wasn't Richard's wife but just some "black harlot, that he has openly lived with for twenty years . . . is his conduct less shameful. . . . Is it less disgraceful to have thrust forward a negro concubine as the honored recipient of the extorted courtesies of his guests than a negro bride? It is less infamous to have attempted to push a bevy of mulatto bastards upon fashionable society than a household of colored but legitimate sons and daughters?"[22]

Of course, it was slavery, racism, and white supremacy that made interracial marriages "shameful," "disgraceful," "infamous," and illegitimate in the eyes of white Americans. It was the laws of racial slavery that made Black women vulnerable to becoming sex slaves, "concubines," and "harlots" and turned Black children into "bastards." After condemning Richard not only for having had such a relationship but for not having the grace to hide it, the *Journal* then criticized him for bribing two greedy white men into marrying his "mongrel" daughters by giving them "two extensive and valuable farms," thereby "spurning the laws of the land" and bringing "outrage" to the "feelings of every man and woman who retains a lingering sense of decency."[23]

The *Journal* was similarly "outraged" that certain papers had dared to compare Richard Johnson with Thomas Jefferson. While Jefferson had his faults, the *Journal* was quick to point out that he was careful not to run around flaunting them:

> *He* never lived in open intercourse with an odoriferous wench, treating her and requiring others to treat her as the wedded partner of his bosom; *he* never reared a family of mulattoes under his roof and essayed to place them in the highest spheres of fashion. . . . *He* never took advantage of the necessities of his white fellow-citizens and bribed them with countless sums of gold to make such **beasts** of themselves before the open eyes of the whole world as to stand up in the church, clasp the **sable paws** of negresses, and pronounce the sacred vows of wedlock. (Bold type mine.)[24]

Interracial relationships, it seems, were doomed either way. Sex with a Black woman out of wedlock was disgusting. Such women were "harlots" and "concubines." Marrying a Black woman was worse. In fact, a white citizen who united in holy matrimony with a "negress" was no better than an animal, willing to debase himself by taking the "sable paws" of a subhuman creature for profit. The only thing to do, then, was not to have interracial sex at all, or at least be a gentleman and lie about it. And this is why men like Henry Clay and Thomas Jefferson are still revered. Because they didn't live in "open intercourse" with Black women; treat them as the "wedded partners" of their hearts and the mothers of their households; rear their biracial children overtly under their roofs; or attempt to insert their Black families into the "highest spheres of fashion."[25]

As the papers battered his daughters, his dead wife, and his private life, Richard put a plan in motion to try to stop the attacks on him and his family. In a letter to fellow Democrat Francis P. Blair dated June 16, 1835, Richard dwelled at length on the "assaults of my enemies upon my domestic concerns" and their "exaggerated and false statements." To combat this, Richard reached out to several ministers who had known him for many years and asked them to write letters on his behalf. These character references would appear in print or be sent to Blair directly for dispersal. First and most important among these was the letter of Rev. Thomas Henderson, who had lived in or near Richard's family for twenty-three years. According to Richard, Thomas's statement alone would "silence every heart but those of devils."[26]

Richard then spent several pages addressing the accusations against him, which included everything from being too lenient with his slaves to atheism and drunkenness. The main complaint, however, was his relationship with Julia Chinn and the existence of their two daughters. What is striking is how Richard talked about all three women without *ever once* using their names or admitting his relationship to them. He stated that the "objections and abuse about my home matters has grown out of party politics, and the only evidence upon which they have so infamously abused me is the manner in which I have raised and educated two females, which they suppose were the children of one of my slaves. If I had cut their throats, or treated them as slaves, or sold them to Negro buyers I might have avoided every imputation but treating these two children *as a Christian* has been the whole of my offendings."[27]

"Two females." "Two children." Not "Imogene and Adaline," "my children," or "my daughters." After years of introducing the girls to every guest at Blue Spring and putting his relationship with Julia on public display, Richard, under attack and desperate to ascend to the vice presidency, tried to step back his connection to his daughters and their mother. Additionally, he threw out phrases meant to shame people: had he "cut their throats" or "sold them to Negro buyers" he would have been left alone, but he was being mistreated because he behaved like "a Christian." It's not surprising that a lawyer and a politician defaulted to such (omissions of) language. Richard may have loved Imogene and Adaline, and it appears he did, considering he had them educated, arranged good marriages for them, and gave them vast estates, but he was still a man of his time. As open as he was about some things, including having his daughters play the piano for the Marquis de Lafayette when the general visited Blue Spring Farm, Richard had the girls educated at home instead of sending them to a women's finishing school.[28] He knew how honest to be—even in a letter to a supposed ally. In this he was like Adam Tunno of Charleston, South Carolina. Everyone in town knew that the wealthy Madeira merchant was the partner of Margaret Bettingall, a Black woman who may have been enslaved, and that the couple lived together and had children together. And though Adam left Margaret and their daughters substantial estates in his last will and testament, he never once admitted his connection to them in that document. Even after death, he never acknowledged in writing that these Black women were his family.[29]

Richard went on to tell Blair that both "children" were now "married to as respectable men as in Scott county or Kentucky and out of my way. They were educated at home they were never sent to school, to avoid the appearance even of wishing to push them on society. A stranger would not know from looks that they were coloured—they injure no one; they are respected where known and no attempt ever made to push them into society."[30] It's doubtful this statement would have lessened white people's fears. That the women were light enough to pass for white was a problem; it broke down the most visible barrier keeping Black people separate and subservient. Still, Richard was sure to say the women were married and "out of my way," no obstacle to his political goals. Because Adaline lived at Blue Spring and Imogene was essentially next door, they were clearly still a big part of his life. One wonders how his daughters would have felt had they read this letter. Two nameless burdens, now "out of the way."

What, though, of Julia? Richard does, eventually, mention her, although he never admits to having been in a relationship with her. After his discussion of the two children, he goes on to say that "their mother died with the cholera 3 years ago—last 15 years of her life a member of the Baptist church at the Great Crossings as irreproachable as any member in it and as much respected in her place as a woman could be."[31] That's it. "Their mother." Not "my wife" or "Julia." There is no name or age. No mention of who her parents were, where she was born, or that the church she attended had been founded by his own parents. Nothing about how she had run his plantation and businesses for over two decades during his lengthy absences each year in Washington, DC. No tribute to the many lives she saved from cholera before succumbing to it herself. And he managed to get her date of death wrong: she had been dead only two years. If Richard's discussion of his daughters seemed calculated, his mention of Julia was stone-cold. She was a dead slave whose date of death he couldn't even get right. She was, quite literally, a ghost. Gone and forgotten.

Thomas Henderson did write the statement Richard mentioned in his letter to Francis Blair. It was published in the *Daily Globe* on July 7, 1835. Thomas's letter is notable for many things, one of which is that it shows considerably more warmth toward Imogene and Adaline than Richard's letter to Blair. Thomas, too, though, tried hard to downplay the very public relationship between Richard Johnson and Julia Chinn. His letter began by comparing Richard's situation to that of the "immortal" and "most distinguished patriot" Thomas Jefferson, who frequently had reports published about him "to the world and circulated abroad" that were "untrue and ill founded." Given what Virginians knew about Sally Hemings in Jefferson's day, and what DNA evidence has revealed in the twenty-first century, Thomas perhaps protested too much. Still, he obviously wanted to make the connection between the two men clear before he focused on Richard and his link to the women in question.[32]

After discussing how long he had known Richard and his "pious" parents, Thomas raised the issue of "the circumstance of two females raised by him, the children of a colored woman, and said to be his—whether true or false I know not." For Thomas, what mattered was not the paternity of the girls, whom he did not name, but the "kind and tender manner" in which they had been raised. They were "creatures of God" who didn't choose to bring themselves into the world, and he believed that Richard should be credited for raising them as he did, instead of having sent them to the slave quarters or off to some cotton farm, "supposing they were his children." If they were someone else's children, he was to be commended for not having placed "two such girls as they are in some degraded condition so common in our country." This was Thomas's nod toward the "fancy trade" as it was known: a booming, domestic trade in attractive, often light-skinned, enslaved women who were sold at high prices to become prostitutes in the urban South or the mistresses of wealthy white men.[33]

Thomas had developed a long-term relationship with the two young women in question. He worked closely with their mother at Choctaw Academy for many years. Additionally, both he and Richard believed that all persons, free and enslaved, should have enough education to read the Bible for themselves. And Kentucky, unlike many other slave states, didn't prohibit teaching bondspersons how to read. After he took charge of Choctaw Academy, Thomas thus spent his evenings, at Richard's request, giving lessons to the house staff at Blue Spring, as well as the two aforementioned girls, helping them learn to read the scriptures. However, he "soon discovered such uncommon aptness in those two girls to take learning, and so much decent, modest, and unassuming conduct on their part, that my mind became much enlisted in their favor. At that age, nor even now, a stranger would not suspect them to be what they really are—the children of a colored woman. I continued to give them lessons until their education was equal or superior to most of the females in the country." Thomas concluded by saying that the girls were now "both married to respectable men, and independently situated." He did not mention that their "respectable" husbands were white or that both couples were landowners and slave owners, courtesy of Richard M. Johnson.[34]

CHAPTER SIX

As for Julia Chinn, Thomas informed readers that the girls' mother was one of the many laborers who had come to Richard as an inheritance from his father's estate. She had been raised by Jemima Suggett Johnson, Richard's mother, "one of the most exemplary and pious of women." He then stated that Julia, whom he never named, was

> a good servant, faithful, obedient, and humble; and appeared to know her place and her business, both at home and abroad, as such. She always, so far as I could ever discover, filled her place faithfully as a servant, with others, in waiting in the house, and performing the necessary business thereof. All the difference that could ever be discovered between that woman and other servants was, that she, from her age, experience, and skill, seemed to be at the head and was the chief manager of the domestic concerns of the house.

According to Thomas, Julia was also for many years a regular member of a "large and respectable Baptist church" that he himself attended, and she was known as a "pious, humble Christian to the day of her death." He finished by saying that since she was dead and gone, "why all this slander, at this late day, is a matter of some surprise."[35]

Thomas's letter revealed that he believed Adaline and Imogene to be intelligent, virtuous, kind, humble, and decent young women. In 1835, although they were married and living in their own homes, they would have been no more than twenty-one and twenty-three years of age, respectively. Thomas had, in many ways, been a role model to the girls and helped raise them; given how often Richard was away, and for how long, he may have felt like an uncle toward them. This is very much in line with what we already know about his relationship with them.

His description of Julia is harder to swallow, given what we know about her life at Blue Spring, her work with Thomas at Choctaw Academy, and his interactions with her. From "knowing her place" to the description he gives of her, particularly that it was only her "age, experience, and skill" that set her apart from the other bondspersons on the farm and made her the "chief manager of the domestic concerns of the house," the picture that would have likely come to the minds of those not personally familiar with Julia is an Old South stereotype: the older, heavyset, asexual "Mammy." That image would be made notorious a century later in the movie *Gone with the Wind* and immortalized on packages of Aunt Jemima pancake mix.[36]

Julia was certainly in charge of household affairs at Blue Spring. But the image of her as a "faithful, obedient, and humble" servant who "knew her place" and who was no different from any other enslaved laborer at Blue Spring Farm, except for age and experience, doesn't sit right. This was the woman who had entertained President Madison and General Lafayette. The person from whom Thomas had to request money for academy matters, who organized the farm's hospital during the cholera epidemic, and who ran the household staff. The well-dressed lady who attended Great Crossing Baptist Church, turned heads at electioneering parties at Choctaw Academy, and did business with local vendors. Mistress of the parlor at Blue Spring, Julia Ann Chinn was no more than forty-three years old when she died and could have been as young as thirty-six.

It was necessary, however, for Thomas Henderson to assure voters that Richard's house was one of "profound order, decorum, and strict discipline." This meant stating that Blue Spring was a regular site of religious meetings, asserting that Richard never used "intoxicating or ardent spirits," and denying that *any* of his servants differed in status or treatment from any of the others. Above all, it meant making clear that Blue Spring Farm was a place where white people were in charge and everyone knew their place. Julia Chinn, then, couldn't stand out. At all. She had to be just like any other enslaved laborer Richard inherited from his father. She couldn't be literate, authoritative, or business savvy. She certainly couldn't be young, well dressed, or beautiful.[37]

Richard's attempts to fix things didn't help matters. In fact, Thomas's letter was seen by many people as nothing more than a well-dressed lie. The *Richmond Whig* responded that "the intelligent reader will perceive that he [Henderson] knows all about it and is guilty of . . . unqualified suppression of the truth with the intent to deceive."[38] And things were about to get worse for the Johnson family, after a story that had surfaced a few days earlier in the *Maysville Eagle* began to circulate more widely.

Under the title "Amalgamation," the *Eagle* reported on July 2 that "last week, a couple of half breed Indian youths, from Col. Johnson's Choctaw School, passed through this place with two of the Colonel's mulatto girls (slaves), whom they had induced to elope with them. One of the couples passed themselves off as husband and wife—the others acting in the capacity of servants." Not only had the four run away; they had also taken one of Richard's carriages and $1,500 in cash. The route the foursome took made it likely that after clearing Maysville, they would have crossed the river into the free state of Ohio. After that, they would have headed for the Canadian border, where slavery had been outlawed in 1833, and where US slave catchers couldn't follow them. While the Native men were blamed for "inducing" the enslaved women to leave with them, ultimately the greater fault was believed to lie with Richard. The boys' sexual and racial morals had been "corrupted" by their time at Blue Spring, a clear jab at Richard's relationship with

Julia Chinn. It's also suggestive that the two women were listed as "mulatto girls," which, when paired with the title "Amalgamation," told readers that interracial sex was happening at Blue Spring on a wide scale and in various ways.[39]

With small variations, the *Eagle* and, a few days later, the *Louisville Journal* and the *Kentucky Sentinel* all agreed that two Native men and two enslaved women had run away together from Blue Spring with a variety of stolen goods and cash. The *Lexington Observer* received inside information as early as July 1 that one of the runaways was Richard Johnson's current sexual partner, concluding, "We understand that he not only lost his *first* wife by the Cholera two years ago, but has recently been deprived of his *second* one by the base ingratitude of an Indian, who was lately a student of Choctaw Academy." While the paper didn't directly name Parthene as the "second wife," the editors were clearly making the case that Richard, far from being a man who had had *one* relationship with *one* Black woman, was a habitual amalgamationist.[40]

A week later, the *Observer* published a letter written by a resident of Georgetown dated June 24 containing key details about the runaways. It was then that folks in Fayette County came to know that Johnson's "second wife, Madame Parthene, a yellow woman, has eloped with one of his Indian students, carrying with her a check for $1000, and cash to the amount of $300, which she took out of her titled husband's drawer—she having possession of his keys. The name of the Indian is Jones, and he is a fine looking copper-faced savage." Apparently, John Jones and another student, George Hunt, left Blue Spring with a carriage and two horses.[41]

Parthene's relationship with Richard appears to have been far less consensual than the one that had existed between him and Julia, if one can even use that word within the context of slavery. Like Parthene, Julia was very young when she and Richard began their partnership; there was a large age gap between the couple; she remained enslaved for the duration of her life; and she was light-skinned. In all these ways, Richard, now fifty-five years old, remained true to form in this new pairing, taking up with a young, enslaved, "yellow woman," who grew up with his daughters, who were twenty-one and twenty-three years of age in 1835. And like Julia, Parthene had possession of Richard's keys, access to his money and other goods, and the ability to leave Blue Spring with her cousin to visit with friends on a Sunday.

All of these latter things suggest a certain level of trust, power, and privilege, a reflection of Parthene's position in Richard's life. It is also a testimony to the Chinn family's overall authority and station within the farm's laboring hierarchy. Because Parthene, like most of the house staff, was a Chinn. In fact, she appears to have been Julia Chinn's niece. Evidence suggests that Julia's brother, Daniel

Chinn, was Parthene's father.[42] Parthene, then, was Imogene and Adaline's first cousin. None of the newspapers noted that "Mrs. Johnson" was one of Julia's nieces, however. If they knew this very disturbing fact, they kept it to themselves.

Unlike Julia Chinn, Parthene was clearly not happy with her role as "Mistress of the Parlor" and pushed back against it. Having grown up on the farm as part of the household staff, educated alongside her cousins, and protected by her aunt, sex with Richard held no appeal for Parthene, no matter what privileges it may have brought. She wanted a different life, and she escaped to pursue her dreams. Those dreams may have included John Jones. An Anishinaabe man who taught at Choctaw Academy, John was studying law under Richard and had helped Julia save many lives at Blue Spring during the cholera epidemic. He also may have been Parthene's lover, which led her to risk running away with him. Richard certainly believed that John had seduced one of Julia's nieces, presumably Parthene, for he later stated, "His course is doubly dishonorable towards me, after my distinguished friendship towards him."[43]

This could explain Richard's response to the fugitives. Like an enraged lover *and* owner, he sent his overseer, Edward Pence, brother of his son-in-law Daniel, after the foursome. Pence discovered the quartet had left Lexington on Monday, but he eventually caught up with them just a few miles from Lake Erie in northern Ohio. After a hard-fought battle, Edward and his men managed to recapture both women. The newspaper accounts, however, now claimed that the women had been *kidnapped* by a band of "Puttawatomie and Miami Indians" and that the battle was fought with great desperation, as the kidnappers were unwilling to "yield their rich and beautiful prizes." Afterward, the Native Americans supposedly followed the Kentuckians back as far as Columbus, where they succeeded in recapturing both women. However, after another fight, they lost "Mrs. J——." The Kentuckians, supposedly battle-weary and worn down from fatigue, hunger, and thirst, gave up on trying to recapture Julia's unnamed niece until reinforcements could be sent. However, "Mrs. J. has before this been restored to the *fond embraces* of her distracted husband, and we hope in a few days to be able to announce to our readers that Miss Chinn has also been restored to the arms of her distressed and agonizing parents."[44]

The counternarrative here is striking. "Madame Parthene" didn't run away; she was kidnapped by "savage and dangerous Indians." Several things don't add up, however. If she were kidnapped, it's unclear why Parthene took $1,300 from Richard before leaving that Sunday, the equivalent of about $44,000 in 2023 currency.[45] There's also the question of why the Native men and the enslaved women left at separate times, and with stolen goods, in what appears to have been a carefully thought-out and well-executed plan. Additionally, it seems clear that Edward Pence and his party of slave catchers had been ordered by Richard to prioritize capturing Parthene. In fact, they never did catch her companion, "Miss Chinn," likely her sister or a cousin. Finally, after Parthene was seized for the second time, she was held in the Columbus jail before being brought back to Kentucky! It appears she couldn't be trusted not to run away, and she was closely guarded all the way back to Blue Spring, which makes the story of kidnapping highly suspicious.[46]

Richard couldn't allow anyone to believe that Parthene had planned this, that she despised him and desperately wanted to get away from him and her life at Blue Spring Farm. He had to come up with a cover story for her escape. Enter kidnapping by Indians. Such a tale actually makes sense for a man whose parents were among the first settlers to Kentucky during the frontier phase and whose family withstood Native attacks on their settlement in what is now Louisville (where Richard was born) as well as at their home in Scott County. At that home, surrounded by a heavy stockade and known as Johnson's Station or Johnson's Fort, Richard grew up in a time and place where people carried their guns to church in case of attacks by local Indigenous groups angered by the unending waves of white settlers flooding onto their homelands.[47] He himself had risen to fame for having supposedly killed Tecumseh in battle during the War of 1812. While he now claimed to be a friend of the Choctaw Nation, the disciplinary issues at Choctaw Academy were a constant source of frustration for him, and he longed to be able to flog the school's students. At the end of the day, it wouldn't have taken much effort for Richard to have turned the escape into a situation where "valuable servant girls" were stolen by "dangerous and desperate Indians."[48]

Parthene was far from happy to be back at Blue Spring. When she returned, under guard, Richard, far from receiving her with "fond embraces," had her "pretty considerably scourged." Afterward, she found herself "reduced from the parlor to the kitchen." Whipped and then demoted from the Big House to overseeing the farm's food and fires, it would seem that Parthene was a willing participant in the escape from Blue Spring. And whether John Jones was her lover or just a friend who wanted to help her get free, Parthene's sexual relationship with Richard doesn't appear to have been consensual. As for how Richard felt about her now that she was back, all those "*kind feelings* with which it was said his bosom once overflowed" had apparently vanished.[49] Richard's reaction to Parthene's resistance might explain why Julia Chinn never openly rebelled against the man she had lived with for over two decades. She, better than anyone, would have known how he might react if she were to ever try and leave him and what could happen to her and her children. She likely decided it was too high a risk.

The facts as they stand are as ugly as any tale from the antebellum South. It appears that almost as soon as Julia was in her grave, if not before, Richard Johnson forced his dead wife's niece, his daughters' cousin, to have sex with him.[50] Two years later, she ran away from what was essentially an incestuous relationship with a fifty-five-year-old man, a man she had grown up with and perhaps saw as an uncle. In fleeing, she gave up all the privileges she had acquired from the relationship: the clothing, the cash, the keys, and any bit of control. Her "uncle" then went to great expense to hunt her down and bring her back and risked conflict with both the Miami and the Potawatomi by blaming them for her kidnapping. Having long proclaimed himself a friend to Native peoples, Richard was quick to throw them to the wolves to protect his image and reclaim his property. Upon Parthene's capture, she was beaten, likely had salt poured on her open wounds, and was then sent to the kitchens.[51] Richard, it seems, was willing to do whatever it took to show Parthene, and everyone else at Blue Spring Farm, who was master. It didn't matter that Parthene was Imogene and Adaline's cousin and had once been a favored member of the house party. Parthene, then, knew she was taking a great risk in trying to escape. This suggests that whatever she was running from was bad enough to make the risk worthwhile.

That Parthene was Julia's niece is suggested by two things. First, she was a member of the house party, and most of the household staff were Julia's kin. Additionally, an article published in 1845 in the antislavery newspaper the *Liberator* provides details that support the familial connection. Reprinted from the *New-York Tribune*, "The Workings of Slavery" contains interviews with self-liberated Black people living in Canada, including one Mr. Daniel Chinn. Daniel was listed as both the brother-in-law and the father-in-law of Richard Johnson, because not only had Richard married Daniel's sister, Julia Ann Chinn, but after Julia died from cholera, "Col. Johnson has since lived with one of Mr. Chinn's daughters, as though she was his wife. This . . . would make Mr. Chinn father-in-law of the venerable ex-Vice President of our great republican nation."[52]

The article does not provide the name of Daniel's daughter. Additionally, the piece was written in 1845, ten years after Parthene's runaway attempt. Were Richard and Parthene living together in 1845, or had he taken up with another daughter of Daniel Chinn's? The phrase "has since lived with" could mean that Richard had at one point lived with the daughter in question or that he was living with her in 1845. What the article does make clear is that Daniel wasn't trying to live at Blue Spring after Richard had abused one of his daughters.

Daniel wasn't the only Chinn who was disgusted with Richard. His son, Marcellus, escaped from slavery when Richard took him as his body servant on an electioneering tour to New York during his first vice presidential campaign in

CHAPTER SIX

1835. Although Richard tried to get abolitionist Lewis Tappan to convince the boy to return to him, he never did. Lewis agreed to help Richard, but only if he first signed freedom papers for Marcellus, which Richard refused to do. Here, again, Richard made it clear that he saw himself as master and that Marcellus was his property. Marcellus eventually moved to New Bedford, Massachusetts, and became a sailor. Richard then took Daniel with him on his second electioneering tour as his body servant, believing *he* would never run away, but Daniel fled while the group was in Detroit and made the short journey to freedom, crossing over into Canada. Despite one letter from Richard asking him to return, and another one that threatened him, Daniel stayed in Canada and never returned to the United States.[53]

Richard's supporters, including Thomas Henderson, had consistently praised him for the kind and loving manner in which he treated Julia and his daughters, although we don't know how the couple's relationship started, how Julia actually felt about Richard, or her reasons for participating in the relationship. Certainly, her desire to give her descendants more opportunities than she herself had would have influenced her decisions to engage or stay in a partnership with Richard. That being said, no matter how he may have treated this one family, the interview with Daniel Chinn sheds additional light on Richard's overall character. In particular, "his conduct in becoming the father of children by three women, the sisters of Mr. Chinn's wife ... and then selling them all, both the women and his own children, to James Peak, to be carried off in slavery, as Mr. Chinn states that he did, may not be quite so highly commended."[54]

Richard was no different from other enslavers. He may have had a more consensual alliance with Julia Chinn, Daniel's sister, but he also had a highly coercive union with at least one of Daniel's daughters and possible sexual relations (and children) with three of Daniel's sisters-in-law, the sisters of his wife, Patience. Furthermore, he may have sold all three of Patience's sisters, and the children he had by them, to James Peak, one of his local creditors and a textile merchant, much as Henry Clay had done with his mistress and their children.[55] Whether it was so he could hide the evidence of his behavior or due to his financial troubles, this wasn't out of the ordinary for Richard. Former Johnson bondsperson Addie Murphy said she "saw slaves sold, hand-cuffed in twos," and we know that Richard sold some of the enslaved women at Blue Spring for having sex with the students from Choctaw Academy. That act served to punish the women involved while helping Richard, who was always in debt, raise much-needed funds.[56] In fact, financial pressures led Richard to mortgage Daniel and Patience Chinn at one point, even though they were Julia's closest kin. At the end of the day, while Richard may have cared for Julia and their daughters, it doesn't appear to have changed his feelings about or his behaviors toward Black women, or Black people, as a whole. They were still his property to do with as he saw fit, body and soul. He was first, last, and always an enslaver.

One wonders how Adaline and Imogene felt about their father sleeping his way through their relations, including their cousin, a girl they had grown up with, gone to school with, and worked with. Adaline Johnson in particular had spent countless hours with Parthene, sewing and mending clothes for the boys of Choctaw Academy. The situation would have affected her in particular, both emotionally and practically, because Adaline still lived at Blue Spring. It's hard to imagine that the girls hadn't spent a good amount of time talking about everything from religion to romance growing up, as girls do, while they patched up pants, studied their lessons, walked to and from church, ate meals together, and lay awake at night. What happened to Parthene had to have shaken Adaline. It certainly upended Patience Chinn's life. Her family had been destroyed: Daughter raped, beaten, and banished to the kitchens. Sisters, nieces, and nephews sold away. Son and husband fled. It's safe to say that Blue Spring Farm was no haven for Black people, even if their last name was Chinn.

While the furor over the runaways eventually died down, the press didn't lessen its attention on the Johnson family. This was a presidential election; it had national stakes. And while northern states didn't have legalized slavery, that didn't make them pro-Black. Racism was a national problem. The *Providence Journal*, for instance, mused, "How would it look in the eyes of civilized Europe and the world, to see the Vice President, and his yellow children, and his wooly headed African wife, in the city of Washington, mingling in all the giddy mazes of the most fashionable and respectable society in the country?" Given that these arguments were about keeping the Johnsons out of the halls of the upper class ("the giddy mazes of the most fashionable and respectable society in the country") and about what the "civilized" elites of Europe and other global powers would think of the United States if Richard won the election, broader tactics were needed to bring the masses over to the Whig Party.[57]

One such tactic was a cartoon that was almost certainly drawn by Edward William Clay and published by Henry R. Robinson of New York City as a single-sheet, lithographic print. The two men, who worked closely together during these years, had conservative Whig sympathies and both were anti-abolitionists. In the late 1830s, Clay created a series of racist, sensationalistic cartoons warning New Yorkers of the dangers of racial "amalgamation." The style of these and other known Clay images are similar to the anti-Johnson cartoon.[58] Titled "An Affecting Scene in Kentucky," the image, held by the Library of Congress, is seen below.

CHAPTER SIX

Cartoon, "An Affecting Scene in Kentucky."
Originally published in a nineteenth-century newspaper, this image can be found in the online collections of the Library of Congress.

Seated in a chair with his hand over his face, a clearly distraught Johnson lets a copy of conservative Whig James Watson Webb's *New York Courier and Inquirer* fall to the floor and moans, "When I read the scurrilous attacks in the Newspapers on the Mother of my Children, pardon me, my friends if I give way to feelings!!! My dear Girls, bring me your Mother's picture, that I may shew it to my friends here."

On the far right are his daughters, Imogene and Adaline. Visibly brown-skinned, they wear elegant dresses with puffed sleeves, stockings, shoes, and earrings. Their hair is swept into "updos," and one carries a handkerchief. The other holds a painting of a dark-skinned Black woman wearing a traditional African or West Indian head wrap and says, "Here it is Pa, but don't take on so." The second daughter says, "Poor dear Pa, how much he is affected." A man standing behind them, likely meant to represent a less-educated westerner who reveres Richard for his war record, exclaims, "Pickle! Pop!! and Ginger!!! Can the slayer of Tecumseh be thus overcome like a summer cloud! fire and furies. oh!"

Flanking Johnson are a tall, gaunt abolitionist to our right, and a shorter, well-dressed, free Black man to our left. The white abolitionist has a comforting hand on Richard's shoulder. Holding a copy of the *Emancipator* out of Hartford, Connecticut, under his left arm, a newspaper sponsored by the abolitionist

154

Lewis Tappan of New York City, the man says, "Be comforted Richard; all of us abolitionists will support thee." The free Black man, in the dialect that all Black people were assumed to speak in, pledges "de honor of a Gentlemen dat all de Gentlemen of Colour will support you." On the far left is a portly postmaster who, remembering Richard's faithfulness during the Sunday Mails Battle, states, "Your Excellency, I am sure all of us Postmasters and deputies will stick to you; if you promise to keep us in office."[59]

The image reveals that in the eyes of the opposition, none of Richard's supporters were men of good character. They all lacked respectability: abolitionists, free Blacks, ignorant frontiersmen, and opportunistic political appointees. It's also telling that the illustrator portrayed Julia as a dark-skinned, turban-wearing "other," someone who wasn't from here, although by all accounts she was native-born and brown-skinned at best, referred to as a quadroon or octoroon by many due to the lightness of her skin color. More terrifying to white audiences would have been the fact that her daughters were dressed like ladies. Blurring the lines between slave and free, Black and white, this was similar to portrayals of Black people in other Clay cartoons and appears to represent the social upheavals anti-abolitionists warned would come with amalgamation: poor whites and free Blacks in positions of power and Black women parading around as the equals of white ladies. What's striking is that Imogene and Adaline, known to have been light enough to pass for white, were visibly brown-skinned in this cartoon. Portraying them as white would have been going too far for Clay and Robinson, however. White people needed to *see* the dangers being highlighted in the cartoon. Julia is thus Blacker than she was in real life, and her daughters are browner. The point was to paint all three women as outsiders who were crossing into white spaces and to thus inspire white folks to rise up and stop racial and social amalgamation from going any further.

It isn't surprising that one of the persons in the cartoon is a free Black man. This was a concern that many people had about Richard: Given his attitude toward his daughters, what would his future position be on rights for free Blacks? During the Missouri Compromise debates, Johnson had originally favored abolition societies. Still, he voted in favor of the Compromise of 1820, which admitted Maine to the United States as a free state and Missouri as a slave state, and when he became a candidate for the vice presidency, he toed the party line, favoring states' rights. One wonders, though, about a story in the abolitionist newspaper the *Emancipator*, which claimed that when Johnson visited New York City, "he took much pains to express to some of the gentlemen of color his deep interest in the question of their rights and prospects, as all he should leave behind him at death (his daughters) were identified in destiny with them."[60] While antebellum newspaper articles are full of discrepancies, it makes sense that Richard was anxious about his daughters and their future after he was no longer alive to protect them.

As the calendar turned to 1836, the press, both local and national, didn't stop in its attempts to smear Julia and her daughters and keep Richard out of office. Most rehashed the same tired rants about the couple, but a few were slightly more innovative in their insults. Perhaps the most creative were the minstrels who penned the song "Johnson's Wife of Old Kentucky." It's doubtful Richard and his daughters were amused by the ditty that made its way around the pubs:

> The wave that heaves by Congo's shore
> Heaves not so high nor darkly wide
> As Sukey in her midnight snore
> Close by Tecumseh Johnson's side.[61]

It was then, in the midst of one of the most vicious political campaigns of the nineteenth century, that Adaline Johnson Scott died. Did reading all the ugly newspaper coverage about her family contribute to her untimely death? It certainly couldn't have helped her stress levels. Adaline was about twenty-one years old when she passed away, and she'd been married for just over three years. Given the timing of events, it's quite possible that she died in childbirth or shortly thereafter. If so, it was probably her second pregnancy, since she had given birth to a son, Robert Johnson Scott, named for Richard's father, in 1834.[62]

Adaline's death devastated Richard, emotionally and practically, because he had come to depend on her for handling many of the daily affairs at Blue Spring Farm and Choctaw Academy since Julia's death in 1833. Grief-stricken, Richard wrote,

> As to the removal of the store, that I must leave to the wishes and opinions of Mr. Pence and Mr. Scott and to future events and consequences resulting from the death of Adaline. I thank you, and all who administered to that lovely and innocent child in her final and awful hour. She was a source of inexhaustible happiness and comfort to me. She was mild and prudent. She was wise in her counsel beyond her years and obedient to every thought and every advice of mine for her whole life. I do not recollect that she ever done an act that even ruffled my temper—She was a firm and great prop to my happiness here—but she is gone where sorrow and sighing can never disturb her peaceful and quiet bosom. She is happy, and has left me unhappy, in mourning her loss, which perhaps, I ought not to do, knowing what a happy change she has made.[63]

Unlike in his correspondence with Francis Blair, Richard's attitude toward Adaline here is paternal and personal. This letter suggests that Richard and his daughter had a strong bond and that Adaline was a "good daughter" who was deferential to her father and knew her place. It's possible that Richard was visualizing Adaline through grief-colored glasses that exalted her beyond reality, but his description doesn't differ from what Thomas Henderson wrote about Adaline and her sister in 1835. Even-tempered, sensible, intelligent, mature, and obedient, Adaline Johnson Scott was the quintessential antebellum woman. In life she had brought Richard much comfort and happiness, and her passing brought him great sorrow.[64]

Losing Adaline during the campaign was difficult for Richard. And while the negative newspaper coverage likely didn't help, the knowledge of her father's sexual transgressions with her cousin Parthene may have also played a role in Adaline's death. This seems to have weighed on Richard, who compared his grief to that of King David in the Bible, who lost his firstborn son. While Richard states that, like David, he had to reconcile himself to the will of God, there may have been more to his identification with the biblical king. David's son died because he lusted after and slept with Bathsheba (a married woman), got her pregnant, and then had her husband, Uriah, murdered in order to hide his actions. Although David was loved by God, even he had to pay a price for such a long string of sins; God took his firstborn son.[65]

In 1845, Daniel Chinn would outline a litany of evils that Richard Johnson had committed during his life, including the sexual assaults and sales of Daniel and Julia's family members. Perhaps Richard wondered if Adaline's death was the blood price that God demanded of him. Given what we now know about the connections between stress, high blood pressure, and the mortality rates of pregnant women, particularly Black women, we can't rule out the possibility that Julia's death, Richard's subsequent actions with numerous women at Blue Spring, including Parthene, and the constant attacks against their family in the press all combined to place an unbearable strain on Adaline. A hypertensive disorder of pregnancy, such as preeclampsia, may well have been a factor in her untimely death.[66]

The press didn't let down in its attacks against Richard after Adaline's death, but he still became the ninth vice president of the United States. It wasn't simple, however.[67] Although the Van Buren ticket won the election, they lost several southern states, including Richard's home state of Kentucky. And when it came time for the electoral college to vote, the delegates from Virginia cast their ballots for Van Buren but refused to do the same for Johnson, leaving him one ballot short of the majority required to ascend to the vice presidency. According to the Twelfth Amendment, this meant the Senate had to officially select the vice president, choosing from among the top two vote getters in the election. When the Senate voted, Johnson won the majority of the votes, thirty-three to Francis Granger's sixteen; he thus became the United States' first vice president chosen by the Senate. He remains the nation's only vice president elected in this manner.[68]

Though the Senate chose Johnson, this was done along strict party lines, and it quickly became clear that the Democrats had no real love for him. Given how many states they had lost, the party now saw him as a liability, and Democratic opposition to him began almost immediately. As early as October 1837, Senate doorkeeper Edward Wyer was heard to say that "of all the vulgar men in the world, the most vulgar man, in his judgement, was the Vice President of the United States." Richard had little pull with President Martin Van Buren, and as party leaders in 1838 prepared for the election of 1840, John Quincy Adams remarked on "Colonel R. M. Johnson, whose Vice Presidential chair, it is said, is gently to be drawn from under him at the next Presidential election."[69]

It seems odd that people were still so disgusted by Johnson's relationship with Julia Chinn in 1838, given that she had been dead for five years. Perhaps the "vulgarity" was in reference to Parthene, who disappears from the traditional archives after being recaptured and flogged in 1835. Apparently, it had nothing to do with either woman. Sources reveal that Richard Mentor Johnson began *another* sexual relationship with *another* young, enslaved, Black woman while he was the sitting vice president of the United States. The evidence comes to us from Amos Kendall, Richard's close friend since 1815. The two men were from the same small town in Kentucky, and Amos had at one time been the editor of their local paper, the *Georgetown Patriot*, which the Johnson family controlled. Richard and Amos even lived in the same boardinghouse in Washington, DC.[70]

In 1839, Amos was postmaster general of the United States. He had served in both the Jackson and Van Buren administrations. That summer, Richard was living in Kentucky during the congressional break, overseeing affairs at home during a financial crisis. He had recently built a spa, White Sulphur Spring, which he opened to raise money and help offset his debts. It became a popular resort that attracted wealthy guests and was known for its beautiful and romantic scenery, fine fishing, high-quality dining, and well water of pure, white sulfur. The hotel on the property was a frame building over 200 feet long and two stories high, with a double porch. Many such places were built in Kentucky in those days, and the rich and famous came from far and wide to take the waters, both for recreation and for their health.[71]

In August 1839, Amos Kendall received a letter from a friend who had visited Richard's resort and tavern. After reading it, Amos sent the letter on to President Van Buren, along with one of his own. The letter from his friend, whose name was withheld, first addressed the business Richard had opened. The anonymous friend had apparently spent an evening there and was surprised to find Johnson helping to actually run the place: "The Vice President of these United States, with all his civic and military honors clustering around his time honored brow, is or seems to be happy in the inglorious pursuit of tavern keeping—even giving his personal superintendence to the chicken and egg purchasing and watermelon selling department."[72]

While the letter writer looked down on Richard for running the tavern himself, and enjoying it, this was nothing compared to his feelings on Richard's new partner: "But in truth the old Colonel . . . devotes much too much of his time to a young Delilah of about the complexion of Shakespeare's swarthy Othello. This is said to be his *third wife*, his second, which he sold for her infidelity having been the sister of the present *lady*. She is some eighteen or nineteen years of age and quite handsome—plays on the piano, calls him my *dear Colonel* and I believe *my dear* is returned, and is said to be very loving and devoted."[73]

While these opening lines on the subject of Richard's latest interracial relationship appear neutral, perhaps even complimentary, given that the woman in question is said to be "quite handsome," the underlining of certain words, such as "third wife" and "lady," reveals the letter writer's true feelings about a habitual amalgamationist who attempts to place Black women on par with white women. The final paragraph makes the writer's position crystal clear: "I have been less than I now am, but neither now, nor at any time, would I so act in defiance of public opinion for all the honors Col. Johnson has enjoyed twice told. How can he expect this to countenance and sustain him when he seems to have lost all self respect and openly and thoroughly lives in adultery with a buxom young *Negro wench*?"[74]

For the anonymous letter writer, Richard was beyond redemption. He had no self-respect because he was acting in "defiance of public opinion" and "openly" living in "adultery" with a "Negro wench." The writer's usage of the slur "wench" made it clear what he thought of the young woman. The fact that he referred to her as a "young Delilah" is also telling. Likely a reference to the story of Samson and Delilah in the Bible's book of Judges, not only did naming Richard's new partner a Delilah imply that Black women were deceitful temptresses who seduced and ultimately betrayed their lovers, but the moral of the tale of Samson was a cautionary one for powerful men: heroes who dishonor their vows will eventually be destroyed. The tale, then, isn't just about the treachery of women; it's one that speaks of self-ruin by great leaders, men such as Richard.[75]

This letter ended Amos and Richard's quarter century of friendship. As Amos stated in his own letter to Van Buren, "I will take care in as prudent a way as I can to wash my hands of any future responsibility for his support." Deeply angered

CHAPTER SIX

by Richard's behavior, Amos considered him to have lost all "self-respect" and "decency" and to be, at this point, completely "disreputable." Amos told the president that when he had visited Kentucky the previous fall, he had heard stories that Richard was in another interracial relationship, but he thought it was just gossip. Richard had promised Amos that the habits of his younger days were over, and Amos himself "did not doubt that if practiced or renewed, it would be in such a manner as to avoid public reproach; but it seems that I was entirely mistaken. He seems encouraged by his elevation, as if it were the seal of public approbation to his conduct in that respect."[76]

Clearly Amos hoped that Richard's amalgamationist ways had ended, or that if he did decide to take up with another Black woman, he would do so in a manner avoiding "public reproach," like other enslavers. That he would hide it. It was not to be. Richard's election to the vice presidency apparently made him feel untouchable. Of course, it's possible that Amos's friend was mistaken by what he saw in 1839, but that seems unlikely. In October 1840, a woman named Catherine L. Bragg was traveling through Kentucky and wrote a letter to her friend Catherine C. Gould, who lived in Connecticut. Having just finished an eleven-day stagecoach journey, Bragg mentioned that the trip went better than anticipated and that they made some very "pleasant acquaintances but never felt quite so much *honored* as on the last day of our route. We rode from Maysville to Paris with Mrs. Johnson the Vice President's wife & her two milk & molasses children. This is the third wife I understand. His first was a real full blooded *negro*, the second a large, stout yellow woman & this one is a light yellow with black freckles—everyone to their taste."[77]

Bragg's letter supports the one written by Amos Kendall's friend claiming that Richard had a third Black wife, but it also raises some questions. This "light yellow woman with black freckles" doesn't match the description of the woman "about the complexion of Shakespeare's swarthy Othello" described by Amos's friend. Eyewitness descriptions of Black folks are notoriously unreliable, however, so it's quite possible that both letters are referring to the same woman. Julia herself was described in a multitude of ways by the antebellum press. If it is the same woman, that would make her the sister of Richard's second "wife," Parthene Chinn. That would make the first wife Julia Chinn. Parthene, who was probably Julia's niece, was known to be light-skinned, or "yellow," which fits Bragg's description of wife number two. Julia, however, was not, by any account, a "real full-blooded negro." She was referred to by those who knew her as being brown, "mulatto," or light-skinned; some people even said she was an "octoroon." Still, since Catherine Bragg had never met Julia and was using hearsay to describe her, this, too, can be excused.

What is less easy to dismiss is Bragg's reference to the third Mrs. Johnson's "two milk & molasses children." The phrase suggests the children in question were mixed race. If these were the woman's own children by Richard, this is an important revelation. Richard was sixty years old in 1840. This third woman, according to Amos Kendall's friend, appeared to be eighteen or nineteen years of age in 1839. There was thus a forty-year age gap between the pair. If the woman that Kendall's friend wrote about in 1839 is the same person Catherine Bragg met in 1840, she was about twenty years old and already the mother of two children. And if she was Parthene Chinn's sister, she was also Julia's niece and Imogene and Adaline's first cousin.

It's disturbing enough to consider that Richard had moved on from a decades-long partnership with Julia, which appeared to have been built on some semblance of mutuality, to a forced sexual relationship with Parthene, who was likely his dead wife's niece, a situation bad enough to make the young woman run away from Blue Spring. And after she was captured, Richard didn't just have Parthene flogged; according to Amos Kendall's friend, he sold her for having had an affair with John Jones. But now he had taken up with yet another niece of his late wife, Daniel Chinn's other daughter, Parthene's sister, and perhaps had children by her. Richard clearly had a type. Young, light-skinned, enslaved, and under his control.

This sounds like the worst kind of antebellum story, complete with a lecherous, old, white man who preys on young Black girls at the center of the tale. It is reminiscent of the abuse experienced by Celia, purchased by sixty-year-old Robert Newsom to be his sex slave when she was only fourteen, or of the sexualized terror that Harriet Jacobs began experiencing at the hands of her enslaver, Dr. Flint, when she was only twelve. Jacobs, who eventually escaped to the North and published her life story, engaged in a relationship with a white man named Mr. Sands that produced two children, all to try to keep Flint from molesting her.[78] If Richard's behavior fell in line with that of men such as Newsom and Flint, and it appears it did, it explains why Daniel and Marcellus Chinn both eventually fled the Johnson plantation. Blue Spring Farm appears to have been a different place in 1840 than it was when Julia Chinn was alive, although it's hard to know how Julia felt about her life or about Richard. Their partnership may well have been emotionally, if not physically, coercive, particularly at the start, especially if Julia was only fourteen years old when the couple's alliance began and Richard was in his thirties.

It's possible that Catherine Bragg was wrong, and the woman she met on the stagecoach wasn't Richard's new sexual partner. Or that she was involved with Richard but these weren't her children. Perhaps this wasn't the young "Delilah" from 1839 but a different woman altogether. She may have been older and the children her own but from a prior relationship. On the other hand, this may have been Parthene's sister, raising her nieces and nephews now that their mother was gone, having been sold as punishment for having dared to run away with her lover. But no matter who this new "wife" was, it makes sense that she chose the path of least resistance. She played the piano to entertain Johnson and his guests, called Richard "my dear Colonel," and was "very loving and devoted."[79] What choice did she have if she wanted to avoid Parthene's fate? If she *was* Daniel Chinn's daughter, this woman had already lost a sister, her father, and her brother, Marcellus. She couldn't afford to lose her home and whatever family she had left.

While the details about the woman on the stagecoach and the children traveling with her remain shrouded in mystery, the fact that Richard was in the midst of another relationship, with another enslaved Black woman, wasn't a secret. It explains why race and sex played a key role in yet another presidential election, and why Andrew Jackson withdrew his support for Richard in 1840. Jackson feared that Richard would take down the Democrats this time, and although he still supported Martin Van Buren for the presidency, he suggested James K. Polk of Tennessee for vice president. The Democrats were so divided over a vice presidential candidate that Van Buren ended up running alone that year, despite Jackson's warnings to the party to unite around a two-person ticket. In total disarray, each state chose its own vice presidential candidate.[80]

Richard's enemies had been trying to force him to retire as early as 1839. John Catron, the onetime Tennessee judge who had tried to convince Andrew Jackson to withdraw his support from Richard in 1836, now lived in Frankfort, Kentucky. Catron wrote to James K. Polk in November 1839 and told him that Richard "had adopted another mistress—a young hearty black wench—and the thing is openly admitted." He assured Polk that Richard had no friends left in Kentucky because his affairs with enslaved women disgusted even the local Democrats. Richard's old friends Amos Kendall and Francis P. Blair, both Kentuckians, had deserted him. Former congressman Cave Johnson of Tennessee, no relation to Richard, stated that Ohio would join Kentucky Democrats in rejecting Richard.[81]

Although the noose was tight around Richard's neck, he refused to "go gentle into that good night." He decided to run for the vice presidency on his own, along with several other Democratic candidates. Johnson still had friends in many places, and he had not been sitting idle while his party worked to get rid of him. Instead, he quietly gathered his supporters and went on a long speaking campaign. Large enough crowds turned out in places such as Michigan and New York to encourage the aging colonel that he had a chance to win the election. He could even be persuaded on occasion to tear open his shirt and show off his old war wounds. Giving rambling, at times incoherent speeches, Richard was looked down on by many of his peers. He still, however, appeared to have what some referred to as "a disgusting popularity" with the masses.[82]

Although Richard appeared at times to be losing his grip on reality, he understood why he had been shunned by his own party. He wrote to his Democratic colleague Humphrey Marshall in May 1840 and addressed the issue head on: "As to myself, relative to the reelection to my present office you have seen my letter which was placed before the convention. It is impossible for me to change my Course—I am now perfectly happy in the reflection, that no state will vote for me, where I am not their first choice, & thus I am, as I wish to be, put on my trial before the people of each state, where I shall be the choice of at least 20 out of the 26—but more or less, *it is my bride, to be forced of my own political party upon none*" (italics mine).[83] There was no doubt that Richard understood that this election was about interracial sex and that it was his "bride" as much as it was he who was being "put on trial" before the voters.

The press continued its attacks on Richard right up until the election. In November 1840, the *Louisville Weekly Journal* reflected, "We begin to think, from the Vice President's late displays in Ohio and Indiana, that his marriage was really and truly an affair of the heart. His heart and his wife are of a color." The same paper poked fun at Richard's desire for Black women and his homesickness after being on the campaign trail for so long. "So strong is the good Colonel's attachment to home, that after the absence of a month or two, the bare sight of a wench makes him shed tears."[84]

It's no surprise that Richard didn't win the vice presidency in 1840. Van Buren didn't win the presidency either. William Henry Harrison and John Tyler received 234 electoral votes to Van Buren's 60 and Richard's 48. What is surprising is that Richard not only lost Kentucky; this time he even lost his home district. The men of Scott County seemed unwilling to receive another public tongue-lashing like the one they had received in 1836, when the *Lexington Observer* noted, "But what shall we say of Scott? . . . She has given a majority of 447 votes for a man for . . . Vice President, who has tried to place a negro woman and her female offspring upon a level with white women. . . . How can such men . . . look at their wives and daughters in the face."[85]

While the economic panic of 1837 didn't help the Democrats in the election of 1840, and their inability to unify around one vice presidential candidate was a problem, the fact is that their public engagement in and over matters about interracial sex hurt them, and it destroyed Richard Johnson's national political career. In many ways, it was the ghost of a Black woman named Julia Chinn that brought them all down. In the United States, even wealthy and powerful white men could lose everything if they chose to disregard the playbook that existed about Blackness and interracial sex and blatantly flaunted their private lives in public spaces.

On March 2, 1841, Richard left his post as president of the Senate. He would never again hold national political office, although he would remain a force in local and state affairs. Indeed, he would be elected to represent Scott County in the Kentucky House of Representatives in August 1841 and would repeat his victory in August 1842. Whatever years Richard Mentor Johnson had left on this earth would be spent in Kentucky, trying to recapture his glory days.

As for Julia Chinn, she had worked hard to make the world a bigger place for her descendants than it was for her. Her sacrifices ensured that her daughters were well educated, wealthy, and married to white men before she died. As her husband's days began to draw to a close, the tactics of negotiation that Julia had engaged in for decades began to bear fruit, both good and "strange," for her children and grandchildren.[86] In some ways, their lives appeared to be a narrative of upward social mobility. In others, they were a stark testimony on the lengths to which some Black folks felt forced to go in post–Civil War America in order to avoid the brutalities of racial violence and Jim Crow segregation. Collectively, their stories also reveal the socially constructed nature of race and its malleability over time.

CHAPTER SEVEN

END OF DAYS

Privilege, Property, and Passing(s)

*N*ovember 19, 1850. A messenger had brought the news to the farm: Richard Mentor Johnson was dead. It wasn't entirely unexpected. He had been declining for weeks. This was his second stroke. The doctors had warned him to rest after the first one, but he refused to stay in bed. She remembered her mother telling her how he had done much the same thing after almost dying in the Battle of the Thames during the War of 1812. That time, he had gotten up on crutches after just a few short weeks, determined to get back to Washington, DC, back to Congress. This time, it was the Kentucky Statehouse in Frankfort instead of the Capitol Building in DC. Attempting to conduct business on the statehouse floor in his weakened condition, however, Richard eventually collapsed and had another stroke.[1]

She heard that nobody had come to visit him during his final days. Not his brothers, not his nephews. Perhaps she should have gone to see him. It wasn't a long trip. They could have all gone. It might have done him some good to see them. The journey to Frankfort would have been complicated, however. It still was. This was about more than just geographical distance. Attending the funeral would be . . . difficult. For so many reasons. He more than anyone would have understood that. She sighed. Mother and Adaline had been gone these many years, both taken too soon. Parthene too. She involuntarily flinched at the thought. This was different, but it was still the end of an era. Imogene touched the pendant that lay at her neck. She would mourn her father in her own way, away from hostile, prying eyes.[2]

Richard Mentor Johnson spent his remaining years in Kentucky, but he never stopped hoping, or trying, to get back to Washington. A lifelong politician, he had his supporters. As late as 1847, there were still those who thought he could win the presidency. In a letter to Senator John J. Crittenden, Thomas Metcalfe, the former governor of Kentucky, wrote, "It begins to be believed that our old friend Col. Richard M. Johnson will be the nominee on the part of the democrats. If so, the sympathies of the country would now run greatly in his favor, and [he] will be hard to beat."[3]

While flattering, the truth was that such sentiments were just the final echoes of a long and storied career. Like most of the "war hawks" of his generation who had fought for and in the War of 1812, the passage of time was telling on Richard, and over the next five years, all the great statesmen of his day including Henry Clay, John C. Calhoun, and Daniel Webster, would pass away. As for Richard, he had retired to his home in 1844 and remained there until he was elected to the Kentucky state legislature again in 1850. According to Judge James Kelly, nobody ran against Richard that year because everyone liked him, and he was impossible to beat at home.[4]

Despite such compliments, these last years were hard on Richard. In debt for most of his adult life, he had taken out more loans during his vice presidency to finance his lavish lifestyle. Always a fan of good food, wine, and parties, he had rented a new home in Washington, DC, and he entertained there in grand style. With Choctaw Academy close to empty and no money coming in, his spending habits, and his creditors, finally caught up with him; he had to sell Longview Plantation, his residence in Kentucky since returning from Washington in 1841. Thankfully, Blue Spring was in the hands of Adaline's widower, Thomas Scott, which protected it from Richard's creditors. While selling Longview was upsetting for Richard, it was far worse for the twenty-four enslaved persons he put on the market. Debt and death always put the enslaved at risk of being mortgaged or sold to pay bill collectors and fulfill inheritances. Richard's case was no exception. He had attempted, he said, to hold on to those he had "raised or inherited, and who I wished to set free at my death," among whom were some of his own relatives, first cousins to his daughters. Sadly, even they were not safe from the auction block. When it came down to his own well-being, or splitting up Black families, Richard, like most enslavers, protected himself. In 1847, Richard sold ten of his most valuable laborers, although he claimed they were able to choose "their own masters in the neighborhood," which kept them near friends and loved ones. He said it was the best he could do for them. It's unclear whether those sold included any of his and Julia's kinfolk.[5]

As late as the fall of 1850, people in Kentucky proposed that Johnson, now seventy years old, should run for governor of the state, but Richard's personal race was almost done. When he took his seat in the statehouse on November 8, 1850, he was "suffering from the effects of a protracted and dangerous illness from which little hope had been entertained of his recovery." He actually went to Frankfort against the advice of his physicians; he'd had a stroke, and his doctors told him that he wasn't ready to return to work. The effects of that first stroke were clear to his colleagues, some of whom said that he appeared to be "laboring under an attack of dementia, which renders him totally unfit for business. It is painful to see him on the floor attempting to discharge the duties of a member."[6]

A few days later, Richard had another stroke. This one left him paralyzed, and his doctors said there was no chance of recovery. On November 19, 1850, Representative Lucius Desha rose up in the statehouse and announced that Col. Richard Mentor Johnson had died at 4:00 a.m. that morning at his lodgings in the city of Frankfort. Coming as it did at such an early hour of the morning, Richard's death wasn't announced in area papers until the next day, November 20, the same day as his funeral.[7]

Richard was buried at Frankfort Cemetery, alongside Kentucky's most famous citizens and with much pomp and ceremony, honoring his many years of service to the state. His colleagues in the statehouse, as well as members of the Masons and the Odd Fellows, organized the funeral, and the governor directed that all public offices on the capitol square be closed during the services. Upon news of Richard's death, Kentucky state representatives James Irwin and Lucius Desha sent a note to the mayor of Lexington. They informed him that they were "superintending the procession to be formed for the interment," which would be held the next day. The mayor was then asked to invite "the City authorities of Lexington, and such military companies as may be willing to be in attendance on the occasion."[8]

Although the "lateness of the hour at which the above letter came to hand last night, prevented any regular action of the Mayor and Council in time to meet the emergency," Richard's funeral was still well attended.[9] All legislative and executive business was suspended, and most private businesses closed their doors out of respect. The lobbies and galleries of the statehouse overflowed with persons of all backgrounds as Richard's coffin lay draped in flags in front of the

Speaker's chair. Henry Clay gave a speech about his longtime colleague and occasional rival. And then, after an "eloquent, striking, and impressive sermon" by the Reverend Stuart Robinson, a long and "imposing" procession made its way to the cemetery as minute guns fired at regular intervals along the way. Because Richard had been a Mason, the Masonic service of interment was conducted at the gravesite by members of that order.[10]

It all sounds magnificent, respectful, and grand. A letter Senator Fitch Munger wrote to his sister, Mary, however, casts an entirely different light on the event:

> Col. Johnson was buried yesterday with great pomp and ceremony & with as much of the Military as the shortness of time would permit. The Corps was brought to the Capitol & Mr. Robinson gave a sermon.... Clay spoke.... There was a Masonic graveside service ... and the Odd Fellows in procession.... One thing I regretted, not a relative of his was present except a Nephew, & he did not take his place as a mourner— No one to shed a tear— A Nephew passed through the place in the morning, but did not stop. Some of his Relations were in town during his illness, but did not call on him— Rev. John T. Johnson, who is a brother, knew of his illness, but did not care to see him. Such lack of attention on the part of his relatives is unexplained. I am the more pleased from this fact that the Legislature made the parade it did.[11]

Munger was able to comment on the number of relatives who attended the funeral because the organizing committee had set up a special section for family members to sit in during the service at the state capitol and a place for them to walk during the processional to the graveyard.[12]

Not one of Richard's relatives attended his funeral except for a nephew. This may have been Jetson, who used to "drive his Uncle Dick to Lexington. He was fond of his uncle," and apparently Richard once gave him some sound advice, telling him to "always act the gentleman whether the other fellow does or not."[13] If it was Jetson, then he was "gentleman" enough to show up to his uncle's funeral but not "fond" enough of Richard to take his place as a recognized mourner. Still, he attended, unlike the nephew who "passed through" town but didn't stay for the service. He certainly did more than the local relatives who chose not to visit Richard when he was ill, including his brother John T. Johnson, who had attended Great Crossing Baptist Church with Julia and Richard for many years.[14]

While Munger claims that the lack of attention by Richard's relatives is "unexplained," it's not surprising that the white Johnsons didn't show up to his funeral or visit while Richard lay dying. It can be summed up in two words: Julia Chinn. While the Johnsons never publicly spoke out against Julia or her daughters while Richard was alive, the couple's relationship was a long-standing source of shame for the family. Richard quarreled with his mother about Julia shortly after the couple's oldest daughter was born. Jemima Johnson wanted Richard to sell Julia and Imogene and get on with his life. To "be sensible" and forget about them. When he refused, it caused a rift between Richard and his mother, who passed away in 1814, the same year that Julia and Richard's younger daughter, Adaline, was born.[15] And while Richard's sister Sally and her husband, William Ward, lived at Blue Spring for several years before moving to Indian Territory, Lexington newspaper editor Nicholas L. Finnell noted that he had long avoided discussing Richard's personal life in the press because he didn't want to offend "the feelings of the numerous respectable relations of Col. Johnson."[16] All of this may explain why Richard's funeral was held with such haste and why state officials and members of the Masons and the Odd Fellows organized the service: the Johnsons likely didn't want to be involved, and a quick funeral would have provided excuses for why relatives were "unable" to attend.

Richard's death led the Johnson clan to display their true feelings. While their absence at the funeral was telling, after his death, Richard's two remaining brothers, including John, who had refused to visit Richard before he died, went to court to have Richard declared dead. After proving their brother was deceased, they stated that he had left no will and said he had no descendants living, in order to lay claim to his estate, thereby disinheriting their niece and Richard's only direct survivor, Imogene. The courts noted that "satisfactory proof was this day made in open court, that Col. Richard M. Johnson . . . died on the 19th day of November 1850 in the city of Frankfort, Kentucky. It was further proved that he left no widow, children, father, or mother living; and that John T. Johnson and Henry Johnson are his only living brothers, and that he left no sister living—which is ordered to be certified." John and Henry's behavior suggests they considered Julia and Richard's relationship to be a stain on the family that needed to be erased. It would explain why they didn't attend their brother's funeral and then colluded with the courts to have Imogene's very existence erased: "He left no . . . children . . . living." Imogene, alive and well in Scott County, did not, then, inherit any portion of her father's estate.[17]

While no will for Richard Mentor Johnson has been discovered, it's possible that John and Henry Johnson destroyed any will that Richard left behind, along with his other papers and personal documents. It's hard to believe that a lawyer and forty-year career politician didn't have a will. On the other hand, Richard, who had given both his daughters substantial estates when they got married in the early

1830s and who continued to transfer property to them and to his grandchildren over the course of his life, may not have felt a will was necessary. Knowing both the law and his brothers as well as he did, he may have realized that it was safer to transfer property to his daughters and their husbands via notarized deeds while he was alive or give them gifts of cash, as opposed to leaving them inheritances. Wills could be contested by angry family members. Richard might have thought it best not to test that option. There is also the chance that his first stroke caught him unawares and that he never recovered enough, mentally, to draft his last will and testament before suffering the second stroke and passing away.

Imogene, Adaline, and their children were fortunate that Richard had transferred most of his property to them before he died. Whatever was left, however, his brothers took. The US census for 1850 reveals that Richard owned real estate worth $10,000 when he died, roughly $382,000 in 2023 currency. He also owned seven enslaved laborers, down from forty-four in 1840. Of the seven, five were over the age of sixty, and one fifty-year-old man was deaf. Given their ages, these last remaining persons were likely those folks whom Richard had known since childhood, people he had "raised or inherited." There were no children and no women of childbearing years. This wasn't a productive labor force by antebellum standards. Richard had thus divested himself of the majority of his workers by 1850. He had already sold ten of his slaves to pay down his debts in 1847. He likely transferred the rest of his bondspeople to Imogene before his death. What Richard still had was some valuable land, and his brothers made sure to keep that from their niece. While this may have been partly due to greed, given the Johnson family's substantial landholdings in Kentucky, it's more likely that it was because they wanted to keep the land in the family; they didn't see Imogene and her children as "real" Johnsons. At heart, this was about slavery, Blackness, and (il)legitimacy.[18]

As for Imogene Johnson Pence, given her history, it's not surprising that she didn't attend Richard's funeral. She may have worried about pushback from the press if she showed up and took her place as an official mourner. With all the ugly media attention that she, Julia, and Adaline had received over the years, one can't rule this out. Of course, the Pences may have attended the funeral but chose not to enter the area marked off for relatives. They may have wanted to remain hidden from both the press and any white Johnson family members in attendance. Considering how Richard's white relations had behaved during his final illness, and how they had treated Imogene and Julia over the years, including wanting to sell them when she was born, she may not have wanted to see the white Johnsons at her father's funeral.

Anna Claypoole Peale (American, 1791–1878), *Colonel Richard M. Johnson*, 1818. Watercolor on ivory, 6.98 × 5.46 cm (2¾ × 2⅛ in.). Museum of Fine Arts, Boston, Emma F. Monroe Fund, 68.619. This pendant remained in the Pence family until it was sold by Brenda Brent Wilfert's grandfather.

Photograph © 2023 Museum of Fine Arts, Boston.

There is another possibility. Perhaps Imogene didn't attend her father's funeral because she was angry with him. She may have been relieved that he was dead. It's possible that what happened to her cousin Parthene marked her in ways unseen. Maybe she blamed Richard for Adaline's death. The fact that she named her firstborn son after her father and wore a locket painted with Richard's image (which she passed down to her children) suggests she was close to him, but that could have been a facade Imogene maintained to ensure the financial stability of her family. In this, as in other things, she may have been her mother's daughter.[19] Or maybe Imogene both loved and resented Richard. Families are nothing if not complicated. And sometimes, death brings freedom to the living.

Richard's death in 1850 marked the closing of an era in Kentucky politics. It wasn't the end of the story of his and Julia's family, however. Thirty-eight years old, Imogene Johnson Pence was still living in Scott County the year her father passed away, as she had since her birth in 1812. And while Adaline Johnson Scott had died in 1836 at the age of twenty-two, she left behind a husband, Thomas West Scott, and one son, Robert Johnson Scott, born around 1834. Although the two branches of the family would part ways the year after Richard died, a unique set of circumstances continued to connect them. Both lines of the Chinn-Johnson family tree began in prosperity, carrying forth the inheritance so carefully crafted for them by their mother and grandmother, Julia. Additionally, although everyone knew that Imogene and Adaline Johnson were Julia and Richard's daughters, and the newspapers had spent years dragging the Johnson women through the mud for being Black, by 1850, the Scott and Pence descendants had crossed the color line and were living as white people. One branch of the family did this away from Kentucky, in Illinois and Missouri. The other did it at home, in Scott County. Both sets of family members had the privileges of light skin, freedom, education, and wealth to aid in their transition. But what led them to take such measures? What did they gain by passing for white? And what, if anything, did they lose in the process?

Thomas West Scott continued to live at Blue Spring Farm after Adaline's death in 1836, and he helped manage affairs there along with Imogene's husband, Daniel Pence. Thomas remained close to his father-in-law even after remarrying in December 1840, taking a local white woman, Catherine Fitzgerald, as his new bride. Born a mile from Lexington in October 1822, Catherine was the daughter of a slaveholding farmer and only eighteen years old when she married Thomas, then thirty-two. Despite the new marriage, Richard transferred another piece of land to Thomas in the late 1840s. This land was specifically meant to provide for Thomas's oldest son, the only living child that Adaline had given birth to before she passed away. This was Julia and Richard's grandson Robert Johnson Scott, named for Richard's father.[20]

By 1850, Thomas, now forty-one and a farmer by trade, was still living in Scott County with Catherine, then twenty-seven. That year Thomas owned $32,000 in real estate (over $1.2 million in 2023 dollars) and thirteen enslaved laborers. The couple headed a large household that included Catherine's seventy-four-year-old mother, Lucretia Fitzgerald, and seven children: Helen, aged nine; Josephine, six; Eugene, four; Mary, three; Thomas W., two; and baby Catherine, seven months old. The oldest child in the house was Robert, Adaline's son, who was sixteen that year. Along with the rest of the family, Robert's racial designation on the census was left blank, which meant he was coded as white.[21]

In 1851, shortly after Richard's death, the Scott family pulled up stakes and moved to Rushville, Illinois. It's unclear why they left Kentucky, but Thomas had lived in Rushville when he was younger, before he married Adaline. Additionally, his parents had relocated to Illinois from Kentucky in 1832, the same year that Thomas and Adaline were wed.[22] It's possible that Thomas wanted to be near his aging parents or that he was looking for a fresh start after Richard died. Perhaps he wanted to give his oldest son the chance to be judged on his merits and abilities, not his lineage. Regardless of the census records, everyone in the area knew that Robert's maternal grandmother, Julia Chinn, had been an enslaved Black woman.

By 1860, Thomas, who was fifty-one that year, was still farming, although he also ran a general loan and brokerage business in Rushville. He owned $28,200 worth of real estate and $2,500 in personal property. Catherine was thirty-seven and there were eight children living at home. They ranged from sixteen-year-old Josephine to two-year-old Mentor Scott, who was almost certainly named for Richard Mentor Johnson. Helen, now nineteen, no longer lived with Thomas and Catherine. She may have been married by this time and living with her husband. Adaline's son, Robert Johnson Scott, was also missing from Thomas and Catherine's household in 1860. Robert, who would have been twenty-six that year, was likely married and in his own home by this point, like his half-sister Helen.[23]

While it's not clear where Robert was living in 1860, ten years later he was in Brookfield Township in Linn County, Missouri. That year Robert J. Scott, a thirty-five-year-old white man who was born in Kentucky, was working as a physician. Although he wasn't as wealthy as his father, he owned real estate valued at $4,000 (almost $92,000 in 2023 dollars) and had personal goods worth another $2,050. There were four other people living in the Scott household that year, including Robert's second wife and three children. His wife, Emma, was white, and she was nineteen years old. Born in New York, her occupation was "keeping house," and she was stepmother to Robert's three young children from his first marriage: Edward Bion, who was eleven years old; Thomas Frederic, aged nine years; and Fannie (later Frances), who was seven. All three children had been born in Illinois, and both boys were in school in 1870. Robert had thus lived in Illinois until at least 1863, given his daughter's age. It's possible that he relocated to Missouri after the death of his first wife, hoping to start over.[24]

Robert Johnson Scott wed at least once more during his life, marrying a woman named Maud Crawford on September 11, 1880.[25] He was single when the census takers came by earlier that year, however, because Emma had already passed away. Still in Brookfield, Robert listed his age as forty-three and his birth date as "ca. 1837."[26] Given that his mother, Adaline Johnson Scott, died in 1836, this is incorrect. While it's possible that he didn't know his exact birth date, it's more likely that Robert did this deliberately: he hadn't made such errors in the past, and he had listed his age on the 1870 census as thirty-five, not thirty-three.[27] He may have been trying to erase any connection to his Black mother and to his enslaved grandmother, Julia Chinn. The social context of the day would have given him ample cause to hide his personal history.

The end of the Civil War had given Black folks hope that things would improve for formerly enslaved people in the United States. Radical Republicans initially appeared to be committed to what could be called Black Reconstruction: legal, political, economic, and social justice for African Americans in a reformed United States. The passage of the Thirteenth Amendment outlawing slavery, followed by the Fourteenth Amendment, which established citizenship for Black people, and then the Fifteenth Amendment, which gave Black men the right to vote, suggested that a new day was coming. As the years went on, however, it became clear that northern whites were more committed to a quick, political reconstruction of the North and the South, which would enable the nation to move toward economic prosperity. The federal government, weary of hearing about equality and justice for Black people, focused on forgetting the war and making money.

The increase in lynchings and rapes against Black people by white supremacist groups; laws disenfranchising Black voters, including literacy tests, poll taxes, and grandfather clauses; segregation policies; a lack of employment and educational opportunities for formerly enslaved people; fraudulent sharecropping contracts; and wholesale stealing of elections by southern Democrats all signaled to African Americans that little had changed since 1860. The deal crafted between Republicans and Democrats in 1877 to ensure that Rutherford B. Hayes won the presidency, which included pulling the last of the Union troops out of the South, was the final nail in the coffin. The era known as Political Reconstruction came to an end; southern Blacks understood that they had been abandoned. As the Freedmen's Bureau was dismantled, what little help Black folks had been receiving in the form of direct aid and legal help from the federal government vanished. Southern "Redemption" had arrived, and with it came the "one-drop rule" of racial (re)construction and the formal outlawing of interracial sex. A large portion of the nation was no longer safe for anyone with any Black ancestry, no matter how small or how far removed—if it had ever really been safe at all.[28]

The larger US social context in the 1870s may help explain why Robert Johnson Scott, who lived in a former slave state, distanced himself from his Kentucky kinfolk and from his deceased Black mother and enslaved Black grandmother in particular. This was the New South. Jim Crow America. Robert was educated and propertied. He had married more than one white woman, and he had several white-presenting children enrolled in Missouri schools. A practicing physician, he had lived his entire adult life as a white man. Under the new order, however, if Robert's lineage were discovered, his whole existence, and that of his children, would instantly change. His home, his medical practice, his marriage, and potentially his very life could be taken away. He could lose everything he had built. Because the one-drop rule would code him and his children as Black. The hammer of segregation would come down on them. Instantly.

Robert had a lot to lose. When the census was taken in early 1880, Robert, widowed for the second time, was still working as a physician. He also headed up a household of ten persons, including four of his own children: (Edward) Bion, aged twenty-one; (Thomas) Frederic, eighteen; (Fannie) Frances, fifteen; and Ira, the only child born in Missouri, who was nine. Given Ira's age and place of birth, Emma, Robert's second wife, was probably his mother. Bion and Frederic, now using their middle names, were still in school, although all four Scott children had attended classes that year. In addition to his children, three members of the Bond family lived with Robert. They were thirty-two-year-old Henrietta Bond, a white female servant, and her two daughters, Emma, aged seven, and five-year-old Hattie. The children were both listed as boarders. Two other servants, a white woman named Emma Scrivner and a white man named Sylvester Trowbridge, both of whom were twenty years old, rounded out the Scott household that year. Robert was clearly a man of means: not only did he practice medicine, but he also sent his children to school and retained no fewer than three, white, live-in servants to help keep his home running. One has to wonder if Robert refused to hire Black servants because of his own background. He may have had moral objections to having African Americans labor for him, given his family's heritage of slavery. Regardless, Robert lived a life of privilege, all of which would have disappeared, or been greatly altered, had his connection to Julia Chinn and Adaline Johnson been discovered.[29]

Twenty years later, "R. J. Scott" was still practicing medicine in Missouri. That year, Robert, widowed yet again, owned his home, free and clear. Now aged sixty-two, according to the census, Robert was the head of an eight-person household. Living with him in 1900 were his children by his third wife, Maud. They were daughter A. J. Scott, aged sixteen; son Stone J. Scott, who at thirteen was already a farm laborer; Robert Bruce Scott, ten; and Ruth R. Scott, who was seven. Robert's son from his second marriage, Ira, was also living at home that year. Ira was now twenty-nine and a farm laborer, like young Stone. Maggie Scott, Ira's thirty-five-year-old, Scottish-born wife, and the housekeeper, Ella Haight, aged thirty-two, were the final two members of the household.[30]

It's curious that full names were recorded for everyone in the Scott home that year except for daughter A. J. and Robert himself. A. J.'s initials are suggestive. It's very likely that she was named to honor Robert's deceased mother, Adaline Johnson Scott. Her middle name could have also been Julia. Robert's desire to keep this information out of the census may have prompted him to list his daughter by her initials. It might also explain why he began using his own initials instead of his full name. It's possible that he was trying to hide his connection to the Johnsons. If so, it would reveal a deep fear of even the most tenuous link to his Black past, despite naming his daughter Adaline. In a nation that had recently committed itself to segregation via the *Plessy v. Ferguson* decision, federally enshrining "separate but equal" as the law of the land, Robert may have decided that no risk was worth taking, no matter how small.[31]

The year 1900 was the last time that Adaline's son appeared in the federal census records. The *Directory of Deceased American Physicians, 1804–1929*, states that R. J. Scott, born in 1838, was an "allopath" who died in Brookfield, Missouri, on December 11, 1905, from "angina pectoris." In layman's terms, this means that Robert Johnson Scott, who was actually about seventy-one years old when he died (not sixty-seven, as listed), was a regularly trained medical doctor and that he died of a heart attack.[32]

Had Adaline and Julia been alive, one can assume that they would have been proud of the fact that Robert became a physician. An educated man, he was a property owner, his children went to school, and he was successful enough to employ white servants. One wonders, of course, how his mother and grandmother would have felt about the fact that Robert was living undercover as a white man in Missouri, far removed from his kin. They certainly would have understood how difficult life was for Black men in Jim Crow America, given everything they themselves had experienced. Maybe that's why Robert didn't stay in Scott County when his family moved to Illinois. He was seventeen at the time. He didn't have to leave, but perhaps he didn't want to remain in a place where everyone knew he was Julia Chinn's grandson. That might also explain why he didn't stay in Rushville, where people knew he was born of Thomas Scott's first marriage to a Black woman. Moving to a place where he had no family and changing his date of birth might have been the only way out that Robert could see: the one way he could be a doctor, marry whom he wanted, and give his children a more secure future. The way to be truly free. It's curious, however, that at least two of his sons appear to have been working not as professionals but as farm laborers in 1900, despite the educational and racial advantages their father was able to give them by cutting the ties to his own history and heritage.

Julia Chinn, an enslaved Black woman whose choices were constrained due to time, place, and social position, would have understood Robert's desire to help his children. Like her own mother before her, she strove to make the world bigger for her daughters than it was for her, ensuring they were educated, propertied, and married to men who had access to legal citizenship. Her grandson's story in some ways thus stands as a continuation of that narrative of upward social mobility. It was Julia's sacrifices that made his achievements possible. His existence, however, is also a testimony to the realities of the one-drop rule and life under segregation. R. J. Scott was a man who could never go home, for fear of discovery. Not to Illinois, and not to Kentucky. The violence of Jim Crow, anti-Blackness, and white supremacy forced Robert to choose a life of secrecy and lies as opposed to one surrounded by his family of origin. We have no way of knowing if he felt the trade-off was worth it or if he sometimes ached for all he had lost, fearing that he may have "sold his birthright for a mess of pottage."[33]

Unlike her younger sister, Imogene Johnson Pence lived to a ripe old age. And while Adaline's branch of the family left Kentucky in 1851, Imogene's remained there for a good long while. She had married a man from a local family named Daniel B. Pence in June 1830, when she was just eighteen. The couple then moved to a large piece of land adjacent to Imogene's childhood home at Blue Spring Farm, land given to them by Julia and Richard shortly after the pair wed. It was here that they built a neoclassical, two-story brick house that is still standing today; here that they made their home for the next five decades; and here that they raised their family. While two of the couple's children died young, the other four grew to reach adulthood.[34]

The training and well-being of their children was of utmost importance to Imogene and Daniel, so much so that they built a schoolhouse on their property, hired a private teacher who lived with them, and had their children educated at home. It makes sense that Imogene, who was educated at Blue Spring by Thomas Henderson when he was the headmaster of Choctaw Academy, preferred not to send her children away to school. When the Pence children were young, white mobs burned several free Black schools in the region. As for sending them to a white school, that could have led to harassment from children and teachers alike. Everyone in Scott County knew the Pence family's background, and Imogene, like Julia and Richard before her, would have wanted to protect her children from any racism or violence.[35]

The Pence Family Farm, aerial view, Georgetown, Kentucky.

Image courtesy of the Brenda Brent Wilfert private collection.

In addition to being the place where they raised and educated their children, their home was also where the Pence family conducted business. Daniel was a farmer, and the Pences used slave labor to work their plantation. This isn't surprising: Daniel's father, George, owned slaves, although he appears to have never held more than three persons at one time. In fact, by 1840, George Pence owned no enslaved laborers at all.[36] Daniel's in-laws, however, were slaveholders on a different scale. As early as 1810, Richard Mentor Johnson owned twelve people. This number only grew over the years. By 1820, Julia and Richard owned seventy-two laborers, and in 1830, the couple owned forty-five enslaved persons, sixteen of whom were women between ten and thirty-five years of age. Several of those women, then, would have been of childbearing age.[37] Julia and Richard transferred some of their human chattel to Imogene and Daniel when the younger couple wed in 1830, at the same time that they gave them the land on which they lived. The Pences needed workers to toil in the hemp and tobacco fields that made up the bulk of Kentucky's agricultural production. This explains the sharp decrease in the number of bondspersons the Johnsons owned that year as compared to 1820.[38]

These gifts from her parents meant that Imogene and her husband began married life from a position of financial strength, which they were able to build on and pass down to their children. The fact is that the wealth, status, and very freedom of Imogene Johnson Pence and her children, who were themselves descended from enslaved Black people, was grounded in the captivity and sweat of other Black people. In the Old South, power and position rested on real property: land and laborers. Julia Chinn spent her entire life sacrificing and negotiating to ensure that her daughters would never have to work for other people. That they would never *be* property but that they would, instead, *hold* property. In this, she succeeded. It is a sad testament to the reality of the society in which Julia and Imogene lived that wealth was predicated on and in Black bodies. That to secure the safety, freedom, and financial health of their own families, Black people in the antebellum South often had to be willing to hold other Black people in bondage. This was the twisted core of racial capitalism and white supremacy laid bare.

Information from Imogene's account ledger reveals that she and Daniel began transferring property to their fifteen-year-old daughter, Amanda Malvina, and her new husband, Robert M. Lee, a farmer, in 1848. While much of what they gave the pair were household goods including silverware, dishes, bedding, and furniture, Imogene and Daniel also gave the young couple cash and real property that would be critical to their long-term success. This included livestock—and seven enslaved laborers. Ranging in age from two-year-old Isaiah to twenty-two-year-old Sarah and twenty-three-year-old Jack, the bondspersons the Lees acquired comprised five young children, who would become good workers, and a young couple instantly able to toil in the fields and who had years of reproductive productivity ahead of them. Sarah and Jack could have been a married couple, happy to be moving to a new home together, or they, and any of the children who came with them, could have been torn from existing familial structures. There is no way to know. What we do know is that the value of the seven persons totaled $2,600, about $99,000 in 2023 dollars.[39]

Amanda Malvina, who went by her middle name, wasn't the only Pence child to benefit from her parents' wealth and generosity. Her sister, Mary Jane, and her husband, Josiah Pence (the couple were second cousins), also received help from Imogene and Daniel. In 1850, fifteen-year-old Mary Jane and her farmer husband acquired goods that helped the newlyweds set up their first home, including furniture, silver, candlesticks, carpeting, bedding, and towels. Like her sister, Mary Jane also acquired horses, mules, and cows, along with seven enslaved laborers. The market value of those seven people came to $2,550, only fifty dollars less than the value of the workers given to Malvina. Unlike her sister, however, Mary

Jane received six young children, ranging in age from two-year-old Richard and five-year-old Silas all the way up to twelve-year-old Allen and thirteen-year-old Bluford. The latter two children could have been put in the fields on arrival, while Silas might have begun training as a houseboy. Only one adult was transferred to Mary Jane: twenty-year-old Eliza. While she would need a partner to reproduce, Eliza had many childbearing years ahead of her, and she would have been able to perform a range of domestic and agricultural chores for Mary Jane and Josiah as soon as she arrived. It's unknown whether Eliza was taken from a husband or other family members on Imogene and Daniel's farm when she was given to Mary Jane; whether the young children transferred with her were related to her in any way; or whom these bondspersons may have been forced to leave behind when they had to move.[40]

Not only were Imogene and Daniel wealthy, but they, like Julia and Richard before them, were generous to their daughters and grandchildren. Malvina's oldest child, Mary Elizabeth, was born June 23, 1851. Sometimes called Lizzie, Imogene's granddaughter married a man named Virgil W. Easley in 1868. In 1870, Imogene and Daniel gave Lizzie a set of chairs as well as seventeen dollars in unspecified "different articles." Four years later, "Mary Easley" received $500 from her grandparents, "by the wish of her Mother, Malvina Lee," and when Mary's house burned down, her grandparents helped her start over, providing furniture, food, livestock, and funds so she could purchase a new home.[41]

Similarly, Mary Jane's daughter Annie (born Anna Mary Pence on May 21, 1857) was given ten dollars' worth of goods by her grandparents in 1869, while her brother Willie (born William H. Pence on May 13, 1852) received a cow and a horse in 1870.[42] When Annie married James L. Jackson in November 1875, she received $100 in cash from her grandparents to purchase furniture and "wedding clothes," as well as eight sheep and an assortment of towels, linens, and bedding. Over the next few years, Imogene and Daniel gave "Annie Jackson" gifts of cash, as well as a variety of household goods, meat, livestock, and "the rent of the mill" one year. The rent money alone amounted to $200. As late as 1879, the year Imogene's account book ends, the Pences were still providing their kinfolk with gifts of cash and livestock.[43]

It's important to note that among the practical gifts of livestock and housewares that the Pences passed down to their daughters and grandchildren, they also transferred items that were status symbols. These included things such as buggies and gold watches. Even the household goods were made of high-quality materials, including mahogany furniture, silver tableware, ornate clocks, store-bought carpets, and "fine" blankets.[44] It would have been important for Imogene in particular to ensure that her descendants owned things that reflected their wealth and social standing. She surely remembered how their neighbors, and the antebellum press, made constant, ugly comments about the Johnson women's elegant dresses and about the fact that Julia and her daughters had the nerve to ride around in carriages, as if they were the equals of white women.[45] Passing down mahogany furniture, gold jewelry, and buggies to her kin was thus a fairly pointed statement to the larger community that the Pences were a family of worth and respectability, equal to their white neighbors in every way.

While the younger members of the family likely appreciated everything they received from Imogene and Daniel, the most significant item the senior Pences transferred to their daughters, apart from enslaved laborers, was land. In the Old South, "real" property was everything. Wealth was measured in terms of how much real property one owned, which meant bondspersons, houses, and land. While household items enhanced the quality of one's daily life, it was real property that made you a plantation owner and a slaveholder. These were the highest social statuses one could attain in the Old South, and with them came privilege and protection. It was unlikely that your neighbors would see you as a threat to the southern way of life if you were integrated into that way of life as a slaveholding plantation owner. This kind of cover would be especially important for mixed-race families such as the Pences, who traced their ancestry back to an enslaved Black woman.

That the elder Pences had enough money to buy prime farmland and enslaved laborers for their daughters as wedding gifts is significant. It's also worth noting that the land they acquired was Johnson family property. When Thomas W. Scott, Adaline's husband, moved to Illinois in 1851, he still owned thirteen enslaved persons and $32,000 worth of land in Scott County (over $1.25 million in 2023 currency). This included Blue Spring Farm, Imogene and Adaline's childhood home.[46] Imogene and Daniel purchased part of the Blue Spring property for their daughter Malvina and her husband, Robert Lee, for $6,270 ($242,000 in 2023 dollars) and paid for it in five installments between January 1850 and January 1854. Imogene and Daniel also bought land from Thomas for their daughter Mary Jane and her husband, Josiah. They began making payments on that land in 1854 and finished paying on it in 1857 for a total of $4,034. When added to land they purchased from Daniel's side of the family for $1,908, the land Imogene and Daniel gave to Mary Jane was valued at $5,942, just $328 less than the land they had purchased for Malvina.[47]

There's no question the Pences were wealthy if they could afford to be so generous to their daughters. It's also clear that they wanted to keep Blue Spring in the family and assure their children a place among the South's landed gentry. The information from Imogene's account book, compelling on its own, is reinforced by data from the US census. In 1850, Imogene and Daniel owned thirty enslaved laborers, ranging in age from a nine-month-old girl to a forty-eight-year-old man. Of these thirty persons, fourteen were adults and sixteen children. Bondspersons over fourteen years of age were considered to be adults and classified as "full hands." Additionally, the group was split almost down the middle in terms of gender: there were fourteen male hands and sixteen female hands. This distribution held across generations: there were seven adult men, seven adult women, nine girls, and seven boys. Not only did Imogene and Daniel have a labor force that was currently productive; they were raising future workers who would be able to perform various tasks as young as age six, and they had a group that was positioned to reproduce. In fact, with five women already aged eighteen or older, and three fully grown men among their laborers, the Pences could look forward to years of productive reproduction.[48]

This was a valuable labor force. Using the prices provided in the account book (from the transfers of enslaved persons to their daughters) as a guide, the Pences' bondspeople appear to have been worth roughly $12,000 in 1850, or about $463,000 in 2023 currency. That is more than twice the amount of wealth in laborers than what the couple transferred to Malvina and Mary Jane together.[49] And this wasn't the entirety of their property, since it doesn't account for personal goods or real estate. In 1850, Imogene and Daniel controlled land valued at $30,000. Malvina and Robert, who lived with Malvina's parents that year, owned real estate worth $6,000 (or $231,000 in 2023 dollars). Imogene and Daniel's estate in 1850, without the inclusion of any personal property, was thus worth $42,000. That would be about $1.62 million in 2023 currency.[50]

The senior Pences weren't comfortable or well-to-do—they were millionaires by today's standards. And they were millionaires not just because they were landowners but because they were slaveholders. It was enslaved labor that had allowed Robert and Jemima Suggett Johnson to work and expand their original land grant, pass land on to their children, arrange advantageous marriages for their offspring, and turn the Johnson clan into one of the most powerful families in all of Kentucky. It was enslaved labor that had enabled their son Richard Mentor Johnson to work the land at Blue Spring, entertain in lavish style, maintain a Native American boarding school, get out of debt by mortgaging his bondspeople, live away from his farm for six months every year, and provide substantial dowries for his daughters by Julia Chinn. And it was enslaved labor that provided those same daughters and their families with land, workers, social status, and the money to purchase luxury goods. The enslaved labor of a mother whose sacrifices helped them acquire their education, their positions, and their very freedom.

The history of this nation is such that the freedom of some Black southerners was birthed, shaped, and solidified by the continued bondage of others, those with whom they ought to have shared common cause but from whom they were separated by the twisted structures of white supremacy. One couldn't keep up one's land in the South without workers. And the workers were enslaved. One also couldn't become an open abolitionist in the Old South. Not if one wanted to remain free. Or alive. So some Black people became enslavers. They focused on what they felt was best for their families. They weren't thinking about the larger Black "community," and they weren't revolutionaries trying to overthrow the system. Neither heroes nor victims, instead these folks worked to secure their own positions and survive within the system in a time and place where their options were limited. Because from their perspective, there seemed to be no other way up. Or out.

The fortunes of the extended Pence family continued to prosper after 1850. By 1860, Mary Jane and Josiah were living in their own home and had four children. Mary Jane was a "housekeeper," a stay-at-home wife and mother. The family had nine enslaved laborers and owned $20,000 in real estate and another $6,000 in personal property. Valued at $942,400 in 2023 currency, the estate likely included the seven enslaved persons transferred to the younger couple by the senior Pences in 1850 and the Blue Spring land purchased for them from Thomas Scott. Malvina and her husband, Robert, had also improved their position by 1860. That year, the Lees, also living on their own, had a daughter named Mary, owned $8,200 in real estate, and held $6,900 in personal property. The estate, worth roughly $547,300 in 2023, would have included their thirteen enslaved laborers (counting the seven people that Imogene and Daniel gave them in 1848) as well as the piece of Blue Spring property purchased for them from Thomas Scott. Like her sister, Malvina was also a "housekeeper."[51]

Imogene, fifty-eight, and Daniel, sixty-five, were doing well in 1860. That year, the couple owned seventeen laborers, $46,000 in real estate, and $5,600 in personal property. Ten years later, when many former slaveholders had been bankrupted by the Civil War, the senior Pences held real property assessed at $43,350 and personal property worth $5,700. This was still a loss. The total value of Imogene and Daniel's property in 1860 was $51,600, about $1.87 million in 2023 currency. In 1870, their property was appraised at $49,050, or $1.13 million in 2023 currency. The couple were still millionaires by our standards, able to hire three male farm laborers to work for them. Two of these men were Black, and all three lived with the Pences. Imogene and Daniel's household also contained three domestic servants that year, all of whom were Black women. This was in addition to the couple's two sons: Frank, who was twenty, and Edward, who was twelve and still in school. Despite the disruptions of the Civil War and the devaluation of the US dollar, Imogene and Daniel were still wealthy, and their land and home continued to be maintained by Black labor.[52]

The war led to varying degrees of financial loss for all the Pences. In 1870, Mary Jane and Josiah still had four children at home. William was eighteen and worked as a farm laborer, while Anna, thirteen, was in school. Daniel and Emma, seven and two, respectively, didn't yet attend school. The family still owned $20,000 in real estate, but their personal property only amounted to $2,650. Their estate would be worth about $520,000 in 2023 currency. The junior Pences had thus lost about 45 percent of the value of their estate in the decade following the Civil War. Malvina and Robert Lee fared a bit better. In 1870, the couple had only one child, six-year-old Robert, living with them, and while their personal goods were worth only $1,300, they owned $17,800 in real property. Their $19,100 estate would be worth roughly $438,600 in 2023 dollars. Malvina's family had thus lost roughly 20 percent of the value of their estate since 1860. Although this was better than Mary Jane's household, it was still a substantial loss.[53]

While Imogene, Daniel, Mary Jane, Josiah, and Amanda Malvina all appear in the 1880 census, there is no information on property or estates in that census. That year, sixty-eight-year-old Imogene and seventy-six-year-old Daniel lived with their two grown sons: Frank, who was thirty, and Edward, who was twenty-one. Both men were farmers, like their father. Mary Jane, who was forty-five, and Josiah, fifty, had several of their children living with them in 1880, including twenty-eight-year-old William, who worked as a miller; eighteen-year-old Daniel B., a farmer; and Emma, who was thirteen. Their twenty-two-year-old daughter, Anna Jackson, and her thirty-year-old husband, James Jackson, a farmer, also lived with them. Rounding out the household were a twelve-year-old Black houseboy named Stephen Brown; a twenty-year-old Black house girl, Ellen Mitchell; and Ellen's three-year-old daughter, Alice. Malvina, who was forty-eight and widowed, lived with her two sons: five-year-old D. Franklin and fifteen-year-old Robert, both of whom farmed and went to school. The final member of their home was the cook, a forty-year-old Black woman named Ellen Stepp.[54]

The Pences were still doing well in 1880: the men farmed their own land, the children went to school, and they had Black women and men working for them. This might explain why, despite the increasing racial prejudice after the end of Reconstruction, they decided to stay in Kentucky. Their wealth and local connections gave them opportunities in Scott County they wouldn't necessarily find elsewhere. Josiah Pence, for example, developed and patented a horse-drawn seed-gatherer, and he later helped Cyrus McCormick invent the mechanical reaper, which helped revolutionize agricultural production. He and Mary Jane lived comfortably, and they entertained famous, and infamous, guests at their home, including Frank and Jesse James. The Jameses' parents were from nearby Stamping Ground, and though Frank and Jesse grew up in Missouri, they came back to Kentucky to visit family and friends. Two of Josiah's brothers were members of the James gang, having ridden with Frank and Jesse during the Civil War, which brought the Jameses into the Pences' orbit.[55]

Their money and connections didn't just enable the Pence family to live and entertain in style. These things also allowed them to cross the color line and live as white people. As early as 1850, Imogene, Daniel, and all of their children appear in the US census records as white persons—not free people of color, but white.[56] This occurred at the height of antebellum slavery, in their home county, where everyone knew that Imogene was the daughter of Julia Chinn and Richard Mentor Johnson and where the newspapers had spent decades dragging Julia, Imogene, and Adaline through the mud for being Black. Daniel Pence, of course, *was* white, although many of his peers felt he had lost his membership in the race when he stooped so low as to marry the daughter of an enslaved woman. It's possible that the census takers in Scott County were strangers who didn't know, or couldn't tell, that Imogene and her children had African ancestry. Or perhaps they knew but quietly decided to list everyone in the household as white. Of course, depending on what percentage of African heritage Imogene and her children had, they may have *been* white under the law in antebellum Kentucky. Given that Julia died enslaved, however, unless Imogene was formally manumitted by Richard, technically speaking, she and her children would have been enslaved until the Thirteenth Amendment was passed after the end of the Civil War.[57]

Although census takers listed all the members of the Pence family as white, that doesn't necessarily mean that their neighbors saw them as white. Working from the understanding that race is socially constructed, the question is only partly about whether Imogene and her children conducted themselves as or believed themselves to be white people. The other part hinges on whether the white community accepted them as white persons, thus completing the construction. In the Old South, embracing racially mixed or ethnically ambiguous persons as white was done on a case-by-case basis and was grounded in large part on a person's performance of respectability.[58] Evidence from postwar Kentucky suggests that many of the same folks who had once behaved as if Julia, Imogene, and Adaline were nothing short of lepers decided, at the very least, to ignore Imogene and her lineage. Others became sincere friends of the Pences. Their shift in behavior was due in no small part to Imogene's decades-long labors as a wife and mother of impeccable Christian virtue and exemplary moral character.

CHAPTER SEVEN

Great Crossings merchant Maj. Fabricus C. McCalla was among those white locals who became close friends with the Pences. The major lived at Longview, the plantation that had once belonged to Richard M. Johnson. He knew the Pences well and considered them to be neighbors and friends. McCalla wrote to Daniel the year before the major passed away. In his letter McCalla, who had been ill and housebound, reached out to Imogene and Daniel for cabbages, saying that it was easy for him to ask for such a thing because the Pences always made him feel that if he had something they wanted, they would not hesitate to ask. He went on to say:

> It is so pleasant to have Friends near in whom you have perfect confidence and implicit trust! How the hardships and troubles of life are lessened and divided by the aid and services of true friends and also the joys and blessings of life increased and multiplied by having Friends to impart them to and enjoy them with us. I have been wonderfully blessed in the number and character of the dear, kind friends God has raised up around me and I try to feel grateful and thank him daily for so blessing me—and oh if I could feel worthy of them I would be so happy, but they are my friends, nevertheless, and among them all I do not feel that I have any worthier or truer or more generous and kind than you and your highly esteemed wife.

McCalla ended by sending the family his Christmas wishes and said if his niece's chicken salad came out to his liking, he would send some to Mrs. Pence, but that it would have to be "mighty nice in my judgment if I do so."[59] McCalla clearly respected Daniel and Imogene. The couple, who had his confidence and trust, were his "true friends." It's hard to imagine how he could have paid Imogene any greater compliment than when he referred to her as Daniel's "highly esteemed wife," someone who deserved the very best, even if the item in question was chicken salad.

The major wasn't the only person who held Imogene and Daniel in high regard. On August 20, 1873, Rev. Richard Montgomery Gano baptized Imogene and Daniel along with their son Daniel Franklin Pence (Frank) and their granddaughter Anna Mary Pence. Gano then baptized their daughter Mary Jane in 1886. The son of John Allen Gano, one of the first Baptist ministers in Kentucky, Richard Montgomery Gano was born in June 1830 and served at the First Christian Church in Georgetown. He was, at various points in his life, a physician, an ordained minister, a farmer, a politician, and during the Civil War, a brigadier general in the Confederate army. Gano was, then, a high-ranking former Confederate officer.

And given that he was born, raised, and educated in Kentucky, he would have known Imogene's family history. But he still baptized her and her descendants. By 1873, Gano apparently felt that the manner in which Imogene conducted herself was more important than her mother's status as an enslaved person or than the fact that the Pences would have been seen by many folks as an interracial family in the face of rising segregationist ideas and one-drop policies. It is, in many ways, reminiscent of how Silas Noel had treated Julia Chinn and her daughters so many years before, at Great Crossing Baptist Church.[60]

Imogene's devotion to God appears to have been sincere and well known. When she passed away in 1883, the editors of the *Georgetown Weekly Times* ran a very complimentary obituary. According to the paper, Imogene, who was almost seventy-two when she died, "had been an invalid for many years." Despite this, she "bore her afflictions with Christian fortitude" and always "expressed a willingness to go at any time her Savior might call her." An "exemplary member of the Christian Church, a devoted mother, faithful wife, and a woman of rare intellectual attainments," Imogene was laid to rest on the Pence farm, surrounded by a "large circle of friends" who came to pay their last respects.[61] The Stamping Ground paper reported on October 17 that Elder H. W. Ford had preached the funeral service for Imogene on October 14. It concluded by letting its readers know that the deceased was "a lady of rare and gifted intellectual attainments, and highly respected by all who knew her."[62]

Shunned by white people as a child, homeschooled in secret, and humiliated by the press for the first thirty years of her life, Imogene Johnson Pence apparently spent the last three decades of her life as a "highly respected" white woman and beloved member of her community. An "exemplary" Christian "lady" with many friends, Imogene was applauded for all the things that nineteenth-century white women were supposed to be. She never complained about her troubles, loved the Lord, was devoted to her children, and was a faithful helpmeet to her husband. She was also "a lady of rare and gifted intellectual attainments." Given how both papers phrased it, this was uncommon and thus worth noting. It seems that by the time she died, her white peers in Scott County had come to see Imogene the way that Rev. Thomas Henderson had back in 1837, when he wrote that Adaline and Imogene had an "uncommon aptness . . . to take learning" and that they were "so decent, modest, and unassuming" in their conduct that his "mind became much enlisted in their favor." He thus continued to teach them "until their education was equal or superior to most of the females in the country."[63]

Imogene's loss was mourned by many, none more so than her husband and children. Buried in the family cemetery on the Pence farm, the inscription on her headstone made it clear how much her family valued her:

CHAPTER SEVEN

IMOGENE

Beloved Wife of
DAN'L B. PENCE

BORN
Feb. 17, 1812

DIED
Oct. 4, 1883

Oh Mother dear a shore farewell
That we may meet again above
And rove where angels love to dwell
Where trees of life bear fruits of love.[64]

Imogene's performance of respectability had helped solidify her hold on whiteness. Marriage to a white man aided her family's transition across the color line, but for nineteenth-century women such as Imogene, education, wealth, motherhood, and religious piety were central in their quest for respectability, the construction of whiteness, and acceptance by their local white community. Unwavering in her commitment to her husband, to her children, and to her Savior, Imogene Johnson, born the daughter of an enslaved Black woman, died Imogene Pence, the free white wife of a free white man.

That man, Daniel B. Pence, never remarried, and he continued to live on the property that had been his home with Imogene for over fifty years. His family and neighbors remained close by; he needed their support as the years went on. His sight began to fail after his wife's death, and in June 1885, Daniel had a cataract removed from his right eye. Dr. Williams and Dr. Ayres, oculists who practiced in Cincinnati, performed the surgery.[65] Despite this procedure, at some point in the years before his death in 1891, Daniel B. Pence went completely blind. He was still interested in his farm, however, and in the health of his crops. His grandson William Collis Pence, the son of Frank Pence, remembers that as a boy, he would often lead his grandfather, "who was then blind and in old age, down from the house at Great Crossing to the fields to feel the ears of corn and how well they were coming in."[66]

When Daniel passed away on April 24, 1891, he was remembered in the *Georgetown Times* as an "Aged and Excellent Man." Eighty-six years old, Daniel B. Pence had once been reviled in the press as a man "greedy of money, but insensible to shame" for marrying Imogene Johnson, a Black woman and the daughter of a slave. In death he was lauded as "a good citizen, and punctual in all business affairs.

Headstone of Imogene J. Pence, Georgetown, Kentucky.

Image courtesy of the Pence Family private collection.

He was a member of the Christian Church, and for several years before his death had been totally blind. He was a warm friend of the TIMES.... Until his health began to fail, he never failed on the first day of January of each year... to call at the office and pay for his paper.... This was characteristic of his dealings with all men."[67] Elder Hiram Ford, who had preached at Imogene's funeral service, also conducted Daniel's funeral. And like his wife, Daniel was laid to rest in the family burial ground on the Pence farm. The men of his family, across generations, stood as his pallbearers. They included his son-in-law Josiah Pence; his oldest son, Frank Pence; his younger son, Edward H. Pence; his grandsons William H. Pence and Daniel B. Pence Jr.; and his grandson-in-law Virgil W. Easley.[68]

The last of his siblings to pass away, Daniel's death marked the end of yet another era.[69] While Julia and Richard's descendants continued on with their lives, right down to the present day, many, if not most, of the twentieth-century Pences would have no knowledge of the enslaved Black woman who pioneered their family line. Indeed, they had no idea that their family traced back to a vice president of the United States. National attitudes toward Blackness, slavery, and interracial

Headstone of Daniel B. Pence, Georgetown, Kentucky.

Image courtesy of the Pence Family private collection.

sex all played a role in erasing Julia Chinn and her daughters, Imogene Johnson Pence and Adaline Johnson Scott, from US history textbooks as well as from the memories of their own families. Anti-Black racism and white supremacy together worked to keep their stories buried for over a century.

While the Pences crossed the color line as far back as 1850, the family remained in Scott County, Kentucky, for many years. They knew the truth of their heritage, as did their neighbors. It was, as they say, an open secret. At some point, however, as younger Pences left Kentucky and struck out for other parts of the country, some folks decided to stop sharing the family story with their children and grandchildren. William Collis Pence remembered walking his grandfather, Daniel B. Pence, down to the fields. He shared those stories of his childhood at Great Crossing with his son, Frank Durham Pence.[70] Frank, however, like Robert Johnson Scott before him, left Kentucky, and he never told his children their family history while they were growing up. His daughters Margaret and Harriet, whom I was privileged to meet and interview for this book, had no knowledge of their Kentucky connections until they were grown women, married and with children of their own. The two sisters, who grew up in Cincinnati, Ohio, are the direct descendants of Julia Ann Chinn through Julia and Richard's oldest daughter, Imogene Johnson Pence, and her husband, Daniel B. Pence. Raised as white women, Margaret Pence Brooks and Harriet Pence Gray are Julia Chinn's great-great-great-granddaughters. They are also only five generations removed from slavery.[71]

The Chinn-Johnson-Pence saga is truly a tangled and somewhat tortuous web. Filled with pain, secrets, violence, and shame on the part of some folks because of the country's history of race-based chattel slavery and anti-Black racism, it is also a narrative of sacrifice, resilience, courage, and survival. It is the story of people like you and me: flawed, imperfect, human, and struggling to stay alive. To succeed. It's the story of women and men trying to make a better life for themselves and for their children, often at great costs. It is, at its core, the story of an American family.

EPILOGUE

PAST MEETS PRESENT

History and Memory

Born in *1939*, Brenda Brent Wilfert grew up in Lexington, Kentucky. She had no idea of her family's connection to Julia Chinn and Richard Johnson as a child, however. A white woman, she can't say for sure that this was because of race but admits it's possible because her mother, named Imogene, "was, shall we say, 'social minded.' My birthday parties were announced in the newspaper, and I went to social dancing school at the right age, and on to belong to the Junior Cotillion. My family didn't have any money, but we appreciated nice things, were attractive and intelligent."[1] I would say she's right; that race is what kept her mother and maternal grandmother, Grace Maria Pence Jackson, from telling Brenda and others in the family the truth about their ancestry. In a nation where Jim Crow raged and the one-drop rule was practiced, both by law and by custom, Brenda would have found it impossible to join the "right" sorority at the University of Kentucky in the late 1950s had she mentioned to people that her family traced its lineage back to a vice president and his enslaved Black wife.[2]

Although Brenda grew up just a few miles from Georgetown, she didn't know that she was related to Julia and Richard until she was a grown woman. She also didn't have any real interest in her family history until then, either. At some point in the mid-1980s she reached out to her uncle Claude Jackson, who lived in California, hoping to get his help identifying the people in some pictures she had. Brenda's mother had passed away in 1979, and since the photos were from her mother's side of the family, Brenda hoped that Claude, her mother's brother, might be of assistance. Although she hadn't had much contact with him over the years, Claude did send her some information. This included a partial sketch of the family tree, some pages copied from the Pence Family Bible (Pence was her maternal grandmother's maiden name), and photocopied pages from Leland Meyer's 1932 biography of a man named Richard Mentor Johnson. Brenda had never heard of Johnson before. According to Brenda, Claude acted like he was "telling tales out of school," admitting that the family had "partially Negro heritage."[3]

Brenda now knew that she was related to Richard Johnson, and that there was Black ancestry in her family, but the exact nature of it wasn't clear to her. She doesn't remember if she spoke to her uncle about Julia Chinn or if she read Meyer's book. What she does know is that when her father passed away years later in 1998, her stepmother, who was getting ready to sell their house, found a box of Brenda's mother's things up in the attic and sent them to her. It was this box that sent Brenda "down the rabbit hole." That box contained several items, including an album filled with unlabeled photographs, a leather wallet stamped with the words "D. B. Pence's Book, 1831," an 1872 letter to "Mr. Pence" from someone called "The Major," and a slave wanted ad/reward poster signed by D. B. Pence. Brenda, then almost sixty years old, went to work trying to identify the people in the photo album, uncover who "D. B. Pence" was, and figure out who "The Major" may have been.[4]

By the late 1990s, the internet had revolutionized the way people did research. Teaching herself how to use a computer at the age of sixty, Brenda went online to put together her family tree and used sites such as Ancestry to try to discover the identities of "The Major" and "D. B. Pence." Her research led her to a man named Richard Pence in Fairfax, Virginia, who had been collecting information on every US-born Pence for several years. He was a wealth of knowledge, and he put her in touch with distant cousins she had never met who lived near Cincinnati, Ohio. Descendants of her maternal grandmother Grace's brother, William Collis Pence, the Pence sisters Margaret and Harriet provided Brenda with information she had never seen, including data from the family Bible, account books, pictures, and more. The women eventually met in Kentucky and together they visited the Pence house in Great Crossing where Imogene Johnson Pence and Daniel Pence had lived with their children. It was the box in the attic, then, that helped Brenda Brent Wilfert finally put together the full story of her heritage and fill in

The Pence Family Farm, 1990s, Georgetown, Kentucky.

Image courtesy of the Pence Family private collection.

the missing pieces of her family tree, from Julia Ann Chinn and Richard Mentor Johnson down to the present day.[5]

Brenda's first cousin, William "Bill" French Jackson, stumbled upon his family history in an equally remarkable fashion. Bill's father was the Uncle Claude from Brenda's story. Claude Jackson was born and raised in Lexington, Kentucky, but Bill, born in 1948, moved to California when his parents divorced in 1950 and grew up in Los Angeles. He knew nothing of his family connections to Julia or Richard as a child. In 1976, his father came to see Bill, then living in the Washington, DC, area. During his visit, Claude randomly suggested to his son that they drive out to Kentucky to visit whatever family remained in the area, maybe go to some graveyards, and do some research on the family. The pair ended up spending a day in Georgetown and found themselves at the Georgetown Library and Historical Society. While there, they met some folks who helped them investigate their family tree. It was at the Georgetown Library and Historical Society on that day in 1976 that the two men discovered their connection to Julia Chinn and Richard Mentor Johnson. Bill was twenty-eight years old.[6]

One of the puzzling things about this story is that Claude Jackson was born and raised in Lexington. Born in 1913, Claude would have been living in the area with numerous other members of the Pence clan, all direct descendants of Julia and Richard through their daughter Imogene and her husband, Daniel Pence. Imogene and Daniel had six children, and Daniel himself didn't pass away until 1891. Yet Claude, according to Bill, "claimed surprise when we discovered this" in 1976. One wonders if Claude had always known the truth but didn't quite know how to tell his son the family history. Perhaps the "impromptu" research trip to Kentucky was his way of letting his son in on the family secret without admitting to his part in keeping it from him. We can't know for certain because Claude has since passed away.[7]

Bill remembers feeling "totally elated" upon discovering his connection to Richard Johnson. "A history major in college, I wanted to become a history professor, and I was all about the early presidents and all of that. I was, of course, very familiar with Martin Van Buren. I had never heard of Richard M. Johnson. I was delighted because I thought, 'Gosh, I'm related to a vice president.... How exciting this is.' I was very proud at that moment." I then asked Bill how he felt when he realized that he was also related to Julia Chinn, an enslaved Black woman whom Richard had most likely owned. He responded:

> Spending the time that I did in Kentucky as contrasted to growing up in Los Angeles, I was always amazed at the racial divide that existed in Kentucky at that time, as compared to what I was accustomed to in Los Angeles. In Los Angeles I ran with a group of guys; they were my best friends. Craig Beck was a Mormon, Leonard Titus was Black, and Jimmy Ito was Japanese. Steven ... was Chinese ... Leonard Jelly Rojo was Spanish, and ... David Garfield was Jewish. We were all friends, and I was a kid and we all had ... you know, crazy names for each other, but literally there was no racial tension, let alone animosity, when I was growing up in Los Angeles. Then when I would come to Kentucky and stay with my grandparents in Sharpsburg, Kentucky, a little town of population 300, we lived on what was known as Main Street or Front Street, and the Blacks lived on the next street over, which had a name for the street, I don't recall what it was, but everybody called it Back Street. And yet when I was in Kentucky the general banter was always "Oh well ... we all have Black blood in our history." That was the general banter at the time. So that's why I found it humorous or funny when I found out the news because I said, "Oh, well, it is true!" You know, I really was not put off, you know, in any way. If anything, I viewed it as more historical. But ... just to give the full perspective on the matter ... as I went forward and talked about

Richard M. Johnson, I realized that . . . I made that connection very clearly and talked about it a lot, but . . . I have been more guarded over time about the association of my . . . three-times-removed great-grandmother, depending on who I was talking to, especially if I'm talking to people in Kentucky.[8]

Bill's early excitement at uncovering his relationship to Richard and Julia turned to caution. He found out that certain members of his own family were not happy to discover they had African American lineage. His guard really went up after some hurtful incidents with his first wife, who was from Georgia. Bill had told her before they got married about his connection to Julia, and she appeared unbothered by it. The pair wed in 1980. Repeated remarks over the years made it clear that she was uncomfortable with Bill's Black heritage, however; one incident still stings. Getting ready to take his then wife out for dinner one night, Bill asked if there was anywhere in particular she wanted to go that evening. When she said no, he said, "'Well, come on now, we're free and white.' It was just something that flowed out of my mouth at the time, and she immediately looked at me and she said, 'Well, almost white.'"

> ACM: So, you were saying, "We're free and white. We can go anywhere we want."
>
> BJ: Yeah . . .
>
> ACM: And her response was "Well, almost white."
>
> BJ: "Well, almost."
>
> ACM: I see.
>
> BJ: So frankly, that hurt. I mean . . . she just wasn't the sort who had that great a sense of humor . . . where it would come off light-hearted. I mean . . . there was something there. Obviously, she had thought about it.
>
> ACM: Even though it was four or five generations back.
>
> BJ: Yeah. And, interestingly, within about nine months we were separated and divorced. . . . I won't say it was a direct result of that, but I will say that I'm talking to you about it today. That was thirty years ago.
>
> ACM: It really stuck with you.

BJ: Right. So, I was kind of guarded, you know, thereafter, about who I shared that information with, probably pretty much up until the time that I married my current wife.[9]

When I asked Bill why he thought this history had been erased from family memory, why he and his father hadn't known about their connection to Julia and Richard until 1976, he was hesitant to draw any firm conclusions. We spoke about how the communities in that part of Kentucky are still quite small and that very few generations had actually passed since Imogene Johnson Pence's death, when you stop to think about it.[10] It's also quite revealing that in every generation of the family there has been an Imogene, including Brenda Wilfert's mother. In fact, Brenda believes that her middle name, Gene, may be a watered-down version of "Imogene."[11] So while the family had at some point decided not to discuss their Black heritage, they also appear to have resolved to honor Imogene's memory, if not Julia's. Although Bill didn't want to speculate about the erasure of Blackness, his answer still sheds light on the matter: "You know . . . it's a closeted secret. It is not something that people were necessarily proud of. Now, for whatever reason, whether it's out of embarrassment because of enslavement, things like that. What it stems from, I don't know either. But I know that it's certainly been hush-hush in our family, and whenever it comes up in other families that I'm aware of, it's just as hush-hush."[12]

"It is not something that people were necessarily proud of." Perhaps from "embarrassment because of enslavement." It could have also been due to the existence of interracial sex. Perhaps it was anti-Black racism. Whatever it was, it wasn't just Brenda and Bill's branch of the family that had erased Julia Chinn from memory. Through Brenda I met her distant cousins, the two sisters living in Ohio who had carried the Pence name from birth but who, growing up, had no idea who Imogene and Daniel Pence were, let alone Julia Chinn or Richard Johnson. Harriet Elizabeth Pence Gray and Margaret Ellen Pence Brooks were born and raised in Cincinnati. Born in the early to mid-1950s, the Pence sisters thought that their family had always lived in Ohio until their older sister, Mary, went away to college at Morehead State University, in Kentucky. While there, Mary met someone from Great Crossing, or a town close by. Margaret remembers that this prompted their father to comment "that we had family from there and that was really, I think, that was the extent of that, just knowing that we had family from there. I think I remember looking it up on a map wondering where it was, but other than that, I don't remember talking about it at all."[13]

It wasn't until Margaret went to college at Eastern Kentucky University in the mid-1970s in Richmond, a town not too far from Georgetown, that the subject came up again. At that point, her father said something to her about Richard Mentor Johnson. Margaret isn't sure if her father mentioned that a book had been written about Johnson or if she went looking for the book on her own initiative, but she remembers going to the library at Eastern Kentucky and finding Leland Meyer's 1932 biography on Richard and bringing it home for her father one weekend. She remembers thinking that he knew the book existed but that he'd never seen it for himself. She believes her father read the book that weekend, and

> on the page where it did talk about Julia Chinn, I know that he had made an asterisk by her name and he had written in the bottom of it, and ... I think he had probably written some descendants of Julia Chinn and marrying a Pence and I think he had probably written the descendants down underneath him, the people that really Daddy knew, probably his father and his grandfather. And I remember thinking it was awful that he was writing. Not awful, but just "Wow, he is writing in a library book!" And so, then I just took the book back and put it back on the shelf at Eastern. I think that's when I first really became aware that we were related to a vice president.

Harriet, like Margaret, remembers this being the first time she knew about her connection to the famous Kentucky politician and thinking how exciting it all was.[14]

I asked both women if this was when they also became aware of who Julia Chinn was, that she was an enslaved Black woman and the mother of Imogene Pence, their great-great-grandmother. They both said no. Harriet said her father must have known, since he read the book, but she doesn't remember hearing about Julia at the time, that surely she would have remembered something so significant. When I asked Margaret if she read the book that she brought home for her father that weekend, she said no. She was around twenty years old at the time and she said, "It just must not have interested me as much, I guess ... you know." Harriet added that it was seen as something that was more for their father. "I think it was presented to Daddy. Like, this is something Daddy would be interested in. Because he likes history, and it's his family. . . . It really doesn't concern us."[15]

Frank Pence didn't tell his daughters about Julia and Richard after he read Leland Meyer's book that weekend. As Harriet said, her father must have known, but no conversations were sparked as a result of that book being brought home, either by Frank or his daughters. There was an occasional comment in the years that followed about Richard Johnson being the man who supposedly killed

Tecumseh, "but there was never any mention of the other ancestor the Pences were descended from.... It makes no sense when you think about it now," says Harriet. Margaret just remembers thinking "that I was pretty impressed that I was a descendant of the vice president. I don't know... if I ever even thought about who the woman was.... It was just being related to a vice president."[16] Margaret and Harriet's behavior isn't all that surprising. In a society shaped by patriarchy, where women have traditionally taken their husband's names upon marriage and children are given their father's surnames at birth, we have been conditioned to look to who our male ancestors were and what they accomplished, as opposed to the women in our family lines. Unless you were raised in a culture that honored and valued the contributions of women, why would you think about the wife of your famous forefather?

It wasn't until 1990 that Harriet and Margaret came to realize that Richard's wife was a Black woman named Julia Chinn. One day, Harriet got a phone call from her mother. She was by this point married with children of her own. Mom called to tell Harriet that Frank, her father, had been at a used bookstore in downtown Cincinnati and saw a book called *Famous Men of Kentucky*.[17] He opened it up, found Richard Johnson in the book, and discovered that Johnson had a common-law wife and two daughters. Frank purchased the book and brought it home, and "according to Mother, he was quite surprised to learn this information, that she was a woman of color, she was African American, she had been a slave. And then, that was how I found out. It's inconceivable to me that Daddy didn't know all along. He *had* to have known. He was an avid reader. I'm *sure* he read that; he *saw* that. It just simply wasn't talked about. So, probably, I don't even think there was an awful lot of communication between Mother and Dad."[18]

I believe Harriet is right: Frank Durham Pence knew the truth long before reading that book in the store in downtown Cincinnati that afternoon in 1990. He had, after all, read the Meyer book that Margaret had brought home from college back in the 1970s. But, as Harriet mused aloud, "he then just... you know... he put that information away, set it on a shelf and then didn't really think about it himself maybe until he saw that book again? I don't know... how that went on in his mind. But it does seem very strange that it wasn't... that information wasn't brought out to us especially before that... but it just wasn't."[19] Perhaps by 1990 Frank Pence felt the world had changed enough or that his daughters were old enough to know the truth. We'll never know his reasoning, as he has since passed away.

When I asked the women how they felt about being descended from an African American woman, and an enslaved one at that, their insights were telling. Margaret remarked, "If you think long and hard enough about it, there were a lot of people who were descended from slaves and just didn't know about it. We happened to be a family that knew about it." Harriet concluded, "I mean there's lots of people who *knew* up to a very late time in the 1800s, who lived, and they never talked about it. Why? It just didn't make sense. I mean . . . I understand probably . . . socially . . . in that place and time in Kentucky . . . they didn't want to talk about it, and it must have carried on in the family that they just stopped talking about it."[20]

We then discussed why they thought this had become a family secret, and the Pence sisters directly addressed issues of race and slavery. Harriet was pretty forthright in stating that it was probably because Julia "was Black. And that maybe they still talked about her being a slave. I don't know how much slavery was still talked about after the Civil War was over. But my grandfather, he was born in 1885, and there were tons of people who were still alive who had been slaves. So I would think that slavery had to have been part of it, but . . . but the Black part also . . . people just didn't talk about it."[21]

The question of how other people responded to the news that the Pences had Black ancestry brought back some difficult memories. As with Bill Jackson, there was one family member who had a problem with it: Harriet's now ex-husband. The sad thing about it is that he directed his "jokes," which were really racist commentary, toward the couple's young son. The boy was only eight or nine years old at the time, and he had no way of comprehending what his father was saying to him. Harriet stated that some of the things her then husband said "were not nice at all. Like to my son: 'Well, you know, maybe you really are gonna like watermelon.' I am not making it up."[22]

Margaret remarked that her former brother-in-law had probably heard a lot of racist things while growing up. Although the man was born in Ohio, his family was originally from North Carolina; it's where his father had been raised, and all his relatives had Black housekeepers and nannies. And while he claimed the revelation about his wife's family wasn't an issue, all his commentary, coded as "jokes," proved it *was* a problem. He also pointedly told Harriet that "we will not be talking about this story. We will not be telling the cousins and the aunts and uncles in North Carolina. This is not something we should talk about."[23]

But Harriet clued into something true about her former husband's family. About southern families. Really about all old American families that strikes at the very heart of this book:

> But when you go to North Carolina—and his family was a very old family in North Carolina . . . they had, I am sure, slaves— . . . and [at] one of the old graveyards, there's . . . the white Grays on this side, and a row of hedges and these are all Black Grays on this side. So

EPILOGUE

> I'm like, "You know . . . you can't tell me that, you know . . . you're making a big deal about this thing, but you know as well as I do, I'm sure that there's crossovers here. You just don't have the proof."

And I said to her, "Or maybe the older family members did. They just don't talk about it, maybe." Margaret immediately chimed in, "Right, right." Because you either have to acknowledge that there is a biological kinfolk connection or that at some point, one side of the family had owned the other side of the family. Or both. None of these scenarios is appealing for some people to admit or have to deal with.[24]

While sex across the color line, slavery, and slave ownership have been difficult topics for some folks to discuss, others have faced these truths head on. William H. McIntyre Jr., was a man who wanted to talk about everything, no matter how uncomfortable the subject. Born in Georgetown, Kentucky, in 1931, Mr. William was a husband, a father, and a veteran of the Korean War. And from the time he was about ten years old, he remembered his great-uncle Buddy McIntyre sitting him and the other children down at family reunions and telling them stories, including the fact that their family traced itself back to a white man named Col. Dick Johnson and a woman known only as "the African." Uncle Bud told young William that the woman in question was completely Black and hadn't been in the country very long. He also said that she had been purchased as a slave by Colonel Dick. It wasn't until he was older that Mr. William came to realize that Colonel Dick was Col. Richard Mentor Johnson, the man who became the ninth vice president of the United States.[25]

The McIntyres are an old Kentucky family. They've been in Scott County for many generations. They identify as African American, but Mr. William was clear that he didn't have a problem with the fact that he had white ancestry; he was proud of his heritage, both sides. Uncle Bud told him that he should never forget his lineage and that he shouldn't be ashamed of having white relatives. According to Mr. William, however, not everyone in the McIntyre clan felt the same way. Uncle Bud was the only person from Mr. William's grandparents' generation who told the children the old stories. Other folks were uncomfortable discussing such matters. Mr. William said there appeared to be "a stigma" attached to having such conversations because of slavery and interracial sex.[26] Apparently these relationships from the past can lead to discomfort on both the white and the Black sides of racially mixed families, although for different reasons. For many white-identified families, it's the acknowledgment that their ancestors were enslavers. For Black families, it's facing the trauma of the sexual violence that was done to their forebears.

The uneasiness that some of the McIntyres had with this history went beyond just an unwillingness to talk about it. Some folks who came to the larger family reunions apparently didn't accept Mr. William's side of the family because of their white ancestry. When I asked Mr. William why he thought this was, his answer wasn't directly about slavery, nor was it about the fact that many enslavers had raped Black women:

ACM: What is it about the fact that you're a descendant of Richard Johnson that makes them so uncomfortable?

WM: You think that Black folk resent some Black folk because they're too Black.

ACM: Mmmm.

WM: Some resent you because you're too light.

ACM: So, you think a lot of it had to do with skin color issues.

WM: Yes.

Mr. William claimed that "you find out that a mixture of black and white makes a good-looking family. And a lot of people would get upset if you was too nice looking. And way back then, there was a lot of good-looking people in my family." In his opinion, this led to resentment among certain members on the other side of the McIntyre clan, who referred to his side of the family as the "half-white side" and commented negatively about some of them, including Mr. William, having blue eyes. His remarks here allude to another serious issue that has developed as a result of slavery, racism, and white supremacy: the obsession some Black folks have with light skin, often equating Eurocentric features and/or whiteness with beauty, also known as colorism.[27]

As much as white families have struggled to come to terms with their Black heritage because of generations of secrets, it is clearly no less easy for some Black families who have always known the truth. The United States makes it complicated because these are stories shrouded in pain due to anti-Black racism and our centuries-long refusal to accept our histories of settler colonialism, slavery, and interracial sex. It's additionally difficult for the McIntyre family because, unlike the Pences, who trace back to Julia Chinn and can establish their lineage with a paper trail through her daughter Imogene Johnson Pence, Mr. William's family line goes back to a woman who remains unnamed and for whom there are no definitive records. This isn't to say that oral testimonies aren't important.

EPILOGUE

Family histories, passed down from generation to generation, are critical sources of information and should be reinforced by and used alongside other materials, just like all records. No source is without subjectivity or bias. To discount everyday objects, art, music, poetry, interviews, buildings, land, and oral traditions as sources is a western mind-set that privileges the written word and performs violence anew on Black women and other groups who have already experienced archival erasure at the hands of settler colonials.[28]

Not everyone agrees. There are members of Mr. William's own family who don't believe in oral culture, including a cousin named David who knows "quite a bit of history" and who, according to Mr. William, "disputes me a lot of times on the things that I say." As far as Mr. William was concerned, however, the family histories were important. They mattered, and "regardless of who says it's not true or whatever, I believe it because Uncle Bud said so." This was also why he didn't feel the need to take a DNA test to prove his ties to Richard Johnson. Some members of the Pence family have been tested so that they can find other descendants from across the nation. Mr. William, however, had a different philosophy on testing, which was linked to a reverence for his elders and to Black traditions of storytelling:

> WM: And I asked Uncle Bud, "Uncle Bud, can this be proven?" He said, "A lot of this stuff cannot be proven. It's an oral history."
>
> ACM: Right.
>
> WM: It's not written down. Just like a lot of folks' history is not written down. But it's a fact. All they have to do is take blood samples and do a blood thing.
>
> ACM: Oh, DNA testing.
>
> WM: DNA test, yeah. Yes, indeed, but I don't think I'd be willing to do that, because I've heard that I'm a descendant of Richard Johnson, and that's enough for me. I don't have to prove it. I'm just going by what Uncle Bud said. And back then, the old folk in the family was just like God.
>
> ACM: I understand.
>
> WM: And whatever they said was a fact.[29]

For Mr. William, who passed away at the age of ninety on February 2, 2022, Uncle Bud was the griot of the McIntyre family.[30] Griots originated in the thirteenth century in the Mande Empire of Mali, and for centuries they have told and retold the history of that empire, keeping their stories and traditions alive. In West African societies today, griots are historians, storytellers, praise singers, poets, and/or musicians. A repository of the oral tradition, griots are often seen as leaders due to their positions as advisers to royal personages. They keep records of all the births, deaths, and marriages through the generations of a village or family.[31] Great-Uncle Bud performed this role for Mr. William's family. Neither of William's parents wanted to discuss the old stories, and his grandfather, Uncle Bud's brother, passed away the year Mr. William was born. It was left to Uncle Bud and another great-uncle, Ron, to keep the records, tell the stories, and be the family historians. According to Mr. William, they were wonderful historians; indeed, they told so many stories, he couldn't remember them all. His respect for them, and the traditions in which they stood, meant he felt no need to take a test to prove his connection to Richard Mentor Johnson. Uncle Bud said it was so. And that was enough.[32]

As with so much of the history of Black women from the pre–Civil War era, we often have to be content with more questions than answers. With frustrating silences and gaps. With having to tell ourselves that what we've found is "enough." We simply don't know how many women Richard Johnson had sexual relationships with. Nor do we know exactly how many children he had. There are the tantalizing snippets from Catherine Bragg's 1840 letter, as well as the one that Amos Kendall's unnamed friend wrote in 1839, both of which claim that Richard had at least three Black "wives."[33] Antebellum newspapers suggest that one of these women was Parthene, who was likely Julia's niece. The third woman may have been Parthene's sister. Did either Parthene or her sister have children with Richard? Catherine Bragg wrote that she met "Mrs. Johnson the Vice President's wife & her two milk & molasses children" while on a stagecoach from Maysville to Paris, Kentucky, in 1840.[34] She never mentions the woman's first name, how old her children were, or if they were actually Richard's offspring, but there is some evidence to suggest that Richard had children with another Black woman after Julia passed away in 1833.

This story takes us across the river, to Lancaster, Indiana, northwest of present-day Madison. Here, in 1848, a group of antislavery advocates, many of whom were from New England, established the Eleutherian Institute, up on a peaceful hill. Founded to educate all students regardless of "sect, sex, or color," some of the pupils at Eleutherian College, as it came to be known, were self-liberated Black folks who had crossed the Ohio River from nearby Louisville, Kentucky. Wealthy southern enslavers also sent their Black children to the school, which

Eleutherian College from northwest in evening, Madison, Indiana.

Image courtesy of Wikipedia Commons, the free Media Repository. See https://commons.wikimedia.org/wiki/File:Eleutherian_College_from_northwest_in_evening.jpg.

had an excellent curriculum, including Latin and modern languages, and aimed to train teachers and preachers. Not an inexpensive college, it is said that two of the young ladies who attended Eleutherian, Lucy and Georgiana Jefferson, were Thomas Jefferson's granddaughters.[35]

Among the names of the many students listed in the college's 1857–58 *Catalogue* is one Theodore Johnson of Frankfort, Kentucky. Young Theodore, a person of color, claimed that he was the son of Col. Richard Mentor Johnson, former vice president of the United States. His statement was supposedly supported by the ongoing payment of his college tuition through drafts drawn on a Louisville bank by the administrators of Richard's estate. A bright scholar, Theodore remained at Eleutherian until he enlisted in the Sixth Indiana Regiment as a private during the Civil War. Serving as a white man, he died in February 1863 in a hospital in Munfordville, Kentucky, several months after the Battle of Munfordville, also known as the Battle of Green River. He was only eighteen years old.[36]

Who was Theodore Johnson? His age in 1863 makes him too young to have been one of the "milk & molasses children" spotted on the stagecoach by Catherine Bragg in 1840. The Theodore who died in Munfordville wouldn't have been born until 1845. Census records from Scott County, Kentucky, in 1850 give us some clues. Richard, who was sixty-nine years old that year, had six people living with him when the census taker came calling. Three of those six persons had the last name Jusan. Malvina Jusan was twenty-one years old; Adelaide was six; and Theodore Jusan was five years old, making his year of birth 1845, the same as the Theodore who would die at Munfordville in 1863. All three of the Jusans were listed as "mulatto." Ten years later, fifteen-year-old Theodore Johnson was living in Lancaster, Indiana, in the household of one Reuben Walter. The census taker in 1860 recorded that Johnson, a "mulatto male" was a student and noted that he was born in Kentucky.[37]

While not definitive, the census materials, when linked to the records from Indiana, are suggestive. Malvina Jusan may have been Richard's final sexual partner, and Adelaide and Theodore her and Richard's children. After Richard's death, it's possible that John and Henry Johnson, who became the administrators of their late brother's estate, sent Theodore to school at Eleutherian and paid for his education out of the funds from Richard's estate.[38] This may have been to satisfy Richard's final wishes to help his son, to guarantee that Theodore was removed from the area, or both. While the Johnson men were unable to physically relocate Imogene Johnson Pence and her family away from Scott County, they may have tried to ensure that none of their brother's other "mistakes" remained nearby to embarrass them or cause trouble for their family. What isn't clear is what happened to Malvina or Adelaide Jusan after Richard's death. While Theodore likely died without heirs, if his sister grew to womanhood and married, there could be other Johnson descendants alive today who descend from her line.

There are many other stories like this one. Obie Taylor Sr., for example, also traces his family line back to Julia Chinn. The Taylors, who are African American, are descendants of Julia through Mama Nell, Obie's great-grandmother. From the time he was a child, Obie was told that he was related to Richard Johnson. "I never really knew how, but I had always heard those kinds of stories before within the family." When he got older, Obie started asking his great-aunts and great-uncles questions about the connection. His great-aunts were the ones who helped him to put the pieces together. They told Obie that their mother, his great-grandmother Nellie Pence Taylor, was the daughter of Edward Herndon Pence and Amanda Thomas, a woman of color. Amanda, who worked on the Pence farm, appears to have been Ed's sexual companion before he married his wife, Ida.[39] Ed was the son of Imogene Johnson Pence and Daniel B. Pence. This makes Nellie Pence Taylor the great-granddaughter of Julia Chinn. Obie Taylor Sr., then, is the four-times-great-grandson of Julia Chinn, six generations removed from slavery.

Like William McIntyre's story, the information in the Taylor family is based on oral testimony. There are no corresponding records. Obie, who has become the family genealogist, has spent time trying to figure out who Amanda Thomas was and where she came from. Even Mama Nell's early records are a mystery. He knows she was born in 1891. She passed away in 1985 at the age of ninety-four in Stamping Ground, Kentucky, and had two sisters named Betty and Susan, also the daughters of Ed and Amanda. Both Betty and Susan relocated to Ohio, where they married and raised families of their own. Obie has discovered, however, as many researchers have, that records on African Americans in the nineteenth century were neither complete nor always accurate. There are frustrating gaps and issues we deal with as Black historians, particularly with census records:

> Sometimes they [census takers] would just completely alleviate [sic] whole families. They wouldn't even knock on the door and say, "Well, who's here," or if they did, they may say you had "two males and two females" and an age. And that's it in terms of no names or anything like that. So, it makes it kind of hard to really, you know . . . validate some of the statements that you make. But from my standpoint, coming from a direct family member who has that close tie, it's not generations down by any means, it's their mother, saying, "Hey, this is my father, and this is my mother." I feel very comfortable accepting that [Mama Nell's parentage] as being factual.[40]

As historians of the Black experience know, the work we do often leaves us with more questions than answers. Brenda Wilfert, the genealogist for her branch of the family, has concluded that "the joy in studying genealogy has to be found in the quest itself. . . . Wherever the answers lead us is at best a secondary source of entertainment." Brenda did some digging on Amanda Thomas after listening to Obie Taylor's oral history recording. Her research into the Pence family papers revealed that a woman named "Aunt Mandy" lived with the Daniel Franklin Pence family as a nanny and cook. Daniel Franklin (Frank) was also a son of Imogene and Daniel B. Pence. "Aunt Mandy" is most likely Amanda Thomas. Born enslaved to the senior Pences, she was eventually freed by them and continued to work for the family. At some point she married a man named Thomas and they lived together on the Pence farm. By age fifty, Amanda had given birth to nine children, seven of whom were still living. Two of these children were listed in the 1900 census records as Mary E. and Susan. Brenda posits that the *E* may have stood for Elizabeth, and this could be Mama Nell's sister Betty. By 1900, Amanda Thomas was a widow. Mama Nell does not appear in the census records by name until 1910. That year, she was nineteen and married to Harrison Taylor, Obie's great-grandfather. It's unclear why Betty and Susan appear in the 1900 census with Amanda, but Nellie does not. When it comes to archives, to paper, there are constant gaps and frustrating silences. But for Obie, as for Mr. William, his elder had said it was so. And that was enough.[41]

As I wrap up this book, I know in my heart that the work is never really done. At some point you have to lay down your pen (or walk away from your computer) and leave certain things for others to take up. That is both the anguish and the beauty of the labor I am engaged in. There is always something for the next person to do. Shortly after I sent this manuscript off to my editor, I was contacted by a lovely lady who lives in Washington, DC. Professor Phylicia Fauntleroy Bowman earned her PhD from American University, spent the early part of her career in international relations, and is now researching the neighborhood where she grew up in the District of Columbia. Her family has a long and rich history. Both the women and the men have acquired college degrees for seven generations, going back to the 1850s. That is a stunning achievement for a Black family that can trace itself directly to enslavement in the United States, and it's a legacy that Dr. Bowman is justifiably proud of.[42]

Professor Bowman reached out to me because she was doing research online and learned that I was writing a book about Julia Chinn. She's been compiling sources on her family history for a number of years and has information that the woman who began her family line, Lucy, was an enslaved woman who may have been owned by Richard Mentor Johnson. Family histories state that Lucy was the sexual partner of a vice president of the United States and had at least one child by him, named Maria. Professor Bowman credits Julia Chinn with encouraging Richard to sell Lucy and her children, including Maria, to a new owner. That man, Sanford Mitchell, in turn, manumitted Lucy in 1832. It was Lucy's freedom and subsequent marriage to Henry Alexander, who freed all five of her children (who he claimed were his own), that laid the foundation for the educational attainment and success of the Alexander descendants, including Dr. Bowman.[43]

The stories of Julia Chinn, Lucy Alexander, Amanda Thomas, Malvina and Adelaide Jusan, as well as women whose names we don't yet have, such as William McIntyre's ancestress, known only as "the African," all deserve to be told to the best of our abilities. A part of Lucy's story has been recounted by Dr. Adele Logan Alexander, who also traces her family line back to the Alexanders.[44] More work

EPILOGUE

remains to be done, however, on Lucy and on countless other Black women. It's why I'm always surprised by people who comment, "What more can we say about slavery in the American South?" My response is "We've only just begun to unpack it. To understand the richness, the diversity, and the complexity of it all. Really, we haven't even scratched the surface."

During one of our phone conversations about Julia and Richard in 2018, Brenda Wilfert said to me, "I'm for throwing it [the truth] all out there."[45] William McIntyre agreed: "I would love to see a roundtable in the library of people getting together, sitting there chatting, and just opening up.... Ask any question that you want to ask. And I would like to see a dialogue like that in Scott County and all over the country."[46] Not everyone shares their viewpoint. Scott County officials had the chance to name a new school after Richard Johnson a few years ago. It caused a lot of debate, and ultimately the decision was voted down. While conversation centered on the fact that it didn't seem right to name a school after a slaveholder, Brenda doesn't think that's why the decision went the way it did. I have my doubts as well. There are enough monuments to Henry Clay in Kentucky to make one speculate that the discomfort had more to do with Richard's public relationship with a Black woman and the way in which he "raised, educated, protected, and recognized his daughters" by Julia Chinn.[47]

"When it came to the two girls, he [Richard] was certainly unusual," says Brenda. And ultimately, that's what did him in. There was "really no coming back from the Julia thing," she mused, "otherwise, he might have become president."[48] She may be right. Mr. William agreed with her about one thing: how Richard handled his relationship with Julia continues to affect his reputation in the present. When I asked him why he thought there were no Johnson statues or schools in Scott County today, he was forthright with me:

> WM: If he had not taken up with a Black woman, there would be statues of him. But he was ostracized because he took up with that Black woman and made it known. Now there was others....
>
> ACM: Henry Clay did the same thing.
>
> WM: He didn't come public with it....
>
> ACM: You think that's part of the reason why we don't have monuments and schools?

WM: Yes, that's the reason why. Exactly the reason why. See, I enjoy chatting with people about stuff like this. But a lot of people will not open up and talk to you about stuff like this.[49]

For Brenda Wilfert, William McIntyre, and me, one thing seems clear: our nation's ongoing discomfort with slavery, "amalgamation," and Blackness lies at the heart of why Julia's story, and the stories of so many other interracial families, have been ignored for so long and continue to be sidestepped by those who would rather just forget. It's past time that Julia and her daughters were restored to their rightful place in US history and in the larger story of the Pence family. I would suggest that it's time for Scott County, for Kentucky, to name a school not in honor of Richard Mentor Johnson but in memory of Julia Ann Chinn, without whose coerced labor Choctaw Academy would have never been the success it was for as long as it was.[50]

POSTSCRIPT

THE SEARCH FOR JULIA, REDUX

*A*s this manuscript nears completion, there are still so many loose threads, as is always the case. In particular, we have yet to find Julia's and Adaline's graves. While I'm positive they were buried on Blue Spring Farm, the property is no longer in the family's possession, and the original house and its cemeteries have vanished. It seems fair to say that if Richard Mentor Johnson had lived a more "conventional" life, we wouldn't have, quite literally, lost the vice president's wife.

It is my hope that the publication of this book will generate enough interest to have ground-penetrating radar brought out to Blue Spring to locate Julia's and Adaline's graves. We can then mark the locations with stones in order to honor their memories. I have long been troubled by the lack of any one site where we can go to recognize and remember Julia Chinn. She is both everywhere in Scott County and nowhere. Like the beautiful patchwork quilt pictured on the front of this book, under which her grandson Daniel Franklin Pence slept, her story is scattered in fragments across a dozen archives and physical places, from Washington, DC, to New Jersey, Ohio, Kentucky, Kansas, and Arizona. By themselves, the remnants do not look like much. But when stitched together, the larger picture comes into clearer focus and presents the image of an extraordinary life.

POSTSCRIPT

For me, then, it's important that we find Julia's final resting site as a way to publicly proclaim, once more, that *Black women's lives, and stories, matter.*
Amrita Chakrabarti Myers
Bloomington, IN
April 16, 2023

Daniel Franklin Pence quilt. Part of the Pence Family private collection.
Photo courtesy of the author.

Acknowledgments

Recovering Julia's story has been more than a decade-long journey. Along the way I've met many amazing people and visited a multitude of places. Julia Chinn has quite literally changed my life. That being said, I hope folks will extend me grace if I forget to mention them in the paragraphs below. Charge it to my head and not my heart and know that I appreciate you.

This book began "way back when" because I had a conversation with a colleague. It is because of her that I decided to pursue Julia's story, and she was generous enough to share her manuscript on Choctaw Academy with me prior to its publication. I am grateful for Christina Snyder. She is a brilliant scholar, and I am fortunate to know her.

This book has benefited from the generosity of several Bluegrass historians. When you do the kind of work I do, it's important to understand that there are local folks who know a whole lot more about the area than you do. A whole lot. Dr. Lindsey Apple, Ann Bolton Bevins, Ellie Caroland, Albert Hart, Dr. James C. Klotter, and Dr. William "Chip" and Candy Richardson all provided invaluable assistance. I met Drs. Apple and Klotter when I was first thinking about this project, and they helped to get me situated in Kentucky. Mr. Hart invited me into his home and was kind enough to give me a copy of his book *Richard M. Johnson and the Hostile Press*. The Richardsons allowed me access to their part of the original Blue Spring property, on which the last remaining Choctaw Academy building stands. Ann and Ellie have become very dear to me. They've introduced me to numerous people, answered countless emails, opened up their personal archives to me, taken me around to various sites, loaned me books, and mailed me materials more times than I can count. There are no words for the debt I owe them.

Through Ann and Ellie, I met and interviewed several descendants of the Johnson family including Margaret Pence Brooks, Harriet Pence Gray, William "Bill" French Jackson, William McIntyre, Obie B. Taylor Sr., and Brenda Brent Wilfert. Brenda is a treasure. A lay historian, her archives are a wonder, and I was blessed to fly out to Arizona and spend a week with her and her husband, Tom, go through her papers, and interview her for this book. She then put me in touch with her cousin Bill in Kentucky, as well as the Pence sisters Margaret and Harriet, who live in Ohio. Margaret and Harriet gave me access to their family's archival materials, which, when added to Brenda's records, allowed me to tell the story of the Chinn-Johnson family after 1850. It is no small thing to entrust your family's documents, and stories, to a stranger. I am deeply grateful that all the descendants listed here chose to share their homes, their thoughts, and their records with me.

A project of this nature requires structural support. I was fortunate to receive assistance from various offices at Indiana University in addition to external organizations and agencies. Grants from IU's Center for Research on Race and Ethnicity in Society, the College Arts and Humanities Institute, the Institute for Advanced Studies, and the New Frontiers program helped me travel to archives across the country. Fellowships from the Kentucky Historical Society in Frankfort and the Filson Historical Society in Louisville enabled me to undertake research at those particular facilities. A true blessing was a major fellowship from the American Council of Learned Societies, which allowed me to take a year away from teaching and service and write a full first draft of the manuscript. I was fortunate to spend my leave at the James Weldon Johnson Institute (JWJI) at Emory University in Atlanta. I am grateful to Dr. Andra Gillespie, Kali-Ahset Amen, and the staff of the JWJI for making my year at Emory such an amazing experience.

My cohort at the JWJI in 2017–18 was truly phenomenal. My work, and my life, is so much the better for having met and spent time in the presence of Taina Figueroa, Derek Handley, Felipe Hinojosa, Justin Hosbey, Alexandria Lockett, Alison Parker, Ashante Reese, Kyera Singleton, and Charissa Threat. Y'all are a treasure.

Julia's story is scattered in archives across the country. In addition to examining materials in the private collections of Margaret Pence Brooks, Harriet Pence Gray, and Brenda Brent Wilfert, I spent significant time at numerous public facilities. Thank you to all the wonderful archivists and librarians at the Filson Historical Society and the Southern Baptist Theological Seminary (Louisville); the Kentucky Department of Libraries and Archives and the Kentucky Historical Society (Frankfort); the Georgetown and Scott County Museum, Georgetown College, and the Scott County Public Library (Georgetown); the Lexington Public Library–Main Branch and the University of Kentucky's Margaret I. King Special Collections Library and William T. Young Library (Lexington); and the Library of Congress (Washington, DC). Special thanks to Walter Bowman, Glenn Crothers, Mark Furnish, J. P. Johnson, Reinette Jones, Sarah-Jane Poindexter, and Kathy Vaughan-Lloyd, who went above and beyond in assisting me with my research.

On my many sojourns in and through Kentucky, Melissa Schroeder-Stein, her wife, Kelly Schroeder-Stein, and their wonderful children regularly provided me with a place to lay my head, to the point where their guest room was dubbed

"Aunt Amrita's room." I am forever grateful. Anastasia Curwood and her partner, Carol Skricki, also gave refuge to their friend from across the state line. Thanks to my KY Crew for making my time in the Bluegrass so enjoyable. And for making me realize that I really do like bourbon.

I've had some brilliant students who've helped me with this project over the last several years. Dr. Charlene Fletcher converted all of my earliest research photographs from a mass of disorganized, numbered documents into named PDF files. For that alone she deserves a medal. Dr. Jazma Sutton spent one summer going through the records of the Bureau of Indian Affairs–Choctaw Academy from the National Archives (on microfilm). And Oti Ogbeide read through a decade's worth of electronic files in order to begin constructing my bibliography. I am so grateful to them all. IU really does have the most wonderful students!

I must thank the members of the US History Workshop at Indiana University who provided helpful critique on an earlier draft of chapter 4, "Disorderly Communion," which I presented in the fall of 2019. Valerie Grim took time out of her busy schedule to give official comments and Janine Giordano Drake sent me useful suggestions, all of which strengthened the piece. The revised paper appeared as an article in the Spring 2020 volume of the *Journal of African American History* (*JAAH*). I owe a debt to *JAAH* editors Pero Dagbovie and LaShawn Harris for believing in my work and to the anonymous reviewers who provided thoughtful feedback on the manuscript.

In addition to the reviewers at the *JAAH*, I am fortunate to have had other folks do heavy lifting for me, time and again. Kali Gross has read my work several times. If not for her, I would have never written a public-facing piece about Julia, which she helped me cut and polish, and which appeared on the Association for Black Women Historians' blog in 2019. Randal Jelks has provided feedback on numerous fellowship applications, and he, Tera Hunter, Leslie Schwalm, and Deborah Gray White have written copious letters for me without hesitation (and sometimes on rather short notice). Deborah said to me years ago, "You never stop being an advisor." She's not wrong, and I truly appreciate her ongoing counsel. Liza Black read chapter 3, "Campus Conflicts," twice and provided critical insight (and readings) on Native communities that reshaped my work on that chapter. Jessica Millward read chapter 2, "Mistress of the Parlor," and pushed me to rethink my terminology (again) around enslavement. And Tiffany Gill, whom I have known for literally half my life, read the *entire* revised manuscript in spring 2022. That's sisterhood. I can't possibly thank her enough for that labor of love, especially given the events that had just transpired in her own life at the time.

I've been fortunate during my years at IU to work with people who have become part of my community. Most are women; many do public-facing work around race and/or gender. It's a privilege to teach with them, both in the classroom and out in the streets. My thanks to Maria Hamilton Abegunde, Liza Black, Maria Bucur, Cara Caddoo, Kalani Craig, Arlene Diaz, Justin Garcia, Karen Inouye, Sarah Knott, Krista Maglen, Marissa Moorman, Michelle Moyd, Leah Shopkow, Candis Smith, Maisha Wester, Cindy Wu, and Ellen Wu. You are framily.

There are folks around Btown whom I genuinely admire and respect. They love the people, and they're doing the work to try and make life better for Black and Brown folk, both here and across the nation. It's a privilege to serve alongside them in community spaces and to learn from them in a variety of ways. They are Black Brilliance. Jada Bee, Dana Black, Nicole Bolden, Jennifer Crossley, Martin Law, Jacinda Townsend, and Lauren Volpp: I see you.

Getting this book out was a communal effort. It really was. Nobody taught folks of my generation anything about agents or trade presses. That wasn't how it was done back then. I'm thus grateful that Tanisha Ford made herself so accessible to answering my many, many questions about this whole process (that's my mentee right there!) and that Ibram X. Kendi and Danielle McGuire were kind enough to broker introductions for me to editors and agents. They didn't have to; they don't even know me that well. I'm also thankful that Katy O'Donnell took the time to read my one little chapter way back in 2018 and saw enough promise in my work to introduce me to several agents. And that Ayesha Pande of Pande Literary signed me to her agency. Ayesha has always believed in me, and in Julia. She was an editor with the trades for many years before she opened her agency, and she invested a lot of time into helping me find my narrative voice. I owe her a lot. As much as I owe my editor Debbie Gershenowitz and the team at Ferris and Ferris–UNC Press. Debbie G. has an amazing rep in the field. She is known for being a fierce editor, but I have found her to be wise and fair. Her instinct for what works is unerring. Partnering with her was unquestionably the right decision. I am also very appreciative of the time and energy that the two external readers for the press put into my manuscript as it neared completion. Their helpful insights have made this a stronger final product.

When things have gone sideways in my world, I've been fortunate to have friends to call on, both near and far. For holding me down and lifting me up in ways too numerous to mention (including taking me to the hospital on occasion), I am sending love out to Abegunde, Dana Black, Nicole Bolden, Cara Caddoo, Karen Costa, Arlene Diaz, Stephanie Evans, Justin Garcia, Tiffany Gill, Mandy Gott, Ricky Jones, Debbie Kincade, Shannon King, Jessica Millward, Marissa Moorman, Michelle Moyd, Alison Parker, Mary Wiggins, Stephanie Wright, and Ellen Wu. Sisters Abegunde, Steph E., Tiff, Deb, JMil, Mary, and Steph W., and Brother Rex have carried me through some valleys. I love y'all. You're a blessing.

ACKNOWLEDGMENTS

Throughout this entire process, my family has continued to cheer me on from the sidelines. My cousins in Philly provide me with a place of refuge whenever I need to escape the pressures of small-town life, and my parents have patiently awaited the publication of a book that never seemed to be done. My weekly phone calls with my octogenarian father in Edmonton, Alberta, inevitably end with some version of "I'd like to see you finish this before I die." No pressure there! Much love to Tamali, Surojit, and Sid Das; Anindita, Tilak, Neil, and Aakash Sen; and Amal, Sukla, and Anita Chakrabarti. A very special high-five paw to my road dog and princess puppy, Shiloh. Shi has now seen me through to the finish line of two books. Her unconditional love, sweet presence, and gentle demands for cuddles and walks have kept me sane (and healthy!) over the years. And while she's gone from being a frisky youngster to a graying, dowager duchess, she's still my baby and the best writing partner I could ever ask for. I love you, Shi-Bear.

It's doubtful Julia ever thought anyone would write a book about her, because she was just a regular person. Everyone has a story to tell, however, if we are willing to listen. This book is dedicated to two women who had stories to tell. Neither lived a glamorous life. Time, place, and social space meant they had few opportunities. They were just regular people. But like Julia, they sacrificed and made ways where there seemed to be none so their descendants could go further in life than they ever would. One was married at the age of twelve, the other fourteen. One gave birth to ten children, seven of whom survived to adulthood. The other had five children, four of whom reached maturity. Neither received much of an education, because they lived in a time and place where girls were expected to be wives and mothers. Each, however, was fiercely dedicated to ensuring her children went to school and earned good grades. Both were stern women, even as elders, and were a bit frightening to their grandchildren.

It wasn't until one of those grandchildren was much, much older that she came to realize the enormous burdens these women carried. One had lost everything in a civil war, became a refugee, and had to start over again in a new city with her then six children and a husband who was still off fighting with the resistance. In fact, there was a long stretch of time when she thought her spouse was dead. The other spent years not only looking after her own family but helping to care for her widowed mother and younger sisters, living in an extended kinship household that was taxing on her and her husband, both emotionally and financially.

I didn't know either of my grandmothers very well. My maternal grandmother died from cancer when I was only eleven. My paternal grandmother passed when I was nineteen. What I can tell you is that, growing up, everyone talked about my grandfathers and their achievements. No one, however, said very much about my grandmothers and everything they had accomplished. Because, well, patriarchy.

ACKNOWLEDGMENTS

This book is dedicated to Nilima Chakraborty. Married at fourteen, her hard work and constant insistence on excellence ensured that all four of her living daughters made it to college. Three of them, including my mother, eventually earned their master's degrees.

This book is also dedicated to Usharani Chakraborty. Married at twelve, while she didn't have the opportunity to obtain much of an education, her children became teachers, accountants, and engineers. Two of her sons, including my father, attended school abroad.

Both of my grandmothers labored for the duration of their lives. They scrimped, saved, and sacrificed. They often went without, hoping and praying that all they could not attain for themselves would come to fruition for their descendants.

It is because of them, that I am.

Notes

ABBREVIATIONS

BBWPC	Brenda Brent Wilfert private collection
Argus	*Argus of Western America*
CPIIC	Consumer Price Index Inflation Calculator, Official Data Foundation, Alioth Finance, www.in2013dollars.com
Craig Papers	Lula Craig Papers, "History of Nicodemus Colony," Colonel Richard M. Johnson Section, Kenneth Spencer Research Library, University of Kansas, Lawrence, KS
ECPC	Eloise Caroland private collection
FHS	Filson Historical Society, Louisville, KY
FPB	Francis P. Blair
GCBC	Great Crossing Baptist Church
Henderson Letter	"Letter of Thomas Henderson," *Daily Globe (Washington)*, July 7, 1835, Thomas Henderson Papers, Filson Historical Society, Louisville, KY
Henderson Papers	Thomas Henderson Papers, Filson Historical Society, Louisville, KY
KDLA	Kentucky Department of Libraries and Archives, Frankfort, KY
KSCL	Margaret I. King Special Collections Library, University of Kentucky, Lexington, KY
Ledgers	Ledger Books of Great Crossing Baptist Church, Southern Baptist Theological Seminary, Louisville, KY
LOKR	*Lexington Observer and Kentucky Reporter*
Observer	*Lexington Observer*
PFF	Pence Family File, Kentucky Historical Society, Frankfort, KY
PFPC	Pence Family private collection
RMJ	Richard Mentor Johnson
SCPL	Scott County Public Library, Georgetown, KY
Sentinel	*Kentucky Sentinel*
TH	Thomas Henderson
Vertical Files: Pence	Vertical File Collection, Pence Family, Kentucky Historical Society, Frankfort, KY

A NOTE ON TERMINOLOGY

1. For discussions on "slave" vs. "enslaved," see "Sampler: A Note on Terms," in Miles, *All That She Carried*, 287–90; and Dunbar, *Never Caught*, xi.
2. Du Bois, *Philadelphia Negro*, 1.
3. Cooper and McCord, *Statutes at Large*, 7:290, 293–94.
4. Hunter, *Bound in Wedlock*.
5. Lucas, *History of Blacks in Kentucky*, 109.

PREFACE

1. "Ward Hall: Kentucky's Grandest Greek Revival Mansion," Ward Hall Preservation Foundation, accessed January 9, 2023, www.wardhall.net.
2. See chap. 3 of this book for information on Choctaw Academy. See also "Save the Choctaw Academy," Facebook, accessed January 9, 2023, www.facebook.com/Save-the-Choctaw-Academy-356091604736264.
3. For information on the Johnson family and GCBC, see chap. 4 of this book; Birdwhistell, "At the Big Crossing," SCPL; and Meyer, *Life and Times*. See also Bevins and Snyder, *Scott County Church Histories*, 6–7.
4. Meyer, *Life and Times*, 363; "Johnson Said to Have Had Negro Common Law Wives," *Georgetown (KY) Graphic*, February 13, 1958, 6.
5. Tom Eblen, "Preservationists Rush to Save Long-Forgotten Native American School," *Lexington (KY) Herald-Leader*, April 15, 2016, 1A, 2A. See also "Save the Choctaw Academy."
6. RMJ to TH, March 24, 1830, December 31, 1825, Henderson Papers.
7. Ashland: The Henry Clay Estate (website), accessed December 20, 2022, https://henryclay.org.
8. On the deaths of Imogene Johnson Pence and Daniel B. Pence, see chap. 7 of this book. See also photo of headstones, PFPC; "Obituary of Daniel B. Pence," *Georgetown Times*, April 29, 1891, ECPC; Notated Pence Bible Pages, ECPC; and Family Bible Pages, Vertical Files: Pence.

INTRODUCTION

1. Brenda Brent Wilfert, telephone interview, May 14, 2018.
2. Much of this information comes from Craig Papers, 1–5. This is an oral history that was gathered from Julia and Richard's former enslaved laborers after they had moved to the all-Black colony of Nicodemus, Kansas, in the 1870s.
3. Much of the information on Julia and her daughters comes from letters found in Henderson Papers.
4. Ledgers; letters in Henderson Papers; Meyer, *Life and Times*, 317.
5. Meyer, *Life and Times*, 422; Ford and Weinberg, "Slavery, Interracial Marriage," 58.
6. See Rothman, introduction to *Notorious in the Neighborhood*, esp. 6. On toleration for relationships at the local level, see Leslie, *Woman of Color*; Myers, *Forging Freedom*, chap. 6; and Schafer, *Anna Madgigine Jai Kingsley*.

7. On the distinction between toleration versus tolerance, see Hodes, introduction to *White Women, Black Men*.

8. Lucas, *History*, 109.

9. See, e.g., Alexander, *Ambiguous Lives*; Gordon-Reed, *Thomas Jefferson*; Gordon-Reed, *Hemingses of Monticello*; Hodes, *White Women, Black Men*; Leslie, *Woman of Color*; Miles, *Ties That Bind*; Rothman, *Notorious in the Neighborhood*; and Schafer, *Anna Madgigine Jai Kingsley*.

10. Meyer, *Life and Times*.

11. For examples of other rural or small-town stories, see Rothman, *Notorious in the Neighborhood*, esp. chap. 2, for the story of Nancy West and David Isaacs; and Schafer, *Anna Madgigine Jai Kingsley*.

12. See Roark et al., *American Promise*, 3rd. ed., chap. 14.

13. Snyder, *Great Crossings*.

14. Christina Snyder, conversation, Bloomington, IN, summer 2010. I am thankful for the discussions I had with Christina about Julia and Richard and for her help in connecting me with folks in Scott County, including Ann Bevins. I am particularly indebted to her for sending me her then unpublished manuscript (now book), *Great Crossings*. It was an invaluable resource as I wrote the first draft of *The Vice President's Black Wife*.

15. Meyer, *Life and Times*; Foreman, "Choctaw Academy," 453–80; D. G. FitzMaurice, "19th Century Kentucky Veep Overdid the Vice Part," *Lexington Herald-Leader*, June 27, 1989, section D; Wikipedia, s.v. "Richard Mentor Johnson," last modified December 30, 2022, https://en.wikipedia.org/wiki/Richard_Mentor_Johnson.

16. Myers, *Forging Freedom*.

17. Stephanie Camp notes it is unlikely that new sources on slavery will come to light, thus we must think expansively and creatively about the sources we do have. Camp, introduction to *Closer to Freedom*.

18. Richard Mentor Johnson Papers, 1808–1847, Library of Congress, Washington, DC.

19. The information from Kentucky comes from nine different facilities: the Filson Historical Society and the Southern Baptist Theological Seminary, both in Louisville; the Kentucky Department of Libraries and Archives and the Kentucky Historical Society, both in Frankfort; the Scott County Public Library and the Georgetown and Scott County Museum, both in Georgetown; and the Lexington Public Library, Main Branch, the Margaret I. King Special Collections Library, and the William T. Young Library, all in Lexington, the latter two at the University of Kentucky.

20. See chap. 7 of this book. I have long wondered if Richard's brothers destroyed his will. It's possible, especially if Richard had left his remaining property to his surviving daughter, Imogene Johnson Pence, and her husband, Daniel Pence.

21. See, e.g., Mary Maillard, "Julia Ann Chinn (ca. 1790–1833)," BlackPast, February 3, 2014, www.blackpast.org/african-american-history/chinn-julia-ann-ca-1790-1833; Meyer, *Life and Times*; and Snyder, *Great Crossings*. I published a piece in 2019 on Chinn and Johnson, discussing her erasure from historical memory. See Amrita Chakrabarti Myers, "The Erasure and Resurrection of Julia Chinn, U.S. Vice President Richard M. Johnson's Black Wife," *Association of Black Women Historians* (blog), March 3, 2019, https://abwh.org/2019/03/03/the-erasure-and-resurrection-of-julia-chinn-u-s-vice-president-richard-m-johnsons-black-wife.

22. See Morgan, epilogue to *Laboring Women*. See also Fuentes, *Dispossessed Lives*.

23. In doing this kind of reconstructive work, I follow in the footsteps of other historians of Black women, especially scholars of slavery. Some I have already named, including Adele Logan Alexander, Stephanie Camp, Marisa Fuentes, Annette Gordon-Reed, and Jennifer Morgan. Tiya Miles's compelling work on source and method in *All That She Carried* has also been very useful. Additionally, while I use the term "informed speculation," the work I do is indebted to that of Saidiya Hartman, who coined the term "critical fabulation," the combining of archival research with critical theory and fictional narrative to fill in the blanks left in the historical record. See Hartman, "Venus in Two Acts," 1–14.

24. Hemings has been written about in detail by Annette Gordon-Reed in two prize-winning books. See Gordon-Reed, *Thomas Jefferson*; and Gordon-Reed, *Hemingses of Monticello*.

25. There haven't been many books written about long-term Black female/white male relationships in the Old South. In addition to the work done by Gordon-Reed on the Hemings/Jefferson family, see Alexander, *Ambiguous Lives*; Leslie, *Woman of Color*; Rothman, *Notorious in the Neighborhood*; and Schafer, *Anna Madgigine Jai Kingsley*. For other types of interracial relationships, see Gaul, *To Marry an Indian*; Hodes, *White Women, Black Men*; and Miles, *Ties That Bind*.

26. On the "one-drop rule," see Hickman, "Devil," 1161–265; and Yaba Blay, "How the 'One Drop Rule' Became a Tool of White Supremacy," *Literary Hub*, February 22, 2021, https://lithub.com/how-the-one-drop-rule-became-a-tool-of-white-supremacy. See also "Loving v. Virginia," History Channel (website), November 17, 2017, www.history.com/topics/civil-rights-movement/loving-v-virginia. It wasn't until 2000 that people could self-identify as more than one race on the federal census. See Betsy Ladyzhets, "How the US Census Has Measured Race Over 230 Years," *ScienceNews*, March 12, 2020, www.sciencenews.org/article/census-2020-race-history.

27. William "Bill" French Jackson, interview, Cincinnati, OH, July 13, 2016.

28. Harriet Pence Gray and Margaret Pence Brooks, interview, Cincinnati, OH, July 13, 2016.

29. See Wikipedia, s.v. "Critical race theory," last modified January 17, 2023, https://en.wikipedia.org/wiki/Critical_race_theory.

30. Steve Contorno, "DeSantis Administration Rejects Proposed AP African American Studies Class in Florida High Schools," CNN, January 19, 2023, www.cnn.com/2023/01/19/politics/ron-desantis-ap-african-american-studies/index.html.

31. See Gabrielle Dean, "Dr. Martin Luther King, Jr.'s Beloved Community," *Sheridan Libraries and University Museums Blog*, Johns Hopkins University, January 21, 2019, https://blogs.library.jhu.edu/2019/01/dr-martin-luther-king-jr-s-beloved-community.

32. There have been debates over whether abolitionist and women's rights activist Sojourner Truth ever said "Ar'n't I a Woman?" The sentiment, however, holds. See "(1851) Sojourner Truth 'Ar'nt I a Woman?'" BlackPast, January 28, 2007, www.blackpast.org/1851-sojourner-truth-arnt-i-woman.

33. On Payton Gendron and the shooting of ten Black people at Tops Friendly Markets in Buffalo in May 2022, see Wikipedia, s.v. "2022 Buffalo shooting," last modified January 8, 2023, https://en.wikipedia.org/wiki/2022_Buffalo_shooting. Dylann Roof murdered nine Black people at Emanuel AME Church in Charleston, South Carolina,

in June 2015. He admitted that he wanted to start a race war. He is now serving life in prison without the possibility of parole. Wikipedia, s.v. "Dylann Roof," last modified January 2, 2023, https://en.wikipedia.org/wiki/Dylann_Roof. Gendron expressed support for Roof and for "replacement theory" in his manifesto. Replacement theory is a white nationalist, far-right conspiracy theory first posited by French author Renaud Camus. The original theory states that, with the cooperation of "replacist" elites, white European populations are being replaced with nonwhite peoples, particularly those from Muslim nations, through mass migration, demographic growth, and a drop in the birth rate of white Europeans. Wikpedia, s.v. "Great Replacement," last modified January 1, 2023, https://en.wikipedia.org/wiki/Great_Replacement. The argument in the United States is that nonwhite individuals are being brought here to "replace" white voters in order to achieve a political agenda. This is often touted by anti-immigration groups, white supremacists, and others. See "The 'Great Replacement' Theory, Explained," National Immigration Forum, accessed January 9, 2023, https://immigrationforum.org/wp-content/uploads/2021/12/Replacement-Theory-Explainer-1122.pdf. White supremacists claim that the influx of immigrants, and people of color specifically, will lead to the extinction of the white race. See Dustin Jones, "What Is the 'Great Replacement' and How Is It Tied to the Buffalo Shooting Suspect?," NPR, May 16, 2022, www.npr.org/2022/05/16/1099034094.

34. Eileen Sullivan and Katie Benner, "Biggest Domestic Terror Threat Comes from White Supremacists," *New York Times*, May 12, 2021, https://www.nytimes.com/2021/05/12/us/politics/domestic-terror-white-supremacists.html; *Threats to the Homeland*.

CHAPTER ONE

1. Julia's middle name is in "The Workings of Slavery," *Liberator*, July 25, 1845; and in Johnson Ancestry II Binder: Richard Mentor Johnson, BBWPC. Henrietta's name is in Craig Papers, 1–5.

2. Bevins, *Slaves and Free Blacks*, 1.

3. Meyer, *Life and Times*, 18–20, 26, 28–29. Richard was the fifth of Robert and Jemima's eleven children and the first one born in Kentucky. May, "Johnson Family." See also transcription in Johnson Family Papers, SCPL; and Snyder, *Great Crossings*, 43.

4. Meyer, *Life and Times*, 28–29, 34, 40–44.

5. Smith, "Slavery and Abolition," 81; Lucas, *History*, xiv. Kentucky had a total population of 220,955 in 1800. Black persons thus made up 18 percent of the state that year. See Wikipedia, s.v. "Demographics of Kentucky," last modified February 3, 2023, https://en.wikipedia.org/wiki/Demographics_of_Kentucky.

6. Lucas, *History*, xvii–xviii.

7. Lucas, 16–17.

8. Lucas, 2–3.

9. Bevins, *Slaves and Free Blacks*, 22; Lucas, *History*, 13. For dollar conversion, see CPIIC, accessed January 6, 2023, www.in2013dollars.com/us/inflation/1849?amount=5.

10. Meyer, *Life and Times*, 26; Lucas, *History*, 14.

11. Lucas, *History*, 14–15. There were dairy cows at the Station. Meyer, *Life and Times*, 27. A peck is eight dry quarts, or a quarter of a bushel. See Sheela Prakash, "Know Your

NOTES TO CHAPTER ONE

Nomenclature: What's a Bushel and a Peck?" Kitchn, August 30, 2016, www.thekitchn.com/know-your-nomenclature-whats-a-bushel-and-a-peck-234710.

12. See White, *Ar'n't I a Woman?*; and Jones-Rogers, *They Were Her Property*. Additionally, oral testimonies of formerly enslaved people collected by the federal government in the 1930s contain examples of such behavior. See Slave Narrative Collection, Library of Congress, Washington, DC.

13. The law of maternal heredity, also known as *partus sequitur ventrem*, was passed by the Virginia General Assembly in December 1662. See Encyclopedia Virginia, s.v. "Negro womens children to serve according to the condition of the mother, 1662," last modified August 17, 2021, https://encyclopediavirginia.org/entries/negro-womens-children-to-serve-according-to-the-condition-of-the-mother-1662; and Jacobs, *Incidents in the Life*.

14. Hemings Family Tree in Gordon-Reed, *Hemingses of Monticello*, 668. On "kinlessness," see Morgan, *Reckoning with Slavery*.

15. Thomas Jefferson himself considered "the labor of a breeding woman as no object," for "it is not their labor, but their increase which is the first consideration with us." Their "increase" meant their children. King, *Stolen Childhood*, 2.

16. Description of Julia in Craig Papers, 1–5.

17. Lucas, *History*, 14, 16, 10, 3–5.

18. Wright, *Lexington*, 73, 5; Smith, "Slavery and Abolition," 84; Lucas, *History*, 10, 5.

19. Lucas, *History*, 44.

20. Lucas, 6; Bevins, *Slaves and Free Blacks*, 22; Bevins, "Great Crossings."

21. Hatfield, "Richard Mentor Johnson," 125; Meyer, *Life and Times*, 318.

22. White, *Ar'n't I a Woman?*, 92; King, *Stolen Childhood*, 22–24; Lucas, *History*, 10–11, 7.

23. King, *Stolen Childhood*, 44–45, 52–53; Lucas, *History*, 33.

24. See Stephanie Camp's discussion of enslaved women and their three bodies, particularly the third body of pleasure. Camp, *Closer to Freedom*, chap. 3. See also Lucas, *History*, 34.

25. Lucas, *History*, 35. For Lexington population numbers, see Wikipedia, s.v. "Lexington, Kentucky," last modified April 12, 2023, https://en.wikipedia.org/wiki/Lexington,_Kentucky#Demographics.

26. Lucas, *History*, 101.

27. Lucas, 102.

28. Robert McAfee, a friend of Richard's, said Johnson read law with the Honorable James Brown in Lexington in 1800. Brown was a professor at Transylvania Law. Johnson's name doesn't appear on the Transylvania list of graduates in 1824, however, which included all graduates from 1802 onward. Other records from Transylvania do not include his name. Meyer, *Life and Times*, 291. Richard briefly practiced law after being admitted to the bar and before he was elected to the state legislature in 1804. Snyder, *Great Crossings*, 44. For Julia's 1790 birth date, see Johnson Ancestry II Binder: Richard Mentor Johnson, BBWPC. The 1796 birth date is in Craig Papers, 1–5.

29. Craig Papers, 1–8.

30. On enslaved families and separation, see Berry, *Price*, esp. 6; Bailey, *Weeping Time*; Taylor, *Driven toward Madness*; and Miles, *All That She Carried*, 5.

31. Craig Papers, 1–8.

NOTES TO CHAPTER ONE

32. For information on housekeepers and mistresses, see Myers, *Forging Freedom*, esp. chap. 2. We can estimate when the couple began having sex by when their first child was born. See Imogene's date of birth in "Record of Births," Pence Family Bible, PFF.

33. The phrase "little commonwealths" is from Demos, *Little Commonwealth*.

34. Craig Papers, 1–8.

35. Craig Papers, 1–8. The Craig Papers is an oral history collection. In the introduction to the chapter on Richard Johnson it states that "Johnson was a Kentuckian. We get his story from slaves who lived on his Kentucky plantation. They were a part of the [Nicodemus] colony that came to Graham County, Kansas, in the [18]70s. Among them were Mrs. Mary Johnson, her son Joseph and his family—Thomas Johnson and his family, Beverly, Herring, Hiram, Travis, and John Samuels." While these were people who would have known Julia and Richard well, the fact that over sixty years had passed between the time the events recorded in the oral history took place and the founding of Nicodemus could explain the confusion with certain facts. Richard's father, Robert Johnson, died in October 1815 without a will. Robert's date of death was recorded on his tombstone at GCBC: "Col. Robert Johnson / husband to / Jemima Johnson / was born July 17, 1745 / died 15 of October 1815 / aged 70 years." See also Meyer, *Life and Times*, 48. Jemima Johnson died in 1814, predeceasing her husband by just over a year. Meyer, *Life and Times*, 47.

36. Young and Middleton, *Heirs Apparent*, 120; Kennedy, *Rediscovering America*, 341, 343.

37. Lindsey Apple, "Richard Mentor Johnson (1781–1850)," 86, BBWPC; Schenkman and Reiger, *One Night Stands*, 76–77; Stimpson, *Book about American Politics*, 133. Ward Hall, a Greek Revival manor in Scott County, Kentucky, was the home of Junius Richard Ward, Richard's nephew. Now on the National Historic Register, Ward Hall is open for tours. See "Ward Hall: Kentucky's Grandest Greek Revival Mansion," Ward Hall Preservation Foundation, accessed December 19, 2022, www.wardhall.net.

38. For family letters, see Henderson Papers. While Richard lived in Washington, DC, for thirty-four years, he spent most of those years at the home of Rev. O. B. Brown. He had no home of his own in that city until 1836, when he ran for the vice presidency: "Rich. M. Johnson, Esq. has rented a large and fashionable house on the Capitol Hill. The house is to undergo a thorough repair, and that whispering old damsel, Gossip, says that he will entertain upon a large scale." This house, where he lived from 1836 to 1840, was on Maryland Avenue, east of the Capitol. In 1840 he was once again living at Mr. Brown's house. *LOKR*, July 27, 1836; Meyer, *Life and Times*, 294, 311–12.

39. See letters in Henderson Papers. For Julia's date of death, see entry, July 6, 1833, 2:265, Ledgers; and Meyer, *Life and Times*, 339–41.

40. Letter, October 8, 1840, Catherine L. Bragg Papers, FHS; Ford and Weinberg, "Slavery, Interracial Marriage," 57; "Johnson Said to Have Had Negro Common Law Wives," *Georgetown Graphic*, February 13, 1958, 5; Mary Maillard, "Julia Ann Chinn (ca. 1790–1833)," *BlackPast*, February 3, 2014, www.blackpast.org/african-american-history/chinn-julia-ann-ca-1790-1833. Newspapers from the era referred to Julia in a variety of ways: jet black, swarthy, dusky, yellow, etc.

41. Kennedy, *Rediscovering America*, 341–43.

42. While race-based chattel slavery was hereditary and passed down through the female line, which expressly revealed kinship on the one hand, colonizers and enslavers

created the myth of "kinlessness" on the other hand in order to justify commodifying African-descendant peoples, giving rise to racial capitalism. Turning to the logics of numeracy, listing human beings as numbers and dollar amounts in ledgers and account books, Black folks became data, kinless for the purposes of purchase and resale. Western notions of value and race thus grew up together, as racial capitalism denied enslaved folks their humanity, kinship, and affective ties while simultaneously relying on kinship to reproduce and enforce slavery through enslaved women's bodies. See Morgan, *Reckoning with Slavery*.

43. Craig Papers, 6–8.

44. John Wilson interview, 16, Draper Manuscripts, Truman State University Archives, Kirksville, MO; Hart, *Richard M. Johnson*, 20; Henderson Papers.

45. Entry, April 20, 1828, 2:169–70, Ledgers.

46. Kelly, "Judge James Y. Kelly Manuscript," 477.

47. RMJ to Humphrey Marshall, May 1840, Humphrey Marshall Papers, FHS; Henry Burke, "Window to the Past: Richard Mentor Johnson," Lest We Forget, compiled by Bennie McRae Jr., accessed January 6, 2023, http://lestweforget.hamptonu.edu/. I have never seen the press release Burke quotes in this piece. Kentucky law did not recognize marriages between whites and "negroes or mulattos." But state law also defined a mulatto as someone who had "one fourth, or other larger part of negro blood." If Julia Chinn had less than 25 percent African ancestry, as some sources assert, referring to her as an "octoroon," then by legal standards she would have been "white." Of course, if she were legally enslaved, Julia would have been socially and culturally "Black" in the eyes of the larger society in which she lived. See Maillard, "Julia Ann Chinn"; Ford and Weinberg, "Slavery, Interracial Marriage," 57; and Letters to the Editor, *OAH Magazine of History*.

48. Post, "Kentucky Law Concerning Emancipation," 344–46.

49. The methods through which Black women could acquire manumission were severely constrained. While discomfiting to analyze, relationships with men of influence were one tool in their limited kit. See Millward, "'Relics of Slavery,'" 22–30. See also Myers, *Forging Freedom*, chaps. 2, 5, 6.

50. McLaurin, *Celia, a Slave*, 24, 28.

51. McLaurin, 33–35.

52. Schafer, *Anna Madgigine Jai Kingsley*, 2.

53. Schafer, 14–15.

54. Schafer, 21, 24, 25–26.

55. Schafer, 33–35.

56. Alexander, *Ambiguous Lives*, chap. 2.

57. Gordon-Reed, *Thomas Jefferson*, 108–16.

58. Gordon-Reed, 172–74.

59. Leslie, *Woman of Color*, 1, 136–39, 38, 44–46.

60. Leslie, 75, 104, 140–46.

CHAPTER TWO

1. An account from 1927 says that Lafayette *may* have stopped by Johnson's tavern, and "perhaps a barbecue at Blue Lick," before arriving at Cincinnati on the morning

of May 20, 1825. Accounts from the era reveal that Lafayette definitely stopped at Blue Spring. *Sunday Herald-Post*, March 27, 1927, Filson Historical Files: "Lafayette, Marquis de (General)," FHS. Richard did have a tavern on his property. Snyder, *Great Crossings*, 41, 57; editorial, *Lexington Gazette*, May 19, 1825, Richard M. Johnson Folder, Johnson Family Papers, FHS.

2. Stedman, *Bluegrass Craftsman*, 74–76; Ann Bolton Bevins, "Victory Lap Brings Lafayette to Scott County," *Georgetown News-Graphic*, July 20, 2008, 2B; Snyder, *Great Crossings*, 42; Meyer, *Life and Times*, 316.

3. Stedman, *Bluegrass Craftsman*, 76; Meyer, *Life and Times*, 317; *LOKR*, July 1, 4, 1835.

4. Stedman, *Bluegrass Craftsman*, 76; Snyder, *Great Crossings*, 41.

5. For more on women and work in the late eighteenth and nineteenth centuries, see Boydston, *Home and Work*; Miller, *Needle's Eye*; and Jacqueline Jones, *Labor of Love*. See also Snyder, *Great Crossings*, 57.

6. See letters of Abigail Adams to John Adams in Butterfield, *Adams Family Correspondence*. A number of women fought during the Revolution disguised as men, including Deborah Samson. See Ellet, *Women*; and Hanaford, *Daughters of America*. The final quote in the paragraph is from an essay titled "On Matrimonial Obedience." Written by "A Matrimonial Republican," it was originally published in *Lady's Magazine* in 1792. In Kierner, *Contrast*, 119–20.

7. See Kelley, *Learning to Stand*; and Murray, "On the Equality."

8. African Americans were barred from obtaining an education in many southern states in the pre–Civil War era. In the North, they had to open their own schools in many locales, often in conjunction with Black church denominations, and faced deep hostility from a northern populace committed to maintaining racial hierarchies, with or without slavery. For an in-depth examination of Black women's educational labors in the antebellum period as students, teachers, and activists, see Baumgartner, *In Pursuit of Knowledge*.

9. Pease and Pease, *Ladies, Women, and Wenches*; Salmon, *Women and the Law*; Myers, *Forging Freedom*, 103–6, 156, 173.

10. Various letters, Henderson Papers. For a detailed discussion of Choctaw Academy, Julia's handling of school issues and Blue Spring's financial matters, and relations between the farm's Black people and the academy's students, all of whom were young boys or men, see chap. 3 of this book. Chap. 2 mentions the academy only in brief because it is the focus of the next chapter.

11. Meyer, *Life and Times*, chap. 3.

12. For Daniel, see "The Workings of Slavery," *Liberator*, July 25, 1845. Julia's financial responsibilities are discussed in chap. 3 of this book.

13. For detailed information on Richard's military exploits in the War of 1812, see Meyer, *Life and Times*, chap. 3; Cleaves, *Old Tippecanoe*, 112, 120, 134, 158, 173–74, 202; Stimpson, *Book about American Politics*, 125, 130; and Schlesinger, *Age of Jackson*, 140–41.

14. Meyer, *Life and Times*, 137–39. On Julia's medical skills, see RMJ to TH, December 9, 1825, June 1834, Henderson Papers. Imogene married in June 1830, shortly after she turned eighteen years old. Adaline married in November 1832. Adaline likely also married at eighteen, which means she was probably born in 1814. That means Julia would have gotten pregnant when Richard was home recuperating after the Battle of the Thames in late fall 1813. "Daniel B. Pence and Imogene Johnson were married June 6th,

1830," in Pence Family Bible, PFF. Adaline's marriage announcement is in Clift, *Kentucky Marriages*, 72.

15. Schafer, *Anna Madgigine Jai Kingsley*, 25–26, 33–35.

16. On Fort George Island, Anna Kingsley lived with her children in the "Ma'am Anna House" from the 1820s until 1838. This dwelling was sixty feet away from the house that her husband, Zephaniah, occupied. Built of tabby bricks on the first floor and wood frame above, the dwelling had a kitchen and parlor on the first floor and bedrooms on the second. Schafer, *Anna Madgigine Jai Kingsley*, 45–49. For Julia Chinn's house at Blue Spring, see RMJ to TH, March 24, 1830, December 31, 1825, Henderson Papers.

17. Leslie, *Woman of Color*, 44–45; RMJ to TH, March 24, 1830, December 31, 1825, Henderson Papers.

18. Snyder, *Great Crossings*, 51, 56.

19. RMJ to TH, December 8, 1825, Henderson Papers. Richard didn't hire an overseer for Blue Spring Farm until 1828. Until then, Julia and Thomas handled plantation matters as a team, with Thomas responsible for slave discipline. For a detailed discussion of this, see chap. 3 of this book.

20. RMJ to TH, n.d. and January 13, 1826, Henderson Papers.

21. As late as 1842, Thomas was a minister at Center Ridge Baptist Church in Grant County. He died at his home near Crittenden, Kentucky, on April 26, 1846, and is buried in the family burial ground in the orchard. Emma Rouse Lloyd, *Clasping Hands with Generations Past* (privately printed by Wiesen-Hart, 1932), 83, 87, 96, in Finding Aid Folder, Henderson Papers; War Department to TH, March 13, 1841, Henderson Papers.

22. RMJ to TH, December 31, 1825, Henderson Papers. See also Lucas, *History*, 35; and May, *Yuletide in Dixie*.

23. RMJ to TH, December 31, 1825, January 13, 1826, March 24, 1830, Henderson Papers. For a larger discussion on the lives of white southern plantation mistresses, see Glymph, *Out of the House*; and Jones-Rogers, *They Were Her Property*.

24. On Patience and her daughters, see chaps. 3, 6 of this book. We know Thomas Henderson tutored the house staff, along with Adaline and Imogene, at night. See Henderson Letter.

25. "Miss J****** . . . was dressed in the most brilliant manner." The anonymous writer claimed Choctaw Academy yielded Richard "a clear profit of fifteen or sixteen thousand dollars a year, and enables him to dress his family so fine that many of his poorer neighbors are beginning to give up the little *colorable* objections they have heretofore had to associating with them." *Observer*, August 2, 1832. On the Johnsons and GCBC, see chap. 4 of this book.

26. Snyder, *Great Crossings*, 116.

27. While none of Julia's letters have been recovered, Richard refers to them in his letters to other people. See, for example, RMJ to TH, December 31, 1825, Henderson Papers.

28. Richard mentions that Julia wrote to him in his letters to Thomas. RMJ to TH, January 13, February 10, 1826, Henderson Papers. It's quite possible that when he died, Richard's surviving brothers destroyed the letters that Julia and their daughters had written to him over the years, as well as all of his other papers, which explains why none of these records have materialized. It also explains why there is no significant Richard M.

Johnson collection in Washington, DC, or anywhere in Kentucky, despite his having been in political office for well over four decades.

29. RMJ to unknown, March 12, 1834, Henderson Papers. For a detailed account of Julia's labor for Choctaw Academy, see chap. 3 of this book.

30. *Kentucky Gazette*, July 9, 1819; Meyer, *Life and Times*, 314.

31. *Argus*, August 4, 1824.

32. Myers, *Forging Freedom*, 178.

33. *Argus*, August 4, 1824; Meyer, *Life and Times*, 315.

34. Stedman, *Bluegrass Craftsman*, 76.

35. For Richard's parents, see chap. 1 of this book. Richard's brothers James Johnson and John T. Johnson served in the federal House of Representatives, and brother Benjamin was a federal district judge. The Johnsons regularly obtained government contracts and favors for family members and allies, and their financial interests in local newspapers, such as the *Georgetown Patriot*, only added to their influence. Additionally, Richard's sister Sally married William Ward, connecting the Johnsons to a powerful planter family with land in Kentucky and Mississippi. Meyer, *Life and Times*, chap. 1 and 324–26.

36. Johnson Papers; Snyder, *Great Crossings*, 48–50.

37. Meyer, *Life and Times*, 318. Meyer cites a "manuscript in his possession" that was signed by Katherine Stout Bradley, Katie Bradley Rice, and Alfred M. Bradley Jr.—lineal descendants of James Suggett, who was Richard Mentor Johnson's maternal grandfather. See also McQueen, *Offbeat Kentuckians*, 16, 18.

38. For details on Richard's sexual behavior after Julia's death, see chap. 6 of this book.

39. Snyder, *Great Crossings*, 1, 3–4. For more on the school, including its inception, see chap. 3 of this book.

40. *Observer*, August 2, 1832; Hart, *Richard M. Johnson*, 17. "Daniel B. Pence and Imogene Johnson were married June 6th, 1830," Pence Family Bible, PFF.

41. Craig Papers, 8.

42. For white education in the Old South, see Hyde, *Schooling*.

43. RMJ to TH, December 16, 17, 1825, Henderson Papers.

44. RMJ to TH, December 2, 8, 16, 1825, February 16, 10, 1826, Henderson Papers.

45. RMJ to TH, January 6, 1826, Henderson Papers.

46. RMJ to TH, January 13, 1826, Henderson Papers. For information on employment and poverty of free Black women in the Old South, see Myers, *Forging Freedom*, chaps. 3 and 4. See also Snyder, *Great Crossings*, 67.

47. Tim Talbott, "Slavery Laws in Old Kentucky," ExploreKYHistory, accessed January 9, 2023, https://explorekyhistory.ky.gov/items/show/180.

48. RMJ to TH, January 13, February 10, 1826, December 8, 1825, Henderson Papers.

49. Meyer, *Life and Times*, 318; Henderson Letter.

50. For more on the lives of antebellum Black women, see Alexander, *Ambiguous Lives*; Dabel, *Respectable Woman*; Dunbar, *Fragile Freedom*; Millward, *Finding Charity's Folk*; and Myers, *Forging Freedom*.

51. Before she married, Adaline went by the last name Johnson. See Clift, *Kentucky Marriages*, 72. See also Meyer, *Life and Times*, 317; RMJ to TH, December 8, 1825, Henderson Papers; various articles, *Daily Globe*, July 7, 1835; and *LOKR*, July 1, 4, 1835. On the Bettingall/Tunno family, see Myers, *Forging Freedom*, chap. 6.

52. Addie Murphy to J. C. Meadors, August 13, 1938, 123–24, J. Winston Coleman Papers, KSCL.

53. RMJ to TH, March 28, April 30, 1828, March 8, 1832, Henderson Papers. Like Julia's letters, Adaline's have not survived, but Richard frequently mentions the contents of his daughter's letters in his own.

54. RMJ to Adaline Johnson Scott, December 12, 1833, Henderson Papers.

55. Clift, *Kentucky Marriages*, 72. "Daniel B. Pence was born October 13, 1804," Pence Family Bible, PFF.

56. Snyder, *Great Crossings*, 60.

57. For more on how enslaved people always had a price on their bodies and were constantly at risk of sale, see Berry, *Price*. On the connection between debt, auctions, and the separation of enslaved families, see Bailey, *Weeping Time*.

58. See Myers, *Forging Freedom*, chaps. 5, 6, for the stories of Margaret Bettingall and Sarah Sanders, which speak directly to these issues.

CHAPTER THREE

1. RMJ to TH, January 6, 1826, Henderson Papers; Jack H. Dycus, "Choctaw Indian School," *Lexington Leader*, May 17, 1936, in Filson News Clippings: Schools–KY–Scott County–Choctaw Indian School, FHS. We can deduce that free Blacks in the Bluegrass region were manufacturing and selling alcohol because local laws prohibited them from doing so and fined them $50–$300 when they were caught. Lucas, *History*, 109.

2. RMJ to TH, December 27, 28 [?], 1827, March 24, 1830, Henderson Papers.

3. Choctaw Academy has been written about numerous times over the years, mostly in article form. The most recent, and in-depth, exploration of the school is Christina Snyder's award-winning monograph *Great Crossings*.

4. Snyder, *Great Crossings*, 20–21.

5. Tolerance is acceptance, inclusion, and understanding, whereas toleration is the act of putting up with something. See Hodes, introduction to *White Women, Black Men*.

6. For a discussion of plantation spaces, including the woods and swamplands around farms and homes, as contested, or rival, geographies between the enslaved and their enslavers, see Camp, introduction to *Closer to Freedom*. I use it here to argue that the space on and around Blue Spring became a rival geography between various groups that included not only enslaved persons and Richard Johnson but also the Native students and white teachers of Choctaw Academy, Julia Chinn and her daughters, and the other Black members of the house party, many of whom were related to Julia.

7. Dr. Liza Black, email to author, November 6, 2022.

8. Wikipedia, s.v. "Treaty of Washington City," last modified July 12, 2022, https://en.wikipedia.org/wiki/Treaty_of_Washington_City; Snyder, *Great Crossings*, 36, 14.

9. *Lexington Gazette*, November 4, 1825, Johnson Family Papers, Richard M. Johnson Folder, FHS; Snyder, *Great Crossings*, 14, 38; Meyer, *Life and Times*, 361. In the long run, of course, we know this strategy failed because the Choctaw were still removed from their lands.

10. Emma Rouse Lloyd, *Clasping Hands with Generations Past* (privately printed by Wiesen-Hart, 1932), 87–88, in Finding Aid Folder, Henderson Papers. Richard and his

brother James Johnson were in debt because of a series of unfortunate business deals, including an ill-fated Yellowstone expedition in 1819. "Johnson Said to Have Had Negro Common Law Wives," *Georgetown Graphic*, February 13, 1958, 6. That Richard hoped the school would help him get out of debt is also in Meyer, *Life and Times*, 336–37.

11. Lloyd, *Clasping Hands*, 87, Henderson Papers.

12. RMJ to Maj. John T. Johnson, December 31, 1825; and to TH, December 2, 1825, both in Henderson Papers.

13. Tom Eblen, "Preservationists Rush to Save Long-Forgotten Native American School," *Lexington Herald-Leader*, April 15, 2016, 2A; Ron Bryant, "Academy for Indian Boys Near Georgetown Briefly Flourished," *Kentucky Gazette*, December 21, 2005, 8; Meyer, *Life and Times*, 363; Dycus, "Choctaw Indian School," FHS.

14. RMJ to TH, December 2, 8, 1825, Henderson Papers. Five hundred dollars would be roughly $15,200 in 2023. CPIIC, accessed April 8, 2023, www.in2013dollars.com/us/inflation/1825?amount=500. See also n10 in this chap.

15. Lloyd, *Clasping Hands*, 92, Henderson Papers. See also RMJ to TH, January 13, 1826, December 31, 1825, Henderson Papers.

16. RMJ to TH, December 9, 1825, June 1834, Henderson Papers.

17. For more on women and medicine on antebellum plantations, see Fett, *Working Cures*. See also Cooper Owens, *Medical Bondage*.

18. RMJ to TH, February 26, 1826, Henderson Papers.

19. RMJ to TH, March 28, 1828, March 4, December 13, 1826, Henderson Papers.

20. For a broader discussion of capital and credit in antebellum America, see, e.g., Kamensky, *Exchange Artist*; Mihm, *Nation of Counterfeiters*; and Bodenhorn, *History of Banking*.

21. RMJ to TH, February 26, 1826, Henderson Papers. Ten dollars in 1826 would be roughly $303 in 2023. See CPIIC, accessed April 8, 2023, www.in2013dollars.com/us/inflation/1826?amount=10.

22. RMJ to TH, January 6, 13, 1826, December 19, 1827, Henderson Papers.

23. See, e.g., Child, *Boarding School Seasons*; Lomawaima, *They Called It*; and Adams, *Education for Extinction*. While these authors focus more on the postbellum period, the blueprints for the policies of cultural eradication they illuminate were designed in the early nineteenth century.

24. See chap. 2 of this book for Imogene's education. On white women's education in the nineteenth century, see Kelley, *Learning to Stand*; and Nash, *Women's Education*.

25. See chap. 2 of this book for more on Richard's debts and overall financial situation.

26. Meyer, *Life and Times*, 320; RMJ to TH, December 19, 1827, Henderson Papers. For inflation calculation, see CPIIC, accessed April 8, 2023, www.in2013dollars.com/us/inflation/1827?amount=100. For Rood, see Snyder, *Great Crossings*, 225.

27. RMJ to Callender Irvine, August 4, 1827, Choctaw Academy Folder, SCPL; RMJ to TH, March 28, 1828, Henderson Papers.

28. RMJ to TH, April 30, 1828, March 8, 1832, Henderson Papers.

29. RMJ to TH, April 16, 1834, Henderson Papers.

30. See chaps. 5 and 7 of this book for additional details on Adaline's husband and son.

31. RMJ to Adaline Johnson Scott, December 12, 1833, Henderson Papers.

32. RMJ to TH, March 20, 1828, March 8, 1832, Henderson Papers. See chap. 6 of this book for details on Adaline's health issues and death.

33. For information on Imogene's husband and children, see chap. 7 of this book.

34. See "Richard M. Johnson," 1810, 1820, 1830, and 1840 US Federal Census databases, Ancestry.com; and 1850 US Census–Slave Schedule, Scott County, Kentucky, Pence File, ECPC. See also 1850 US Census, District 2: Scott County, Kentucky, roll M432_218, p. 453A, image 372, Kentucky Census Records, KDLA.

35. On the free Black communities of Louisville and Lexington, see Lucas, *History*, chap. 5.

36. For more on slavery in Indian nations, see Snyder, *Slavery in Indian Country*. Ideologies about colorism, racial hierarchy, and anti-Blackness that permeated certain Indigenous nations were a by-product of settler colonialism and the racism that Native nations themselves experienced at the hands of Europeans. While Native groups had long enslaved one other as prisoners of war, generational, race-based, chattel slavery was introduced to them by colonizing nations, along with accompanying ideas about race, racial hierarchy, and anti-Blackness. For more on these issues, see Miles, *Ties That Bind*. See also Guilbault, "Creating a Common Culture."

37. Sarah Deer posits that Indigenous communities learned about sexual violence from Europeans and Americans, who raped Native women from the first days of contact. In particular, Deer argues that Native Americans did *not* use rape as a tactic of war and were shocked that settler colonials did. See Deer, *Beginning and End*, esp. chap. 3.

38. RMJ to TH, January 6, 1826, Henderson Papers; Dycus, "Choctaw Indian School," FHS. See also Lucas, *History*, 109.

39. RMJ to TH, December 27, 1827, Henderson Papers.

40. Deer, *Beginning and End*, chaps. 2, 3. See also Morgan, *Reckoning with Slavery*.

41. RMJ to TH, December 28 [?], 1827, Henderson Papers.

42. RMJ to TH, March 24, 1830, Henderson Papers.

43. RMJ to TH, March 24, 1830, Henderson Papers.

44. RMJ to TH, March 24, 1830, Henderson Papers.

45. RMJ to TH, December 28 [?], 1827, Henderson Papers. The term "wench" was used in antebellum America to refer to Black women, particularly enslaved women. Developed in the colonial era, it was a term that set Black women apart from (white) ladies, who were seen as virtuous and chaste wives and mothers, whereas wenches were hypersexual, promiscuous, immoral temptresses. The stereotype of the Jezebel grew up hand in hand with this term. See White, *Ar'n't I a Woman?*, chap. 1. See also Kathleen M. Brown, *Good Wives, Nasty Wenches*.

46. Addie Murphy to J. C. Meadors, August 13, 1938, 123, J. Winston Coleman Papers, KSCL.

47. RMJ to TH, March 24, 1830, Henderson Papers. While my reading of the document suggests the student's name was Joe, Christina Snyder concludes that the name of the student involved with Lucinda was Isaac Folsom. There is a Joseph Pitchlynn Folsom and an Isaac Pitchlynn Folsom in the records. The letter from March 24 doesn't fully spell out the name of the student. Blurry, it is abbreviated to just three letters. It could be Jos. or Isc. or even Isa (which could be short for Isaiah). See Snyder, *Great Crossings*, 117, 284, 287–88. For rival geographies, see Camp, *Closer to Freedom*, 8.

48. See Snyder, *Great Crossings*, 116, 224, 240. Imogene married Daniel in 1830. For more on the Pences, see chap. 7 of this book.

49. RMJ to TH, January 16, 1828, Henderson Papers.

50. See chap. 4 of this book for information on GCBC. The school building was "40 paces" from the main house. Conversion at Kyle's Converter, accessed January 6, 2023, www.kylesconverter.com/length/paces-to-feet. See also Snyder, *Great Crossings*, 117.

51. RMJ to TH, March 28, 1828, Henderson Papers.

52. RMJ to TH, March 7, 1828, Henderson Papers. See also Snyder, *Great Crossings*, 120.

53. RMJ to TH, March 7, 1828, Henderson Papers. Robert and Jemima Johnson had eleven children. Sally was their fourth child and second daughter. William Ward was the federal government's agent in Indian Territory and married to Sally Johnson. Thomas L. Johnson: Genealogy of the Johnson Family, FHS. See also Snyder, *Great Crossings*, 50–51, 56.

54. RMJ to TH, March 8, 19, 20, 1828, Henderson Papers.

55. RMJ to TH, March 7, 1828, Henderson Papers.

56. RMJ to TH, n.d., document A H497 17, Henderson Papers. This letter would have been written in March or April of 1828, given the timing of Riddle's expulsion.

57. Ward to TH, April 12, 1828, Henderson Papers.

58. See n49 in this chapter and text in accompanying paragraph.

59. See n45 in this chapter and text in accompanying paragraph.

60. RMJ to TH, March 1, 1830, Henderson Papers. See also Snyder, *Great Crossings*, 99–100, 109–10.

61. RMJ to TH, March 24, 1830, Henderson Papers. Julia and Rose both passed away from cholera around the same time. Their deaths are recorded in the GCBC ledger books. Entry, July 6, 1833, 2:265, Ledgers.

62. RMJ to TH, March 24, 1830, Henderson Papers. For more on the historical construct of Black women as wenches and Jezebels, see White, *Ar'n't I a Woman?*, chap. 1; and Kathleen M. Brown, *Good Wives, Nasty Wenches*.

63. RMJ to TH, January 28, 1831, Henderson Papers.

64. Lloyd, *Clasping Hands*, 88, 92, Henderson Papers; Meyer, *Life and Times*, 374. There were approximately 200 students at Choctaw Academy in 1831. "Johnson Said to Have," 6. Eight hundred dollars is just over $27,400 in 2023. See CPIIC, accessed January 6, 2023, www.in2013dollars.com/us/inflation/1831?amount=800.

65. John Wilson interview, 15–16, Draper Manuscripts, Truman State University Archives, Kirksville, MO; RMJ to TH, February 14, 1831, May 27, 28, 1834, Henderson Papers.

66. RMJ to TH, January 10, 1835, May 4, 1834, Henderson Papers.

67. For more on Imogene's life after her marriage, see chap. 7 of this book.

68. RMJ to TH, December 7, 1835, Henderson Papers.

69. RMJ to TH, April 30, [1833?], Henderson Papers. A comment on p. 1 of the letter mentions, "You have lived with me as the chief of the Choctaw Academy eight years." The letter's date does not include a year, but because the school opened in 1825, the comment suggests the letter was written in 1833.

70. For more on the resistance of washerwomen, see Hunter, *To 'Joy My Freedom*. A postbellum study, it highlights that Black women's resistance tactics after the war were a continuation of those begun during slavery. See also Camp, *Closer to Freedom*.

71. RMJ to TH, April 30, [1833?], Henderson Papers. If this letter was written in 1833, "Mr. Pence" could refer to either the overseer, Edward Pence, or his brother Daniel Pence, Imogene's husband.

72. RMJ to Adaline Johnson Scott, December 12, 1833, Henderson Papers.

73. See nn16–18 in chap. 2 in this book.

74. RMJ to unknown, March 12, 1834, Henderson Papers. On the cholera epidemic and Julia's role in it, see chap. 5 of this book.

75. RMJ to TH, March 14, 1834, Henderson Papers.

76. RMJ to TH, March 16, 1834, January 14, 1835, Henderson Papers.

77. RMJ to TH, June 1834, Henderson Papers.

78. RMJ to TH, March 14, June 17, 1834, Henderson Papers.

79. RMJ to TH, April 25, 29, 1834; and to Adaline Johnson Scott, December 12, 1833, Henderson Papers.

80. For a detailed discussion of Adaline's death, see chap. 6 of this book. See also RMJ to TH, February 26, 1836, Henderson Papers.

81. War Department to TH, March 13, 1841, Henderson Papers. See also Lloyd, *Clasping Hands*, 92, 94, Henderson Papers.

82. Rouse, "Colonel Dick Johnson's," 116.

83. Camp, *Closer to Freedom*, 8.

CHAPTER FOUR

1. Birdwhistell, "At the Big Crossing," 17, 20, SCPL.

2. Entry, April 20, 1828, 2:169–70, Ledgers. There are four church ledgers, starting in 1793. All material cited herein comes from vols. 1 and 2. Vol. 1 runs 1793–1813 and vol. 2 1813–61. Though the church was founded in 1785, the ledgers begin in 1793. No internal documents appear to exist for the first eight years of the church's existence.

3. On church schisms, see Chesebrough, *Clergy Dissent*; McKivigan and Snay, *Religion*; and Whyte, *Send Back the Money*. For race and southern religion more broadly, see Heyrman, *Southern Cross*; and Irons, *Origins of Proslavery Christianity*. On churches in Kentucky and the border states, see Ford, "Black Spiritual Defiance," 69–106; and McKivigan, "Battle for the Border," 48–71.

4. McKivigan, "Battle for the Border," 52, 62.

5. See Family Bible Pages, Vertical Files: Pence; and Pence Family Bible, PFF.

6. These separate Black services would have been in addition to regular Sunday services, which were attended by all the church's congregants, white and Black. Entry, first Saturday in October 1802, 1:82, Ledgers.

7. Ann Bevins, *Lexington Leader*, August 24, 1963, 3, Vertical File Collection, Scott County Baptist Churches, Kentucky Historical Society, Frankfort, KY. See also Bevins and Snyder, *Scott County Church Histories*, 6–7.

8. Great Crossing was originally called Big Crossing. Both names reference the place where buffalo crossed the N. Elkhorn Creek. See Birdwhistell, "At the Big Crossing," 3, SCPL.

9. The members of Great Crossing helped organize the region's Elkhorn Baptist Association one month after the church was founded. See Meyer, *Life and Times*, 300, 44; and Birdwhistell, "At the Big Crossing," 5, SCPL. The Baptists became the largest denomination in antebellum Kentucky, numbering roughly a quarter million by 1860. The state's next-largest denominations in the antebellum era were the Methodists, with 200,000

NOTES TO CHAPTER FOUR

members, and then the Disciples of Christ and the Presbyterians, each with 100,000 members. Steely, "Established Churches and Slavery," 98.

10. Birdwhistell, "At the Big Crossing," 6, SCPL.

11. See n2 of this chapter. The GCBC ledger books contain a wealth of information about the church in the nineteenth century, including details about its membership and how it dealt with disciplinary issues along lines of race.

12. Entry, first Saturday in June 1815, 2:17, Ledgers; Meyer, *Life and Times*, 301. See also Birdwhistell, "At the Big Crossing," 18, SCPL. Robert's date of death is recorded on his tombstone in GCBC's cemetery: "Col. Robert Johnson / husband to / Jemima Johnson / was born July 17, 1745 / died 15 of October 1815 / aged 70 years."

13. Their commitment to their faith and their connection to Great Crossing meant that the senior Johnsons would have insisted their enslaved laborers attend church on preaching Sundays. On Julia's piety, see Henderson Letter. Information on the first meetinghouse is in Birdwhistell, "At the Big Crossing," 12, SCPL. Church ledgers record the names of enslaved members separately, at the end of lists of names of white members. See Ledgers, 1:4.

14. Craig Papers, 8.

15. Entry, first Saturday in July 1802, 1:78, Ledgers. The gallery was preserved in the church and used as a Sunday school room as late as 1918. Josephine Grauman Marks, "Old Church and Original Records Survive in Scott," April 7, 1918, Filson News Clippings: Churches–Kentucky–Baptist–Scott County, FHS. Setting aside the gallery as seating for Black people in predominantly white churches, regardless of denomination, was common for the era. Voelker, "Church Building," 226.

16. Emma Rouse Lloyd, *Clasping Hands with Generations Past* (privately printed by Wiesen-Hart, 1932), 87, in Finding Aid Folder, Henderson Papers; Henderson Letter. See also entry, first Saturday in October 1814, 2:13, Ledgers.

17. Entry, first Saturday in October 1802, 1:82, Ledgers.

18. Entry, first Saturday in July 1824, 2:108–9, Ledgers.

19. See Stevenson, "'Marsa Never Sot,'" 345–67. See also Ford, "Black Spiritual Defiance"; McKivigan, "Battle for the Border"; and Lucas, *History*, 133–34.

20. The Senate adjourned on March 9 that year and did not resume again until December 5. See "Dates of Session of the Congress," United States Senate, accessed December 17, 2022, www.senate.gov/legislative/DatesofSessionsofCongress.htm.

21. Entry, first Saturday in June 1825, 2:117–18, Ledgers.

22. Birdwhistell, "At the Big Crossing," 13, SCPL; Marks, "Old Church," FHS; Ledgers.

23. Marks, "Old Church," FHS.

24. Marks; Ledgers.

25. Meyer, *Life and Times*, 44.

26. Entry, first Saturday in April 1802, 1:76, Ledgers.

27. Entry, first Saturday in November 1808, 1:140, Ledgers.

28. Lucas, *History*, 118.

29. Entries, May 6, 1826, and first Saturday in July 1826, 2:138–41, Ledgers.

30. Entries, first Saturday in March and first Saturday in May 1825, 2:114–15, 117, Ledgers.

31. Entries, first Saturday in November 1811 and first Saturday in March 1812, 1:165, 167–68, Ledgers.

32. Entry, first Saturday in April 1812, 1:167–68, Ledgers.

33. Newspaper editor Nicholas L. Finnell wrote that he had avoided publishing on the topic of Richard and Julia's relationship for many years, in large part because he didn't want to offend "the feelings of the numerous respectable relations of Col. Johnson." *LOKR*, December 12, 1832.

34. See chap. 3 of this book.

35. Entry, first Saturday in November 1815, 2:21, Ledgers. For Fanny's death, see entry, July 6, 1833, 2:265, Ledgers.

36. The Senate was in session from December 6, 1819, to May 15, 1820. This means Richard wouldn't have been home until late May or early June. See "Dates of Session of the Congress." See also entry, first Saturday in April 1820, 2:65–66, Ledgers.

37. There are no records suggesting Julia Chinn was ever cited by the Great Crossing morals board.

38. "The Sunday Mails Report," *Kentucky Reporter*, February 4, 1829. See also *Argus*, April 7, May 19, June 16, 1830.

39. Entries, first Saturday in May and first Saturday in June 1820, 2:65–67, Ledgers.

40. Entry, first Saturday in October 1826, 2:144, Ledgers.

41. Birdwhistell, "At the Big Crossing," 20–21, SCPL.

42. Birdwhistell, 20.

43. On the Second Great Awakening, see, e.g., Wellman, *Grassroots Reform*; Kruczek-Aaron, *Everyday Religion*; and Clapp and Jeffrey, *Women, Dissent, and Anti-slavery*.

44. Birdwhistell, "At the Big Crossing," 14, SCPL.

45. Birdwhistell, 20.

46. Entry, April 20, 1828, 2:169–70, Ledgers.

47. Congress was in session that year from December 3, 1827, to May 26, 1828. Richard wouldn't have been able to come home until sometime in June. See "Dates of Session of the Congress."

48. Entries, May 3, November 15, 1828, 2:175, 198, Ledgers.

49. Birdwhistell, "At the Big Crossing," 21, SCPL. See also Henderson Letter.

50. Family Bible Pages, Vertical Files: Pence; Pence Family Bible, PFF.

51. John Wilson interview, 16, Draper Manuscripts, Truman State University Archives, Kirksville, MO. Believing Daniel Pence was a "Dutchman" affirms his German heritage (see "Pennsylvania Dutch"). "Dutch" here is likely an Anglicization of "Deutsch," the German word for the German language, not a reference to Holland.

52. Bentz-Pence Family Tree in PFPC.

53. Entry, April 8, 1832, 2:245, Ledgers. See also entries, July 6, August 3, September 6, 1834, 2:282, 284–85, Ledgers.

54. Entries, February 5, March 5, 1831, 2:235–36, Ledgers.

55. Entry, July 6, 1833, 2:265, Ledgers; *LOKR*, July 1, 4, 1835.

56. Imogene Johnson Pence and her husband, Daniel, like other landowners from the era, were buried on their family farm. See chap. 7 of this book. Thomas Henderson was also buried in the family cemetery on his own farm. See n21 in chap. 2 of this book.

57. RMJ to FPB, June 16, 1835, 52–56, esp. 55, Blair-Lee Papers, Princeton University, Firestone Library, Princeton, NJ; "Imogene Pence Obituary," *Georgetown Weekly Times*, October 10, 1883, ECPC.

58. Entry, May 7, 1831, 2:237, Ledgers.

NOTES TO CHAPTER FIVE

59. Entry, first Saturday in December 1841, 2:353, Ledgers.
60. Entry, first Saturday in January 1842, 2:353–54, Ledgers.
61. Entry, first Saturday in April 1842, 2:356, Ledgers.
62. Entry, May 7, 1843, 2:369, Ledgers.
63. Entry, first Saturday in July 1843, 2:370, Ledgers.
64. The seminary was eventually relocated to Louisville and remains there under the name Southern Baptist Theological Seminary. This is where the Great Crossing Ledger Books are currently housed. See Steely, "Established Churches and Slavery," 98; and McKivigan, "Battle for the Border," 62–63.
65. Steely, "Established Churches and Slavery," 99; Ford, "Black Spiritual Defiance," 70.
66. Ford, "Black Spiritual Defiance," 70–72.
67. Entry, first Saturday in August 1843, 2:371, Ledgers.
68. Entry, first Saturday in August 1859, 2:519, Ledgers.
69. In the Roman Catholic Church in the sixteenth century, you could reduce the amount of time you spent in purgatory, or limbo, by paying money to the church for your sins. Called an indulgence, the more you paid, the more time was shaved off of your years in purgatory and the more quickly you entered heaven. See *Encyclopaedia Britannica Online*, s.v. "Indulgence," by Lawrence G. Duggan, July 20, 1998, revised September 29, 2022, https://www.britannica.com/topic/indulgence.
70. For the story of Wall and King, see chap. 3.

CHAPTER FIVE

1. *Kentucky Reporter*, July 20, 1831; Meyer, *Life and Times*, 317.
2. The *Lexington Observer* (*Observer*), later the *Lexington Observer and Kentucky Reporter* (*LOKR*), was known to be anti–Andrew Jackson, anti–Richard M. Johnson, and pro–Henry Clay. See Hart, *Richard M. Johnson*, 17, 21. The paper out of Frankfort, the *Argus of Western America* (*Argus*), unlike the *LOKR*, focused almost exclusively on hard politics and was filled with articles on nullification, Indian removal, and foreign affairs. The *Argus* was also a pro-Johnson paper, run by Richard's good friend Amos Kendall until midway through 1830. It's thus not surprising that there were no mentions of Julia, Adaline, or Imogene in the *Argus*. Even after Kendall left the paper, it remained a pro-Jackson/Johnson paper under new editor and owner Gervas E. Russell.
3. See my introduction for a conversation on sources.
4. *Observer*, July 9, 1831. Judge James Kelly claimed in an interview given later in his life that Julia and Richard's daughters "never circulated among the whites." Kelly, "Judge James Y. Kelly Manuscript," 477.
5. See n2 in this chap.
6. *Kentucky Reporter*, July 20, 1831.
7. For more on public versus private sexual conduct, see Myers, *Forging Freedom*, esp. chaps. 5, 6.
8. RMJ to FPB, June 16, 1835, 52–57, Blair-Lee Papers, Princeton University, Firestone Library, Princeton, NJ.
9. The *Argus* did not comment on the July 1831 barbecue incident. It was, instead, filled with pieces on Peggy Eaton, or the "Petticoat Affair," and reports on the midterm elections, including Richard's reelection to the House of Representatives.

NOTES TO CHAPTER FIVE

10. Hart, *Richard M. Johnson*, 17; *Observer*, August 2, 1832.

11. For more on Black women dressing for freedom and the pushback it engendered, see Camp, *Closer to Freedom*; Stewart, "Fashioning Frenchness," 526–56; Jessica Marie Johnson, *Wicked Flesh*; and Walker, *Exquisite Slaves*.

12. See chap. 4 of this book.

13. *Biographical Review of Cass, Schuyler, and Brown Counties, Illinois* (Chicago: Biographical Review, 1892), s.v. "Thomas W. Scott," 197, in Miscellaneous Binder, BBWPC.

14. *LOKR*, November 29, 1832.

15. *LOKR*, November 29, 1832. For Adaline's marriage, see Clift, *Kentucky Marriages*, 72. Imogene and Daniel's marriage took place on June 6, 1830. See Family Bible Pages, Vertical Files: Pence; and Pence Family Bible, PFF.

16. "Land Grant Indenture between Richard and Edward P. Johnson on One Hand and Adaline J. Scott and Her Husband, Thomas W. Scott," November 9, 1832, deed book L (1832–33), 126, Scott County Deed Books, KDLA.

17. On trusts and guardianships, see Myers, *Forging Freedom*, esp. chap. 6.

18. *LOKR*, December 12, 1832.

19. See Thomas Brown, "Miscegenation," 23.

20. *LOKR*, December 20, 1832.

21. *Richmond Whig*, July 20, 1835.

22. Many works have discussed the trope of the Black Beast Rapist. For one example, see Williamson, *Crucible of Race*. For a public history website that discusses this stereotype, see "The Brute Caricature," Jim Crow Museum, Ferris State University, accessed January 7, 2023, www.ferris.edu/HTMLS/news/jimcrow/brute.

23. *LOKR*, June 24, 1835.

24. *LOKR*, June 6, 1833.

25. For more on the cholera epidemic of 1832–33, particularly with regard to treatment, see Whooley, *Knowledge*.

26. "Deaths from Cholera in the city of Lexington, June 1–Aug 1, 1833: Whites 252, Slaves 184, Free blacks 48," document 1, Cholera Folder, FHS; Sue McClelland Thierman, "Kill or Cure, 125 Years Ago," *Courier-Journal Magazine*, ca. 1957, in Filson News Clippings: Cholera, FHS.

27. "Receipt for the Cholera, July the 28, 1833," document 2, Cholera Folder, FHS.

28. "Observer and Reporter—Extra: The Cholera, June 15," *Argus*, June 19, 1833.

29. *LOKR*, June 27, July 11, 1833.

30. "Choctaw Academy, Cholera: Report of the Attending Physician of the Choctaw Academy," *Argus*, July 31, 1833.

31. "Choctaw Academy, Cholera."

32. RMJ to TH, December 9, 1825, June 1834, Henderson Papers.

33. Snyder, *Great Crossings*, 148.

34. See n2 of this chap.

35. Snyder, *Great Crossings*, 148.

36. Entries, June 1, July 6, 1833, 2:263, 265, Ledgers.

37. *Argus*, August 7, 1833. The printed correspondence on the cholera epidemic ranged from June 24 to July 1, 1833.

38. RMJ to TH, March 12, 14, 1834, Henderson Papers; Meyer, *Life and Times*, 317.

39. *LOKR*, September 4, 1833.
40. Holt to TH, February 24, 1834, Henderson Papers.
41. See Gordon-Reed, *Thomas Jefferson*; and Gordon-Reed, *Hemingses of Monticello*.
42. L. Smith to B. W. Smith, May 25, 1844, L. Smith, FHS.

CHAPTER SIX

1. *Observer*, July 8, 1835 (article reprinted from *Louisville Journal*). Christina Snyder states that the two men departed first with the carriage and trunks. The women left three days later and met up with their companions at a prearranged spot. From there, they made their way to Lexington and then to Ohio. Snyder, *Great Crossings*, 194–95.

2. See chap. 3 of this book for more on Parthene and her work at Choctaw Academy.

3. Julia and Richard's relationship appears to have been the reason Richard lost his Senate seat in 1829. On December 10, 1819, Richard was elected by the Kentucky legislature to serve out the remaining US Senate term of John J. Crittenden. Richard was elected to a full term in 1822, and he went on to serve in the Senate until 1829. He was defeated for reelection in 1828, largely because of his personal life. Although he was popular in his congressional district, as a senator he answered to the state at large, and the plantation aristocracy could not overlook his decision to openly live with an enslaved Black woman as his wife. Johnson attempted to return to the Senate three times, to no avail. He was defeated by Henry Clay in 1831 and 1848 and by Crittenden in 1842. Still, he continued to serve his district in the House of Representatives throughout the 1830s. Richard was a Democratic US representative (1806–19 and 1829–37) before he served as vice president under Martin Van Buren (1837–41). John S. Cooper, "When No One Won: Richard Mentor Johnson," World History (website), July 3, 2017, https://worldhistory.us/american-history/presidential-history/when-no-one-won-richard-mentor-johnson.php; Ford and Weinberg, "Slavery, Interracial Marriage," 57.

4. Other articles attacking Richard included the following, all in *LOKR*: "Johnson recommends a thief for a job," November 18, 1835; "Johnson owes the St. Louis Bank $55,000 says the *St. Louis Republican*," November 25, 1835, and June 29, 1836; "Johnson didn't author the Sunday Mails Report or Kill Tecumseh," December 30, 1835; "Johnson's military exploits minimal at best," May 11, 1836; "Richard M. Johnson a political tool," July 13, 1836; and "Having Richard Johnson preside over the senate is unthinkable," June 8, 1836.

5. See *Argus*, various issues, May 6, 1835–November 16, 1836.

6. *Kentucky Gazette*, July 25, 1835.

7. Jonathan Milnor Jones, "Making," 298.

8. *Sentinel*, March 4, 1835.

9. Meyer, *Life and Times*, 413. Balch owned a plantation in Tennessee that directly neighbored the plantation of Andrew Jackson. During their time as neighbors, the two men became close friends. This friendship helped Balch advance his career as Jackson, and then Martin Van Buren, gave him various political appointments. "Alfred Balch," Florida's 2nd Judicial Circuit Historical Society, accessed January 7, 2023, https://2ndcircuit.leoncountyfl.gov/courtHistory/abalch.php.

10. Jonathan Milnor Jones, "Making," 289–90. See also *Sentinel*, June 3, 1835.

11. Snyder, *Great Crossings*, 201.

NOTES TO CHAPTER SIX

12. Quoted in Cleaves, *Old Tippecanoe*, 294.
13. Cleaves, 306.
14. *Sentinel*, June 10, 1835.
15. *Louisville Journal* quoted in *Cincinnati Daily Gazette*, June 6, 1835.
16. "Col. Johnson & His Calumniators," *Sentinel*, August 8, 1835 (reprinted from *Onondaga Standard*). For more on Taylor, see "Speaker of the House John W. Taylor of New York," History, Art, and Archives, US House of Representatives, accessed January 7, 2023, https://history.house.gov/Historical-Highlights/1700s/Speaker-of-the-House-John-W—Taylor-of-New-York/. Webster, one of the great statesmen of the nineteenth century, has been written about extensively. See Remini, *Webster*.
17. *Sentinel*, August 26, 1835. See also Katie Crawford-Lackey, "Olympian Springs," ExploreKYHistory, accessed January 7, 2023, https://explorekyhistory.ky.gov/items/show/473.
18. *Observer*, July 8, 1835.
19. See n14 of this chap.
20. "The *Georgetown Sentinel*—Col. R. M. Johnson," *Observer*, July 8, 1835 (reprinted from *Louisville Journal*).
21. See chap. 5 of this book.
22. "*Georgetown Sentinel*—Col. R. M. Johnson."
23. "*Georgetown Sentinel*—Col. R. M. Johnson."
24. "*Georgetown Sentinel*—Col. R. M. Johnson."
25. "*Georgetown Sentinel*—Col. R. M. Johnson."
26. RMJ to FPB, June 16, 1835, 52, Blair-Lee Papers, Princeton University, Firestone Library, Princeton, NJ.
27. RMJ to FPB, 55.
28. For Lafayette, see chap. 2 of this book.
29. See Myers, *Forging Freedom*, chap. 6.
30. RMJ to FPB, June 16, 1835, 56, Blair-Lee Papers, Princeton University, Firestone Library, Princeton, NJ.
31. RMJ to FPB, 56.
32. Henderson Letter. On Jefferson, see Rothman, *Notorious in the Neighborhood*; Gordon-Reed, *Thomas Jefferson*; and Gordon-Reed, *Hemingses of Monticello*.
33. Henderson Letter. For more on the fancy trade, see Berry, *Price*; and Walter Johnson, *Soul by Soul*. See also Tiya Miles's discussion of Louisa Picquet in *All That She Carried*, 154–56.
34. Henderson Letter.
35. Henderson Letter.
36. Fleming, *Gone with the Wind*. For more on Aunt Jemima, see Manring, *Slave in a Box*.
37. Henderson Letter.
38. *Richmond Whig*, July 10, 1835.
39. *Maysville Eagle*, July 2, 1835, reprinted in *Lexington Intelligencer*, July 7, 1835. See also Hart, *Richard M. Johnson*, 23.
40. *Observer*, July 1, 1835, quoted in Hart, *Richard M. Johnson*, 24. An anonymous letter writer in the *Journal* apparently called one of the runaways "Madame Johnson." The

editors of the *Sentinel* demanded to know the identity of the letter writer, so that everyone could see "the blackness of his base heart." *Sentinel*, July 8, 1835.

41. *Observer*, July 8, 1835 (article reprinted from *Louisville Journal*). From the *Sentinel* we learn that the two men were from Choctaw Academy, a teacher named John Jones and a student named George Hunt. *Sentinel*, July 8, 1835.

42. For Daniel's connection to Parthene, see "The Workings of Slavery," *Liberator*, July 25, 1845.

43. See RMJ to TH, April 1, 1836, Henderson Papers; and Snyder, *Great Crossings*, 194, 197.

44. "Good News," *Observer*, July 8, 1835.

45. Thirteen hundred dollars would be just over $44,000 in 2023. CPIIC, accessed January 7, 2023, www.in2013dollars.com/us/inflation/1835?amount=1300.

46. Reprint of a letter from Columbus, Ohio, July 6, 1835, in *Vermont Phoenix*, July 24, 1835.

47. See Ann Bevins, *Lexington Leader*, August 24, 1963, 3; and Vertical File Collection, Scott County Baptist Churches, Kentucky Historical Society, Frankfort, KY.

48. The phrase "valuable servant girls" is from Snyder, *Great Crossings*, 195. Snyder here quotes a letter that Richard wrote to federal officials about the runaways.

49. *Observer*, July 22, 1835.

50. See chap. 3 of this book.

51. After being lashed, runaways at Blue Spring had salt poured on their open wounds. Addie Murphy to J. C. Meadors, August 13, 1938, 123, J. Winston Coleman Papers, KSCL.

52. "Workings of Slavery."

53. "Workings of Slavery." See also Snyder, *Great Crossings*, 214-15.

54. "Workings of Slavery."

55. Information on Peak is in Snyder, *Great Crossings*, 213-14. For Clay, see L. Smith to B. W. Smith, May 25, 1844, L. Smith, FHS.

56. Murphy to J. C. Meadors, August 13, 1938, 123-24, J. Winston Coleman Papers, KSCL; Snyder, *Great Crossings*, 213.

57. Thomas Brown, "Miscegenation," 7-8.

58. Ford and Weinberg, "Slavery, Interracial Marriage," 58.

59. For more on the Sunday Mails Battle, see chap. 4 of this book.

60. Snyder, *Great Crossings*, 205-6.

61. Sukey was a generic name often used to refer to enslaved women in the Old South, much like Sambo was used to refer to enslaved men. Song quoted in Schlesinger, *Age of Jackson*, 214.

62. In 1850, Adaline's husband, Thomas West Scott, was a forty-one-year-old farmer living in Scott County with his second wife, Catherine, then twenty-seven years old. There were seven children living in the Scott household that year. The oldest was Adaline and Thomas's son, Robert, aged sixteen years. His next closest sibling was his half sister Helen, aged nine years. "1850 Census for Scott County, Kentucky," 464, Thomas W. Scott Folder, ECPC.

63. Mr. Pence and Mr. Scott were Richard's two sons-in-law, Daniel Pence and Thomas Scott. RMJ to TH, February 26, 1836, Henderson Papers.

NOTES TO CHAPTER SEVEN

64. For the Blair letter, see nn27, 30 in this chapter. See also Henderson Letter.

65. RMJ to TH, February 26, 1836, Henderson Papers. The story of David, Bathsheba, and Uriah is in 2 Sam. 11.

66. Hypertensive disorders of pregnancy remain one of the leading causes of pregnancy-related maternal and fetal mortality worldwide. For more on high blood pressure and maternal/fetal health, including preeclampsia and its treatment, see Garovic et al., "Hypertension in Pregnancy."

67. The full story of Julia and Richard's relationship was printed as late as November 1836. *Observer*, November 2, 1836.

68. Stimpson, *Book about American Politics*, 129–30.

69. Schlesinger, *Age of Jackson*, 297; Stimpson, *Book about American Politics*, 132–33.

70. Extracts from *"The Life of Amos Kendall,"* 147, in Richard M. Johnson Folder, Johnson Family Papers, FHS. See also Meyer, *Life and Times*, chap. 1.

71. Meyer, "'Kentucky Hospitality,'" 378.

72. Unknown to Kendall, August 12, 1839, Martin Van Buren Papers, KSCL.

73. Unknown to Kendall.

74. Unknown to Kendall.

75. The full story of Samson and Delilah is in Judg. 16:1–22.

76. Kendall to Van Buren, August 22, 1839, Martin Van Buren Papers, KSCL.

77. Bragg to Gould, October 8, 1840, Catherine L. Bragg Papers, FHS.

78. McLaurin, *Celia, a Slave*; Jacobs, *Incidents in the Life*.

79. Unknown to Amos Kendall, August 12, 1839, Martin Van Buren Papers, KSCL.

80. Meyer, *Life and Times*, 434, 438–41; Stimpson, *Book about American Politics*, 132.

81. Jonathan Milnor Jones, "Making," 334–35. Blair is the person Richard had written to about his troubles back in 1835. See nn27, 30 in this chapter.

82. *Kentucky Gazette*, October 29, 1840; Schlesinger, *Age of Jackson*, 297, 435.

83. RMJ to Marshall, May 26, 1840, Humphrey Marshall Papers, FHS.

84. *Louisville Weekly Journal*, November 4, 1840, 2.

85. *Observer*, November 16, 1836.

86. I refer here to the title of the song by Billie Holiday, "Strange Fruit," 1939. Music and lyrics by Abel Meerpool, 1937.

CHAPTER SEVEN

1. Meyer, *Life and Times*, 473. For Richard and the Battle of the Thames, see chap. 2 of this book.

2. Fitch Munger to Mary Munger Carlisle, November 21, 1850, Miscellaneous Files, FHS. Information on the pendant comes from Brenda Brent Wilfert, emails to author, June 1, 2, 2022. The pendant remained in the Pence family until it was sold by Brenda's grandfather W. C. Jackson. It is now in the Museum of Fine Arts, Boston. See Anna Claypoole Peale, *Colonel Richard M. Johnson* (1818), MFABoston, accessed January 10, 2023, https://collections.mfa.org/objects/34030/colonel-richard-m-johnson. I have imagined here how Imogene would have learned of her father's death and responded to it. Using archival documents and items of material culture uncovered in my research, I've filled in the remaining blanks with fictional narrative, engaging in what Saidiya Hartman calls "critical fabulation." See Hartman, "Venus in Two Acts."

3. Meyer, *Life and Times*, 470–71.
4. Meyer, 472.
5. Snyder, *Great Crossings*, 261–62. For information on debt, death, and the separation of Black families, see Bailey, *Weeping Time*. See also Berry, *Price*.
6. Meyer, *Life and Times*, 473.
7. Meyer, 474.
8. *Daily Commonwealth*, November 20, 1850; *Kentucky Statesman*, November 20, 1850.
9. *Kentucky Statesman*, November 20, 1850.
10. *Daily Commonwealth*, November 21, 1850.
11. Munger to Mary Munger Carlisle, November 21, 1850, Miscellaneous Files, FHS.
12. *Daily Commonwealth*, November 21, 1850.
13. Kelly, "Judge James Y. Kelly Manuscript," 477–78.
14. See chap. 4 of this book for more on John T. Johnson.
15. See chap. 1 of this book. See also Craig Papers, 1–8.
16. See chap. 2 of this book; and Snyder, *Great Crossings*, 51, 56. See also chap. 5 of this book; and *LOKR*, December 12, 1832.
17. Meyer, *Life and Times*, 322; order book 13, 136, Fayette County Order Books, KDLA.
18. 1850 US Census–Slave Schedule, Scott County, Kentucky, Pence File, ECPC; 1850 US Federal Census, District 2: Scott County, Kentucky, roll M432_218, p. 453A, image 372, Kentucky Census Records, KDLA. For dollar conversion, see CPIIC, accessed January 8, 2023, www.in2013dollars.com/us/inflation/1850?amount=10000. See also Snyder, *Great Crossings*, 261–62.
19. Names and dates of birth for Imogene and Daniel's children are in Pence Family Bible, PFF. Their first child, Richard M. J. Pence, was born March 18, 1831, and died March 6, 1834. See n2 of this chapter for information on the pendant.
20. "Thomas W. Scott," 1850 US Census, Scott County, Kentucky, 464, ECPC; *Biographical Review of Cass, Schuyler, and Brown Counties, Illinois* (Chicago: Biographical Review, 1892), s.v. "Thomas W. Scott," 197, in Miscellaneous Binder, BBWPC; Scott County Deed Book U (1846–48), cited in Meyer, *Life and Times*, 321.
21. "Thomas W. Scott," 464, ECPC. That $32,000 is roughly $1,222,600 in 2023 dollars. The Scotts were thus millionaires by today's standards. See CPIIC, accessed January 8, 2023, www.in2013dollars.com/us/inflation/1850?amount=32000.
22. For more on the Scott family, see chap. 5 of this book. See also *Biographical Review*, s.v. "Thomas W. Scott," 197, BBWPC.
23. See "Thomas W. Scott," 1860 US Census, Rushville, Schuyler County, Illinois, Thomas W. Scott and Adaline Johnson Scott Binder, BBWPC; and *Biographical Review*, s.v. "Thomas W. Scott," 197, Miscellaneous Binder, BBWPC. Thomas's real estate holdings alone that year would be worth over $1 million in 2023 currency. See CPIIC, accessed January 8, 2023, www.in2013dollars.com/us/inflation/1860?amount=28200.
24. See "Robert Scott," 1870 US Census, Brookfield Township, Linn County, Missouri, Thomas W. Scott and Adaline Johnson Scott Binder, BBWPC. In the census, the children's names are listed as "Edward B.," "Thomas F.," and "Fannie." The boys would go by their middle names (Bion and Frederic) and Fannie would be "Frances" later in life, so I've included them here to minimize confusion. For dollar conversion, see CPIIC, accessed April 6, 2023, www.in2013dollars.com/us/inflation/1870?amount=4000.
25. Brenda Brent Wilfert, email to author, January 24, 2011.

NOTES TO CHAPTER SEVEN

26. See "Robert Scott," 1880 US Census, Brookfield Township, Linn County, Missouri, Robert J. Scott Records, BBWPC.

27. See n24 of this chapter.

28. The material cited on the years 1865–77 can be found in almost any college-level US history textbook. See, e.g., Roark et al., *American Promise*, 8th ed, chap. 16. For deeper reading on Reconstruction, see Du Bois, *Black Reconstruction in America*; Foner, *Reconstruction*; and Foner, *Short History of Reconstruction*. For more on the "one drop rule," see Hickman, "Devil"; and Yaba Blay, "How the 'One Drop Rule' Became a Tool of White Supremacy," Literary Hub, February 22, 2021, https://lithub.com/how-the-one-drop-rule-became-a-tool-of-white-supremacy.

29. "Robert Scott," 1880 Census, Robert J. Scott Records, BBWPC.

30. "R. J. Scott," 1900 US Census, Brookfield, Missouri, Robert J. Scott Records, BBWPC.

31. See "Plessy v. Ferguson," History (website), October 29, 2009, last updated January 16, 2023, www.history.com/topics/black-history/plessy-v-ferguson.

32. *Directory of Deceased American Physicians, 1804–1929*, in Robert J. Scott Records, BBWPC.

33. For a detailed examination of passing and its possibilities, challenges, and losses, see Hobbs, *Chosen Exile*. The quote "a mess of pottage" is from James Weldon Johnson, *Autobiography*, 154.

34. Information on Daniel and the Pence family is in chap. 4 of this book. Dates of birth for Imogene and Daniel's children are in Pence Family Bible, PFF: Richard M. J. Pence, b. March 18, 1831 (d. March 6, 1834); Amanda Malvina Pence, b. February 12, 1833; Mary J. Pence, b. March 11, 1835; Daniel Franklin Pence, b. March 8, 1850; Albert Pence, b. September 19, 1852 (d. August 19, 1853); and Edward Pence, b. July 21, 1858.

35. Snyder, *Great Crossings*, 303.

36. "George Pence," 1810, 1820, 1840 US Census, Pence Census Documents, BBWPC.

37. "Richard M. Johnson," 1810, 1820, 1830 US Federal Census databases, Ancestry.com.

38. On Kentucky's economy, see Lucas, *History*, chap. 1. The year Imogene married wasn't the only year Richard gave her land and property. See RMJ and David Suggett to Daniel B. Pence and Imogene Pence, deed, deed book Q (1840–41), 426, Scott County Deed Books, KDLA.

39. Daniel B. and Imogene Pence Account Book, 2–9, PFPC. The book was kept by Imogene, using the same style of accounting taught to her by Thomas Henderson when she was growing up. Snyder, *Great Crossings*, 303. For dollar conversion, see CPIIC, accessed April 6, 2023, www.in2013dollars.com/us/inflation/1848?amount=2600.

40. Bentz-Pence Family Tree; and Pence Account Book, 10–20, both in PFPC. For more information on children and labor under slavery, see chap. 1 of this book. See also King, *Stolen Childhood*.

41. For dates of birth and marriage, see Pence Family Bible, PFF. See also Pence Account Book, 8, PFPC. The $500 would be worth roughly $13,200 in 2023 dollars. CPIIC, accessed April 9, 2023, www.in2013dollars.com/us/inflation/1874?amount=500.

42. Pence Account Book, 15–16, PFPC.

43. Pence Account Book, 17–20.

44. Pence Account Book, 3, 7, 9, 11, 12.

NOTES TO CHAPTER SEVEN

45. For more on these issues, see chaps. 5, 6 of this book.

46. "Thomas W. Scott," 464, ECPC. See also 1850 US Census–Slave Schedule, ECPC. For dollar values see CPIIC, accessed April 6, 2023, www.in2013dollars.com/us/inflation/1851?amount=32000.

47. Pence Account Book, 3, 5, 6, 11, 13, 14, PFPC. It's possible that Thomas Scott gave the money from the sale of the Blue Spring land to his and Adaline's son, Robert, since the property was supposed to be held in trust for him until he came of age. Snyder, *Great Crossings*, 304. For Malvina's land value see CPIIC, accessed April 6, 2023, www.in2013dollars.com/us/inflation/1850?amount=6270. Mary Jane's land would be worth roughly $212,800 in 2023 dollars. CPIIC, accessed April 6, 2023, www.in2013dollars.com/us/inflation/1854?amount=5942.

48. 1850 US Census–Slave Schedule, ECPC.

49. Pence Account Book, 2, 10, PFPC. For dollar conversion, see CPIIC, accessed April 6, 2023, www.in2013dollars.com/us/inflation/1850?amount=12000.

50. 1850 US Federal Census, District 2, 453A, image 372, KDLA. For dollar conversions, see CPIIC, accessed April 6, 2023, www.in2013dollars.com/us/inflation/1850?amount=6000; and www.in2013dollars.com/us/inflation/1850?amount=42000.

51. "J. Pence," 882; and "R. Lee," 920, both in 1860 US Federal Census, District 1: Scott County, Kentucky, roll M653_394, Kentucky Census Records, KDLA. For dollar values, see CPIIC, accessed April 6, 2023, www.in2013dollars.com/us/inflation/1860?amount=1510o.

52. "D. Pence," 1860 US Federal Census, District 1: Scott County, Kentucky, roll M653_394, p. 881, Kentucky Census Records, KDLA; "Daniel B. Pence," 1860 US Census–Slave Schedules, Scott County, Kentucky, KDLA; "Daniel Pence," 1870 US Federal Census, White Sulphur, Scott County, Kentucky, roll M593_497, p. 351B, Kentucky Census Records, KDLA. For dollar conversions, see CPIIC, accessed April 6, 2023, www.in2013dollars.com/us/inflation/1870?amount=49050.

53. "Josiah Pence," 329A; and "Robert M. Lee," 352A, both in 1870 US Federal Census, White Sulphur, Scott County, Kentucky, roll M593_497, Kentucky Census Records, KDLA. For dollar conversion, see CPIIC, accessed April 9, 2023, www.in2013dollars.com/us/inflation/1870?amount=19100.

54. "Daniel B. Pence," 65B, Enumeration District 169; "Josiah Pence," 39C, Enumeration District 168; and "A. M. Lee (Amanda Malvina)," 43C, Enumeration District 168, all in 1880 US Federal Census, White Sulphur, Scott County, Kentucky, roll 44, Kentucky Census Records, KDLA. Robert M. Lee died November 19, 1875. See Pence Family Bible, PFF.

55. Snyder, *Great Crossings*, 304.

56. See "Daniel B. Pence," 1850–80 US Federal Census databases, Ancestry.com.

57. The Emancipation Proclamation would not have applied to Imogene or her children because it only impacted those states in rebellion to the Union during the Civil War. Kentucky was "neutral"; thus all of the state's enslaved persons remained in bondage until the Thirteenth Amendment was passed in 1865, abolishing slavery across the nation.

58. On the performance of respectability and social, racial construction, see Hodes, *White Women, Black Men*; and Myers, *Forging Freedom*, esp. chap. 5.

59. See McCalla to Pence, December 23, 1872, Pence Ancestry Binder II, BBWPC.

60. See Pence Family Bible, PFF; Notated Pence Bible Pages, ECPC; and *Handbook of Texas*, s.v., "Gano, Richard Montgomery, 1830–1913," by W. Kellon Hightower, 1976,

revised January 1, 1995, https://tshaonline.org/handbook/online/articles/fga14. For more on Noel and GCBC, see chap. 4 of this book.

61. "Obituary of Imogene Pence," *Georgetown Weekly Times*, October 10, 1883, ECPC.

62. *Stamping Ground Newspaper*, October 17, 1883. Transcription of the article provided by Dr. Lindsey Apple.

63. Henderson Letter.

64. Photo of Imogene Johnson's headstone, PFPC.

65. "Memoranda" page, Pence Bible, PFPC.

66. "The Recollections of Frank Durham Pence, Son of William Collis Pence, as told to Harriet Pence Gray," November 3, 1998; and Bentz-Pence Family Tree, both in PFPC.

67. Thomas Brown, "Miscegenation," 23; "Obituary of Daniel B. Pence," *Georgetown Times*, April 29, 1891, ECPC.

68. Notated Pence Bible Pages, ECPC. See also Family Bible Pages, Vertical Files: Pence; and Pence Family Bible, PFF.

69. Daniel's last remaining brother died in 1878. "Obituary of Joseph Pence," *Georgetown Times*, March 20, 1878.

70. See n66 of this chap.

71. Harriet Pence Gray and Margaret Pence Brooks, interview by author, July 13, 2016.

EPILOGUE

1. David Mills, "The Vice President and His Mulatto," *Undercover Black Man* (blog), April 26, 2007, http://undercoverblackman.blogspot.com/2007/04/vice-president-and-his-mulatto.html.

2. Brenda Brent Wilfert, telephone interview by author, May 14, 2018.

3. Brenda Brent Wilfert, interviews by author, March 14, 2016 (in person), May 14, 2018 (telephone).

4. Mills, "Vice President"; Wilfert, interview by author, March 14, 2016.

5. Wilfert telephone interview, May 14, 2018.

6. Bill Jackson, interview by author, July 13, 2016.

7. "Obituary of Daniel B. Pence," *Georgetown Times*, April 29, 1891; and Notated Pence Bible Pages, both in ECPC; Family Bible Pages, Vertical Files: Pence; Jackson interview.

8. Jackson interview.

9. Jackson interview.

10. "Obituary of Imogene Pence," *Georgetown Weekly Times*, October 10, 1883, ECPC.

11. Wilfert interviews, March 14, 2016 (in person), May 14, 2018 (telephone).

12. Jackson interview.

13. Harriet Pence Gray and Margaret Pence Brooks, interview by author, July 13, 2016.

14. Gray and Brooks interview.

15. Gray and Brooks interview.

16. Gray and Brooks interview.

17. I haven't been able to track down this book despite various searches online and through library database requests. It's possible the name is a bit different from the one Harriet remembers.

18. Gray and Brooks interview.

19. Gray and Brooks interview.
20. Gray and Brooks interview.
21. Gray and Brooks interview.
22. Gray and Brooks interview.
23. Gray and Brooks interview.
24. Gray and Brooks interview.
25. William McIntyre, interview by author, July 28, 2016. Richard Johnson was commissioned a colonel during the War of 1812. He was regularly called "Colonel Dick" thereafter by friends and political enemies alike, or "Colonel Johnson." These names show up in private letters and in the press. See Kelly, "Judge James Y. Kelly Manuscript," 477. Catherine Bragg states in her letter that Richard had three Black wives, the first of whom "was a real full blooded negro." See chap. 6 of this book for more on this subject. This could possibly be a reference to McIntyre's ancestress. See Bragg to Catherine Gould, October 8, 1840, Catherine L. Bragg Papers, FHS.
26. McIntyre interview.
27. McIntyre interview. For more on the historical development of whiteness with beauty standards and the larger issue of colorism, both in and outside of the Black community, see Hobson, *Venus in the Dark*; and Sharpley-Whiting, *Pimps Up, Ho's Down*, chaps. 1, 4.
28. There has been important work done on the violence of the written archives and the need to ask new questions and utilize a wide(r) range of source materials when doing work on African-descended women. I refer here to the work of Camp, *Closer to Freedom*; Fuentes, *Dispossessed Lives*; Miles, *All That She Carried*; Morgan, *Laboring Women*; and Morgan, *Reckoning with Slavery*.
29. McIntyre interview.
30. "William Hatley McIntyre," obituary, *Georgetown News-Graphic*, February 3, 2022, updated April 19, 2022, www.news-graphic.com/obituaries/william-hatley-mcintyre/article_663a0046-850f-11ec-a792-8f60d416a886.html.
31. For more on griots, see Seckou Keita, "My Culture: Griot Tradition," Seckou Keita (website), accessed December 20, 2022, www.seckoukeita.com/my-culture. See also Wikipedia, s.v. "Griot," last modified December 28, 2022, https://en.wikipedia.org/wiki/Griot.
32. McIntyre interview.
33. See n25 of this chap. See also unknown to Kendall, August 12, 1839, Martin Van Buren Papers, KSCL. For more on this topic, see chap. 6 of this book.
34. Bragg to Catherine Gould, October 8, 1840, Catherine L. Bragg Papers, FHS.
35. Thompson, "Eleutherian Institute," 110, 113–14; *Catalogue of Eleutherian College*, 7–8. See also Susan Reigler, "Historic Eleutherian College," Road Trip, in *Courier-Journal* (Louisville, KY), June 10, 2007, in ECPC.
36. *Catalogue of Eleutherian College*, 3; Thompson, "Eleutherian Institute," 114; Breitweiser, "Historic Eleutherian College," 1. I've never been able to confirm payment of tuition from a Louisville bank to Eleutherian on behalf of Theodore Johnson. The Battle of Munfordville, or Green River, was fought September 14–17, 1862. See "Munfordville: Battle for the Bridge," American Battlefield Trust, accessed December 20, 2022, www.battlefields.org/learn/civil-war/battles/munfordville.
37. Copies of census records in Theodore Johnson Research Folder, ECPC; and Theodore Johnson Records, BBWPC.

38. For more on John and Henry Johnson and the administration of Richard's estate, see chap. 7 of this book. Theodore Jusan/Johnson may have been the grandson of Choctaw Academy student Pierre Juzan and Blue Spring enslaved laborer Dicy. It's possible that his mother, Malvina Jusan, was the daughter of Pierre and Dicy, whose relationship took place in the late 1820s. See chap. 3 of this book; and Snyder, *Great Crossings*, 305.

39. Obie B. Taylor Sr., interview by Ellie Caroland, Pass the Word, July 23, 2005. This interview was conducted at the Johnson-Ward Reunion, July 22–24, 2005, Ward Hall, Georgetown, Kentucky. Mrs. Caroland conducted this and other interviews on behalf of the Scott County Genealogical Society. All interviews are open access and on file via Pass the Word, a Kentucky Historical Society oral history project; see Pass the Word, http://passtheword.ky.gov/collection/ward-hall-oral-history-project. Edward H. Pence married Ida Cooper in 1896. See Pence Family Bible, PFF.

40. Taylor interview.

41. Brenda Brent (Gordon) Wilfert, "Edward Herndon Pence, and Amanda Thomas, and Nellie Taylor: Family Ties Research" (unpublished materials, October 15, 2005). Research materials compiled and originally sent to Ann Bevins, then forwarded to the author. The Taylor line of descent from Edward Pence has now been confirmed. Mr. Gulferry M. Taylor, a grandson of Nellie Pence Taylor, contacted Brenda Brent Wilfert after his DNA test matched him to her Ancestry tree online. Brenda called to discuss this with me on February 18, 2023. Gulferry M. Taylor was also interviewed at the Johnson-Ward Reunion, July 22–24, 2005, Ward Hall, Georgetown, Kentucky, by a member of the Scott County Genealogical Society. His interview, like Obie's, is open access and on file via Pass the Word. See n39 of this chapter.

42. Phylicia Bowman, emails to author, April 7, 10, 2022; educational attainment tables for Dr. Bowman's family, provided to author by Dr. Bowman, April 10, 2022.

43. Bowman email, April 7, 2022; Grace Gibbs Brown, interview by Phyllis Fauntleroy, August 7, 1979; and Mason County, Kentucky, deeds of manumission. Transcript and deeds provided to author by Dr. Phylicia Bowman. Subsequent research by Dr. Bowman has led her to believe that Lucy may not have been related to Julia or Daniel Chinn as she once thought, although Lucy's connection to Richard is still unclear. Bowman email, January 2, 2023.

44. Alexander, *Parallel Worlds*.

45. Wilfert telephone interview, May 14, 2018.

46. McIntyre interview.

47. Wilfert telephone interview, May 14, 2018.

48. Wilfert telephone interview.

49. McIntyre interview. See chap. 5 of this book for information on Henry Clay's relationship with an enslaved woman on his plantation.

50. See chap. 3 of this book for more on Julia's roles at Choctaw Academy.

Bibliography

PRIMARY SOURCES

Archives

Filson Historical Society, Louisville, KY
    Catherine L. Bragg Papers, MSS CB
    Cholera Folder, MSS CC
    Filson Historical Files
    Filson News Clippings
    Thomas Henderson Papers, 1824–1841
    Thomas L. Johnson: Genealogy of the Johnson Family
    Johnson Family Papers, Richard M. Johnson Folder, MSS AJ67a
    Humphrey Marshall Papers, 1827–1921
    Miscellaneous Files
    L. Smith, MSS CS
Georgetown and Scott County Museum, Georgetown, KY
Kenneth Spencer Research Library, University of Kansas, Lawrence, KS
    Lula Craig Papers, "History of Nicodemus Colony," Colonel Richard M. Johnson Section
Kentucky Department of Libraries and Archives, Frankfort, KY
    Fayette County Order Books
    Kentucky Census Records
    Scott County Deed Books
Kentucky Historical Society, Frankfort, KY
    Pence Family File
    Vertical File Collection, Pence Family
    Vertical File Collection, Scott County Baptist Churches
Lexington Public Library, Main Branch, Lexington, KY
Library of Congress, Washington, DC
    Richard Mentor Johnson Papers, 1808–1847
    Slave Narrative Collection of the Federal Writers' Project, accessed January 5, 2023, www.loc.gov/collections/slave-narratives-from-the-federal-writers-project-1936-to-1938/about-this-collection
Margaret I. King Special Collections Library, University of Kentucky, Lexington, KY
    J. Winston Coleman Papers
    Martin Van Buren Papers
Princeton University, Firestone Library, Princeton, NJ
    Blair-Lee Papers

Scott County Public Library, Georgetown, KY
    Choctaw Academy Folder
    Ira Vinson Birdwhistell, "At the Big Crossing: The History of Great Crossing Baptist Church, 1785–1985"
    Johnson Family Papers
Southern Baptist Theological Seminary, Louisville, KY
    Ledger Books of Great Crossing Baptist Church
Truman State University Archives, Kirksville, MO
    Draper Manuscripts (Microform Collection)
William T. Young Library, University of Kentucky, Lexington, KY

Private Collections

Amrita Chakrabarti Myers
Brenda Brent Wilfert
Eloise Caroland
Pence Family

Books

Butterfield, L. H., ed. *Adams Family Correspondence*. Vols. 1 and 2. Cambridge, MA: Harvard University, 1963.
Cooper, Thomas, and David J. McCord, eds. *The Statutes at Large of South Carolina*. 10 vols. Columbia, SC: State Company, 1930.
Jacobs, Harriet A. *Incidents in the Life of a Slave Girl: Written by Herself*. Edited by Lydia Maria Francis Child. Boston, 1861. https://docsouth.unc.edu/fpn/jacobs/jacobs.html.
Johnson, James Weldon. *Autobiography of an Ex-colored Man*. 1912. London: Penguin, 1990.
Stedman, Ebenezer Hiram. *Bluegrass Craftsman: Being the Reminiscences of Ebenezer Hiram Stedman, Papermaker; 1808–1885*. Edited by Frances L. S. Dugan and Jacqueline P. Bull. Lexington: University of Kentucky Press, 1959.

Pamphlets, Speeches, Talks

Catalogue of Eleutherian College, 1857–8. Madison, IN: Courier Steam Printing Establishment, 1858. Courtesy of Mark Furnish.
Murray, Judith Sargent. "On the Equality of the Sexes, 1790." *Massachusetts Magazine, or Monthly Museum of Knowledge and Rational Entertainment*, March–April 1790. http://nationalhumanitiescenter.org/pds/livingrev/equality/text5/sargent.pdf.
Threats to the Homeland: Evaluating the Landscape 20 Years after 9/11, Before the Senate Homeland Security and Governmental Affairs Comm., 117th Cong. (2021) (statement of Christopher Wray, Director of the FBI). www.fbi.gov/news/testimony/threats-to-the-homeland-evaluating-the-landscape-20-years-after-911-wray-092121.

Film and Music

Fleming, Victor, dir. *Gone with the Wind*. Culver City, CA: Selznick International Pictures, 1939.
Meerpool, Abel. "Strange Fruit." Performed by Billie Holliday, 1939. New York: Commodore Records.

BIBLIOGRAPHY

Periodicals

Argus of Western America (Frankfort, KY)
Cincinnati (OH) Daily Gazette
Daily Commonwealth (Frankfort, KY)
Daily Globe (Washington, DC)
Georgetown (KY) Graphic
Georgetown (KY) News-Graphic
Georgetown (KY) Times
Kentucky Gazette (Lexington)
Kentucky Historical and Genealogical Magazine
Kentucky Reporter (Lexington)
Kentucky Sentinel (Georgetown)
Kentucky Statesman (Lexington)
Lexington (KY) Herald-Leader
Lexington (KY) Intelligencer
Lexington (KY) Observer
Lexington Observer and Kentucky Reporter
Liberator (Boston, MA)
Louisville (KY) Weekly Journal
Maysville (KY) Eagle
New York Times
OAH Magazine of History
Richmond (VA) Whig
Stamping Ground (KY) Newspaper
Vermont Phoenix (Brattleboro)

SECONDARY SOURCES

Books

Adams, David Wallace. *Education for Extinction: American Indians and the Boarding School Experience, 1875–1928*. Lawrence: University Press of Kansas, 2020.

Alexander, Adele Logan. *Ambiguous Lives: Free Women of Color in Rural Georgia, 1789–1879*. Fayetteville: University of Arkansas Press, 1992.

———. *Parallel Worlds: The Remarkable Gibbs-Hunts and the Enduring (In)Significance of Melanin*. Charlottesville: University of Virginia Press, 2010.

Bailey, Anne C. *The Weeping Time: Memory and the Largest Slave Auction in American History*. New York: Cambridge University Press, 2017.

Baumgartner, Kabria. *In Pursuit of Knowledge: Black Women and Educational Activism in Antebellum America*. New York: New York University Press, 2019.

Berry, Daina Ramey. *The Price for Their Pound of Flesh: The Value of the Enslaved, from Womb to Grave, in the Building of a Nation*. Boston: Beacon, 2017.

Bevins, Ann Bolton. *Slaves and Free Blacks in Scott County History*. Georgetown, KY: Prepared for the Georgetown–Scott County Joint Planning Commission and Kentucky Heritage Council, 1989. Report held at Scott County Public Library, Georgetown, KY.

Bevins, Ann Bolton, and J. Robert Snyder, eds. *Scott County Church Histories: A Collection*. Georgetown, KY: Scott County Bicentennial Committee, 1979.

Bodenhorn, Howard. *A History of Banking in Antebellum America: Financial Markets and Economic Development in an Era of Nation-Building*. London: Cambridge University Press, 2000.

Boydston, Jeanne. *Home and Work: Housework, Wages, and the Ideology of Labor in the Early Republic*. New York: Oxford University Press, 1994.

Brown, Kathleen M. *Good Wives, Nasty Wenches, Anxious Patriarchs: Gender, Race, and Power in Colonial Virginia*. Chapel Hill: Omohundro Institute at University of North Carolina Press, 1996.

BIBLIOGRAPHY

Camp, Stephanie M. H. *Closer to Freedom: Enslaved Women and Everyday Resistance in the Plantation South*. Chapel Hill: University of North Carolina Press, 2004.

Chesebrough, David B. *Clergy Dissent in the Old South, 1830–1865*. Carbondale: Southern Illinois University Press, 1996.

Child, Brenda. *Boarding School Seasons: American Indian Families, 1900–1940*. Lincoln: University of Nebraska Press, 2000.

Clapp, Elizabeth J., and Julie Roy Jeffrey, eds. *Women, Dissent, and Anti-slavery in Britain and America, 1790–1865*. Oxford: Oxford University Press, 2011.

Cleaves, Freeman. *Old Tippecanoe: William Henry Harrison and His Time*. New York: Scribner, 1939.

Clift, G. Glenn. *Kentucky Marriages, 1797–1865*. Baltimore: Genealogical Publishing, 2000.

Cooper Owens, Deirdre. *Medical Bondage: Race, Gender, and the Origins of American Gynecology*. Athens: University of Georgia Press, 2018.

Dabel, Jane. *A Respectable Woman: The Public Roles of African American Women in 19th-Century New York*. New York: New York University Press, 2008.

Deer, Sarah. *The Beginning and End of Rape: Confronting Sexual Violence in Native America*. Minneapolis: University of Minnesota Press, 2015.

Demos, John. *A Little Commonwealth: Family Life in Plymouth Colony*. 1970. London: Oxford University Press, 2000.

Du Bois, W. E. B. *Black Reconstruction in America, 1860–1880*. With an introduction by David Levering Lewis. 1935. New York: Free Press, 1998.

——. *The Philadelphia Negro: A Social Study*. Philadelphia: University of Pennsylvania Press, 1899.

Dunbar, Erica Armstrong. *A Fragile Freedom: African American Women and Emancipation in the Antebellum City*. New Haven, CT: Yale University Press, 2008.

——. *Never Caught: The Washingtons' Relentless Pursuit of Their Runaway Slave, Ona Judge*. New York: 37 Ink/Simon and Schuster, 2018.

Ellet, Elizabeth F. *The Women of the American Revolution*. New York: Baker and Scribner, 1848.

Fett, Sharla M. *Working Cures: Healing, Health, and Power on Southern Slave Plantations*. Chapel Hill: University of North Carolina Press, 2007.

Foner, Eric. *Reconstruction: America's Unfinished Revolution, 1863–1877*. Updated ed. New York: Harper Perennial Modern Classics, 2014.

——. *A Short History of Reconstruction*. Updated ed. New York: Harper Perennial Modern Classics, 2015.

Fuentes, Marisa J. *Dispossessed Lives: Enslaved Women, Violence, and the Archive*. Philadelphia: University of Pennsylvania Press, 2016.

Gaul, Theresa Strouth, ed. *To Marry an Indian: The Marriage of Harriet Gold and Elias Boudinot in Letters, 1823–1839*. Chapel Hill: University of North Carolina Press, 2005.

Glymph, Thavolia. *Out of the House of Bondage: The Transformation of the Plantation Household*. London: Cambridge University Press, 2008.

Gordon-Reed, Annette. *The Hemingses of Monticello: An American Family*. New York: W. W. Norton, 2009.

——. *Thomas Jefferson and Sally Hemings: An American Controversy*. Charlottesville: University of Virginia Press, 1998.

Hanaford, Phebe A. *Daughters of America or Women of the Century*. Boston: B. B. Russell, 1882.
Hart, Albert J. *Richard M. Johnson and the Hostile Press*. Self-published, 2014.
Heyrman, Christine Leigh. *Southern Cross: The Beginnings of the Bible Belt*. Chapel Hill: University of North Carolina Press, 1998.
Hobbs, Allyson. *A Chosen Exile: A History of Racial Passing in American Life*. Cambridge, MA: Harvard University Press, 2016.
Hobson, Janell. *Venus in the Dark: Blackness and Beauty in Popular Culture*. 2nd ed. London: Routledge, 2018.
Hodes, Martha. *White Women, Black Men: Illicit Sex in the 19th Century South*. New Haven, CT: Yale University Press, 1997.
Hunter, Tera W. *Bound in Wedlock: Slave and Free Black Marriage in the Nineteenth Century*. Cambridge, MA: Belknap, 2019.
———. *To 'Joy My Freedom: Southern Black Women's Lives and Labors after the Civil War*. Cambridge, MA: Harvard University, 1998.
Hyde, Sarah. *Schooling in the Antebellum South: The Rise of Public and Private Education in Louisiana, Mississippi, and Alabama*. Baton Rouge: Louisiana State University Press, 2016.
Irons, Charles. *The Origins of Proslavery Christianity: White and Black Evangelicals in Colonial and Antebellum Virginia*. Chapel Hill: University of North Carolina Press, 2008.
Johnson, Jessica Marie. *Wicked Flesh: Black Women, Intimacy, and Freedom in the Atlantic World*. Philadelphia: University of Pennsylvania Press, 2020.
Johnson, Walter. *Soul by Soul: Life inside the Antebellum Slave Market*. Cambridge, MA: Harvard University Press, 1999.
Jones, Jacqueline. *Labor of Love, Labor of Sorrow: Black Women, Work, and the Family, from Slavery to the Present*. 2nd ed. New York: Basic Books, 2009.
Jones-Rogers, Stephanie. *They Were Her Property: White Women as Slaveowners in the American South*. New Haven, CT: Yale University Press, 2019.
Kamensky, Jane. *The Exchange Artist: A Tale of High-Flying Speculation and America's First Banking Collapse*. New York: Viking, 2008.
Kelley, Mary. *Learning to Stand and Speak: Women, Education, and Public Life in America's Republic*. Chapel Hill: University of North Carolina Press, 2008.
Kennedy, Roger. *Rediscovering America*. Boston: Houghton Mifflin, 1990.
Kierner, Cynthia A., ed. *The Contrast: Manners, Morals, and Authority in the Early American Republic*. New York: New York University Press, 2007.
King, Wilma. *Stolen Childhood: Slave Youth in Nineteenth Century America*. Bloomington: Indiana University Press, 1995.
Kruczek-Aaron, Hadley. *Everyday Religion: An Archaeology of Protestant Belief and Practice in the Nineteenth Century*. Gainesville: University Press of Florida, 2015.
Leslie, Kent Anderson. *Woman of Color, Daughter of Privilege: Amanda America Dickson, 1849–1893*. Athens: University of Georgia Press, 1996.
Lomawaima, K. Tsianina. *They Called It Prairie Light: The Story of Chilocco Indian School*. Lincoln: University of Nebraska Press, 1995.
Lucas, Marion B. *A History of Blacks in Kentucky*. Vol. 1, *From Slavery to Segregation, 1760–1891*. Frankfort: Kentucky Historical Society, 1992.

Manring, M. M. *Slave in a Box: The Strange Career of Aunt Jemima*. Charlottesville: University of Virginia Press, 1998.
May, Robert E. *Yuletide in Dixie: Slavery, Christmas, and Southern Memory*. Charlottesville: University of Virginia Press, 2020.
McKivigan, John R., and Mitchell Snay, eds. *Religion and the Antebellum Debate over Slavery*. Athens: University of Georgia Press, 1998.
McLaurin, Melton A. *Celia, a Slave: A True Story*. New York: Avon, 1991.
McQueen, Kevin. *Offbeat Kentuckians: Legends to Lunatics*. Kuttawa, KY: McClanahan Publishing, 2001.
Meyer, Leland Winfield. *The Life and Times of Colonel Richard M. Johnson of Kentucky*. New York: P. S. King and Son, 1932.
Mihm, Stephen. *A Nation of Counterfeiters: Capitalists, Con Men, and the Making of the United States*. Cambridge, MA: Harvard University Press, 2007.
Miles, Tiya. *All That She Carried: The Journey of Ashley's Sack, a Black Family Keepsake*. New York: Random House, 2021.
———. *Ties That Bind: The Story of an Afro-Cherokee Family in Slavery and Freedom*. Berkeley: University of California Press, 2005.
Miller, Marla R. *The Needle's Eye: Women and Work in the Age of Revolution*. Amherst: University of Massachusetts Press, 2006.
Millward, Jessica. *Finding Charity's Folk: Enslaved and Free Black Women in Maryland*. Athens: University of Georgia Press, 2015.
Morgan, Jennifer L. *Laboring Women: Reproduction and Gender in New World Slavery*. Philadelphia: University of Pennsylvania Press, 2004.
———. *Reckoning with Slavery: Gender, Kinship, and Capitalism in the Early Black Atlantic*. Durham, NC: Duke University Press, 2021.
Myers, Amrita Chakrabarti. *Forging Freedom: Black Women and the Pursuit of Liberty in Antebellum Charleston*. Chapel Hill: University of North Carolina Press, 2011.
Nash, Margaret A. *Women's Education in the United States*. New York: Palgrave-Macmillan, 2017.
Pease, Jane H., and William H. Pease. *Ladies, Women, and Wenches: Choice and Constraint in Antebellum Charleston and Boston*. Chapel Hill: University of North Carolina Press, 1990.
Remini, Robert V. *Daniel Webster: The Man and His Time*. New York: W. W. Norton, 1997.
Roark, James L., Michael P. Johnson, Patricia Cline Cohen, Sarah Stage, Alan Lawson, and Susan M. Hartmann, eds. *The American Promise: A Compact History*. Vol 1, *To 1877*. 3rd ed. Boston: Bedford/St. Martins, 2007.
Roark, James L., Michael P. Johnson, Francois Furstenberg, Sarah Stage, and Sarah Igo, eds. *The American Promise: A History of the United States*. Vol. 1, *To 1877*. 8th ed. New York: Macmillan, 2020.
Rothman, Joshua. *Notorious in the Neighborhood: Sex and Families across the Color Line in Virginia, 1787–1861*. Chapel Hill: University of North Carolina Press, 2003.
Salmon, Marylynn. *Women and the Law of Property in Early America*. Chapel Hill: University of North Carolina Press, 1986.
Schafer, Daniel L. *Anna Madgigine Jai Kingsley: African Princess, Florida Slave, Plantation Slaveowner*. Gainesville: University Press of Florida, 2003.

Schenkman, Richard, and Kurt Reiger. *One Night Stands with American History: Odd, Amusing, and Little-Known Incidents*. Rev. ed. New York: William Morrow, 2003.

Schlesinger, Arthur M., Jr. *The Age of Jackson*. Boston: Little, Brown, 1950.

Sharpley-Whiting, T. Denean. *Pimps Up, Ho's Down: Hip Hop's Hold on Young Black Women*. New York: New York University Press, 2008.

Snyder, Christina. *Great Crossings: Indians, Settlers, and Slaves in the Age of Jackson*. London: Oxford University Press, 2017.

———. *Slavery in Indian Country: The Changing Face of Captivity in Early America*. Cambridge, MA: Harvard University Press, 2012.

Stimpson, George William. *A Book about American Politics*. New York: Harper and Brothers, 1952.

Taylor, Nikki Marie. *Driven toward Madness: The Fugitive Slave Margaret Garner and Tragedy on the Ohio*. Athens: Ohio University Press, 2016.

Walker, Tamara. *Exquisite Slaves: Race, Clothing, and Status in Colonial Lima*. London: Cambridge University Press, 2017.

Wellman, Judith. *Grassroots Reform in the Burned-Over District of Upstate New York: Religion, Abolitionism, and Democracy*. New York: Routledge, 2000.

White, Deborah Gray. *Ar'n't I a Woman? Female Slaves in the Plantation South*. Rev ed. New York: W. W. Norton, 1999.

Whooley, Owen. *Knowledge in the Time of Cholera: The Struggle over American Medicine in the Nineteenth Century*. Chicago: University of Chicago Press, 2013.

Whyte, Iain. *Send Back the Money: The Free Church of Scotland and American Slavery*. London: Cambridge University Press, 2012.

Williamson, Joel. *The Crucible of Race: Black-White Relations in the American South since Emancipation*. London: Oxford University Press, 1984.

Wright, John D., Jr. *Lexington: Heart of the Bluegrass*. Lexington, KY: Lexington Historical Publishing Company, 1994.

Young, Klyde, and Lamar Middleton. *Heirs Apparent: The Vice Presidents of the United States*. 1948. Whitefish, MT: Literary Licensing, 2011.

Journal Articles and Book Chapters

Letters to the Editor. *OAH Magazine of History* (July 2009): 4.

Breitweiser, Lynda Jae. "Historic Eleutherian College." *Voice of Freedom: Newsletter of the Underground Railroad Research Institute* 4, no. 1 (Spring 2007): 1.

Brown, Thomas. "The Miscegenation of Richard Mentor Johnson as an Issue in the National Election Campaign of 1835–1836." *Civil War History* 39, no. 1 (March 1993): 15–30.

Ford, Bridget. "Black Spiritual Defiance and the Politics of Slavery in Antebellum Louisville." *Journal of Southern History* 78, no. 1 (February 2012): 69–106.

Ford, Tanisha C., and Carl R. Weinberg. "Slavery, Interracial Marriage, and the Election of 1836." *OAH Magazine of History* 23, no. 2 (April 2009): 57–58.

Foreman, Carolyn Thomas. "The Choctaw Academy." *Chronicles of Oklahoma* 6, no. 4 (December 1928): 453–80.

Garovic, Vesna D., Ralph Dechend, Thomas Easterling, S. Ananth Karumanchi, Suzanne McMurtry Baird, Laura A. Magee, Sarosh Rana, et al. "Hypertension in

Pregnancy: Diagnosis, Blood Pressure Goals, and Pharmacotherapy." *Hypertension* 79, no. 2 (December 15, 2021): e21–e41. www.ahajournals.org/doi/10.1161/HYP.0000000000000208.

Hartman, Saidiya. "Venus in Two Acts." *Small Axe* 12, no. 2 (2008): 1–14.

Hatfield, Mark O. "Richard Mentor Johnson: 9th Vice President, 1837–1841." In *Vice Presidents of the United States, 1789–1993*, 121–34. Washington, DC: US Government Printing Office, 1997.

Hickman, Christine B. "The Devil and the One Drop Rule: Racial Categories, African Americans, and the US Census." *Michigan Law Review* 95, no. 5 (1997): 1161–265.

Kelly, James Y. "The Judge James Y. Kelly Manuscript: Mr. James Y. Kelly's Reminiscences about 'Dick Johnson' Taken Down as He Spoke, April 2, 1929, to Leland W. Meyer." Appendix to Meyer, *Life and Times*, 477–78.

May, J. B. "The Johnson Family." *Kentucky Historical and Genealogical Magazine* (May 1899): 26–35.

McKivigan, John R. "The Battle for the Border State Soul: The Slavery Debate in the Churches of the Border Region." *Ohio Valley History* 12, no. 2 (Summer 2012): 48–71.

Meyer, Leland Winfield. "'Kentucky Hospitality' as Extended by Colonel Richard M. Johnson and His Fellow Citizens." *Register of the Kentucky Historical Society* 29, no. 89 (1931): 372–78.

Millward, Jessica. "'The Relics of Slavery': Interracial Sex and Manumission in the American South." *Frontiers* 31, no. 3 (2010): 22–30.

Post, Edward M. "Kentucky Law Concerning Emancipation or Freedom of Slaves." *Filson Club Quarterly* 59, no. 3 (July 1985): 344–46.

Rouse, Shelley D. "Colonel Dick Johnson's Choctaw Academy: A Forgotten Educational Experiment." *Ohio Archaeological and Historical Publications*, vol. 25 (1916): 88–117.

Smith, Gerald L. "Slavery and Abolition in Kentucky: 'Patter-Rollers' Were Everywhere." In *Bluegrass Renaissance: The History and Culture of Central Kentucky, 1792–1852*, edited by James C. Klotter and Daniel Rowland, 75–92. Lexington: University Press of Kentucky, 2012.

Steely, Will Frank. "The Established Churches and Slavery, 1850–1860." *Register of the Kentucky Historical Society* 55, no. 2 (April 1957): 97–104.

Stevenson, Brenda E. "'Marsa Never Sot Aunt Rebecca Down': Enslaved Women, Religion, and Social Power in the Antebellum South." *Journal of African American History* 90, no. 4 (2005): 345–67.

Stewart, Whitney Nell. "Fashioning Frenchness: Gens de Couleur Libres and the Cultural Struggle for Power in Antebellum New Orleans." *Journal of Social History* 51, no. 3 (Spring 2018): 526–56.

Thompson, William C. "Eleutherian Institute: A Sketch of a Unique Step in the Educational History of Indiana." *Indiana Magazine of History* 19, no. 2 (June 1923): 109–31.

Voelker, David J. "Church Building and Social Class on the Urban Frontier: The Refinement of Lexington, 1784–1830." *Register of the Kentucky Historical Society* 106, no. 2 (Spring 2008): 191–229.

Unpublished Materials

Bevins, Ann Bolton. "Great Crossings." Chap. 10 of unpublished manuscript.

Guilbault, Alexis. "Creating a Common Culture of Slavery: Native, Black, and White Unfreedom in the Ohio River Valley, 1700–1865." PhD diss., Indiana University Bloomington, 2021. ProQuest Dissertations and Theses.

Jones, Jonathan Milnor. "The Making of a Vice President: The National Political Career of Richard M. Johnson of Kentucky." PhD diss., University of Memphis, 1998. ProQuest Dissertations and Theses.

Index

Italic page numbers refer to illustrations.

Adams, Henry, 113
Adams, John Quincy, 158
Alexander, Adele Logan, 209
Alexander, Henry, 209
Alexander, Lucy, 209
amalgamation, 3, 63, 74, 102, 126, 127, 137, 147–48, 153, 155, 159, 160, 211
American Baptist Missionary Convention, 113
antislavery advocates, 92, 113, 151, 205
"anti-sumptuary laws," 123
Ashley (enslaved girl), 30

Balch, Alfred, 138
Baptist churches, 92, 113. *See also* Great Crossing Baptist Church
Barrow, David, 92
Battle of Munfordville (Battle of Green River), 206
Battle of the Thames, 43–44, 95, 165
Bentz, Anna Barbara Bullinger, 108
Bentz, Johann Georg, 108
Bettingall, Margaret (Tunno), 51, 57, 143–44
Bevins, Ann Bolton, xv–xx
Billy (enslaved by Martin Hawkins), 101
Black, J. D., 106
Black, Liza, ix
Black Baptist movement, 113
Black Reconstruction, 174
Black women: lack of right to own property, 46; limitation of female privilege, 5, 73; maternal love, 30, 33; outlines of female privilege, 4–5; stereotypes of, 76, 82, 83, 103, 146, 234n45. *See also* slavery
Blair, Francis P., 121, 143–44, 157, 162
Bluegrass region, KY, 15, 17, 20, 21, 24
Blue Spring Farm, *19*, 41, 166; 1827 attack on, 61–62; conflict with Choctaw Academy, 77–78; current state of property, xvi–xxii, *xvii*, *xxi*, 213; hiring of overseer at, 76–77, 78; importance of enslaved labor to, 71–72; Lafayette's visit in 1825, 39–41, 52; ownership of after Richard's death, 181–82; Richard and Julia's roles, 48; Thomas Henderson's role, 48
Bond, Emma, 175
Bond, Hattie, 175
Bond, Henrietta, 175
Boone County, KY, 47
Bourassa, Joseph, 131
Bowman, Phylicia Fauntleroy, 209
Bragg, Catherine L., 160, 161, 205, 207
Brooks, Margaret Ellen Pence, 190, 198–202
Brown, Stephen, 184
Bryan, John, 106
Bullinger, Anna Barbara (Bentz), 108
Burton, Zerelda, 111

Calhoun, John C., 43, 166
Cameron, Daniel, 14
Carlisle, Mary Munger, 168–69
Catron, John, 138, 162
Cave, Susanna, 93
Cave, William, 93
Celia (enslaved by Robert Newsom), 35–36, 161
Chace, Jacob (enslaved by Richard M. Johnson), 48
Chace, Sandy (enslaved by Richard M. Johnson), 48
Chinn, Daniel (enslaved by Richard M. Johnson): at Blue Spring during attack of 1827, 61, 74, 76; brother of Julia Chinn, 151–152; criticism of Richard Johnson, 151–52, 157; evident paternity of Parthene, 148–49, 151; flight to Canada, 151, 152; Great

Chinn, Daniel (*continued*)
    Crossing Baptist Church, 95; as Richard Johnson's body servant, 49; marriage to Patience Chinn, 43, 49, 59, 61, 76, 107, 152; mortgage by Richard Johnson, 59, 152; paternity of and surname, 23; relocation to Blue Spring, 29, 30, 43
Chinn, Julia Ann: authority and privilege, 88–90; birth and childhood, 17; Blue Spring Farm duties, 43, 46, 49–50, 66–67, 86, 131; business acumen and domestic/financial management, 42, 54–55, 67–68, 86, 87; Choctaw Academy duties, 66–67, 70, 132; cholera epidemic and death, 85, 110–11, 131; clothing, 122–23; complicity in enslavement, 14, 48–50; contemporary significance of, 10–15; "conversion experience" and baptism, 91, 95, 106–7; domestic training and skills, 24–26, 50–51; grave, xx, xvi, 213; in Henderson's letter of reference for Johnson, 146–47; hospitality at Blue Spring Farm, 51–52, 54, 122–23; lack of substantive information regarding, 6, 118, 190; lifelong status as enslaved person, 34–35, 45, 53; literacy, 50–51; medical skills, 66, 87, 130–31; motherhood, 32, 55–56; mother's name, 30, 226n31; overview of life, 2–3; relocation to Blue Spring Farm in 1810, 29–30, 31; rumors of wedding to Johnson, 33–34, 102; separate residence of, 45–46, 85; sexual relationship with Richard Johnson, 31–32, 33–34, 102; sister of Daniel Chinn, 151–52; social status, 58–59, 73
Chinn, Marcellus (enslaved by Richard M. Johnson), 151–52, 161–62
Chinn, Patience (enslaved by Richard M. Johnson): Blue Spring domestic duties, 43, 49; at Blue Spring during attack of 1827, 61; Choctaw Academy "Coffee Riot," 80–81; Choctaw Academy duties and service, 89; and corporal punishment of enslaved persons, 76; Great Crossing Baptist Church, 103; marriage to Daniel Chinn, 43, 49, 59, 61, 76, 107, 152; mortgaged by Richard Johnson, 59, 152; Parthene's relations with Richard Johnson, 153
Chinn family: Black or mixed-race, 88, 148; white, 23

Choctaw Academy, 3, 6, 42, 45; background and history, 62, 63–66; cholera epidemic, 129–30; closure of, 88; "Coffee Riot," 81; conflict with Blue Spring Farm, 77–78; curriculum, 65; discipline problems and violence, 61–62, 72–75, 81–84; electioneering barbecue held at, 122–23; food and coffee at, 80–81; Henderson as headmaster, 47, 54, 64–66; importance of enslaved labor, 71–72, 89–90; John Riddle rebellion, 78–79; Julia's role, 50–51; laundry and clothing, 84–85, 86; management after Julia's death, 85–87; medical duties, 87; religious aspects, 69; relocation to White Sulphur Spring, 82–83; remaining building, xix, xvi, *xviii*; student performances, 54; students' views of Johnson, 89
Choctaw Nation: land encroachment by white people, 63–64; slavery, 62–63, 78
cholera epidemic, 85–86, 110–11, 128–32
Clarke, Lewis George (enslaved person), 24–25
Clay, Edward William, 153–55, *154*
Clay, Henry, xx, 43, 45, 133, 140, 142, 152, 166, 168, 210
colonialism, 75, 80, 88. See also settler colonialism
color line: "crossing" of, 2, 134, 172, 185, 188, 190; and interracial sex, 4, 139, 202. *See also* amalgamation
corporal punishment, 74, 78. See also violence: physical
Craig, Newton, 111
Crawford, Maud, 173, 175
critical race theory (CRT), 12
Crittenden, John J., 166

Daniel (field hand, enslaved by Richard M. Johnson), 48, 50
Davis, Benjamin, 105
Democratic Convention (1835), 137–38
Desha, Joseph, 39
Desha, Lucius, 167
Dickson, Amanda America, 37–38, 45
Dickson, David, 37–38, 45–46
Dickson, Elizabeth, 37
Dickson, Julia Frances (enslaved by Elizabeth Dickson), 37–38, 45–46
Dickson, Rose (Julia Dickson's mother, enslaved by Elizabeth Dickson), 37

INDEX

Dicy (enslaved by Richard Mentor Johnson), 76, 250n38
Dillard, R. T., 106–7
DNA testing and evidence, 145, 204
Drake, Daniel, 128
DuBois, W. E. B., ix

Easley, Mary Elizabeth Lee, 180
Easley, Virgil W., 180, 189
education of women, 41–42
Eleutherian Institute (College), 205–6, *206*, 207
Elkhorn Association of Baptist Churches, 92, 93
enslaved persons. *See* slavery

Famous Men of Kentucky, 200
Fanny (enslaved by Richard M. Johnson), 81, 103, 110, 111
Fayette County, KY, 21, 148
femes covert, 42
femes sole, 42
Fifteenth Amendment, 174
Finnell, Nicholas L., 120, 126, 131, 140, 141, 169
First African Baptist Church (First ABC), 113–14
First Amendment, 115
Fitzgerald, Catherine (Scott), 172–73
Fitzgerald, Lucretia, 172
flogging, 74, 78. See also violence: physical
Folsom (in relationship with Lucinda), 76, 234n47
Folsom, Daniel, 76, 81
Ford, Hiram (H. W.), 187, 189
Fourteenth Amendment, 174
Frahern, Washington, 70
Frankfort, KY, xvi, 21, 128–29, 137, 140, 157, 165, 167, 169, 206
Frayham, William, 70
free Blacks, x, 10, 17, 20, 23, 25, 36, 37, 45, 50, 56, *57, 61*, 72, 73, 91–92, 106, 113, 121–22, 154–55, 177, 209
Freedmen's Bureau, 174

Gano, John Allen, 186
Gano, Richard Montgomery, 186–87
Garner, Margaret, 30
Gendron, Payton S., 15

Georgetown, KY, *19*, 20, 21, 39–40, 52, 82, 92, 93, 117, 119, 123, 128, 129, 186, 195, 198, 202
Georgetown Light Infantry, 52
Gone with the Wind (film), 146
Gould, Catherine C., 160
Granger, Francis, 158
Gray, Harriet Elizabeth Pence, 190, 198–202
Grayson, Stephen, 107
Great Crossing Baptist Church, 20, 47, 49–50, 69, *97*; cemetery, 93, *94*; censure of Richard Johnson, 104–5; charges against parishioners, 108–10; "conversion experience" and baptism of Julia Chinn, 91, 95, 106–7; current building and cemetery, xvi, *xviii*; "disorderly communion" incident, 98–99; enforcement of attendance, 104–6; Great Kentucky Revival of 1800, 106, 107; history of, 92–95, *94*; interracial marriage, 92–93; Revival of 1828, 91, 92, 105, 106–7; Second Great Awakening, 106; segregation and racial issues, 95–98, 100, 111–15; "sins" and rule enforcement, 99–105; "slave missions," 113–14; Robert and Jemima Suggett Johnson and, 20; wedding of Imogene Johnson and Daniel B. Pence, 108
Green, Duff, 138–39
griots, 204–5

Haight, Ella, 176
Hancock County, GA, 38
Harkins, George, 79
Harris, Kamala, 13
Harrison, William Henry, 44, 163
Hatch, Samuel, 129–31
Hawkins, Martin, 101
Hayes, Rutherford B., 174
Hayes, Rev., 34
Hemings, Elizabeth, 23
Hemings, Sally, 10, 23, 37, 133, 137, 145
hemp cultivation, 17, 21, 24, 41, 45, 72, 178
Henderson, Nancy M. (Terrill), 47
Henderson, Thomas, 33, 34, 46–49, *47*; Blue Spring Farm duties, 48–49; Choctaw Academy duties, 55–56, 77–78; cholera epidemic, 129–31; departure from Choctaw Academy, 88; discipline at Choctaw Academy, 82, 83; duties as tutor at Blue Spring Farm, 50, 55–57, 107, 136, 145, 187; Great Crossing Baptist Church, 96, 106; as headmaster of

INDEX

Henderson, Thomas (*continued*)
  Choctaw Academy, 64–66, 68, 74, 82–83; letter of reference for Johnson, 143–47
Henrietta (enslaved by Robert and Jemima Suggett Johnson), 17, 21–25, 27, 43, 48, 51, 66, 95, 98, 106, 107; Julia and Daniel's move to Blue Spring Farm, 29–30
Henry County, VA, 47
history: family history and oral history, 203–4, 208; reconstructive research, 7–8; reliability of oral history, 32
Holt, Jacob H., 132
Hunt, George, 148
Hunt, Susan, 36–37
Hunter, Tera, x

Illinois, 10, 123–24, 172, 173, 176, 177, 181
Indian Removal (1786–1830), 63–64, 88
interracial sex, 35–38; contemporary stigma, 202–3; and fear of violence, 127; local resistance to in Kentucky, 117–19, 122–23, 125–26, 132–34; national opposition to, 136–43, 153–56, 163–64; outlawing of in post–Civil War South, 174–75; resistance to, 3–4; social rules for, 4, 10, 120, 126, 132, 133, 136; and social status, 119–21; toleration of, 4
intersectionality, race and gender justice, 12–13
Irwin, James, 167

Jackson, A. Claude, 194, 195–96
Jackson, Andrew, 51, 88, 136, 137, 138, 158, 162
Jackson, Anna Mary "Annie" Pence, 180, 184, 186
Jackson, Grace Maria Pence, 193, 194
Jackson, James L., 180, 184
Jackson, Ketanji Brown, 13
Jackson, Rachel, 137
Jackson, William "Bill" French, 1, 11, 195, 196–98, 201
Jacobs, Harriet, 23, 161
James, Frank, 185
James, Jesse, 185
Jefferson, Georgiana, 206
Jefferson, Lucy, 206
Jefferson, Thomas, 23, 34, 37, 132–33, 137, 142, 145, 206
Jerry (field hand, enslaved by Richard M. Johnson), 48

Jerry (Choctaw Academy cook, enslaved by Richard M. Johnson), 50, 86
Jim Crow era, 164, 175–77, 193
Johnson, Adaline (Scott). *See* Scott, Adaline Johnson
Johnson, Ann, 111
Johnson, Cave, 162
Johnson, Edward C., 48
Johnson, Henry, 7–8, 169, 207
Johnson, Imogene (Pence). *See* Pence, Imogene Johnson
Johnson, James, 44
Johnson, Jemima Suggett: Great Crossing Baptist Church, 20, 93, 95; Henrietta, 17; Julia's role as housekeeper of Blue Spring, 30; Julia's role as house servant, 24; opposition to Richard's relationship with Julia, 31–32, 33, 53, 169; opposition to Richard's relationship with poor white woman, 53; ownership of Julia, 2, 17; piety of, 146; settlement in Kentucky, 20; and slavery, 182; training of Julia, 25, 26, 50–51, 66, 146
Johnson, Johnathan J., 101–2
Johnson, John T., 7, 66, 101, 168, 169
Johnson, Nancy, 111
Johnson, Richard M., Jr., 40
Johnson, Richard Mentor: acknowledgement of daughters' paternity, 2, 32; archival material and lack of, 7–8, 118; attitudes concerning Native Americans, 74, 89, 150; attitudes concerning Black women, 76, 83, 103, 152–53; birth and early life, 20, 28–29; Blue Spring Farm, 29, 51–52; burial site, xvi; Choctaw Academy, 64–65, 79; correspondence with Julia, 50, 55; coverage of in textbooks, 5–6; declining health and death, 165–66, 167; division of estate after death, 169–70; education, 28; 1840 election, 162–63; election by Senate after electoral college defeat, 157–58; escape of bondservants during election campaigns, 151–52; family's resistance to Julia, 31–32, 33, 53, 169; financial situation, 13, 53, 59, 64, 152, 158, 166–67, 170; Fourth of July barbecue, 117–18, 119–20, 121, 141; funeral arrangements, 167–68; Great Crossing Baptist Church, 95, 104–5; grief following Adaline's death, 156–57; grief following

264

Julia's death, 131–32; interracial sex with Parthene, 135–36, 148–51; interracial sex with unknown woman, 158–62, 207; interracial unions and marital history, 2–3, 33–34, 53–54, 152–53; legacy and reputation, 210–11; local opposition to daughters' marriages, 141–43; local reactions to interracial union, 132; opposition from Democratic party, 158, 162–63; political involvement, 143–45, 164, 166–67; political opposition to, 136, 158, 162–63; residence in Washington, DC, 32–33, 158; return to US House of Representatives in 1814, 44; as slaveholder, 13, 72, 103, 166–67, 178, 182; social and family background, 52–53; "socially Black" status, 96; opposition to as Van Buren's running mate, 136–43; vice presidential campaign, 153–58; War of 1812 service, 43–44, 95, 150

Johnson, Robert, 2, 17, 20, 52, 93, 182; burial site, 95; elected positions in Scott County, 20; establishment of Blue Spring Farm, 29; Great Crossing Baptist Church, 20, 93

Johnson, Sally (Ward), xv, 46, 64, 169
Johnson, Theodore (Jusan), 206–7
Johnson, William (storekeeper), 67
Johnson, William (brother of Richard), 95
Johnson/Chinn union: local resistance to, 3, 117–19, 122–23, 132–34; national opposition to, 136–43, 153–56, 163–64
Johnson's Fort (Johnson's Station), 20, 21, 22, 25, 26, 27, 28, 29, 43, 51, 66, 93, 95, 97, 150
Jones, John, 131, 148, 149, 150, 161
Jusan, Adelaide, 207, 209
Jusan, Malvina, 207, 209
Jusan, Theodore (Johnson), 206–7
Juzan, Pierre, 76, 250n38

Kansas, 32, 55

Kelly, James Y., 34, 166
Kendall, Amos, 158–60, 161, 162, 205
Kentucky: Bluegrass region, 15, 17, 20, 21, 24; Constitutional Convention, 20; enslaved population, 20–21; Frankfort, xvi, 21, 51, 128–29, 137, 140, 157, 165, 167, 169, 206; Georgetown, *19*, 20, 21, 39–40, 52, 82, 92, 93, 117, 119, 123, 128, 129, 186, 195, 198, 202; in late eighteenth century, 17, 20; Lexington, 21, 27, 39, 44, 51, 72, 98, 113, 128–29, 167, 193, 195; Louisville, 20, 72, 98, 113, 141, 150, 205, 206; map of, *18–19*; Scott County, xv, 6, *19*, 20, 21, 28, 34, 47, 93, 104, 106, 120, 122, 124, 144, 150, 163, 164, 181, 185, 187, 207, 210–11; slave codes, 34–35; State Constitution, 20, 35, 52; state law and interracial marriage, 92, 108

King, Peter, 61–62, 73, 74, 76, 78, 79, 115, 136
Kingsley, Anta "Anna" Madgigine Jai, 36, 44–45
Kingsley, Zephaniah, Jr., 36, 44–45, 46

Lafayette, Marquis de, 39–41, 52, 143, 147
Lee, Amanda Malvina Pence, 179, 180, 181, 182, 183, 184
Lee, Mary Elizabeth (Easley), 180, 183
Lee, Robert (son of Malvina and Robert M.), 184
Lee, Robert M., 179, 181, 182, 183, 184
Lewis (enslaved by Richard M. Johnson), 81
Lexington, KY, 21, 27, 39, 44, 51, 72, 98, 113, 128–29, 167, 193, 195
Linn County, MO, 173
Long, G. B., 113–14
Long, Samuel, 83–84
Longview Plantation, 166, 186
Louisville, KY, 20, 72, 98, 113, 141, 150, 205, 206
Loving v. Virginia, 11
Lucinda (enslaved by Richard M. Johnson), 76
Lucy, (enslaved by Richard M. Johnson), 81, 110
manumission of slaves, 34–35, 228n49
Marshall, Humphrey, 163
Matilda (enslaved by J. J. Johnson), 101–3
McAfee, Jackson, 107
McCalla, Fabricus C., 186
McCormick, Cyrus, 184
McIntyre, Buddy (Uncle Bud), 202, 204–5
McIntyre, William H., Jr., 202–5, 208, 209, 210–11
Metcalfe, Thomas, 166
Meyer, Leland, 194, 199, 200
miscegenation. *See* amalgamation

Miss Margaret (worked at Choctaw Academy, racial and free status unclear), 70, 77
Missouri, 10, 35, 172, 173, 175, 176, 185
Missouri Compromise debates, 155
Mitchell, Ellen, 184
Mitchell, Alice, 184

INDEX

Mitchell, Sanford, 209
Monroe, James, 51
Montgomery County, MD, 123
Movement for Black Lives, 12
multiracial lineage, acknowledgment of, 11
Munger, Fitch, 168–69
Murphy, Addie, 58, 152
Murray, Judith Sargent, 41–42

Native Americans, 63–64, 88; Johnson's attitudes concerning, 89, 150. *See also* Choctaw Academy; Choctaw Nation; Indian Removal

Newsom, Robert, 35–36, 161
Noel, Silas M., 91, 107–8, 123, 187

"one-drop rule," 11, 174–75, 177, 187, 193
Outon, Thomas, 110

Parthene (enslaved by Richard M. Johnson): Blue Spring Farm duties, 61, 70–71; Choctaw Academy duties, 84–85, 86, 87; escape attempt, 135–36, 148–50, 153, 161; paternity of, 148–49, 151; relations with Richard Johnson, 135–36, 148–51, 160
patriarchy: challenges to at Choctaw Academy, 78–79; and interracial sex, 35, 38; and nineteenth century marriage, x, 41–42
Peak, James, 152
Pence, Adam, Jr., 108
Pence, Adam, Sr., 108
Pence, Amanda Malvina (Lee) (daughter of Imogene and Daniel), 179, 180, 181, 182, 183, 184
Pence, Anna Mary "Annie" (Jackson) (daughter of Mary Jane and Josiah), 180, 184, 186
Pence, Daniel B., Jr. (son of Mary Jane and Josiah), 184, 189
Pence, Daniel Brown (husband of Imogene), 77, 92, 108, *109*, 121, 123, 124, 125, 126, 149, 172, 177; baptism of, 186; burial site, xxii; death of, 188–89, *190*; descendants of, 194, 196, 198, 207; as slaveholder, 178, 182; wealth of, 179–85
Pence, Daniel Franklin "Frank" (son of Imogene and Daniel), 183, 184, 186, 188, 189, 208; quilt, 213, *214*
Pence, D. Franklin (Amanda Malvina's son), 184

Pence, Edward H. (brother of Daniel Brown Pence), 50, 77–78, 82, 86–87, 149–50
Pence, Edward Herndon (son of Imogene and Daniel), 183–84, 189, 207–8
Pence, Emma (daughter of Mary Jane and Josiah), 184
Pence, Frank Durham (father of Harriet and Margaret), 190, 199–200
Pence, George, 108, 178
Pence, Imogene Johnson, 4, 61, 121, 122, 124, 177; baptism of, 186; birth and childhood of, 32, 43, 44, 55, 58, 102; in Blair letter, 143–44; burial site, xxii;; clothing, 40, 57, 122–23; crossing of color line by, 185, 188; death and obituary, 111, 187–88, *189*; descendants of, 2, 11–12, 190, 193–211; education and tutoring of, 33, 49, 50, 55–57, 66, 69, 136, 187; Edward H. Pence (brother-in-law), 77; family farm, 177, 178, 187, 195; father's distancing from, 143–44; father's death and estate, 7, 165–66, 169–71, *171*; during father's vice presidential campaign, 139, 154–56; gifts and inheritance for descendants, 179–81; as go-between for father and Thomas Henderson, 68–69; Great Crossing Baptist Church, 90, 92, 98, 103-5, 108; known as Richard Johnson's daughter, 2, 57, 132-33, 172, 185; Lafayette's visit to Blue Spring Farm, 40; as landholder, 181–84; in Henderson letter, 144–46; marriage, 54, 77, 84, 92, 108, 123–26, 177; as mother, 177; as Parthene's cousin, 148–49, 151, 153, 161; recognition in Kentucky society, 57–58; as slaveholder, 13, 125, 178–79, 182–83; social status, 58–59, 118–19, 185–88; wealth of, 125, 136, 183–84; work responsibilities, 58, 71
Pence, Josiah, 179, 180, 181, 183, 184–85, 189
Pence, Mary Jane, 179–80, 181, 183, 184–85, 186
Pence, Robert (son of Malvina), 184
Pence, William Collis, 188, 190, 194
Pence, William H. "Willie" (son of Mary Jane and Josiah), 180, 184, 189
Pence (Bentz), Adam, 108
Pence family farm, 177–78, *178*, *195*
Pitchlynn, Peter, 62, 88
Plessy v. Ferguson, 176
Poindexter, George, 34, 140
Polk, James K., 162

INDEX

Pratt, William H., 113
Prentice, George D., 139

racialized ideologies: Black-white binary, 11; erasure of Black people (archival and literal), 2, 7, 8, 11, 15, 23–24, 169, 174, 190, 198, 204; kinlessness, 24, 33, 74–75, 89, 226n14; race as social construct, 2, 10, 72, 164, 185; racial status as "open secret," 190; racism, 7, 9, 11, 14, 35, 38, 142, 153, 177, 190–91, 198, 201, 203; slavery following condition of the mother, 23, 127; "socially Black" status of whites, 96. See also white supremacy
rape. See violence: sexual
real estate and wealth, 125, 181
Reconstruction period, 174, 184
Redemption (era), 174
Republican Motherhood, 41–42
Revival of 1800 (Great Kentucky Revival), 106
Revival of 1828, 91–92, 105, 106–8
Richardson, Chip, xvi
Riddle, John, 78–80
Riddle, William, 78, 81
Robinson, Henry R., 153, 155
Robinson, Stuart, 168
Roof, Dylann, 15
Rose (enslaved woman), 30
Rose (enslaved by Richard M. Johnson), 81, 110
Russell, Gervas E., 140, 141

Sayre, Nathan, 36–37

Schuyler County, IL, 123
Scott, Adaline Johnson, 3, 4, 55; burial site, xx, 213; birth and childhood, 55, 58, 169; in Blair Letter, 143–44; clothing, 57, 40, 122–23; correspondence with father, 58, 70; death of, 88, 156–57, 172; deed to Blue Spring Farm, 125; duties after Julia's death, 87–88; duties at Choctaw Academy, 58, 61, 62, 70–71, 77, 84–85, 86; education and tutoring of, 33, 49, 50, 55–57, 66, 187; father's distancing from, 143–44; and father's relationship with Parthene, 136, 148–49, 151, 153; during father's vice presidential campaign, 139, 154–56; Fourth of July barbecue, 3, 117–18, 119–20, 121–22, 141; and Great Crossing Baptist Church, 90, 98, 103–5; health issues, 71; in Henderson letter, 144–46; known as Richard Johnson's daughter, 2, 132–33; Lafayette's visit to Blue Spring Farm, 40; local resistance to, 125–26; marriage and family, 3, 70–71, 84, 123–25, 172–73; recognition by society, 57–58; Robert J. Scott (son), 172–77; role at Blue Spring Farm, 70, 71; as slaveholder, 13, 125; social status, 58–59, 120–21; wealth of, 136, 170
Scott, A. J., 175, 176
Scott, Amos, 123
Scott, Catherine (Fitzgerald), 172–73
Scott, Edward Bion, 173, 175
Scott, Emma, 173, 175
Scott, Eugene, 172
Scott, Fannie "Frances," 173, 175
Scott, Helen, 172, 173
Scott, Ira, 175–76
Scott, Josephine, 172, 173
Scott, Maggie, 176
Scott, Mary, 172
Scott, Mentor, 173
Scott, Nancy West, 123–24
Scott, Robert Bruce, 175
Scott, Robert Johnson, 70, 172–77
Scott, Stone J., 175–76
Scott, Thomas Frederic, 173, 175
Scott, Thomas West (husband of Adaline), xx, 123–24, 125, 166, 172–73, 181, 183
Scott County, KY, xv, 6, 19, 20–21, 28, 47, 93, 104, 106, 120, 124, 144, 150, 163–64, 172, 181, 184–85, 207, 210–11
Scrivner, Emma, 175
Second Great Awakening, 106, 108
segregation, 11, 164, 174, 175–76, 177
settler colonialism, 9, 12, 63, 64, 72, 75, 80, 88, 89, 90, 93, 203–4
sex: between white men and enslaved women, x, xx, 31–32, 33–34, 35–38, 76, 85, 101–2, 103, 108, 120–21, 126, 132–33, 136, 140, 142, 147–53, 158–62, 210; fear of between white women and Black men, 127
slavery: and abolition crisis, 112–13; care of children, 21, 35; and corporal punishment, 25, 74, 76, 78; and current moment, 11–14; "disciplinary issues" with enslaved persons, 46, 48–50; domestic servants contrasted with field hands, 24–25; and debt, 53, 59,

slavery (*continued*)
  166, 170; and education, 72; end of, 174; enslaved children's daily life, 24, 25–27; enslaved peoples' clothes, living conditions, and diet, 21–23, 30, 57–58; enslaved persons as form of wealth, 125, 179–80, 182–83; escape of enslaved women, 147–50; fancy trade, 145; historians' reconstruction of enslaved women's lives, 6–7; "housekeepers," 30–31; in Kentucky, 17, 20–21, 35, 47, 73, 145; labor, 21, 40, 52, 58, 62, 67, 71–72, 80–81; loss of slaves as wealth after Civil War, 184; manumission, 34–35; and medicine, 66; and religion, 9, 91, 92, 95–96, 97, 98, 100–102, 103, 106, 107, 110, 112; and recreation, 26–27; and sale, 152, 167, 170; seamstresses, 33, 50, 51, 67, 70; self-freed people, 151–52; and separation of enslaved families, 24–25, 29–30; sex between white men and enslaved women, 31, 34, 35–38, 161; slave hiring, 28; social status of enslaved *vs.* Indigenous persons, 80–82, 83; social status of mixed-race families vs. white families, 73–74, 115; washerwomen, 84; weekend and holiday routines, 24, 26–27, 48; white fear of Black male/white female sexual relations, 127
Smith, A., 113–14
Snyder, Christina, 6
Snyder, Pauline, 127
Southern Baptist Convention, 113
State Convention of Colored Baptists, 113
Stedman, Ebenezer, 40
Stepp, Ellen, 184
Suggett, James, 93
Suggett, Jemima (Johnson). *See* Johnson, Jemima Suggett
Suggett, John, 93
Sunday Mails Battle, 105, 155
surnames and identity, 23–24

Tappan, Lewis, 152, 155
Tarrant, Carter, 92
Taylor, Harrison, 209
Taylor, John W., 140
Taylor, Nellie Pence "Mama Nell," 207, 208, 209

Taylor, Obie, Sr., 207–8, 209
Tecumseh, 44, 52, 150, 154, 156, 199–200, Terrill, Nancy M. (Henderson), 47
Thirteenth Amendment, 174, 185
Thomas, Amanda, 207, 208–9
Thomas, Clarence, 14
tolerance *vs.* toleration, 4, 93, 119
Treaty of 1825 (Treaty of Washington City), 64
Trowbridge, Sylvester, 175
Tunno, Adam, 51, 57, 143–44
Tunno, Margaret Bettingall, 51, 57, 143–44
Twelfth Amendment, 157–58
Tyler, John, 163

Van Buren, Martin, 1, 5, 132, 136, 137, 139, 157, 158–59, 162, 163, 196

violence, 2, 23, 48–49, 74–76, 83, 164, 177, 191; archival and scholarly, 7–8, 23–24, 204; against Black men (post–Civil War), 127; at Choctaw Academy, 61–62, 63, 73, 78–79, 81–82, 88–89, 123; physical, 13, 25, 27, 46, 48, 74, 76, 78, 82–83, 89, 103, 135, 150–51, 153, 158, 161; settler colonial, 9; sexual, 4, 23, 25, 35–36, 37, 45, 75–76, 81–83, 153, 157, 174, 202–3

Walker, Herschel, 14
Wall, David, 61–62, 73–74, 76, 78, 79, 115, 136
Walter, Reuben, 207
Ward Hall, xv–xvi, xvii, xx, 32
Ward, Junius Richard, xv
Ward, Matilda Viney, xv
Ward, Sally Johnson, xv, 46, 64, 169
Ward, William, xv, 46, 64, 78, 80, 169
War of 1812, 43–44, 53, 95, 150, 165, 166
Webb, James Watson, 154
Webster, Daniel, 140, 166
Weed, Thurlow, 137
White Sulphur Spring, 32, 82, 84, 158
white supremacy, 2, 9, 12, 13, 14, 15, 114, 142, 174, 177, 179, 183, 190, 203; challenges to at Choctaw Academy, 78–79, 88. *See also* racialized ideologies
Whitley, William, 44
Wilfert, Brenda Brent, 2, 193–95, 198, 208–9, 210–11
Wilson, John, 34

women: civic roles, 41; and education, 41–42; rights for married *vs.* single women, 42; rights in post-Revolutionary America, 41–42; as sexual property, 75. *See also* violence: sexual

Woodford County, 20
Wright, Walter B., 127
Wyer, Edward, 158